MR. STRANGELOVE

MR. STRANGELOVE

A Biography of

PETER SELLERS

ED SIKOV

WITHDRAWN

HYPERION

NEW YORK

Library of Congress Cataloging-in-Publication Data

Sikov, Ed.
    Mr. Strangelove : a biography of Peter Sellers / by Ed Sikov—1st ed.
       p.   cm.
    Includes bibliographical references and index.
    Filmography: p.
    ISBN 0-7868-6664-0
       1. Sellers, Peter, 1925–   2. Actors—Great Britain—Biography.   I. Title: Mister Strangelove,
    a biography of Peter Sellers.   II. Title.

PN2598.S44 S58 2002
791.43'028'092—dc21
[B]
                                                                                    2002068933

Hyperion books are available for special promotions and premiums.
For details contact Hyperion Special Markets,
77 West 66th Street, 11th floor, New York, New York, 10023-6298,
or call 212-456-0100.

Book design by Oksana Kushnir

FIRST EDITION

10 9 8 7 6 5 4 3 2 1

To Edward Hibbert,
who makes my work possible.

To Bruce Schackman,
who makes the rest possible.

C O N T E N T S

Some forms of reality are so horrible we refuse to face them, unless we are trapped into it by comedy.
To label any subject unsuitable for comedy is to admit defeat.

—Peter Sellers

PART ONE

DOWN THE RABBIT HOLE

1925–57

"Who in the world am I? Ah, that's *the great puzzle!"*

In 1924, a low-end music hall performer called Peg Sellers gave birth to a baby boy. She named him Peter. Peg had long been dominated by her imposing impresario of a mother, Welcome Mendoza, and she was eager to focus her own fierce maternal drive on the tiny boy. But Peter Sellers died quickly and was buried and never mentioned again.

Welcome Mendoza was, truly, the outlandish name with which Peg Sellers's mother was born, though she changed it twice along the way: first to Marks when she got married, then to Ray when she elbowed her kids onto the music hall stage. Showmanship and aggression ran strong in this family. Welcome Mendoza Marks, who started calling herself Belle Ray when she became a vaudeville manager, was the granddaughter of the most renowned Jewish prizefighter of the eighteenth century.

Strange to say, there were many brawling Jews in that era: Aby Belasco, Barney "Star of the East" Aaron, Lazarus the Jew Boy, the curiously named Ikey Pig. . . . But the best of them, the strongest and scrappiest, was Daniel Mendoza, whose fabulous life in the ring was set up, however indirectly, by a gang of Jewish killers. In the spring of 1771, a flourishing group of circumcised thieves (led by a doctor, of all people) was busily breaking into Chelsea houses and successfully removing items of interest. The crime spree came to an abrupt end in June when, in the midst of a heist, they made the mistake of killing somebody's servant. The doctor and his gang were quickly apprehended, tried, convicted, and hanged, but the rest of London's Jewish population felt a more long-lasting effect. "I have seen many Jews hooted, hunted, cuffed, pulled by the beard, spit upon, and barbarously assaulted in the streets," a contemporary wrote. "Dogs could not be used in the streets in the manner many Jews were treated."

Daniel Mendoza was five years old at the time of the Chelsea murder, the consequence being that throughout his childhood and adolescence no Jewish boy in London was safe from Christian harassment. Daniel was naturally tough, even belligerent, and he learned to protect himself. When he got older he trained other boys to fight as well, and eventually, as Mendoza's contemporary noted, "it was no longer safe to insult a Jew unless he was an old man and alone." Thrashing others was not Daniel's first career choice, however. After his bar mitzvah he set himself on course to becoming a glassmaker, but his apprenticeship came to a quick end when he couldn't help but beat up the glazier's son. He moved on to assist a greengrocer but spent so much time physically avenging the grocer's wife against the insults of shoppers that he soon moved on again, this time to a tea shop, where he responded to a customer's complaint about the service by clobbering him—for forty-five minutes. The bruised patron, however, had sense. He responded not with legal action but with sound advice: He convinced Daniel to become a professional fighter.

Until his great-great-grandson surpassed him in both fame and fortune, Daniel Mendoza was his family's brightest star. (The great-great-grandson acknowledged this fact in several of his films by hanging portraits of Mendoza in the background; a certain inept French detective, for instance, is an admirer of Daniel Mendoza.) The prizefighter left a curious series of personality bequests. Like his descendent, Mendoza liked to assume other identities if his own grew dull. Mendoza and his friends once decided to go out on the town in the guise of seamen and were promptly arrested, having been mistaken for group of sailors who had just jumped ship. Like his descendent, Mendoza didn't quit show business after facing a hostile audience. There's the story of Mendoza showing up at a Purim pageant and being hired on the spot to perform; the audience booed, the manager refused to pay, and Mendoza, never one to back down from a dispute, simply persisted in his demands until he got his fee. And he was inevitably the victim of trouble, never the cause. As described by a contemporary, he "always was the injured party. In his own estimation, never was there such a mild mannered man as he. The fights just seemed to seek him out." Can a sense of victimization be genetic?

Mendoza made and lost a vast amount of money in his life. His abiding concern for the box office led him to stage one of several grudge matches with his archrival, Richard Humphreys, on the riverbank, specifically to keep gatecrashers away. He never imagined that they would simply arrive by boat, a fact that bugged him for the rest of his life. The Prince of Wales introduced his friend Mendoza to his father; thus Daniel Mendoza rode the royal carriage to Windsor Castle and met George III. They strolled on the terrace together, the King of England and the street fighter from the East End. It was the first time the monarch had ever spoken to a Jew. After winning his first professional bout and earning the sum of five guineas, he went on in 1785 to whip a fighter called Martin the Butcher in a record twenty minutes and earned, thanks to the patronage and friendship of the Prince of Wales, more than £1,000—a fantastic sum at the time.

Mendoza tended to spend more than he earned, a common enough failing, and more than once he spent time in debtors' prison. As he aged, prizefighting had to be supplemented with catering. Process serving. Recruiting soldiers. Innkeeping. Inciting a mob. Baking. Mendoza died in 1836 at the age of seventy-three, leaving a wife, eleven children, and no money.

Daniel's son Isaac married a woman named Lesser, who bore Welcome. Welcome married Solomon Marks and bore Peg. Peg married Bill Sellers. In 1925 Peg and Bill had another baby to replace the dead one. They called him Peter, too.

• • •

Welcome Mendoza Marks was prolific and shrewd, not only as a business-woman but as a mother. She birthed, fed, and raised a total of eight sons— George, Harry, Chick, Alfred, Lewis, Dick, Moss, and Bert—and two daughters, Cissie and Peg, whose real name was Agnes. When Solomon Marks died, Welcome was dynamic enough to corral her ten offspring at a house at Cassland Crescent, Hackney, and press upon them the idea of a family theater troupe and management company. She called it Ray Brothers, Ltd., having decided that Belle Ray was a more fitting name for a woman of the theater, though everybody around her called her "Ma."

Ma Ray was Mama Rose with skill, better luck, and more children. She never aimed at art. Commerce was her goal, and the more the better. From nothing, she came to manage forty other vaudeville companies in addition to her own, though Ray Brothers, Ltd., was always her chief concern. The company survived, even thrived, but the hard fact was, vaudeville was already on its way out. As clever as Ma was as a theater manager, a more prescient enterprise would have been the business of motion picture exhibition. And even within the slowly declining world of the English music hall, Ray Brothers were never top-notch. They don't seem to have ever played London—only provincial theaters, a heavy component of which were summer seaside resorts.

A German inventor sold Ma her big inspiration: a large but transportable water tank. In it, barely clad nymphs (her daughters) would frolic for the pleasure of an audience (mostly men) who hadn't come to see Shakespeare. Ma called her first revue "Splash Me!" It was prurient, and it sold well. The only problem, her grandson later claimed, was that the tank broke one evening and "eventually drowned the band. . . . Seriously drowned!" (Asked by the interviewer how someone could be "unseriously drowned," the grandson was vague: "Yes, anyway . . .")

Neither Peg nor Cissie Marks was a beauty, but they were young and in good enough shape, and they could always be supplemented by any interchangeable showgirl willing to appear nearly naked and drench herself for pay on a music hall stage. Historically, aquacades have not ranked high in the aesthetic hierarchy of live performance, but even in its own category "Splash Me!" challenged good taste, particularly when Ma directed the girls to eat bananas underwater. With "Splash Me!," audiences throughout southern England knew precisely what they had come to see. So did local officials. But Ma got around whatever Watch Committee happened to have jurisdiction by tinting the water lighter or darker depending on the degree of likely censorship in that particular venue. Always cagey, she took a preemptively patriotic posture during World War I by dyeing the tank water red or white or blue and daring the prudes to criticize such a public-spirited celebration.

Water was not Ma Ray's only medium. For many years she got her daughter Peg to stand onstage in a flesh-toned leotard. This seems to have been the essential point of the act, though its artistic justification took the form of Peg's brother Bert projecting slides on her body that miraculously dressed her as any number of famous ladies—Queen Victoria, Elizabeth I, the Statue of Liberty. Peg appeared in other forms as well. One in particular, a chestnut skit starring Peg as a libidinous charwoman, served well as the warm-up for the water tank.

They were theater people, the Marks/Rays, and Ma was not overly concerned with her children's sex lives, though she's said to have set a strict moral tone during work hours. Peg attempted marriage with a fellow named Ayers, but it didn't work, and soon she was single again and back with Ma. In 1921, with Peg a divorcee pushing twenty-five, Ma felt the need to go

husband hunting on her daughter's behalf. An added incentive for the ma-
triarch was that her car, an enormous showy red thing, needed a driver.
And so she found Bill Sellers.

• • •

They were playing Portsmouth. Her new production (either "More
Splashes" or "Have a Dip!," there's some dispute) had just opened at the
King's Theatre. It was the Roaring Twenties in England, which is to say
that the tank water was clear and the censors weren't troubled. Peg and Ma
were seated in a café listening to the piano player's rendition of "I'm Forever
Blowing Bubbles," and Ma liked what she heard. She asked the man if he
could drive a car and promptly hired him.

Bill Sellers—actually "Seller" at the time—was a Yorkshireman (Bin-
gley, to be precise), a fact that couldn't have worried Ma Ray, and he was
a Protestant, which might have bothered her but didn't. Bill did not possess
a powerful personality. And it may have evaporated further after he married
Peg. The writer and comedian Spike Milligan, who met him in the 1940s,
once described him: "Bill, I think, is kept in the clothes cupboard. I see his
cigarette smoke filtering through the keyhole. Poor Bill—the original man
who never was; he looked a pasty white and reminded me of those people
at Belsen."

• • •

Peg and Bill married in London at the Bloomsbury Registry Office in 1923.
The marriage certificate lists the bride as "Agnes Doreen Ayers, formerly
Marks"; the groom's name is down as "Seller." The ceremony was brief and
the reception nonexistent, since Ma spirited Peg off immediately afterward
to perform the charlady routine while Bill rushed off in another direction
to play the piano for another act. They moved—Peg and Bill and Ma—
into a rooming house in Highgate, North London.

Peg's first pregnancy began soon thereafter. She kept performing. They
were on tour in Dublin when the baby was born and died. According to
Bert Marks's wife, Vera, "We were told that we were never, never to refer
to that child. It was as if he had never existed." But by remaining entirely
unspoken, of course, baby Peter's death came to dominate the family's
emotional life for years to come.

Peg's second pregnancy began at the end of 1924, and once again it
did not stand in the way of her performing schedule. Neither did labor.

She was onstage in the middle of a routine in Southsea on the evening of September 8, 1925, when contractions began, and, trouper that she was, since she had no understudy she went right on with the show. After the curtain fell Bill hauled her into the big red heap of a Ford, got her back to their lodgings, and summoned an obstetrician. And so Richard Henry Seller, the second boy they called Peter, was born. One week later Peg was back onstage.

Peter Sellers, a showbiz baby, was carried onstage two weeks into his life by the vaudevillian Dickie Henderson, who encouraged the audience to join him in singing "For He's a Jolly Good Fellow." Little Pete instantly burst into tears and the audience erupted into laughter and applause. From Pete's perspective, this emotional scenario was played out more or less consistently until his death in 1980.

• • •

"Fun Showers." "Mermaids." "Ripples." Hampshire. Kent. Suffolk. Trunks, rooming houses, Ma, and the inevitable water tank. . . . Baby Pete was schlepped around with Ray Brothers, Ltd., and never had a home. He was pressed into theatrical service at the age of two and a half when Peg secured the little blond boy into a cute white-tie-and-tails outfit complete with a top hat, thrust a cane into his tiny hands, and forced him onstage to sing the sappy "My Old Dutch." The boy detested the bit and made his criticism physical by stomping on the hat.

Matriculation at Miss Whitney's Dancing Academy in Southsea was equally short-lived (discipline problems). But when the child cared to perform his own routines on his own schedule and terms, he was a natural. And he liked it. His Aunt Vera, whom he called Auntie Ve, used to accompany him to the waterfront at Southsea so he could play at conducting an orchestra for amused passersby. She also took him to see *Peter Pan* in London, where, inspired by the onstage Peter's ability to fly, one daring little boy in the balcony attempted to hurl himself off the ledge. Auntie Ve restrained him.

Peg and Bill saw their son as their best ticket to theatrical easy street, a role the son resented. As Auntie Ve once recalled, "They all thought, 'This is where we sit back and Peter will make us a fortune.' " Defiant at an early age, though, young Pete refused to cooperate. Hired for £5 to pose for an advertisement, he shunned all the photographer's directions and then flatly refused to take on any more modeling assignments.

"He was a little monster." This was Auntie Ve on the subject of her nephew. "He had far too many people worshipping him. A good smacking would have done him the world of good." Her husband, Uncle Bert, agreed: "If Peg had to go out of the room for a minute, he would set up a yell you could hear in the Portsmouth dockyards on payday."

Discipline played no role in Peter Sellers's upbringing. Once, after he pushed one of his aunties into the fireplace—with a fire in it—Peg's response was simply to say that "it's the kind of mischief any boy would get into at his age." After all, she was his mother.

• • •

Still, it was a peculiar kind of worship, since Peg alternately doted on and abandoned the boy according to her own needs. She gave him whatever he wanted when she was there, but then she went off on tour and left him in the care of one of the aunts. Peg and Bill did bring Pete along with them sometimes, but their care of him was still sporadic, not to mention risk-prone. In the midst of a fierce Yorkshire winter, with Peg and Bill appearing in something called *The Sideshow* and the child being carted back and forth between a chilly rooming house and the spartan dressing rooms of the Keighley Hippodrome, Pete developed bronchial pneumonia.

The stink of stale fish in strange hotels was the price Peter Sellers paid for staying with his parents when they were working. It was a sad childhood, and he hated it. "I really didn't like that period of my life as a kid," he once declared. "I didn't like the touring. I didn't like the smell of grease paint. It used to hit you when you went into any stage door. Grease paint and baritones with beer on their breath and makeup on their collar. . . . All these voices: 'Hello, how are you, little sonny boy? Are you all right little boy there? (Who is he?)' I used to spend my time sitting in dressing rooms."

There were, of course, moments when Peter found joy in the work of entertainers. One act in particular contributed greatly to young Peter's appreciation of the absurd. He loved Fred Roper's Midgets. They played with trained dogs and jumped through hoops and were the same size as Pete, despite the fact that they had deep voices and smoked cigars. The midget act's merry idiocy spoke to him.

Tragedy provided Pete's salvation from the stinking backstages. Ma Ray died in 1932, and the company quickly slid. Bill and Peg and the uncles were forced to take work with other troupes, and Pete got to stay home a bit more with one or the other of his parents.

• • •

Peter Sellers had just turned six years old in September 1931, when Britain went off the gold standard; by 1932, his cast-adrift parents had discovered a new way of making money. They called it "golding." It was, in essence, a scam. Bill, Peg, and Peg's brother Bert would climb into Bert's car with little Pete in tow; they'd drive out of London to some remote village or other and go house to house convincing the naïve locals that they represented the London Gold Refiners Company, Ltd., a flimflam firm that paid equally fictitious prices for gold. The locals had no idea what their jewelry was worth; Peg did, and she profited. The only "refined" aspect of the company was the phony accents Pete's mother assumed as she relieved people of their bracelets and chains. Although Pete was kept out of sight in the car during these glorified shakedowns, he still claimed as an adult to remember hearing his mother's performances in the gold trade. Even at the time the boy considered them to be a step up from what he had heard her do onstage.

Bill, meanwhile, formed a ukulele duo with a man named Lewis, which meant that he was often on the road. With the already spectral Bill vanishing completely when he went out on tour, Pete was left entirely in his mother's care. The Sellers family's life was made even more transitory by the fact that they kept changing apartments; moving was easier than paying the rent. "I had the constant feeling I was a mole on the lam," Sellers recalled. "I kept longing for another more glamorous existence—for a different me, you might say. Maybe that was the beginning of my capacity for really becoming somebody else."

Still, the Sellerses cut a particular swath as they chased around London: They kept entirely to the north side of the city. The family's locus classicus, established by Ma Ray, was Hackney. Ma lived with Peg and Bill in Islington, East Finchley, and Highgate; after she died the Sellerses moved around in Camden Town. Apart from brute geography, what linked these neighborhoods was their increasing Jewishness. Whitechapel, the East London neighborhood in which Daniel Mendoza lived, was still the center of Jewish life in the city (to the point of being considered a ghetto as late as 1900), but the North London neighborhoods in which the Sellerses housed themselves were attracting more Jews by the year.

All the stranger, then, that it was to St. Mark's Kindergarten that Peg Sellers sent her son. When Pete outgrew St. Mark's, she packed him off to

St. Aloysius, a prep school run by the Brothers of Our Lady of Mercy. It wasn't simple convenience that drove Peg to pick St. Aloysius, and in fact she moved to a small house in Muswell Hill Road, Highgate, specifically to give Peter close access to that particular Catholic school. A telling aspect about all of these shifts in residence is that family and friends—and Peter himself—consistently attributed the decision-making to Peg: Peg choosing the school, Peg moving with Peter, Peg, Peg, Peg. Even when Bill was there he wasn't there. Indeed, according to Peter's son, Michael, while Peg and Peter lived at Muswell Hill, Bill lived separately at Holloway.

On still another occasion, Bill disappeared entirely, and Pete had no idea what had precipitated the departure. After a good deal of time had passed, Peg put Pete in a car, drove to Leicester Square, found Bill standing on the sidewalk as obviously promised, and took him back, leaving Pete utterly baffled.

Pete was not a stupid boy, but he was very much an uneducated one, Peg never having stressed learning as a virtue. Originally enrolled in Form II at St. Aloysius, he was quickly sent back to Form I, an experience he found humiliating. One of his teachers, Brother Hugh, remembered that Pete was upset at his demotion, especially because he was not only older but substantially larger than any of the other boys in his new class. At that point he was almost five feet tall and fairly fat, with coarsening features, dark hair, and all the natural grace and poise of an expanding eleven-year-old. Brother Cornelius recalled that Pete looked as though he was four or five years older than he actually was, a fact that, combined with his educational underachievement, exacerbated his embarrassment.

The most striking feature of Peter Sellers's schooldays is the fact that practically nobody remembered him. As Brother Cornelius said, "One always remembers the troublemakers. But Peter, we didn't notice him at all." Scouring the many profiles, interviews, memoirs, surveys, studies, and incidental trivia about the life of Peter Sellers—and in England there are libraries' worth—one finds reference to only one schoolmate who has ever had anything to say. And what he says is rather weird.

Bryan Connon, turned up by the deft entertainment writer Alexander Walker, appears to have been Pete's only chum at school. "He wasn't much liked," Connon told Walker. But that wasn't a big problem, Connon continued, because "he seemed to have no need of friends. The retreat home to Peg was always open to him—it was the one he preferred to take." Peg's son *had* to go to school, and so he *might* make a friend there, but Pete's friendship with Bryan Connon stopped precisely at her front gate. He never got as far as her doorstep.

Sellers himself reflected on the loneliness of his childhood: "Sometimes I felt glad not to be too close to people. I might have been happier, I suppose. On the other hand, I never had much luck with people over the years."

. . .

Pete was not the only non-Catholic at St. Aloysius, though he was probably the only Jew, and the brothers maintained a liberal policy of accommodation: non-Catholic boys were excused from prayers at their parents' request. The strange thing is that Peg never requested it. And so Peter Sellers learned his catechism. In fact, he mastered not only its language but its cadence and pitch, all in perfect imitation of the Brothers of Our Lady of Mercy chanting in chapel. This skill prompted Brother Cornelius to scold Pete's recalcitrant classmates: "The Jewish boy knows his catechism better than the rest of you!" The problem was, of course, that it wasn't his catechism.

One of the few constants, apart from his mother, was the BBC.

The loyal electromagnetic friend of lonely boys, the radio carried more than simple entertainment into the restricted world within which Peg had barricaded her son. There was nothing radical on the BBC's airwaves, but the middlebrow comedians and variety acts that formed, along with news and sports, the backbone of British broadcasting showed Peter Sellers a way out of his mother's tight domestic trap. However little he understood it at the time (or ever), the blandly funny Misters Muddlecombe, Murgatroyd, and Winterbottom, the stately bands, the hours of forgettable patter—all were a subtly defiant rejection of Peg and her otherwise incessant grip.

He particularly loved the variety show *Monday Night at Seven*. (The title and time were later changed to *Monday Night at Eight*.) Pete listened to it every week, as did Bryan Connon, though always in separate houses. On Tuesdays they'd discuss it in exacting detail on their walk home from school, with Peter tossing off all the best comedy bits against Bryan's straight-man backboard. "He had a gift for improvising dialogue," Connon remembers. "I'd be the 'straight' man, the 'feed,' and all the way up Archway Road I'd cue Peter and he'd do all the radio personalities and chuck in a few voices of his own invention as well." The fun would last only as long as the walk, though, for once they reached Peg's gate it was all over. Pete said good-bye and that was the end of that.

• • •

With its heavy quotient of solitude and an awkwardness both physical and social, Peter Sellers's youth might necessarily have carried along a third component: sexual immaturity. But no. Describing his adolescence to Alexander Walker, Sellers described his own youthful randiness: "I found out how much I liked girls and how much they liked me—or said they did."

It started early. Not coincidentally, his entrance into school marked the first opportunity Pete had to spend a few hours away from Peg—and with girls his own age. It was in kindergarten that he fell for a child he nicknamed Sky Blue. She rejected him, but instead of the expected retreat into despair, Pete pressed forward. In fact, Pete kept after Sky Blue all the way into his twenties. It was all to no avail, and yet he persisted on this doomed quest for at least fifteen years, through several changes of school and neighborhood.

Pete's passion for Sky Blue led him to a dawning awareness of how belittling his mother's treatment of him was. Specifically, Peg was still dressing him in shorts, and he hated them. Not wishing to be regarded as a toddler by Sky Blue, he begged his mother for a pair of boy-worthy trousers to wear to Sky Blue's for tea, and since Peg couldn't bear to say no, she gave them to him. This is the kind of family contradiction that ties boys and girls in knots: Peter Sellers's mother protected, controlled, and belittled him, and she refused him nothing—except normal maturation.

As for the outfit Peg chose for Pete's date, it took the ridiculous form of white ducks—formal, starchy things that humiliatingly made him resemble a tiny aristocrat or waiter. Pete wore the ducks to tea and quickly pissed them in a nervous attack. Since white ducks tend to be rather less impressive with a fresh yellow stain spreading around the crotch, the date was a fiasco.

Even this severe disgrace failed to dampen Peter Sellers's affections, which in itself indicates an unusual psyche for a boy. A less single-minded kid might have given up and moved on, his love turned self-protectively to hate. But Pete was either impervious to punishment or, more likely, a glutton for it, and pressed forward. This time he used performance as his chief means of seduction. In this way Sky Blue became Peter Sellers's first audience—apart, of course, from his devoted mother.

"I found that Sky Blue had a movie hero, Errol Flynn," he recalled. "I'd seen him in *Dawn Patrol* and that was good enough. The next day I put on his voice, his accent, his mannerisms. I even threw in a background of airplane and machine-gun noises for good measure. All to impress Sky Blue." But the girl was a tough audience; the performance wasn't a hit. "She'd switched her affections. Now she was a fan of Robert Donat's. So I went to any Donat films I could find playing—fortunately for me he was a prolific actor—and went through the whole act again with his voice. No luck this time, either."

Rainer Werner Fassbinder once remarked that Steven Spielberg always wanted to be a little boy when he grew up. With Peter Sellers, it was neither a matter of choice nor desire. Consider his formative years: Peg's incessant doting and catering to his every whim; his parents' nomadic existence throughout his childhood; the school shuffle and subsequent demotion at St. Aloysius, which effectively made it impossible to bond with anyone his own age and size; the lack of any religious identity (or, better, the abundance of religions at his disposal); the absent father, both figuratively and literally; the obsessive pursuit of a girl who didn't want him. With whatever degree of intent, Peg and Bill Sellers did a splendid job of creating an emotionally spoiled, spiritually amoebic mama's boy, whose innate and fierce talent for mimicry allowed him not only to perpetuate but to depend on and enjoy his own evacuated personality.

• • •

While the dreariness of Peter Sellers's childhood paved the way only to the awkward joylessness of being the big fat Jew of St. Aloysius, the gray chill of his prep school years yielded, thanks to international politics in the late 1930s, to a dawning awareness of his own potential annihilation. He had just turned thirteen when thoughts of mass suffocation drifted into his head as well as everyone else's in the kingdom. World War II was beginning.

In the last week of September 1938, with Hitler on the brink of attacking Czechoslovakia and the skies of London increasingly dotted with blimps, the government bestowed 38 million gas masks on the British people. Men, women, and children got them; babies, too young to know the difference, were written off.

The historian Angus Calder describes the British people's mood as they tried on their new headgear at the dawn of the new era: "Fitting on these grotesque combinations of pig-snout and death's-head, sniffing the gas-like odour of rubber and disinfectant inside them, millions imagined the dangers ahead more clearly. Symptoms of panic appeared." The imaginative Briton, Calder writes, "saw in his mind's eye not the noble if heart-rending scenes of 1915, not the flower of the nation marching away to fight in a foreign land, but his own living-room smashed, his mother crushed, his children maimed, corpses in familiar streets, a sky black with bombers, the air itself poisoned with gas."

Pete's fourteenth birthday occurred at the end of the week in which Great Britain declared war on Germany. Along with millions of other Englishmen, the Brothers of Our Lady of Mercy ran for cover to the countryside as St. Aloysius was evacuated to a town in Cambridgeshire. Peg, who had opened a Highgate trinket shop at the time, claimed to be unable to move to Cambridgeshire on such short notice.

Perhaps it ought to go without saying, but Peg was unwilling to send her son so far away (two and a half hours by train) without her. So she immediately yanked him out of school, and that was the end of Peter Sellers's education.

She was assisted, however unintentionally, by the government. September 1, 1939, had been set as the date on which children would be required to remain in school to the age of fifteen rather than fourteen, but the war necessitated a postponement. Had it not been for World War II, Peter Sellers might have received at least one more year's worth of education.

But no matter. Peg was very pleased to have him by her side all day long, and that was what counted.

• • •

In September 1939, when the Nazis attacked Poland and England declared war on Germany, the government issued gas masks, mobilized troops, and evacuated nearly 4 million British citizens out of the cities and into the countryside. On the BBC, the immensely popular radio comedian Tommy Handley turned the onrushing catastrophe into an absurd extended joke. Handley's new show, *It's That Man Again*, featured a series of recurring characters with funny voices, a taste for puns, and a brand of humor that would have fallen flat to any audience but the English. In one routine, Handley played the Minister of Aggravation, a joint venture between Agriculture and Information:

> HANDLEY: To all concerned in the Office of Twerps! Take notice that from today, September the twenty-tooth, I, the Minister of Aggravation, have power to confiscate, complicate, and commandeer—
> ASSISTANT: How do you spell *commandeer*, Mr. Hanwell?

HANDLEY: Commandeer—let me see. (Singing:) Comm-on-and-ear, comm-on-and-eer, Tommy Handley's wag-time band! Comm-on-and-eer . . . ! Er, where were we? "I have the power to seize anything on sight!"

ASSISTANT: Oh, Mr. Handpump! And me sitting so close to you!

Fun, filth, and playing to the crowd: Pete was inspired.

England was profoundly rattled by the war, but by and large the British people didn't go berserk at the prospect, their mood at the start of this international catastrophe an improvement over the previous generation's histrionic reaction to the so-called Great War. (The declaration of war on Germany in August 1914 is said to have sparked the stoning of hapless dachshunds in the streets.) In fact, because there was so little combat at first, British wags took to calling it "the Bore War."

Pete helped his mum in her shop. His only friend, Bryan Connon from St. Aloysius, was now his former only friend, having been dispatched along with the other schoolboys to Cambridgeshire. Connon never heard from Sellers again. With no contact with boys his own age, nor any men except his always-in-the-background father—even the celibate monks of St. Aloysius were more spirited role models—Pete's social world now consisted essentially of his mother and the BBC. Together in their North London flat, Pete with his radio and Peg with her trinkets, they endured the coldest winter London had weathered in forty-five years.

And the blackouts. Once a night, for a few minutes at least, everyone in London had to tack thick curtains or dark paper over their windows or face the chastisement of police or patrolling air raid wardens. Blackouts were a matter of national security, of course; lights provided targets for Nazi bombers. But in the Sellers household, blackout curtains served as the physical manifestation of Peg's goal as a mother—they sealed her son away with her. The outside world could never love him as much as she did, so he had to be kept from it in isolation.

As particular as Pete's situation was, however, his countrymen were also experiencing a deep and sometimes morbidly comical sense of disconnection. Plunged into blackness every night, not only were the British people forced to sequester themselves behind dark curtains at home, but the enforced murk of London streets at night led to pratfalls. All told, an astounding one in five people injured themselves during the blackouts—walking headlong into trees and lampposts, bumping against fat people, even just losing their way in the dark chaos of an otherwise familiar lane and tumbling off the curb. Nightlife had suddenly turned into a series of goofily scary and nonsensical comedy routines.

The Bore War, or "funny war" as it was also known, grew less boring in May 1940 when the Nazis' seemingly unstoppable march to the French coast forced the humiliating evacuation of 220,000 British soldiers from the beaches near Dunkirk. The boredom ended absolutely on Saturday, September 7—the day before Pete's fifteenth birthday—when German war planes destroyed London's East End. Other London neighborhoods saw the day's cataclysm as predictive of their own fates. The blitz lasted a full two-and-a-half months, and German ships began massing off the coast of France. The possibility of an outright invasion of England became a much less abstract notion.

When the bombing began, Peg and Pete ran, along with countless other terrified Londoners, to the nearest underground station, which in their case happened to be Highgate. A few weeks later, the Sellers's flat suffered a bit of damage during a bombing raid. The apartment was certainly inhabitable and the shop could have survived, but it was a close enough call to convince Peg to shut the business, pack the trinkets and all the family's furniture, and spirit Pete swiftly and safely away from London.

As their refuge, she chose the town of Ilfracombe on the north coast of Devon. Even apart from the fact that a brother worked in a theater there, escaping to Ilfracombe was a smart move on Peg's part. There was nothing there worth bombing—unless, of course, the Nazis decided to target picturesque seaside resorts for obliteration by firestorm.

The little watering hole of Ilfracombe is seated at the lower verge of one of these seaward-plunging valleys, between a couple of magnificent headlands which hold it in a hollow slope and offer it securely to the caress of the Bristol Channel. . . . On the left of the town (to give an example) one of the great cliffs I have mentioned rises in a couple of massive peaks and presents to the sea an almost vertical face, all muffled in tufts of golden broom and mighty fern." This is Henry James describing Peter Sellers's new location, if not his new home, albeit half a century earlier.

It was in Ilfracombe that Peter Sellers, an unemployed adolescent, returned to the theater, and he did so partly in response to the conflicting influences of his parents. After he became famous, Sellers spoke often about his theatrical grandmother, his mother's performing career, his own bitter childhood backstage, and his profoundly ambivalent feelings about the world of show business. He rarely spoke about his father, who throughout Peter's youth kept up sporadic employment as a musician of little note. But in 1974, Sellers mentioned to Michael Parkinson of the BBC a reflective detail that suggests that Bill Sellers was not simply a blank slate on which his wife and son wrote nothing. Bill's confidence in Peter, at times at least, bore an inverse relation to Peg's: Peg's was infinite, Bill's could be utterly void. Was it in defiance of Bill's paternal defeatism that Peter pursued his career? "Dad was convinced always that I was going to be a road sweeper," Sellers told Parkinson with a laugh. "And he always was very encouraging: 'So you'll turn out to be a bloody road sweeper, will you? I'll tell you that!' "

"See," Peter continued, "my mum very much wanted me to go into the theatre." So that is what he did.

Through the nepotism of Stanley Parkin, a family friend who operated an Ilfracombe theater and hired Peg's brother to work there, Pete got his first job: janitor at ten shillings per week. Promotions followed, as suited an adolescent: box office clerk and usher; assistant stage manager and lighting operator; and, eventually, actor, though as he told Parkinson, only in bit parts "like (officious servant voice) 'Your carriage is without!' or (decrepit old man voice) 'Hello!' or something like this—minor niddly tiddly poo things."

Because of the upswing in touring companies during the war, young Pete also got a glimpse or two of real theater. Ilfracombe was hardly comparable to the prewar West End (and there seem to have been no fond memories of Peg ever having taken him to see plays in London), but instead of the carnival acts he witnessed during his early childhood with Ray Brothers, Ltd., Sellers's backstage jobs in Ilfracombe earned him the chance to see a few sophisticated actors playing complex parts: "I saw some very famous actors come to that theatre—Paul Scofield was one in *Night Must Fall* with Mary Clare."

Somehow he made a new friend. When his uncle and Stanley Parkin hired him to work in the theater, they also brought in a boy named Derek Altman, with whom Pete launched his first stage act. They called themselves Altman and Sellers; they played ukuleles and sang and told jokes. Despite winning first prize in a weekly talent show—a cynic might conclude that their jobs as ushers and box office staff at Pete's uncle's theater played some role in this triumph—the duo soon disbanded. During this time, Pete and Derek, having developed a fondness for the novels of Dashiell Hammett, were also inspired to found their own detective agency and even had business cards printed to that effect. An unfortunate incident put a quick end to the enterprise: a humorless adult reached over and ripped Pete's fake mustache off his lip.

• • •

When a swing band turned up at the theater for a weeklong gig, Pete discovered a new talent. He'd heard drums before, of course, but he'd never had the chance to create all that rhythmic racket himself, so one afternoon, when he found a set of drums onstage for Joe Daniels and His Hot Shots, Pete let loose. The bandleader/drummer caught him mid-act. Daniels wasn't angry. Appreciating the teenager's enthusiasm and nascent talent, he ended up giving Pete pointers for the rest of the week, after which Pete begged his parents for drums and steady lessons. Unable to resist his whims let alone his wants, they came through.

Drumming suited him. Banging in time, Pete could envelope himself in a world of near-total abstraction, all in the context of a great deal of noise. What aggression he felt as an awkward fat kid could be expelled, at least in part, by methodically hitting things, all in a socially respectable and even artistic manner—one that might eventually pay off at that, though drummers' lowly status in the music world tended to be fodder for jokes. (Did you hear about the drummer who graduated from high school? Me neither.)

Jokes aside, Peg was pleased by Pete's enthusiasm for a performing art. Bill went along.

• • •

At the time, whole city blocks across Britain were turning to dust. In a single ten-hour period in mid-November 1940, German warplanes dropped hundreds of tons of bombs on the medieval city-center of Coventry, effectively flattening it. The Germans coined a new verb: *to Coventrate*, meaning to devastate the psychological as well as the physical heart of a population. London was so immense that despite hundreds of thousands of bombs raining down on its head it could not be thoroughly obliterated, at least not with the technology available at the time. But Bristol could—and was. (Bristol is about eighty miles away from Ilfracombe as the crow, or German warplane, flies.) So were Birmingham and Southampton. By the beginning of 1941, the people of Britain were taking a sustained hit of the sort that Americans had never experienced in their own land, and the aftershocks of their direct experience of war continued to rumble in the British psyche for many years to come.

Relatively safe in Ilfracombe, Pete turned sixteen in September 1941. In addition to girls, he was developing an interest in communication with the dead. He began turning to the clairvoyant mother of a friend for cheer and solace when the radio wasn't enough. For whatever reasons, disembodied voices spoke to Pete as meaningfully as those that were attached to people close at hand, if not more so. He believed in them.

Meanwhile, the radio show *It's That Man Again* (*ITMA* for short) had become an even bigger hit, and even more exciting to Peter. One writer has gone so far as to claim that Tommy Handley was "probably the most popular man in the country after Churchill." ("That Man," by the way, wasn't Handley; it was Hitler.) Along with *Monday Night at Eight*, *ITMA* was the BBC's attempt to infuse its more steadfast offerings with fast-paced, American-style patter. According to the historian Asa Briggs, "*ITMA* was *vox mundi*, rich in all the sounds of war and with more invented characters than Walt Disney." Pete Sellers of Ilfracombe found it inspiring.

• • •

Given his bedrock peculiarities, one of the most unexpected aspects of Peter Sellers's life is his extraordinary talent for sexual seduction. It began in earnest in Ilfracombe. His scores weren't just the bravado of a deficient adult embellishing his youthful conquests. That Sellers went on to enjoy a rampant sex life with some of the world's most gorgeous women suggests that he really did have something going for him and that women responded to it. Still, even he admitted that his early dates were the product of desperate pretense. Believing that the real Peter Sellers wasn't much of anything, Pete told the girls that he was a talent agent who'd dropped in on Ilfracombe to scout for future stars. "I'd take the girls out to Bull's Point, opposite the lighthouse," he fondly remembered, "and get them to audition for me—songs, patter, dances. The ones who 'won' were generally those with the most talent for being friendly." These performances filled the ever-expanding subdivisions of his personality: "I enjoyed the impersonation for the feeling of power it gave me. Nobody paid that kind of attention to Pete Sellers."

Remarkably, the fake talent agent persona itself wasn't enough to suit him, so Sellers accomplished these missions of love while wearing a trench-coat in imitation of Humphrey Bogart, a hat like William Powell's, and even the beloved paste-on mustache to make him look a little more like Clark Gable, all in addition to the now-standard Robert Donat voice. These overlapping disguises testify to the lengths Peter Sellers went to deny who he was—or wasn't.

• • •

It was 1943, the grim middle of the war, and Pete was approaching the age of conscription. The Irish-born wartime novelist Elizabeth Bowen described the country's mood that year: "Every day the news hammered one more nail into a consciousness which no longer resounded. Everywhere hung the heaviness of the even worse you could not be told and could not desire to hear. This was the lightless middle of the tunnel."

Bill Sellers, being rather at home in a murk with no end in sight, took one of the most decisive actions of his life. With his son turning into a talented drummer, Bill formed a quartet, with Pete on percussion. At first they played only in North Devon, but gigs followed further afield, and by summertime they were all the way up in Lytham St. Annes on the coast of Lancashire. Bill, whose confidence in Peter's future had once been shaky, grew fond of the kid's drumming: "He proved a wizard at it," Bill later said. To enhance the boy's reputation, Bill had business cards printed, citing Pete's profession as "Young Ultra-Modern Swing Drummer and Uke Entertainer." This burst of confidence on Bill's part leads to unanswerable questions: Was Bill's lack of confidence in Peter's abilities actually invented by Peter out of resentment for Bill's frequent absences, or out of loyalty to his darling mother, or simply out of a mischievous desire to embellish a frankly conventional father-to-son chastisement into a weightier tale of Peter's victimization?

No one knows, but the cards appear to have worked, perhaps too well, for soon Pete was heading out on his own. He took a job with a band from Blackpool farther up the coast. Peg was not happy. His band having broken up upon the drummer's departure, Bill joined the Entertainments National Service Association. ENSA had been founded at the start of the war as a network of morale-boosting, ever-touring diversions for soldiers and factory workers. ENSA's mandate was to bring entertainment not only to workers and servicemen within Great Britain but to British workers and servicemen anywhere in the world—a global music hall. By the war's end more than four out of every five British actors, musicians, costumers, comedians, stage managers, acrobats, and clowns had found employment, however temporary, with ENSA. It's an impressive statistic as statistics go, but what it really reflects is the extent to which the British entertainment barrel's wartime bottom had to be scraped. For every great ENSA discovery—Terry-Thomas, Tony Hancock—and every popular ENSA star—Sybil Thorndike, George Formby, Gracie Fields—there were at least six essentially talentless washouts who would never have been allowed onstage had dire conditions not demanded it. For them, World War II was an employment bonanza. "We had to endure them once a month—and endure it was," one Surrey factory worker shuddered when recalling those compulsory amateur hours.

Bill Sellers was in the middle range—a proficient musician who was able to provide his audience with a bit of relief from the tedium of military drills or assembly-line monotony. He assembled still another band, largely from the old band, but with one addition: the ukulele master George Formby being occupied on the top tier of ENSA, Bill settled for George's sister Ethel, a singer who also liked to do a Gracie Fields–like Lancashire-accent comedy routine. Peg, searching for a reason to bring Pete back into the family fold, convinced Bill to get Pete an ENSA job as well.

Pete himself was successfully bribed by the promise of a set of flashy new £200 drums. "They were the finest," Peg told Alexander Walker in the 1960s. "They had to be! Pete wouldn't have looked at them if they hadn't been. With Pete, everything had to be perfect or it wasn't for him. And what Pete wanted, Pete got."

● ● ●

In Taunton he got a girl. As it does for most young men, this triumph, Pete's first home run, took a blend of luck and engineering. But in Pete's case there was an added complication: Peg often accompanied her son and husband on their ENSA tours. According to one fellow ENSA trouper, Peg actually went so far as to sleep in Pete's room with him, leaving Bill to find a bed somewhere else. But when Bill and Pete set up the band in Taunton, Peg stayed at home, fifty long miles away in Ilfracombe.

They were billeted, along with some ENSA showgirls, in a funeral parlor. This made more sense than it may seem at first, since the mortician happened to serve as the local ENSA manager, but still, it was something out of a macabre vaudeville sketch. The doorbell rings, an ENSA trouper answers it, and finds a corpse on the other side of the threshold.

One of the girls was particularly unnerved by the whole experience and found it difficult to sleep with dead people in the house. She confessed her fears to Pete and maternally told him that if he, too, became frightened, he could always join her in her room for solace and support. He took her up on it.

"It was absolutely irresistible," Sellers later declared. "Although I was still pretty young, I was no stranger to the charms of girls. But I'd never had an invitation issued to me in such plausible circumstances. So one night, in pajamas and dressing gown, and armed to the teeth with Robert Donat accents, I found my way along to the girls' room. Feigning fear, and trembling with what I hoped she'd think was fright, I got into bed with her. The only mistake I made was that I didn't take off a stitch in advance—it was a far from ideal state for impetuous lovemaking."

Peter Sellers was no longer a virgin. Quickly thereafter he was no longer an ENSA trouper, either, Bill having discovered his son's sexual success. He dispatched the boy back to Peg.

But drumming had sparked Pete's ambition to the point that even Peg Sellers was forced to contend with the fact that her son couldn't simply stay with her forever doing nothing, and soon he was playing gigs with the broadcast bandleaders Oscar Rabin and Henry Hall. Finding work outside of ENSA wasn't terribly difficult at the time, given the scarcity of musicians during the war. But sometimes he had to take what was available, no matter what. Thus, Waldini and His Gypsy Band—an elderly Welshman and a group of Brits with bandanas on their heads. "Waldini" was no master musician, but he was even worse at finding his way from town to town; getting lost seems to have been one of Waldini's greatest talents. One day, directionless in the middle of a Lancashire nowhere, Pete decided he'd had enough and returned again to Peg.

For Peter Sellers, these back-and-forth shuttlings were his first negotiation between the absolute dependence of childhood and the relative autonomy of young adulthood. All adolescents go through it. But in Sellers's case, his fledgling freedom was doubly crippled by the vacuum that passed for a core self—his ego was made up of multiplying electrons soaring around no nucleus—and a dependence on his mother that verged on obscenity. (Unlike Freud's version of the Oedipus myth, Peter never had to challenge his father for his mother's affections because Bill was figuratively impotent already.) The overgrown boy was turning into an undergrown man, with ludicrous results. At one point he landed in Brighton and took a job at a movie theater. He called Peg one day on the telephone and announced that he had proposed to his landlady's daughter the night before and was now compelled to follow through. Outraged and panicking, Peg and her entourage—Bill, Auntie Ve, and Auntie Cissie—sped to Brighton and yanked him home, whereupon he took a job in a circus and proposed to a girl from the sideshow.

"Although I was on my own at last, I hated the life," he later said. "I felt lonely. I felt trapped. I missed Peg, who'd always entertained me when things were black.

"It put the final seal on my dislike of show business," Sellers went on, "of *having* to entertain. I thought to myself, 'There must be less humiliating ways of being pushed around.' "

He managed to find such a way: by joining the Royal Air Force. That military service turned out to be less a source of complaint for him than entertainment work provides a stark measure of Sellers's ambivalence toward his lifelong career.

• • •

Military service was a national expectation at the time; barring some physical or mental abnormality, one enlisted, and that was it. So it was not
unusual that after his birthday in September 1943, Peter Sellers signed up
with the RAF. Spike Milligan, who heard Sellers's tales some years later,
describes Peg's predictable reaction: "She must have gone through the entire
medical encyclopedia to find a disease that would get Pete back into civvy
street, back into her loving care and protection: 'He's got flat feet! He's got
a flat head! Flat ears! He's even got flat teeth!' " It was all to no avail; Peg's
chubby son became 2223033 Airman Second Class Sellers, P.

Pete was a mama's boy, but he wasn't a coward. Airman Sellers thought
he'd like to be a pilot. This goal might be written off as the glamorous
reverie of a callow dreamer, but it was a wartime dream, which is to say
that when Sellers signed up for military service, real planes were crashing
every day and real pilots were dying. It was a bitter disappointment for him
when RAF doctors found that his eyesight wasn't quite up to the task of
piloting. Turned down for flight training, Pete ended up nothing better
than an aircraft hand.

Sellers's entry into military service was doubly depressing for him since
the other airmen weren't at all dazzled by the fact that he could play the
drums. Pete, who needed much more attention than he got whenever he
was away from his mother, found his mood rapidly sinking.

So Peg stepped in to soothe him. Since he hadn't shipped out yet, she
was free to become a kind of camp follower, trooping after him the way
Marlene Dietrich trails Gary Cooper at the end of *Morocco* (1930), except,
of course, that Dietrich is Cooper's lover, not his mother.

As befitted her role, Peg cooked his meals for him, RAF mess halls not
being good enough for her special boy. And not surprisingly, Peg demonstrated an extraordinary knack for procuring good food for Pete, despite
stringent wartime rationing. Eggs, butter, cream, sugar, tea—all were in
short supply. Peg got them.

Pete soon found a way out of military drudgery by resuming his performing career; it was better to risk demeaning himself onstage and harbor
the hope of applause than to demean himself daily as an aircraft hand. He
approached Ralph Reader, the head of an RAF entertainment unit called
the Gang Shows, and asked to be auditioned. When Reader asked him what
exactly he did onstage, Sellers answered that he played drums and did

Tommy Handley bits from *ITMA*. Entering the auditorium the following day for the audition, Reader had the peculiar experience of hearing himself singing "We're Riding Along on the Crest of a Wave," the Gang Show theme song, to the great amusement of a group of seated airmen who should have been busy cleaning the theater. The airmen noticed the officer and stood at attention; Sellers kept on singing—until he, too, saw Reader staring at him in disbelief. "Well," Pete said resignedly to Reader, "do you want a drink or do I get jankers?"

For a mimic so accurate, jankers—otherwise known as the boot—was unlikely. But when Reader heard Sellers drum, he knew for certain that he had a workable act. Sellers turned out to have other skills. Beyond the drumming, for which Pete was soon showcased, Reader's Gang Shows offered Pete his first chance to be a comedian onstage. Doing short stand-up routines as well as group skits, he played to troops across England before shipping out.

Jack Cracknell, who ran the Gang Show office in London, remembered being bedeviled by a characteristically persistent Peg, who tried every means to convince him—behind her son's back, of course—that Pete should be kept safe within the borders of England.

Once again, she lost. Peter Sellers was sent all the way to India.

• • •

The precise sequence of Peter Sellers's tour of service is vague. As formative as his travels in Asia were to him—think of the many mannerly Indians he impersonated over the years—it's unclear just how much time he actually spent there. Sellers himself once claimed to have spent three years in the East, an impossible length of time given the fact that he also served in France and occupied Germany after the war ended and was back at his mother's house by the end of 1946. As Graham Stark, one of his closest friends, puts it: "He was a great one for the fantasies. He used to boast— God knows why—that he was descended from Lord Nelson!"

However long Peter Sellers spent in Asia—we know he was in and around Calcutta in December 1944—the people he saw and heard there made such an impression on him that he couldn't help but return the compliment by picking up speech patterns that would last a lifetime. These early impersonations may even have included the complete getup, skin tone and all. Sellers once claimed that while in India with the RAF he went so far as to rub brown pancake makeup on his face and hands and wrap his head in a turban so as to pass himself off as a Sikh.

But it was the impersonation of officers—a more dangerous stunt, because he could be court-martialed for it—that became a standard routine during Sellers's military career. He claimed that he'd first pulled the prank on Christmas Eve 1944, in the city of Agartala, most of the way to the Burmese border, in Assam. Sellers's rationale for the stunt was, characteristically, both tortured and foreseeable:

"I'd never spent Christmas Eve in a hot country, and I was far away from home, and I was thinking, 'My mum wants me at home.' " His Pegsickness led to an excess of Christmas cheer: "In those days we were sort of drinking a bit, you know." (Sellers is employing the royal "we.") "We don't drink any more of course—wine, wine, just wine, you know!—and I remember getting very drunk. And I thought, 'I'm a twit to sit here and do this when I could be in the officers' mess.' " So he "found" some insignia of suitably impossible rank and off he went, straight to the officers' club with a new identity.

Since it was the middle of the night, there was "only one lone old twit sitting in the corner." Plowed as he was, the old officer still managed to question Sellers as to how he could possibly have achieved the rank of air commodore at such a young age. After offering several asinine evasions, Sellers came up with this one: "I see in the dark, you know—it's all this rum."

• • •

In late 1944 and early 1945, at the time that Peter Sellers found himself in India, it hadn't been more than a few months since the subcontinent had faced the invading Japanese—a disaster for the Japanese. In fact, there was still intense fighting in parts of Burma in early 1945 when Peter was sent there to drum and tell jokes to exhausted British soldiers. Sellers seems never to have been very near the front, but the same can't be said of his audiences. In England, some of the airmen for whom he performed were regularly flying bombing missions over Germany. In India and Burma, they were fighting jungle fever as well as their fierce enemy. As such, they were a peculiar audience. As soldiers they were tough. As combat-weary men in need of distraction, they were easy.

A bit of personal comic relief occurred for Peter when, somewhere on the subcontinental road show of World War II combat vaudeville, he bumped into none other than the great Welsh "Waldini" and his band of English gypsies. Still in their bandanas, Waldini and his band were gamely crisscrossing India playing their standby Hungarian tunes for homesick British fighting men.

Pete's stint in Asia was necessarily his first extended separation from Peg. Psychologically, he took a notable turn. She remained on his mind, of course, but he wrote to her rarely, if ever. Earlier, when he left her behind to tour around England with his father, ENSA, or the Gang Shows, he'd had no need of pen and paper; the telephone was easier. But now, given the choice between letter writing and nothing, Pete, conspicuously, chose nothing.

• • •

One reason was that Peter was necessarily thrown together with his fellow Gang Show performers, billeted in close quarters, and was rarely alone. One new acquaintance ended up sticking with him for the rest of his life, though with a few years' hiatus after the war.

Dennis Selinger was a theater manager turned RAF gunner. Peter's sharply drawn double nature struck Selinger quickly, just as it struck almost everyone with whom Sellers ever became close: "He was affable, easy, very funny when the mood was on him; at other times withdrawn, uncommunicative."

They met in overheated, overstuffed Calcutta, Sellers fresh from a gig in the jungle, when a turn of events occurred that would seem absurd if not for the anything-might-happen disorder of wartime: The two English nobodies suddenly found themselves treated to dinner by the American movie star Melvyn Douglas, who, being there, was happy to distract two war-weary soldiers.

The Gang Shows provided a good diversion for worn-out, homesick troops, and Pete was getting the attention he required. With Reader the impresario saving the best for last, Sellers's drumming closed the show. A reviewer in the *Bombay Sunday Standard* was impressed with him to the point of clairvoyance: "The 'baby' of the show is Peter Sellers, aged 19, the boy-drummer and impressionist. A big future lies before him."

• • •

"He was a big, fat, curly-haired boy" with "a big, hairy body—like a monkey," says Peter's friend David Lodge, describing the way Sellers looked when they met. They were in Gloucester at the time, fellow Gang Show performers. Lodge recalls their meeting as having occurred just after Sellers returned from Asia, which would place it in 1945. Then again, on another occasion Lodge dated it as occurring in 1944. More important than the exact date is the fact that they got along beautifully, amused each other greatly, and remained the best of friends for the rest of Peter's life.

Given the fact that tense and frustrated men are thrown together during wartime with other tense and frustrated men, military theater often leans in the direction of gender humor. In short, Pete's dress-up routines included drag. Lodge himself made a point of growing a mustache to prevent his own forced march in gowns, but he notes that young Pete's "peaches-and-cream" complexion—a strange contrast to the hairy body—produced a "very convincing woman." But it was Sellers's talent as a drummer more than as a comedian that impressed Lodge: "He was a *great* drummer—as good as Buddy Rich." His were showman's performances, complete with flamboyant riffs and the confident tossing and catching of drumsticks in midair. Aging drummers in Britain may disagree; rumors of Pete's lack of aptitude have surfaced. Unsung English drummers seem to resent the one among their ranks who achieved vast wealth and fame as a movie star, and apparently they denigrate his drumming talent. It doesn't matter. The winner writes the history.

"He behaved like a boy—a rascal, actually," says Lodge, who necessarily got to see Sellers's selfish streak at close range but who, like the other men Sellers grew to trust, saw the tender and vulnerable side as well. They were bunked next to each other in Gloucester. Lodge couldn't help but notice that Pete was being bullied by a loud and burly Welshman who did not appreciate being in such close proximity to a Jew. Sellers, whose temper could erupt violently and without warning, was reacting to these anti-Semitic taunts with undue restraint, so the bluff, muscular Lodge stepped in to assist him. He handed Pete a heavy iron poker and advised him to slam the Welshman over the head with it. "If he won't, I will," Lodge added straight to the Welshman's face. The bully backed off.

What's fascinating about Lodge's tale is not that Sellers was the object of anti-Semitic contempt but that his Jewishness was so evident to a stranger. Did the men question each other about their religions? Or was it simply Peter's nose?

As Lodge soon saw, Pete did possess a volatile temper, and when he exercised it there was no holding back. "Another time he actually broke a chair up, very deliberately, piece by piece, to work out his aggression," Lodge recalls. "I made a note—'If you get on the wrong side of this boy . . .' "

That Lodge quickly gained Peter's trust was made evident by the fact that Peter invited him back home to meet his mother. Peg and Bill were living on Finchley High Road at the time. Lodge, not surprisingly, found his new friend's relationship with his mother "too close for comfort." But, Lodge continues, despite her domination of his emotional life, Peg couldn't control the actions of her willful son. Pete *did* precisely what he pleased. He required her commanding love to survive, but he didn't require her permission for anything.

Only Peg Sellers could see in David Lodge—a tall, broad, athletic serviceman—nothing more than a surrogate for herself. When she discovered that the Gang Show was heading out on tour again, she tried to make Lodge promise to become a kind of nanny for her now fully grown son. Says Lodge, "If she'd been a fella I'd have whacked her."

• • •

Europe was in unimaginable ruins when World War II ended in 1945. Thousands of acres in the heart of British cities had been reduced to rubble—and Britain had *won* the war.

There wasn't enough food, or clothing, or fuel, and these shortages lasted for years. British soldiers, eager to return home from abroad once their enemies had surrendered, were nevertheless compelled to await demobilization on the British military's terms. Since the defeated Germans had to be policed by Allied troops, there were still thousands of British airmen in need of light entertainment. Peter remained in the RAF.

Sellers and Lodge were stationed in a decimated Germany when the officer impersonations kicked up again. "We were based up on the third floor of a big barrack block" in a former Luftwaffe camp in Gütersloh, Lodge remembers. A trace of shock is still left in his voice after all these years. "Out came the makeup box," whereupon Sellers morphed before his eyes into a classical sort of British military man with "a full handlebar mustache, parted hair, lieutenant's bars, wings, and ribbons." Lodge, amazed and appalled at his friend's absolute transformation, asked Sellers where he thought he was going, to which Sellers replied—in a voice unearthed from some forgotten Boer War epic—"I think I'm going to inspect the lads downstairs!"

With the air of a bureaucratic missionary or a sort of military uncle, Peter proceeded to question the boys about the quality of their quarters, their supplies, their food, all with an air of deep concern. Returning to his quarters, he simply couldn't understand Lodge's panicky attitude. "Now they really believe somebody cares about them!" Sellers explained sympathetically.

In telling these tales, Lodge stresses that Sellers still had the lowest possible rank. "He did it because he didn't like himself as he was," Lodge says. "He didn't think he was attractive at all. And he didn't like being a nobody."

There was an infantile streak as well. Lodge tells of sitting in a Paris patisserie with Peter when a tray of cream cakes was set before them: "Very deliberately, Peter took a single bite out of every pastry on it—he was like an immature, undisciplined child who must cram himself with as much satisfaction as he can as quickly as he can."

As far as the chaperoning of Peter was concerned, David Lodge turned out to be a corrupt nanny. He and Pete were males in their twenties; they liked to cat around. In fact, in Cannes they managed to procure some champagne to go with a couple of girls, and everyone got so plastered that the boys creatively talked the girls into crawling around the floor pretending to be feline.

In Toulon, Lodge took it upon himself to rescue Peter from an especially low-life prostititute. Peter had had too much to drink and disappeared. Lodge managed to trace him to a seedy apartment in a bad part of town and burst in to find Peter trying to remove his pants. Fearing for his friend's safety, he grabbed the disappointed Sellers and sped him away.

Women, says Lodge, were particularly easy in Germany. Much to his retrospective shame, the pretty young German girls were helpfully starving, which led the two randy young men to use cookies as bait. ("It was really pathetic," Lodge mutters.) Lodge was—and remains—especially disgusted by Pete's voraciousness with one particular girl, describing her as "desperate" and Sellers himself as "animalistic." There was a comical retribution, though, when Pete got up in the middle of the night to use the bathroom and chose the wrong door in the dark. Wearing nothing but his RAF underwear, he plunged directly out into the street. The door locked behind him, and he had to pound on it furiously to be let back in.

Lodge remembers spending Christmas 1945 with Sellers on the Champs-Elysees. It was a merry time. The war was over, the Allied soldiers were gleeful, and all was right with the world, except that Pete, always on the needy side, had grown a little too dependent on his best friend. When they had to part, having been sent on different entertainment tours, Sellers fell into lonely despair. "I left him in Germany on the Danish border," says Lodge. "He was crying."

• • •

Sellers was back in London working at the Air Ministry on Sloane Square and killing time at the Gang Show headquarters on Houghton Street when his term of service with the RAF ended. He had already returned home to his mother, who somehow managed to reward his survival with a big, new, shiny black American car.

Peg was always adept at pulling money out of a hat, but it took special skill to produce *any* car, let alone a huge American model. It was easy for Peter to park the gleaming heap on any reduced-scale London lane because, apart from the strict gasoline rationing that was still in force, the deprivations of postwar England meant that there were precious few competitors for spots. It was in this car-poor context that Graham Stark, a Gang Show sergeant, arrived at the entertainment unit's headquarters on slim, curving Houghton Street one day and was flabbergasted to see a lowly airman methodically polishing a car so big that it appeared to be a limousine. "The whole thing had an air of a sequence from a Hitchcock movie," Stark writes, "the empty street, the incongruous car, the lone airman silently polishing."

Curious, Stark struck up a conversation with the airman, who boasted that it "only does fourteen to the gallon, but you've got to admit it's a right beauty." ("No concern with petrol rationing, no concern that I was a sergeant," Stark notes. "He just wasn't impressed.") They ended up going out for some tea and war stories, including tales of Peter's life in the theater, after which Peter inquired about the state of his new friend's lodgings. Stark had to confess that he was staying in a one-shilling-a-night flophouse. Peter was appalled.

After a quick call to Peg, he put Stark in the newly polished car and sped him back to East Finchley, where Sellers brought the family's initially skeptical landlady nearly to tears by a torrent of melodramatic pleas. (Poor young officer, served his nation so bravely, jungles of Burma, orphan needing roof. . . .) She immediately offered Stark the empty one-room flat on the floor below Peter, Peg, and Bill. The flat provided a close-range position from which Stark could witness Peter's family dynamic. "He *was* an only child," Stark has said, "but it was an absurd 'only child' "—all the spoiledness and narcissism, only warped.

London itself wasn't itself. The destruction of whole stretches of the city forced many newly homeless residents to become squatters in empty buildings and still-occupied army camps. Mourning was standard, the sullen knowledge still sinking in that the war's dead were not just stragglers on a late steamer from Colombo. There were severe shortages, and therefore strict rationing, of basic foods and supplies. The British people's meat allowance hovered around thirteen ounces per person per week; milk at two pints; cheese at one and one half ounces. They got "sweetie coupons" for candy, and they didn't get many of them. Everybody won a single egg every seven days.

During the winter of 1946, London, never the brightest of cities, was particularly dreary. It scarcely helped that the battery of fierce blizzards and freezing temperatures that season was followed in quick succession by floods during a bleak London spring and a relentlessly gray and rainy summer.

• • •

At the Sellers residence, the inevitable business cards were printed: "Peter Sellers, Drums and Impressions." Peter took work where he could find it, which is to say that he didn't work very much and was supported almost entirely by Bill and Peg.

In his off hours, which appear to have been many, he pursued a girl. He did so with such drive and determination that the words *clinical* and *obsession* come to mind. Pretty, blond Hilda Parkin met Peter in 1946 at a Christmastime ball at the Grosvenor House in London. The Parkin family had been longtime friends of the Sellerses and Rays; it was Hilda's much-older brother, Stanley, who owned the theater in Ilfracombe. "It was a big thing to go to the Grosvenor House," Hilda recalls. "One of the first times we'd been able to go to a big ball for a long time. Peter was really my nephew's friend; my nephew was about my age. And when he told Peter his aunt was coming I don't think he was very pleased. Until we met. And then we had great fun together."

Hilda, who was living in Norfolk at the time, has kept to this day the many letters Peter Sellers wrote to her during their three-year relationship. "I've got 109 letters from Peter, with three proposals of marriage and threats to commit suicide if I broke up with him. Some of the letters were sixteen pages long, and he'd already written one in the morning, and he was writing one now, and he'd just posted one."

From one letter: "Hilda, will you marry me next year? We will both be 22."

From another: "Dearest Hilda—If you ever took it in your mind to pack me in, I'd go completely round the bend."

Another describes the view from his parents' flat on Finchley High Road: "From the window, I can see the backs of rows of dreary looking houses. An overcast sky looks down upon the tax- and cup-tortured England. When I get to the top I'll get you a Rolls Royce! Throw in a few butlers for luck." (By "tax- and cup-tortured England," Sellers is referring to the fact that in the postwar years taxes were as high as food supplies were low. He railed against Britain's new Labor government in other letters, even going so far as to blame Labor for the frigid winter.)

"He was a little fat boy, not that it meant anything," Hilda notes. "I was a trained dancer and acrobat, and I taught him to dance. Peter got on very well with it. He was always kidding, impersonating. . . . We had a thousand laughs. We made some records together, Peter and I [in novelty booths where people could cut their own vinyl]. He used to impersonate me."

He also enjoyed other impersonations: "Often, his letters would arrive with photographs, and in one of them he was dressed up like his mother." This was not done behind Peg's back. *She* took the picture. "In another he was pretending to be his nonexistent sister."

Toward the end of their relationship, Peter paid Hilda a visit in Norwich, where he'd taken the job of carnival barking at one of the Parkins' amusement parks. He checked himself in at the best hotel in town—under the creative name "Lord Beaconsfield"—and went pluckily off to visit his girlfriend. In point of fact, however, the first and only Earl of Beaconsfield was the nineteenth-century British Prime Minister Benjamin Disraeli, with whom Peter, fantastically, had begun to claim family ties.

Hilda: "My family was running this carnival, as you call it—it was an amusement park—and Peter came up to see me. He came everywhere, wherever I was, bless his heart. He said, 'You must come over to the hotel. I've booked in as Lord Beaconsfield.' His mother said there was some back relationship with Beaconsfield, but that line had died out many years ago. There happened to be a lady in that hotel, and someone told her, 'Oh, we have Lord Beaconsfield.' And she said, 'There *is* no Lord Beaconsfield.'

"So they went and looked in his suitcase and found a pack of very cheap cigarettes—Woodbines. Not the best cigarettes! And his pajamas were from Marks and Spencers. When we got there, a couple of fellows came straight up to him. One stayed with me, and one marched him off to the manager's office. He came out a little while later, red-faced, and we both just walked off. I said, 'I thought I was going to be arrested!' "

And what was Peter's first response when confronted by the hotel manager? "When they took him into the office," Hilda says, "he phoned his mother."

According to Hilda, Peg explained that yes, Peter "was always kidding, there was no harm in him, he's not going to hurt anybody, and his uncle is the manager of a big London theater. . . ."

But that was not quite the end of it, according to Hilda: "When he got back to London he had to report to the police. They let him off. I think the police called on them, because I remember he told me that his father had said, 'Here you are, officer—here's the Lord Beaconsfield.' "

"At the end of the three years when we were very good friends, he wanted to get married, he really did. I wasn't thinking of marriage. There'd been a war, and we'd only just finished it. The last thing I wanted to do was get married." So Hilda Parkin told Peter Sellers something he never wanted to hear: "I thought it was fair just to tell him that I wasn't in love with him. He burst out crying. So I cried, too. He kept writing, but I didn't contact him any more. I didn't answer the letters."

• • •

Pete wasn't mortally crushed by the rejection, especially since Margaretta "Paddy" Black, a member of an all-girl Gang Show, appears to have been enjoying a relationship with Peter at the same time he was pursuing Hilda. Paddy recalls accompanying Peter on a visit to one of the Marks/Rays' quite-distant relatives, Gerald Rufus Isaacs, the second Marquess of Reading. (Gerald Rufus Isaacs's father, Rufus Daniel Isaacs, 1860–1935, was lord chief justice of England, ambassador to the United States, and viceroy of India.) After a pleasant discussion of heraldry and cousins far removed, Peter and Paddy headed home, whereupon Peter proudly told her that Gerald Rufus Isaacs's title was hereditary and that he—Peter Sellers—was next in line. If she agreed to marry him, he added pregnantly, Paddy Black stood to become a countess. But the made-up promise of a title wasn't enough.

"As much as I liked Peter," Paddy Black later said, "the idea of getting engaged never entered my head."

At home, a jittery Peg took to her bed whenever Paddy turned up at 211B Finchley High Road. Hilda Parkin had had better luck: "Since they were working and involved with my family, they were quite pleased by it. She was very nice to me." With Paddy, though, Mother made herself so scarce that Paddy assumed she was a bedridden invalid. "Peter?" Paddy would hear a little voice moan from behind a closed bedroom door during these cramped domestic dates.

Then a little louder: "Peeee-ter?!"

• • •

World War II had scared Peg, but certain of Peter's romances threw her into a cold terror. Following her own mother's liberal morality, she didn't expect him to remain chaste. It was his heart's arousal she feared, particularly when the women weren't firmly within her family's orbit. Besides, she was smothering.

David Lodge still remembers the disquieting goodnight phone calls Peter placed to his mother when they were separated: "Good night, Peg. God bless you. Yes, you too. God keep you safe! I love you. Yes, I *do*! Yes, I love *you, too*!"

Lodge also recalls tiny Peg taking him aside one day, looking up at the burly ex-serviceman, and telling him, with profound admiration and not a shred of comprehension, "*You* wouldn't get married and leave your darling mother."

What drove Lodge craziest, though, was the Lady Bountiful air with which Peg thanked him for taking such good care of her Pete during the war. "I'll make things easy for you," she told him, and with a great fanfare of largesse, she arranged for her theater-managing brother-in-law Bert to hire Lodge as an usher.

"She was a pain in the ass," Lodge observes.

After returning from the Lord Beaconsfield escapade in Norwich with humiliation in place of the fiancée on whom he claimed, at least, to pin his future, Peter found himself hanging around the streets of Soho killing time with other unemployed musicians. The musical arranger Wally Stott, with whom Peter would work closely a few years later, remembers meeting him for the first time on the sidewalk on Archer Street: Peter was dressed "in an RAF uniform with a snare drum under his arm." "*All* musicians stand around Archer Street, you know," Sellers himself once noted, "and everyone was getting work but me." (What do you call a guy who hangs around with musicians? A drummer.) Stott, who came to understand Peter very well and like him even more, reflects that "in one of his lives he would like to have been a jazz drummer."

In still another life, clearly, he would have liked to have been noble. Like the pasted-on mustache he used to dress his upper lip in order to become the youngest dick in Devon, Sellers's assumed identity as Lord Beaconsfield surfaced again at, of all places, a middle-class campground on one of the Channel Islands. The camp was owned by Hilda Parkin's brother Stanley; Peter's cousin Dick Ray found work there as well. The job itself was not exactly fulfilling for the talented, impatient young drummer-comedian—crying out "wakey, wakey" to a slew of slumbering tourists wasn't quite the career he had in mind for himself. So Peter decided to add a little sparkle by billing himself as the Fifth Earl of Beaconsfield—that is, until a local reporter spoiled the fun by inquiring as to the circumstances by which someone in *Burke's Peerage* had descended to a downscale campground in Jersey. Even after he was unmasked Peter couldn't quite give it up. He insisted on calling himself simply "the Fifth Earl" until he lost that job, too.

Whether he was Lord Nelson's relative, Disraeli's descendent, the next

Marquess of Reading, or the disembodied doubles of Tommy Handley and the cast of *ITMA*, Peter Sellers was unusually able to sustain multiplying identities and never let them interfere with each other—or with reality, for that matter. As his friends explain it, it was all because he didn't much like himself, a schizoid way to build self-esteem. This is a plausible explanation, but perhaps it was equally the case that Sellers harbored an expanding number of selves and liked *too many* of them. What he didn't like was having to choose one and stick to it.

Was it to keep these propagating identities at bay or to distill them further into a kind of *eaux de folie* that Peter began to believe—insofar as any grotesque fantasy is actually *believed*—in the existence of scurrying little midgety creatures called Toffelmen? Moronic buggers who embraced a philosophy of contradiction, Peter's Toffelmen were creepy but stalwart, rock-bottom pessimists who harbored flickers of hope. With their high, squeaky voices and circus-act entertainment value, they kept Peter company. Who knows when they first knocked on his mental door, or when (if ever) they departed, but when Peter revealed their existence to David Lodge, Lodge was most unnerved. "They were very vulgar," says Lodge. "They were always masturbating."

• • •

The Gang Shows' steady employment having given way to seemingly endless stretches of nothing, Pete was losing hope. A booking at a Peterborough music hall might have bolstered his flagging confidence except for the fact that on opening night, after sharing a cramped dressing room with a blind accordion player and a trick dog act, the waves of hisses that greeted his comedy routine led the manager to fire him on the spot. Luckily for Peter, the headlining singer, Dorothy Squires, came to his rescue and convinced the manager to keep him on, though Squires later said that she'd seen nothing particularly special in Sellers's drab routine. She just felt sorry for him: "He was just another struggling kid, fresh out of the services, very lonely and very scared."

A drumming gig at the Aldershot Hippodrome took a similar downturn. Having been loftily billed as "Britain's answer to Gene Krupa," Peter launched his set only to have the lights go wrong and the accompanying band fall drastically off-tempo. The audience rebelled, loudly. Graham Stark recalls Peter telling him about the fiasco, though for Stark's benefit Peter couldn't help but turn it into a black comedy routine: "As a story of absolute disaster it unfailingly reduced me to tears of laughter," Stark recalls.

With Peter suffering one thudding calamity after another, it's little wonder that he thought about disappearing into still another new identity. At his mother's urging, he considered adopting the stage name "Peter Ray." Hilda Parkin remembers it: "She wanted him to be called 'Peter Ray'—it's in one of my letters. And I said to him, 'You know, "Peter Sellers" sounds much better. It sort of comes to the tongue better than "Peter Ray." ' And there already *was* the star comedian Ted Ray."

As it happened, he kept Sellers but dropped the drums. The big shining car was gone now—who knows where it had come from, and who knows where it went—and since Peter had, after all, chosen to master the most unwieldy musical instrument this side of the piano, the lack of ready transportation made it difficult for him to get from show to show with his cumbersome drum set. "I was playing with a little group called 'The Jive Bombers,' " Peter's story goes. The band was booked in the industrial city of Birmingham, about one hundred miles northwest of London. Peter got there, along with his drums, by hitching a ride with the saxophone player. The Jive Bombers were in mid-session when people began crowding around Peter's drums, helpfully making little percussive noises with their tongues in the middle of his set. Peter's tale concludes: "This fellow says to me, 'Oh say, can ya play "Any Umbrellas"? I said, 'No, no, we don't play that.' He says, '*Why* don't you play it?' I was getting annoyed at this point, so I said, 'Just 'cause we don't play it, that's all.' So he looks at me and says 'Shitface' and walks away. I thought, 'That's it, inn'it? I'm out.' "

• • •

In March 1948, he was standing around Archer Street not knowing quite what else to do when a press agent friend told him that a nearby strip club was looking for a comic. The Windmill, just off Piccadilly Circus, was run by a successfully sordid impresario named Vivian Van Damm. Forbidden by the local morals code from gyrating, Mr. Van Damm's strippers made a show out of stationing themselves around the stage in exalted tableaux of live neoclassical sculpture, each element designed, however roughly, as a contemporary interpretation of a low-grade Venus. The girls were essentially coarser and more modern Peg Rays without the slides and body stockings, and the audiences made do. Already frustrated, the Windmill's crowd was thus a tough one as far as any intervening joke-tellers were concerned, and Van Damm, accordingly, was a harsh auditioner. (Who wants to run a strip club with a clientele bored to the point of rioting? Not Vivian Van Damm.) But Peter was funny enough, and brave enough, to pass Van Damm's test, and so Peter took the job of legitimizing naked women for £30 a week.

Each night, after appearing in small roles in other acts, Peter briefly held the spotlight by himself. He performed a selection of Tommy Handley's *ITMA* voices followed by a song written for him by his father. The audience seems not to have resented Peter's intrusion on the Greco-nudie *tableaux vivantes*, and at the end of the appointed six-week run, Van Damm was impressed enough to add Peter's name to a bronze plaque on the Windmill wall. It was labeled "Stars of Today Who Started Their Careers in This Theatre."

• • •

Some time after the Jersey holiday camp fiasco, Peg had taken Peter by the hand and led him to a Soho office building for a reacquaintance meeting with Dennis Selinger, who seems to have lost touch with Peter after parting ways in Calcutta. After being demobilized, Selinger had returned to London and launched his own theatrical agency. The two men may have been friends in India, but Peg seized control of their reunion, insisting as only Peg could that her son would make a fortune for the hungry young agent. "I was more impressed with Peg than with Pete," Selinger later declared, which was only natural since Peter spent most of the meeting clearing his throat toward no vocal end and fussing over the pristine crease in his pants and the fine leather gloves he held in his nervous hands. Severe clothes rationing, by the way, was still in force.

Selinger agreed to represent Peter, but it appears never to have been an exclusive arrangement, since Peter had at least one other agent knocking on doors for him at the time, and many others followed suit over the years, either in concert with or apart from Selinger. Still, it was Peter himself rather than his agents or his mother who landed the first audition at the BBC. He'd written to request an audition in January 1948, was granted one in February, and in March he appeared on British television on an amateur hour called *New to You*. The act consisted of impersonations and included this little jingle:

I'm glad you've heard my name—it's Peter Sellers!
Peter Sellers can be gay as well as zealous!
And now it's my due, from the program *New to You*,
As one of Britain's up and coming fellas—perhaps.

He needed a writer. In any event, the bit survives only because Peter himself went out and bought a disk-cutting recorder, a rare and expensive machine for the consumer market, simply in order to memorialize the occasion of his BBC debut.

Peter did well enough on *New to You*, but he was not immediately skyrocketed into stardom, and he still needed to find any work he could. When the producer Hedley Claxton needed a straight man to appear with the comedian Reg Varney in his *Gaytime* revue, Peter auditioned. The final tryout came down to Peter and Benny Hill. Benny Hill won.

Peter set his sights, or rather his ears, back on the BBC—not television, which was still minimal in Britain, but radio. After all, he'd been listening to and mimicking BBC programming since childhood. Indeed, by this point he could have trademarked his *ITMA* routines had Tommy Handley himself not already done so. Besides Handley, Peter could do Neville Chamberlain, Winston Churchill, and a host of precise but anonymous American travelogue announcers. His renditions of any number of other BBC powerhouses were flawless. And he could prove it.

The setup: In 1948, Kenneth Horne was the star of a hit radio show called *Much Binding in the Marsh*. Set on an RAF base, *Much Binding* was one of several war-themed comedy shows that were popular that year. The patrician-sounding Horne played the commanding officer; the chirpy-voiced Richard Murdoch played his assistant. Roy Speer was a successful BBC producer.

"I was pissed off—oh, excuse me!, *fed up*, right!—with getting nowhere fast," Peter told Michael Parkinson on the BBC in 1974. "Roy Speer was doing this show called *Show Time*. The compère was Dick Bentley, and there were lots of new acts, you see? I'd written in I-don't-know-how-many times to try to get in on the show. No reply. The secretary said that Mr. Speer 'blah barumpfh hmpf.' So I've got nothing to lose, and I thought, well, I'll phone up. We were doing these impersonations, and one of the big shows on the air was *Much Binding in the Marsh* with Kenneth Horn and Dickie Murdoch. I just thought I'd *do* it. You know, you *do* things at certain times. You've got to get ahead!

You've got to [car noise] *vrummmmm*! So I thought if I stay here I'm dead, [and] even if he kicks my ass out of there it doesn't matter *as long as I make some impression.* So I phone up, and . . . I thought if I click with the secretary, I'll get through, right? So, I said [deep, resonant voice], 'Oh, hello hmmm, this is hmmm Ken Horn. Is Roy there?' Once she said, 'Oh, yes he is, Ken,' I knew that I was alright. So, I got on there and Roy said, 'Hallo, Ken! How are you?' I said, 'Listen, Roy, I'm phoning up because I know that new show you've got on—what is it, *Show Time* or something? Dickie and I were at a cabaret the other night and saw an amazing young fellow called Peter . . . Dickie, what's his name?' [High-pitched twit voice:] 'Uh, Peter Sellers! Sellers!' [Resonant voice again] 'Anyway, it could probably be very good if you probably had him in the show, you know. This is just a tip, a little tip.' He said, 'Well that's very nice of you.' And then he came to the crunch, and I said, 'Uh . . . I, uh . . . It's me, it's Peter Sellers talking and this was the only way I could get to you and would you give me a date on your show?'

"He said, 'You cheeky young sod! What do you do?' I said, 'Well, I obviously do impersonations.' "

Speer was correct. Peter Sellers *was* a cheeky young sod. In other words, he was a natural comedian whose intense insecurity was armored by the hide of a pachyderm. The child who'd gotten whatever he wanted had become an ambitious twenty-two-year-old man who wrote the letters and made the phone calls and white-knuckled his way through one wretched audition after another in pursuit of the blazing career he was convinced he was ordained to have. After his period of postwar malaise, the young Peter Sellers became exceedingly persistent in seeking work that would showcase his enormous talent, and he offended people all along the way.

The piano player at the Windmill found him pushy. A disgruntled Freemason claims that Peter joined the peculiar group in the late 1940s, became an unrepentant social climber, and broke the sacred covenant of secrecy—the code words and wacky handshakes and all the rest. "He bandied the phrases and signals about at the BBC," the bitter Mason reports. By doing so, he continues, Peter greatly embarrassed the good but gullible Masons who had sponsored him in the first place.

Spike Milligan offered a more empathic explanation for his friend's peculiarities. Peter, Milligan once said, "was just a nice, very quiet, and very complex simpleton. He was the most complex simpleton in the world."

• • •

The BBC broadcast Peter's *Show Time* program on July 1, 1948. A little over a week later, Leslie Ayre, the radio critic for the London *Evening News*, gave Peter his first postwar review. It was a very good one with one highly quotable nugget: "In Peter Sellers, radio brings us another really conscientious and excellent artist." An overjoyed Peg framed the whole review and kept it on the wall for the rest of her life. Dennis Selinger did something more practical: He had it reproduced as a three-column ad and ran it in the trades, complete with a glamorous-looking head shot of the suddenly rising young star, the new master of funny voices.

The ad, the review, Selinger's phone calls, and most of all Peter's performances rapidly earned him a slew of variety show bookings and cabaret engagements, not to mention more radio show appearances. Over the course of the next twelve months, Sellers and his proliferating voices turned up on the BBC on *Workers' Playtime*, *Variety Band Box*, *Ray's a Laugh*, *Petticoat Lane*, and *Third Division*. The seamless flow of dissociation his multiple characters produced was remarkable. Men, women, old, young, upper class, working class, the nasal, the clipped . . . Peter's endlessly redoubling accents were so naturalistic that listeners had to remind themselves that they were hearing only one man and not a crowd. And on the radio, at least, whatever genuine Peter Sellers there was tended to get lost. "Well, that's *me!*," Peter announced on one show, only it wasn't his actual voice at all; it was the voice of a bland and anonymous BBC announcer as imitated by Peter.

On the strength of his reputation, the ex-nobody was even able to hook up his friend Graham Stark with steady BBC work as well. Stark and Sellers continued to enjoy each other's company, to the point of developing a double-pickup routine. Along with the disk-cutter, the increasingly gadget-prone Peter owned a then-novel automatic record-changer that accommodated a total of eight records, and so it served as a built-in timing device for two young men on the make. He and Graham would pick up girls and bring them back to Pete's place when Peg and Bill were out. "If we hadn't gotten anywhere with the girls by the fifth, we certainly wouldn't by the eighth," Stark fondly recalls. "This became a catchphrase which Peter and I used to bandy about: 'If you haven't made it by the fifth. . . .' "

• • •

In late 1946, a year and a half before Peter appeared at the Windmill, a bulbous and good-natured Welshman took the stage with an edgy music hall routine. He sang, and not only in the fine Welsh baritone for which he would become world famous. The man sang *both* parts of the sappy Jeanette MacDonald–Nelson Eddy duet "Sweetheart." When "MacDonald" and "Eddy" were forced to sing at the same time, the Welshman yodeled incomprehensibly. But it was a warped shaving routine that caught the audience's interest most dramatically, for the man really did shave himself onstage using a big bowl of warm water, a well-used brush, an old-fashioned cutthroat razor, and ridiculous amounts of shaving cream, after which the comedian drank his filthy shaving water.

Harry Secombe was born in relative poverty in 1921 in the port city of Swansea on the south coast of Wales. His love of singing was established at an early age. According to his brother, the Reverend Frederick Secombe, "Harry's great place for singing was out in the *ty bach*. He used to sit and sing there for hours."

Like so many men his age, Secombe had gone through the war, though in Harry's experience—at least in Harry's *telling* of the experience—World War II tended to be rather more farcical than it probably seemed to others. He recounted one escapade, for example, that is said to have occurred in Medjaz-el-Bab, a tent somewhere in Algeria, where the myopic Secombe espied what he took to be a helmeted Nazi and slapped the enemy dramatically under arrest, only to learn that the Nazi was Randolph Churchill. ("He happened to be facing the wrong way at the time," was Secombe's explanation.)

Young Harry Secombe was amiable but driven. He married a Swansea girl, Myra Atherton, in 1948, and after a short honeymoon in Cornwall, Harry returned to London, Myra to her family in Swansea. They saw each other only when Harry needed to take a break from his heavy performing schedule. They stayed happily married for fifty-three years.

Secombe's six weeks at the Windmill ended with Vivian Van Damm etching Harry's name onto the honored bronze plaque, the one that augured greatness to those who had performed under Van Damm's roof. The gesture may seem to have been a pro forma honor, but bear in mind that in the seventeen months after Secombe appeared at the Windmill, the gruff Van Damm added only three names to the plaque before Peter's—Alfred Marks, Michael Bentine, and Bill Kerr.

When Secombe left the Windmill, the comedy duo of Sherwood and Forest moved in. Sherwood was Tony Sherwood. Forest was Michael Bentine.

Born in 1922 into an upper-crust Peruvian family, the Eton-educated Bentine was, in appearance at least, a sort of Beat-poet Rasputin. With his bushy black mane and beard, he looked, as the musician Max Geldray described him, "as though his parents had invented hair." Bentine's past was suitably shady. He served in the RAF; that much is certain. His exceptional intelligence is also verifiable. But the tales he told of his own exploits, contacts, and secret lives tended to shift so effortlessly from eyewitnessed fact to plausible circumstance to grandiose impossibility and back again that none of his friends ever really knew what to make of him. The pub owner and writer Jimmy Grafton reports: "I have heard him give accounts of exciting incidents as a fighter pilot, bomber pilot, parachutist, commando, member of the Secret Service, even as an atomic scientist. His claims to be an expert swordsman, pistol shot, and archer are substantially true. He is also a qualified glider pilot." Spike Milligan claimed that "he once told me, face to face, that his mother had levitated from the ground, across the dining table, and settled down on the other side."

"Bentine was forever telling people they were geniuses," said Peter Sellers. "I don't know why he did this, but he'd say to *anybody* after a few minutes conversation, 'You're a genius!' And they'd usually believe it, because Bentine is the only one who's had any real education out of the three of us. He was the one who started nuclear physics, and all we could do was get through these three letter words like *cat* and *dog*."

Whatever the actual facts of Michael Bentine's biography may be, he was impulsively creative and recklessly funny. He enjoyed disrupting quiet cafés by suddenly bursting into fake-Russian babble so as to create the illusion that he was a spy (albeit one who couldn't keep his mouth shut). Jimmy Grafton, the publican/writer, remembers being in Bentine's dressing room once at the London Hippodrome when Bentine picked up a longbow and fired an arrow directly at the dressing room door. Because it had been shot from a mighty longbow, the arrow penetrated the wooden door with ease and ended up protruding several inches through to the other side. The reporter who was approaching the door at the time was surely surprised.

• • •

In the summer of 1948, BBC radio's Third Programme was running a comedy series called *Listen, My Children*. (After World War II, the BBC divided itself into three sections: the Light Programme, the Home Service Programme, and the Third Programme, which appealed respectively to working-class, middle-class, and upper-middle and upper-class audiences.) Produced by Pat Dixon, *Listen, My Children* featured Benny Hill, Harry Secombe, and Carole Carr. Smart and funny, the show was popular enough that a follow-up series was quickly planned. It was originally to have been called *Falling Leaves*, but the title was changed to *Third Division—Some Vulgar Fractions*. Two new comics were added to the lineup—Michael Bentine and Peter Sellers.

Peter and his fellow radio comics recorded *Third Division*'s first program in early December 1948. Five more shows were recorded before the end of the year, and they began airing in late January 1949. In the second *Third Division* show, Sellers performed a hilarious sketch—so hilarious, in fact, that Sellers kept it alive for many years thereafter. Written by Frank Muir and Denis Norden, it was a travelogue of a South London neighborhood. "Balham, Gateway to the South" was narrated by an overly enthusiastic, broadly Midwestern American (Sellers), who persistently renders the neighborhood's name in two sharp, twangy stresses—*Bal! Ham!*

With snappy scripts by Muir and Norden, brought to antic life by Sellers, Secombe, Hill, and Carr, *Third Division* was a highly entertaining series of six programs. But it wasn't history-making. That would require the participation of a gaunt lunatic who was living in an attic room over Jimmy Grafton's pub, sharing space with a rhesus monkey.

• • •

Spike Milligan was born in Ahmednagar, India, in 1918, and first appeared onstage at the age of eight in the Christmas pageant of his convent school in Poona. He played a blue-faced clown, arguing shortly before curtain time (to no avail) that his face really ought to have been black. Then, feeling himself unfairly excluded from the pageant's concluding Nativity scene, the boy-clown burst in upon the manger. "I thought the clown should have a place in life," he later explained.

The Milligans moved to England in 1933, when Spike was fifteen. The family was decidedly poor, though no decision had ever been made. Spike joined the war as a gunner in the Royal Artillery, but he was not a natural warrior. In North Africa, his unit proceeded to fire a heavy artillery gun without having dug it in, thereby sending the thing recoiling down a hill, where it narrowly missed a truck occupied by Lance Bombardier Harry Secombe. The burlap covering opened at the back of Secombe's truck and a face popped in. "Anybody seen a gun?" Spike inquired. (Secombe's tale of the event runs like this: "We couldn't get the Germans out of these hills. We kept sending them letters, but they wouldn't go. . . . This huge gun jumped out of the gun pit, and it came pattering over where we were and missed us by a few yards, you know, in this little truck. And I thought, 'They're throwing guns at us.' ")

The comedy of Spike Milligan's World War II took a darker turn when he was blown up at Monte Cassino. His unit was taking cover in an olive grove outside an enemy-held monastery. "I was counting out my Woodbines and reached five when this weird sound hit my ears," Spike remembered. "I can't describe it. It was like a razor blade being passed through my head."

Spike was dispatched to a rehab hospital—the same one to which Harry Secombe had been sent after breaking his eyeglasses. (This is one of Secombe's explanations, at any rate. The other is this: "I had been invalided and downgraded after I got lost in a blizzard.") Whatever it was that put Harry Secombe in the hospital, Harry soon discovered that he and Spike shared the same antic sensibility. Spike described one day: "A crippled sergeant in a wheelchair came round and asked, 'Does anyone do entertainments?' " Spike responded by telling four jokes in quick succession, none of which produced a laugh—"so I picked up an axe and struck Harry Secombe."

Harry told of staying with Spike in a Roman military hostel, men sleeping on every available surface: "There was Spike all tucked up in bed, nice and comfortable with his pajamas on, so I poured a bottle of beer over his head."

In Milligan's case, one suspects that the unbalanced foundation of his worldview, or the solid foundation of his unbalanced worldview, had been formed before the razor sliced through his brain, but the war certainly exacerbated his despair. "I got used to seeing men jumping out of little holes and looking about with binoculars. Men looking out of tanks with binoculars. Always men looking out and throwing things at one another. I thought to myself, 'This is mad.' " Yes, it was. And so was he.

Chronically underhoused after the war, Spike moved into Jimmy Grafton's attic, whereupon his friends dubbed him "the prisoner of Zenda."

The Grafton Arms, the pub on the first floor, had been in the Grafton family since 1848 and was now being operated by Jimmy, fresh back from the war, where he had served as an infantry officer. Grafton was no ordinary publican, however, since he also wrote comedy scripts for BBC radio. But it was not Grafton's scriptwriting talent that initially drew Michael Bentine and Harry Secombe into the pub as patrons. It was the fact that the Grafton Arms served drinks after hours.

Bentine and Secombe had shown up at the pub one day in 1946 or '47 and immediately began complaining about the poor quality of a radio comedy show they had recently heard—*Variety Bandbox*, the author of which was none other than Grafton himself. Then again, Grafton was writing *Variety Bandbox* for the comedian Derek Roy, whom Spike described as "about as funny as a baby dying with cancer."

Since Harry's strange friend Spike began spending a lot of time at Grafton's anyway, Grafton offered him the attic space, where Spike, too, began typing comedy scripts for Derek Roy's new program *Hip Hip Hoo Roy* and peering through a keyhole at a monkey who was living in the next room. Milligan went so far as to claim not only that "Jacko" peed into the pub's pea soup but that he, Spike, actually watched the cook stirring it in. Jimmy Grafton disputes this repulsive accusation, though Grafton himself admits that another pet, a bulldog, came close to biting off Harry Secombe's balls.

But anyway, says Grafton, the monkey was a vervet, not a rhesus, and its name was "Johnny."

Whatever the case may be, Spike's relationship with the monkey was ultimately more productive than his relationship with Derek Roy, since Roy rarely found Spike's scripts very funny and most of them went unused.

• • •

A gang was forming, though none of the members knew it at the time. Peter knew Bentine and Secombe; Spike knew Bentine and Secombe; Jimmy Grafton knew them all. But Peter didn't know Spike, and that was to be the key.

They were living very different lives. While Spike was lodging with a monkey in Grafton's attic and writing scripts for the trash, Peter, flush with his new success as a radio personality and cabaret performer, was growing even more dapper in many new sets of clothes—and cars. Between the summers of 1948 and 1949, he bought and sold four of them. His comedy routines continued to center on impersonations and improvisations, but he'd also begun to court danger onstage by adding a surrealistic twinge to his act. On one occasion he walked brazenly onstage completely shrouded in a plastic raincoat, most of his face covered by the hat he'd yanked down well below its intended level, and delivered his entire routine without showing anything of himself to the audience. Although he was well on his way to becoming the sought-after talent he always knew he was, his very success was serving to intensify the distaste he had always held for the average spectator. They were, after all, the sons and daughters of the good citizens he'd seen gaping at his barely clad mother in Ray Brothers revues. Now that Peter himself was regularly facing the crowds, he was feeling more and more contempt for what he considered to be idiot audiences—"just a bunch of no-brow miners and tractor makers," he once declared.

On October 3 and 10, 1949, two successive Mondays, Peter earned £100 for opening for Gracie Fields at the London Palladium. They were his most important live performances to date, and as the theater manager Monty Lyon recorded in his journal, he was "very well received indeed." Peter's act consisted of a marvelous drag character he'd recently created, the plump and lovely Crystal Jollibottom, a dim-witted sod called Sappy (or Soppy), and a sentimental tribute to Tommy Handley, who had died rather recently. Sellers didn't simply perform these impressions one after the other; he tied them all into a sort of storytelling performance, gliding in and out of the mimicry in an ingratiating and conversational way.

The most extravagant bit was an avant-garde impression of Queen Victoria. This was no mere "We are not amused" queen. No, this was Victoria "when she was a lad."

Rude and hilarious, it involved Peter dressing himself in a ginger-colored beard, an undone corset, and combat boots, and walking to the footlights and announcing, "I'd like to be the first to admit that I do not know what Queen Victoria looked like when she was a lad." He may also have carried under his arm a stuffed crocodile. Accounts differ.

• • •

It was around this time that Harry Secombe was doing a show at the Hackney Empire. Called "a fucking death hole" by one of Spike's knowledgeable friends, the Empire was not known for the kindliness of its audiences, but Harry Secombe's shaving routine, followed by the Jeanette MacDonald–Nelson Eddy duet, were crowd pleasers nonetheless. But it was not Harry's act itself that brought the evening to the level of an historical event. It was what occurred before the curtain went up that mattered—the meeting, in the Empire bar, of Peter Sellers and Spike Milligan.

"He looked like a nervous insurance salesman," was one of Spike's recollections of Peter that evening. Another: "Peter wanted to look like a male model—posh suit, posh collar and tie, Macintosh, gloves he carried in his left hand . . . oh, and a trilby hat" (a soft felt number with a deep crease on top). Milligan was struck by the faintness of Peter's voice ("I thought I was going deaf!") and also by his comportment: "He was quite dignified, apart from the fact that he didn't buy a bloody drink all night. Dignified but skint."

After the show, Milligan, Sellers, and Michael Bentine came around to Secombe's dressing room. For whatever reason, Secombe responded by removing the lone light bulb from its socket and plunging the room into darkness. Milligan re-created the dialogue, notably leaving out his own contributions:

> SECOMBE: Why are you all persecuting me like this? Are you from the Church?
> SELLERS: No, we are poor traveling Jews of no fixed income.
> SECOMBE: Oh, just a minute. (He replaces the bulb.)
> BENTINE: See! See the light! It is a sign!
> SECOMBE: You must help me escape from here. I'm being kept prisoner against my dick!
> BENTINE: You mean will.
> SECOMBE: No, Dick. Will died last week.

They clicked.

• • •

Joking, drinking, deriding other comedians, and carving schemes for professional advancement, Peter could now amuse himself in the company of kindred discontents at the Grafton Arms. The core group—Spike, Harry, Michael, Jimmy, Graham Stark, and the writer Denis Norden—were joined over the next year or so by other rising comedians like Terry-Thomas, Dick Emery, Alfred Marks, Tony Hancock, and even a stray woman, the comedienne Beryl Reid. They'd play pub games of their own invention. "We used to go through this insane mime routine, which kept customers out of the pub for months," Spike recounted. Another game they called "Tapesequences." It was a pseudo-narrative version of "Pass It On" in which one person would start to tell a story into a microphone in a voice so low nobody else could hear it, after which he or she would pass the mike around for the others to continue the would-be tale, which was necessarily nonsense.

At the heart of the group were four men suffering varying degrees of mental distress, a tendency Sellers, Milligan, Secombe, and Bentine codified by nicknaming themselves after the one-eyed mutant lugs in the Popeye cartoons.

Goons.

It wasn't a flattering label. Most people who have seen a few Popeye cartoons are familiar only with the relatively benign Alice the Goon, who in the later years of the series became so upstanding a citizen that she up and joined the Marines. But as the cartoonist E. C. Segar originally drew them, the primordial Goons were hulking, hostile creatures, verbally incoherent, prone to violence. Their charm was their charmlessness. They were butt ugly with brains to match, and Peter and his friends related to them. (The word *goons* also referred to the henchmen, usually dumb as planks, in American gangster movies; more peculiar by far is the fact that *goons* are what RAF prisoners of war called their Nazi guards.)

According to Michael Bentine, it was he who came up with the term. "I was the first of the Goons to make a hit in London's West End," Bentine declared in his memoir, *The Reluctant Jester.* "I have a two-page centre-spread from *Picture Post* dated 5 November 1948, illustrated with pictures of myself and my chairback in action and headed 'What is a Goon?' " ("Chairback" is a reference to one of Bentine's standard comedy acts: appearing on stage armed only with the broken back of a wooden chair, he would proceed to turn himself into a jack of all props, with the chairback becoming in rapid-fire succession a rifle, a saw, a flag, a door, a jackhammer, a pillory, a cow's udder . . .)

According to Milligan, it was he who came up with the term. "It was my idea for us to call ourselves the Goons. It was the name of the huge creatures in the Popeye cartoons who spoke in balloons with rubbish written in them. The name certainly predates the beginning of the war. I started using the [word] 'Goons' in the army."

What can one say, other than what Milligan himself used to interject, in his own voice, after a typically incomprehensible stretch of dialogue in the radio program he, Bentine, Secombe, and Sellers went on to create: "Mmmmmmm—it's all very confusing, really."

In any case, Milligan liked to doodle on his scripts. On one of them, dated November 1949, he drew a Goon. Its head is made up mostly of nose. Its hairy body is shaped like a large fat bullet. It vainly tries to conceal a medieval mace behind its back. The mace, of course, is spiked.

"He taught Laughing and Grief, they used to say."
"So he did, so he did," said the Gryphon, sighing in his turn;
and both creatures hid their faces in their paws.

Spike Milligan's imprisonment in Grafton's zoolike attic came to an end when Spike rented a flat in Deptford, a considerable distance away. After one particular night of joint carousing at the pub, Peter was aghast at Spike having to travel so far just to sleep and invited him to spend the night at his own place, which is to say Peg and Bill's. (Peter had more money than his friends did, not only because he seems to have been paid more for his more-steady work, but also because he still lived with his parents.) He packed Spike into his latest car, a Hudson, drove him to North London, and set him up on a slowly flattening air mattress on the floor, where Spike slept for quite some time.

Spike awoke the first morning to the sound of Peter crying out to his mother, a wail to which Spike grew accustomed. Spike, who was constitutionally unable to stop being funny, did a wicked impression of Peter's plea—a plaintive baby's squeal, except that the baby is postpubertal and his voice has long since dropped. "Pe-e-e-e-g? Pe-e-e-e-ggg-y?!" According to Spike, the object of the squeal would fuss swiftly into the room at the sound of her boy. "Tea, Mum," Peter would order, and off Peg would go to fetch it for him.

While eating scrambled eggs that first morning, Spike noticed a Dürer etching on the Sellers's wall. "It's only a print," said a chain-smoking Bill. "Uncle Bert's got the original."

Spike gasped. "It must be worth a fortune!"

Peg, the dealer in antiques and objets d'art, rushed to the telephone and called her brother in extreme excitement. They'd be over immediately, she said. So they piled into Peter's Hudson and sped to Uncle Bert's only to discover that, no, Bert Marks of North London did not own the famous Albrecht Dürer hare.

"I think Peter Sellers's father was dead, and nobody had the courage to tell him," Spike later opined. "He was like a ghost in the background. Occasionally he would be seen smoking a cigarette. Sometimes he'd play a few tunes on the piano. Very accomplished—smoking and playing the piano at one and the same time. The family was full of talent."

Spike, who slept often at the Sellerses and suffered the wretched air mattress in favor of the loneliness of Deptford, also recalled a distressing but characteristic incident involving Peter, a car, and a car salesman. In Milligan's telling:

Peter was considering the purchase of yet another car that morning, so they drove over to the Star Garage in Golders Green to meet with "a salesman so Jewish in appearance as to make Jewish people look European." (Spike, prone to extracreativity, claimed the man actually had *two* Jewish noses.) The salesman presented Peter with the car in question—a sleek green Jaguar. Peter asked if he could take it for a test drive and drove it all the way to Brighton. Spike expressed concern for the salesman. "Oh, fuck him," said Peter.

Peter, Peg, and Spike dined at leisure at the Grand in Brighton, where Peter paid for the meal with a bum check. "Peter, darling," Peg scolded, "that's very naughty. Will it bounce?" Peter then explained to Spike the relationship he enjoyed with his banker: "I said [to the banker], 'Look—once a month I write all my creditors' names on pieces of paper, screw them up, and put them in a hat. I then draw one out and pay it. If you don't stop bothering me I won't even put your name in the hat.' "

The inevitable denouement: Upon their return to the Golders Green garage late in the day, Peter informed the now-apoplectic car dealer that he wouldn't be taking the Jaguar after all. "Like many people," Spike concluded, "he ended up on the Peter Sellers scrapheap."

Spike could be cruel when discussing his old friend, but it was cruelty born of love. The bond between Sellers and Milligan was forged as solidly as it was because the two men understood each other's hearts as well as their minds. For each of them, nonsensical comedy wasn't simply diverting. It was as restorative as fresh blood, and if it brought with it a bit of cruelty, selfishness, and antisocial behavior, well, that was the price others must pay.

For Spike and Peter, comedy wasn't just comic—it was cosmic. That so few other people knew this spiritual fact only made the two depressives more convinced of its essential truth. Spike's sense of humor, deeply rooted in anguish, found its most appreciative audience in Peter, a childlike, superstitious English half-Jew with too many voices in his head. At first, Peter Sellers was just about the only person who truly got the joke that was Spike Milligan. It was an insane joke, sick and absurd, and it resonated in Peter, who, for his part, showed his appreciation by facilitating its resonance to the rest of the world.

Jimmy Grafton writes in his understated memoir that "all the Goons, like most compulsive comedians, were manic depressives to some degree," with Milligan taking a sizable lead in that particular race. But, Grafton continues, "If Spike was the most manic depressive, Peter was perhaps the next, though not to the same involuntary degree. His periods of elation after a successful performance or when sharing moments of fun with his friends were monitored by a shrewder, more pragmatic mind, as were his darker feelings of frustration."

Because of the Goons' subsequent professional triumphs, Goon minutiae abounds, trailing along with it a number of finer-points debates. It has been universally resolved that Jimmy Grafton, muse, drinkmeister, and friend, took on the Cold War espionage-sounding nickname KOGVOS. But that is where the agreement stops. For what did the acronym stand? King of Goons and Voice of Sanity? Keeper of Goons and Voice of Sanity? King of Goon Voices Society? Take your pick. Whatever his unmelodic title stood for, Jimmy Grafton was a generous fellow who not only perceived his eccentric friends' largely untapped talent but who respected and empathized with them as men, never seizing undue credit and always wishing them well. So good-natured is Jimmy Grafton that he even finds a positive note to strike about someone who never earned the praise and love of Peter's other friends. "I came to like and admire her greatly," Grafton writes of Peg.

• • •

Peter was romantically active as well. "I was introduced to Peter in 1949 by his agent, Dennis Selinger," says Anne Hayes. They met at the BBC's offices on Great Portland Place. "It wasn't instant attraction. That came when I saw him onstage for the first time." Anne was an Australian-born theater student and actress, pretty, blond, charming, and very naïve. She says, from a safe distance, "I suppose I was happy in the beginning. I don't know that I ever thought about it."

It wasn't just Peter's offstage physical appearance that failed to appeal to Anne at first, though he continued to cut a rather large figure. "He was really very fat," she affirms, "about fourteen-and-a-half stone. He had long, wavy hair, and he used to wear these huge suits with great, wide shoulders. He looked a bit like a spiv, really." (In other words, he weighed two hundred pounds and was a very snappy dresser.) Since Peter was given to great displays, a multitude of phone calls ensued from their first meeting, beginning with one placed by Peter the morning after they met in which he insisted that he was already deeply in love with her. Flowers flowed. Telegrams flew. Peter was in flaming pursuit.

His raging displays of affection were paralleled, of course, by an equally intense possessiveness, but in Anne's case Peter's jealousy raged to the point of despising his actress-girlfriend's audiences. On one occasion he appeared backstage before her show and announced that he had taken an overdose— of aspirin. (Peter would have had to have eaten at least 140 standard-issue tablets to have even made himself *at risk* of death by aspirin.) Another evening, when she was performing at the Lyric, Hammersmith, Peter found a better solution to his passionate resentments: "He locked me in the bedroom to stop me going into the theater."

Because of his smothering mother, Peter was a man unable to tolerate any separation from a woman he loved—that is, any separation that he had not initiated himself. He found no difficulty in scheduling his own performances. It was Anne's he found unsustainable. "Peter hated me being in the business," Anne explains, ascribing it not only to Sellers's possessiveness but also to the fact that he, too, wanted to do legitimate theater and couldn't seem to make it happen for himself. His ambition was boundless, but his theatrical training was nonexistent. Besides, at the time he was known strictly as an impressionist, not as an actor.

It was the performing Peter with whom Anne Hayes fell in love, the Peter of infinite color and possibility. It was the everyday Peter she dated, and yet she accepted his proposal of marriage in April 1950. The tantrums, the jealousy, the vigilance, the resentment of her career . . . Anne says she "got used to that in time. You'd think, oh, it was just Peter throwing a tantrum—like a spoiled child, really. At its worst."

"She only wants your body." That was Peg on the subject of Anne.

She was "an old harridan." This is Anne on the subject of Peg. "And the way she kissed him goodbye! I'd think, 'Ugh! Who's engaged to him, you or me?' "

That awful question became less of an idle musing when, all in a period of a few days, Anne broke off the engagement during a spat and threw her triple-diamond engagement ring back at Peter, who handed it over to Peg, who quickly sold it.

• • •

Like everyone, with the notable exception of Jimmy Grafton, Anne blames everything on the harridan. Peg "would allow him *anything*. However badly he behaved as a child, he was allowed just to get away with it. That was instinctive in him. He thought all women would be like his mother." She found his eating habits infantile: "I don't think he knew the meaning of etiquette. He never knew which knife and fork to use, and he was the kind of boy who would immediately grab the first cake off the plate."

Still, Peter was also funny and engaging. His appeal outweighed his ability to enrage or appall, and the bright young couple soon patched things up again despite Peter's notable failure to replace the diamond ring. Not to mention the hostile telephone call Peg placed to Anne's mother: "Anne is going to ruin his life—his whole career! Surely you can recognize this. He is going to be a star. Keep your daughter away from my son!"

Peter Sellers married Anne Hayes in Caxton Hall, in London, on September 15, 1951. Peg made a point of staying home. Bill did, too.

Anne gave up her career. "I would think I probably laughed more with him than with anybody I've known in my life—probably cried more, too," she says in retrospect. "He was amoral, dangerous, vindictive, totally selfish, and yet had the charm of the devil." After all, it could be most entertaining to spend time with Peter and his multiple personalities, as long as his mood allowed it. As Anne used to remark to their friends, "It's like being married to the United Nations."

• • •

In January 1950, Peter and Harry, billed as "Goons," performed a bit of comedy business on the radio show *Variety Bandbox*, but their communal ambitions were running much higher than a single appearance on radio's answer to vaudeville. From Peter's perspective, this drive wasn't for lack of work. His solo career was prospering. In the two years after his initial *Show Time* appearance, Peter Sellers was heard on over two hundred radio broadcasts. He'd been on *Variety Bandbox* any number of times, *Stump the Sto-ryteller* and *Speaking for the Stars*, too, not to mention the comedian Ted Ray's hit show *Ray's a Laugh*. (Late in his life, Sellers credited Ray with teaching him the crucial art of comic timing.) But group Goonishness held a powerful appeal, one that his solo gigs failed to satisfy. Playing four or five separate characters by himself was no longer enough; he needed to multiply voices in collaboration with others—an artistic hunger as well as an appetite to work with a team of good friends. Talk at the Grafton Arms continued to revolve around ways to crack the BBC together.

Because Peter was on the best professional footing at the time, Jimmy Grafton wrote a spec script featuring Peter as the centerpiece, with the other Goons in supporting roles. In fact, the program was called *Sellers' Castle*, and it focused on the stately but broke "twenty-second [a gunshot, a scream] I beg your pardon, the twenty-*third* Lord Sellers" and his schemes to keep his dilapidated residence from being taken from him. The four comedians recorded what they considered the best moments—Bentine and his mad scientist routine, Harry singing, and Spike filling in a bunch of outlandish voices—and through Grafton's agency they got their pilot-of-a-pilot to the BBC producer Roy Speer, who liked what he heard and quickly gave the go-ahead for a full-scale pilot to be recorded. But in a decision worthy of the military, the BBC decided not to assign Speer himself to produce the program but, instead, an inadvertent clown named Brown.

With wisdom born of instinct (comedians are born, not made) and stand-up experience (comedians may be born, but they die repeatedly until they learn what works), the Goons themselves knew that *Sellers' Castle* re-quired the zip of a live, laughing audience. But despite the group's insis-tence, Jacques Brown felt that, no, a studio audience was not at all necessary for this particular comedy recording, and so *Sellers' Castle* was taped in isolation and consequently fell flat. The BBC brass, whom Bentine later described as "a moribund collection of interfering knighthood aspirants," was decidedly underwhelmed by the pilot of *Sellers' Castle*. They found it nutty and incomprehensible and scotched the program, thereby returning the Goons to the morose state with which they were most familiar.

Secombe described their situation coolly: "There was this terrible sense of humor that nobody else really understood." Grafton likewise, though with drier wit: "Spike was still searching for the right formula in between bouts of depression and withdrawal, alternating with occasional music hall appearances."

Enter Larry Stephens, a coscriptwriter for Spike. Grafton, whose memoirs display a sparkling knack for nailing the spirit of things without showing off his insightfulness, describes Stephens as "an ex-commando captain who had seen some tough service in the Far East. He had a natural flair for comedy scriptwriting." Having gone through the war, Stephens understood the Goons. Sellers, Milligan, Secombe, and Bentine possessed the core anarchic attitude; what they lacked was anarchic structure, and Stephens supplied it. "When we first met up we had this thing inside us," Sellers later said. "We wanted to express ourselves in a sort of surrealistic form. We thought in cartoons. We thought in blackouts. We thought in sketches." Stephens helped make this nascent style cohere—to a point.

• • •

In early 1951, the producer Pat Dixon pitched yet another new comedy series to the BBC. It was to be a series of bizarre sketches broken up by musical interludes. The comedians would do funny voices, make funny noises, and generally act strange, and then a jazz band would come on. Dixon was young and driven, and along with Larry Stephens he perceived the coherent incoherence behind Goon humor, the inchoate sense behind the nonsense. Perhaps more important than his appreciation for the Goons' sense of humor, Dixon had earned himself enough of a reputation at the BBC that he could make this pilot happen without Brown-ish interference. A talented young producer named Dennis Main-Wilson assumed the reins.

A pilot was recorded before a live audience on February 4, 1951. Spike recalled the experience: "The audience didn't understand a word of it. God bless the band. They saved it. They all dug the jokes."

The pilot was successful enough that the knighthood aspirants approved the production of a full-fledged series of comedy programs featuring Sellers, Milligan, Secombe, and Bentine, with scripts by Milligan and Stephens as edited by Jimmy Grafton. But with their fingers firmly on the pulsebeat of the bureaucrat in the next office, the BBC executives drew the line at the proposed title. The Goons, needless to say, desired that their series be called *The Goon Show*. The BBC declined, insisting that nobody would know what it meant. The first replacement title proposed was *The Junior Crazy Gang*, but the Goons refused it, citing not only its demeaning blandness but also its pointless reference to an already-existing comedy troupe, the Palladium's Crazy Gang.

The BBC's second idea was revealing: They suggested *Crazy People*. In their own dull way, these executives knew who they were dealing with. This group's comedy really *was* evidence of mental illness.

Sad to say, the BBC's paper-pushers were probably right to deny the Goons their billing of choice, at least at first. After all, the national communications corporation was about to unleash the Goons on an unsuspecting public, and it would take some time to make the show popular. The word *Goon* could only come to mean what the Goons wanted it to mean *on the air*. Even when the series was a big enough hit that the stars were granted their own famous title the following year, the four men who'd named themselves after a species of cartoon morons were *still* faced with at least one clueless BBC planner who asked the question that continued to remain on many listeners' minds. What exactly was this "Go On" show about, anyway?

• • •

Peter was very much employed between the recording of the *Crazy People* pilot in early February and the first program's broadcast in late May. He was busy making movies.

Penny Points to Paradise (1951) came first. Despite its obscene-sounding title, it was little more than a tentative, practically undirected effort to provide employment and exposure for Sellers, Milligan, Secombe, and Bentine. (Also appearing were Alfred Marks, Bill Kerr, and Felix Mendelssohn and His Hawaiian Serenaders.) The 77-minute *Penny* was an insignificantly small movie even by the standards of bilge-budget British independent filmmaking in 1951, and it nearly achieved the supreme ignominy of never even earning a *bad* review let alone a mediocre one. But by virtue of its stars, a term one must use loosely since none of them actually shone at the time, *Penny* survived to become a rare and important bit of Goon juvenilia.

In the film, Spike tells Sellers about some scheme, using a hip slang reference to cash. "Spondulix!" the befuddled Sellers cries. "Dreadful disease!" Spike: "No, major, the *spondulix!*" Spike makes the universal gesture for money-grubbing, prompting Sellers to reply, "In the fingers?! Worst place you can have it! It travels straight up the brain and crumbles the arm! No, no, it travels up the arm and crumbles the brain. Yes!"

We see Sellers doing a pratfall over a garden wall; we see him grasping a rifle being shadowed by an Angel of Death figure in a black shroud; we see him swinging his arm around and rapping Harry Secombe straight across the face.

Peter emerges in a shower cap and towel: "This is a bathroom and not a confounded beehive!" he explains, only to return to the same business a little later and declare, "Madame, this is a bathroom and not a nursery!" (In both cases the towel threatens to slip off, and one notices that David Lodge's description of the youngish Peter was substantially correct: He *was* big, and he was hairy, too, with great tufts of the stuff on his shoulders.)

Sellers shows up again as a fast-talking American salesman, complete with chewing gum: "I represent my friend the Wonder Atomic Aspirin Company, our product is guaranteed to banish *any* headache, take two of these red pills and your headache will vanish, but your hair falls out. [Conspiratorial giggle.] Don't worry though, take two of these green pills and your hair grows again and your eyebrows fall off. . . ."

"It was an awful film," Harry Secombe once said with a hearty laugh, and he's probably right, though Secombe's claim is difficult to prove. Only snippets of the movie have ever been screened since its brief release in the late spring of 1951 to no attention whatsoever.

• • •

More noteworthy if only by degree is *Let's Go Crazy* (1951), a short-subject cabaret show with Peter in the center spotlight. He does five good impersonations in the course of the half-hour film, but singers, tumblers, and a comico-musical group called Freddie Mirfield and his Garbage Men keep breaking in. "Moderate variety filler" was *Today's Cinema*'s seen-it-all-before assessment, though Peter's subsequent superstardom now provides the spark the film lacked when Peter actually made it. It's riveting to see brilliance in the making. In one characteristic skit he's Giuseppe, the cabaret's broadly Italian maître d', who sports a huge handlebar mustache. Giuseppe laboriously attempts to talk a wealthy diner into ordering something Italian, but all the man wants is boiled beef and carrots. Giuseppe weeps.

Even better is Peter's delightful Groucho Marx—not a caricature at all but an appreciative and subtle rendering. Groucho asks the waiter (Spike) if the restaurant serves crabs. Receiving an affirmative response, he hands over a crab and introduces it as his friend.

It's not the gag itself that makes it work; *Let's Go Crazy*'s writing is about as inspired as an elbow. (The waiter appears a little later and bumps a diner. "That was a close shave!," the diner says, whereupon the waiter begins to shave him—a Loony Tunes shave complete with seltzer in the face.) It is instead the warm precision of Peter's style that connects, the odd sort of painterly quality he lends to what is essentially a cheap burlesque. Countless other mimics have been drawn irresistibly to Groucho routines over the years—the stooped, leggy walk; the black Brillo eyebrows; the inevitable cigar incessantly flicked—but, being lesser talents, they tend to out-Groucho Groucho. Peter underplays him, and out of it emanates the essential spirit of Marx.

Peter's Groucho is an aficionado's pleasure, but he could also play to the raucous mob. Toward the end of *Let's Go Crazy* there's an all-too-brief appearance by the proud and robust Crystal Jollibottom. Wearing an absurd boa, she sits on a flaming celery stick. It's the best moment in the film.

• • •

May and June 1951 were bustling months for Peter Sellers. On Monday, May 7, Peter began an eight-week run at the Palladium. Since his last Palladium gig he'd played several other London houses—Finsbury Park, Balham, the Prince of Wales, the Hippodrome. He was by that point a proficient stand-up comedian, impressionist, and crowd pleaser. But as the theater management report pointed out, his audiences' responses were largely if not entirely dependent on their familiarity with radio characters—others' as well as Peter's own—because those were the voices upon which Sellers played.

The manager also noted a certain tendency in Peter's onstage demeanor, one that his friends had been noticing in his private nature: "I think that this act is getting better with each visit and could be exceptionally good if only there was a little more personality."

• • •

On Sunday, May 27, 1951—less than halfway through his run at the Palladium—Peter, along with Spike, Harry, and Michael, showed up at a small studio on Bond Street to record the first official episode of *Crazy People*. It aired the following day at 6:45 P.M. Sixteen more programs followed in the first series, one per week, over the course of the next four months.

As disjointedly manic as *Goon Shows* were in the years to come, the first year of the series was even more so. Each *Crazy People* program was composed of staccato, essentially unrelated comedy skits interspersed with irrelevant jazzy musical numbers—irrelevant to the comedy, that is. The Ray Ellington Quartet, a singing group called the Stargazers, and Max

Geldray on the harmonica provided a form of musical relief from the comedy, though apparently the Stargazers weren't relieving enough because they got bounced in the middle of the second series.

Despite the show's chaotic nature, certain themes began to develop. Druggy in a world before drugs, *Crazy People* was irreverent, illogical, and not a little cynical. Authority was skewered, logic dismembered. The show was a triumph of facetiousness in the service of pointlessness—a philosophical statement. Even its title was inconsistent. BBC program listings called it *Crazy People* for the whole first series, but the Goons themselves insisted on referring to it on the air as *The Goon Show*.

Goon comedy is a mix of pa-dum-pum jokes—Q: "Do you mind if I take a gander 'round the shop?" A: "As long as it's house trained."—with centrifugally disintegrating plots and significantly dumb noises. Like the poetic play of Lewis Carroll, 'twas brillig in a profoundly British way; it was *Alice in Wonderland* after the Great Depression and two devastating world wars. What held it together, increasingly so as the series progressed, was a group of recognizable if distinctively unrounded characters. For Spike, these creations erupted out of the bogs of his emotional landscape. For Peter, they gave a distinct if malleable structure to what had previously been merely feats of impressionism. Milligan later insisted that Sellers's Goon characters were "the boilerhouse of his talent." Spike brought out Peter's loyal side; Peter, he was quick to say, "was instrumental in getting me into the BBC. He was very kind like that." This particular kindness entailed a certain risk on Peter's part. Max Geldray, for instance, reports that Spike stormed into the staid BBC "with all the panache of a walking unmade bed."

As for Peter, he credited Spike with shaping him into a work of art: "[I was] just a vase of flowers," Sellers once said, "and Milligan arranged me."

• • •

Sellers believed, as any performer must, that his characters actually had blood and muscle. "To all of us, they absolutely lived," he claimed. His personalities became British legends.

He was Major Denis Bloodnok, English military man *par infériorité*, whose dimness was only outpaced by his flatulence. (The name stemmed from Peter's use of "nok" to describe a nose; he'd call someone with a pointy proboscis "Needlenok.")

He was Henry Crun, an elderly gentlemen with a crackly, halting voice who forever bickered with Spike's magnificent, equally doddering Minnie Bannister.

He was Hercules Grytpype-Thynne, a devil of an aristocratic villain who harbored a sly, insinuating voice and, in Spike's off-air written descriptions at least, an insistent taste for other men. (Spike writes of Grytpype-Thynne's shady background: "Subject of a police investigation on school homosexuality"; "subject of a military police investigation on homosexuality"; "subject of a prisoners' investigation on homosexuality"; "implicated in homosexuality with a Masai goat herd"; and "recreations: homosexuality.")

And he was the young and endearingly unlovable Bluebottle, who tended to arrive late in the proceedings of whatever muddled story Spike had concocted that week, injecting himself into the midst of the chaos with a high-pitched, nasal, and truly hellish whine: "Cap-i-tan, my Cap-i-tan, I hear my Cap-i-tan call me!" Bluebottle was not a bright boy. He tended to read his own stage directions. "Wooky wooky wooky!" Bluebottle might shriek, after which Peter would squeal, in the same voice, "Make funny face, wait for applause!" And as Sellers told it—and the basic scene has been confirmed by the man himself—*Bluebottle actually did live!*

Peter: "This fellow came over one evening, I'll never forget it. He was tall and wide—he wasn't fat, but he was wide—and he was dressed as a scout leader. In fact he *was* a scout leader. He had a blue briefcase and a scout hat [and] a big red beard and red knee socks and all the insignia, you know. He said—and I'm not kidding, this is how he spoke: [a daffy high-pitched whine, crammed through the sinuses] 'Could I carry in for a moment, please? I have just seen Michael Bentine and he said that I am a genius.'"

Harry Secombe noted that Peter didn't merely *do* the voices. He *became* the characters: "He physically changed as he did the voice. He'd shrink for Crun, and then get very small for Bluebottle." The comedy writer Eric Sykes put it in biological terms: "You'd be in a taxi with Peter, and he'd listen to the taxi driver talking. And when he would get out, he would *be* the taxi driver. But not only in words and voice. His whole *metabolism* would have changed." That Peter was performing Bloodnok et al before a live audience may not have mattered to his style in the least, for like all of Peter's characters, they were just as alive for him when he was alone.

Michael Bentine, meanwhile, played the toothy, chirpy Captain (or

Professor) Osric Pureheart, a variation of the mad inventor character he'd been toying with for several years. Pureheart's notable skill was to invent warped variations of well-known, contemporary British products—a popular new race car, for instance, or an on-the-drawing-board airplane that had been in the news that week. On one episode Captain Pureheart supervised the launch of the *Goonitania*. The following week he led the salvaging of the *Goonitania*.

As befitted his essentially good nature, Harry Secombe played the expansive Neddie Seagoon, hearty and well-meaning, dispatched on important missions he inevitably bungled, rarely comprehending much of anything but never losing hope.

And then there was Spike's Eccles, the prototypical Goon. If Seagoon was a genial British Everydope, Eccles was an inadvertently dangerous Everycretin, a man without a mind. A press item appearing a few days before *Crazy People*'s first broadcast attempted to define to the average Brit in the street what precisely this outlandish-sounding Goon creature was: "Something with a one-cell brain," it explained. Eccles was precisely that human amoeba. Armed with a voice like a Manchester Goofy, Eccles was too stupid to be malicious, too oblivious ever to be considered criminal, and for these very reasons he was terrifying. Eccles was obviously a product of Spike's wartime experiences.

"Gradually," Milligan reflected, "piece by piece, this chemistry of Secombe, Bentine, Sellers, and myself . . . suddenly we were like a magnet drawn toward itself, unexplainably so. We only told lunatic jokes. Everything was lunatic. It wasn't like any other jokes you'd hear." And strangely, week by week, audiences began to embrace them. The Goons' comedy began as a kind of idiolect and turned into widespread slang.

From its genesis in the Grafton Arms, Goon humor was always clubby and fraternal, but thanks to the BBC, now it spread across the airwaves like a social disease, a kind of mental herpes. The *Daily Graphic* predicted as much: "Listeners who like it will, according to the Chief Goons, become Goons of varying degree, depending on the strength of their liking. They will be associate Goons, honorary Goons, and Goon followers." The prophecy was fulfilled. The first *Crazy People* episodes attracted listeners in the 370,000 range, but by the end of the first series of seventeen weekly broadcasts the audience was up to 1.8 million.

Still, only a relative few of these listeners could possibly have realized that they were the first initiates in what would become a fanatical worldwide cult, one that would eventually destroy the minds of millions, including John Lennon, John Cleese, Michael Palin, Elton John, and Charles, Prince of Wales.

• • •

Like children left unsupervised in an isolated orphanage, the Goons developed their own private language, only some of which they shared with their listeners. Secombe recalled the genesis of what became a classic Goon expression, an utterance so devoid of meaning that its very idiocy resonated as profound. Other comedy shows were full of catch phrases, Harry once explained, so Spike decided that the Goons needed one as well: "And he made up 'Ying tong iddle I po,' which means nothing. Within weeks people were saying 'Ying tong iddle I po,' in the street. It frightened us a bit."

"Ying tong iddle I po"—a truly meaningless string of sounds with vaguely Chinese undertones. Because it meant absolutely nothing, "Ying tong iddle I po" was the perfect repeatable nugget of Goonspeak, a motto of linguistic anarchy, a kind of password. Spike inserted it in his scripts randomly, as was of course its very nature:

> SEAGOON: I'm looking for a criminal.
> BLOODNOK: You find your own—it took me years to get this lot.
> SEAGOON: Ying tong iddle I po.

Just among themselves, the Goons' private language could be rather more vulgar. "Secombe read a book on South America," Spike once noted with glee. "There's a South American monkey who, when it's attacked, shits in its hand and throws it at the opposition. So whenever Secombe and Sellers used to meet, one would go '*ptthhp!*' " At this point in the telling Spike reached down to his ass, grabbed an imaginary handful, and hurled the contents aggressively forward. "And the other would go '*mmmhmmmhmmgh!*' " Under threat, the second monkey emitted an equally intense straining sound, reached back and grabbed nothing, and threw his hands in the air in a gesture of abject surrender.

This was how they dealt with one another out of the range of the microphones.

The Goons didn't do comedy the way anyone else did. "Probably," says

Harry, "because we couldn't tell jokes very well. I could never remember the endings."

• • •

With Anne, Peter moved out of his mother's domain and into a penthouse overlooking Hyde Park. Anne had already introduced her best friend, June Marlowe, to Spike over dinner, an evening that was enlivened greatly by the fact that Peter had earlier convinced Spike that it would be a lot more fun if Spike pretended to be Italian. The unsuspecting June spent much of the dinner trying to teach English to the happy immigrant. They soon became engaged.

With the notable exception of Beryl Reid, women were largely excluded from the Goons' professional world, a fact Milligan tended to reiterate with some degree of pride. Spike: "Do you know there were only three women who appeared in *The Goon Show*? The first was Margaret McMillan, a classy girl. I was going out with her at the time." Spike again: "The girls appeared from time to time according to who was dating them. Peter Sellers had one. Her name was Charlotte Greenwood, and I wrote a line for him to say to her: 'You're a dull scrubber!' Peter said, 'I can't say that to Charlotte—I'm going out with her!' " Where was Anne, one wonders? He was married at the time, after all. Or are Spike's recollections to be fully trusted?

• • •

In December 1951, *Charlie Chaplin's Burlesque on "Carmen"* (1916) enjoyed a brief revival run in England, albeit in a newly burlesqued version that wasn't approved by Chaplin. Chaplin had made the film for Essanay as a takeoff on Cecil B. DeMille's 1915 *Carmen*. DeMille's epic melodrama starred Wallace Reid as Don Jose and Geraldine Farrar as Carmen; Chaplin's spoof starred himself as Darn Hosiery with Edna Purviance as the eponymous gypsy, with the cross-eyed clown Ben Turpin doing a turn as the lover of the fat Frasquita.

But with the new release of *Charlie Chaplin's Burlesque on "Carmen,"* English audiences were treated to a burlesque of a burlesque, for Chaplin's comedy now sported a facetious voice-over commentary by Peter Sellers. Chaplin's original two-reeler was left open to this farcical adulteration from the start. He left Essanay soon after filming it, whereupon the company shot new footage and doubled its length without his participation at all. Charlie sued, lost, and was distraught, but as he wrote in his autobiography,

"It rendered a service, for thereafter I had it stipulated in every contract that there should be no mutilating, extending, or interfering with my finished work." There are no reports as to whether Chaplin ever saw or heard Peter Sellers's interference.

As one of the British trade papers sniffed, Sellers "impersonates the characters of the story, plugs away energetically and may amuse the unsophisticated." It would take a few more movies for him to rise above that level.

In March 1952, after being married to Peter for six months, Anne suffered a miscarriage, a tragedy that only served to enflame Peg's maternal instincts. While Anne was recuperating in the hospital, Peg invited Peter to dinner every night, along with a series of his former girlfriends. Ever thorough, Peg is said to have made a point of including one who Peter believed had borne him a daughter (and put her up for adoption) during the war.

Peter Sellers was the painstaking product of a terrible mother, the fucked-up labor of her love. As even his best friends acknowledge, he could be a selfish, childish man, responsive to every need as long as it was his own. His cars, gadgets, and RAF and *Goon Show* buddies (not to mention his mother) occupied at least as crucial a place in his heart as his wife, with the RAF and *Goon Show* buddies (not to mention his mother) outlasting all the others in terms of duration. When, for instance, in the spring of 1952, Peter and Anne moved to a house in Highgate, Spike moved in along with them and stayed until he got married. "He was tired of sleeping under people's carpets," Anne later explained.

There was little restraint in Peter's life. Interests became manias. After Graham Stark became a proficient photographer, Peter, always entranced by mechanical equipment of any sort, grew equally fascinated by his friend's ability to convince beautiful women to pose for pictures. Photography had much to recommend itself—one of his best friends loved it; it involved instruments that could be purchased and replaced; and girls, girls, girls— so Peter swiftly developed a passion for the art. At the very start of it, according to Stark, Peter beelined "to Wallace Heaton's in Bond Street, the Rolls-Royce of camera dealers, and apparently bought every piece of equipment in the shop." Stark claims that Peter even called in sick for a *Goon Show* recording one Sunday so he and Stark could meticulously retouch the breasts and buttocks depicted in one of Graham's bikini-oriented pictures.

At the same time, Peter could be good-hearted and generous, sometimes exceedingly so. He simply could not keep himself from buying gifts for people he liked. *He* wanted things, and so, he concluded, must they. And if, stubbornly, they would not acquire these objects for themselves, he would step in and provide them. "He used to call me when he wanted to go downtown in London," the *Goon Show* harmonica virtuoso Max Geldray remembers. "He would say, 'I'm going to the camera shop'—which he did all the time—'and why don't you come with me?' One particular time he said, 'I'll pick you up in ten minutes.' " Geldray told him, no, he had other errands to do and he'd meet him there, especially because he, Max, needed a new flashbulb for his own camera. When he got there, Peter was admiring a new and very small Swiss camera.

"Look, it has a brighter picture, but the amperage is much lower," said Peter. "And he went on about the thing," Geldray continues. "He said to me, 'Why don't you get it?' "

" 'I don't need it,' " Max replied. "Several hours later, I opened the door of my home, and in the middle of the living room was a package. He and Anne were sitting in my living room. He didn't say anything—he just pointed at the package. I opened it, and there was the new Swiss camera. I said, 'I don't *need* a camera!' He said, 'Yes you do. Yours is broken.'

"He meant the flashbulb. For him, that was 'broken.' "

Technicalities failed to impress Peter. He didn't have time for them. Graham Stark describes the frenzy that accompanied every new purchase: "Pete believed in brute force. He'd tear the box open, ignore the instruction book, and press every button until something worked."

His equipment fever didn't stop at still photography. New movie cameras were also purchased, used, and replaced by still newer and fancier models. Off-hour Goons were a favorite subject of Peter's cinematic eye, as were his wife and mother. As he would continue to do for years to come, he recorded his free time in the form of reel after reel of home movie footage—Harry mugging in a striped bathrobe. Peter hamming it up in a park. A glamorous-looking Anne posed in the driver's seat of a shiny new red sports car. Spike trying to keep hold of a manic dog. A gas station attendant filling Peter's mouth with gasoline. Anne, in a comedy skit, being served a poisoned cocktail by Peter. . . .

"We liked undercranked film," said Harry, the manic, fast-motion effect being characteristically Goonish. And, he also adds, "We were all devotees of Buster Keaton rather than Charlie Chaplin," by which he meant that Keaton's dark absurdity resonated much more deeply than Chaplin's comic ballets, not to mention the fact that Chaplin's Victorian sentimentality had no place in the brutal, existential world of the Goons.

"He had a 16mm camera," Spike noted a little more brusquely. "He was richer than we were—richer by 8mm."

• • •

The second series of *The Goon Show* began in late January 1952. To the Goons' great satisfaction, the title of their program now actually *was The Goon Show*. This victory, like many others, came at a price, one that was paid largely by Spike Milligan. "I was trying to shake the BBC out of its apathy," Spike reflected in the mid-1970s. "And I had to fight like mad, and people didn't like me for it. I had to rage and crash and bang. I got it right in the end, and it paid off, but it drove me mad in the process, and drove a lot of other people mad. And that's why I don't think I could be a success again on the same level—because I just couldn't go through all the tantrums." By July, when the second series finished recording, Spike was twitching in the direction of a mental collapse.

Peter, in contrast, tended to treat his Goon work precisely as the workmanlike job it was. He was always "the most serious of the group," says Max Geldray, but then he could afford to be. Unlike Milligan, Sellers didn't have to face the pressure of writing a hit series comedy script every week only to perform it on the weekend. Instead, Peter showed up on Sundays for the recording sessions, read the script, did the voices, and went back home. His talent, at this point anyway, wasn't agony.

That said, the Goons' joint ambition was, if anything, intensifying. They didn't want to do just radio. Plans for the Goons' first television appearance, *Trial Gallop*, were drawn. The program was scheduled to air in mid-February, but George VI put a crimp in the Goons' schedule for achieving stardom by dying in his sleep at Sandringham on Wednesday the sixth. The Goons' comedy show, which would necessarily have been in bad taste even in the best of circumstances, was canceled. Peter and the others had to wait until July 2 to make their joint television debut; they did so with the one-shot *Goonreel*.

And they still wanted to make a good Goon movie. *Penny Points to Paradise* had apparently taught them little. One can appreciate their artistic ambition, but the execution remained problematic. At the core of the issue was money. It wasn't as though the big British studios—J. Arthur Rank,

Ealing, Hammer—were clamoring for the Goons. They were, at best, interesting new radio stars, still too small to generate movie buzz. If Sellers, Secombe, Milligan, and Bentine were to make another film together, it would have to be rock-bottom cheap. And so, *Down Among the Z Men* (1952).

Filmed in two abrupt weeks in April in a small studio in the northwest London neighborhood of Maida Vale, and faring poorly at the box office upon its release, *Down Among the Z Men* takes the four Goons and, in an apparent effort to broaden their appeal, strips them of most of their Goonishness and replaces it with a low-conventional story, a pretty girl (Carole Carr) who sings two songs, and a dozen tap-dancing chorines. Spike's Eccles and Bentine's Pureheart emerge most clearly from the murk, but Peter's Bloodnok (promoted here from major to colonel) is so anemic a rendition that it takes a few moments to recognize in Bloodnok's introductory scene that the dull-looking gray-haired man sitting behind a military desk is actually supposed to be Sellers's familiar and colorful radio character.

Then again, this was never meant to be art. On the first day of shooting, Peter cornered the director, Maclean Rogers. "I feel," he began, "that the character I am playing has certain undercurrents of repression, which I might best express by having a noticeable twitch." Maclean was blunt: "I've got eight minutes of screen time a day to shoot. Do it quickly."

It's a caper. Spies try to steal a secret nuclear formula. They fail.

Harry Secombe cuts the back off a woman's skirt with a pair of scissors. Michael Bentine pulls Harry's apron down. The best comedy bit is taken by Spike and Harry: "Guerrilla warfare? I know that!," at which point they both begin doing a chimp routine. There's a laughing-gas/crying-gas sketch that would have made even Shemp blush.

The chorus girls, corralled into an earlier Army-camp-workout-turned-dance-number, reappear toward the end of the movie in an ENSA-like evening's entertainment for the camp. Backstage, Carole Carr turns to Spike and Harry. "I'm on next!" she tells them. "As soon as I'm through I'm going over to get the formula back before my second number!"

Inanely—and not in a good way—Colonel Bloodnok takes the stage after Carr's song and proceeds to amuse the audience with an impersonation of an American army officer from a Hollywood movie he saw the week before. It's Peter, not Bloodnok, and it makes no sense, especially since the whole point of the beloved Bloodnok is that he has little talent for anything but intestinal distress. Forced by circumstance, however—the circumstance being that the producer, E. J. Fancey, needed to pull this bit of cheap taffy into a feature-length thread—the bumbling Bloodnok reveals himself to be a cabaret star of exquisite skill. The routine is just an excuse to let Peter shoehorn in an impression routine: a Midwestern American army man and his fast-talking, Brooklynesque subordinate.

Osric Pureheart comes on next with an equally misplaced nightclub schtick. It's Bentine and his old chairback routine.

More disturbing, and consequently a lot funnier, is the fact that *Down Among the Z Men* provides a rare chance to *see* Bentine's Pureheart as well as hear his voice. In addition to Bentine's ridiculous hairiness and drastic British underbite, he gives Pureheart a truly wacky bandy-legged walk, the ghastly gait of a madman with testicular issues.

• • •

The Goons' main focus (for good reason) remained the BBC radio, where *The Goon Show* was evolving artistically from its initial run. It wasn't necessarily better yet, as the Goonographer Roger Wilmut notes. It was increasingly popular with audiences, but it remained relatively unrefined.

Musical numbers by Max Geldray and the Ray Ellington Quartet continued to break each program up into discrete episodes, even as the plots (or what passed for them) became more or less coherent. These interruptions became a standard part of the show for the duration of its long run. They served to regularize the chaos, and they did so in a familiar sort of music hall way that the absurdist *Goon Show*'s rather less-than-intellectual listeners could hook into whenever the senseless noises and bizarre jokes got to be too much. Ying tong iddle I po, and here's Max Geldray with "I'm Just Wild About Harry."

Even Goonish senselessness hadn't quite hit its stride yet. Spike, it comes as little surprise to learn, was a more or less undisciplined writer. And the Goons were all anarchic as performers. They did what they pleased, and what pleased them included mumbling and stepping on each others' lines. The producer, Dennis Main Wilson, was tolerant of their unpredictable behavior as well as their equally lawless comic thrust—possibly to a fault. Only during the third series, after Wilson left and Peter Eton took over as producer, did *The Goon Show* begin to achieve its lasting quality.

Peter Eton was scarcely humorless, but it wasn't easy to make him laugh. It took work and self-restraint. As a result, this new, tough audience of one was therefore able to exercise some control over what Wilmut calls the Goons' "tendency toward self-indulgence." It was not an easy task, though the Goons themselves grew to appreciate the beneficial effect Eton had on them. Harry Secombe credited Eton as being the program's best producer. Before he came on board, Secombe noted, *The Goon Show* had little in the way of shape, and in Secombe's description, the characters all spoke so fast that "it was a gabble." Eton, though, "was great. He used to get quite choleric [and] go all red and shout, 'You bastards sit down!' Peter Sellers would say, 'I'm pissing off,' and Eton would just say, 'Well, go then.'"

Still, Max Geldray declares, no matter who was producing the program, "it was Spike who was the manic and inventive driving force behind every detail of the production." Spike, of course, could also be "one of the most annoying people you could meet." The BBC executives loved the show's success, but as the months went by they grew to despise Milligan, who, as Peter once remarked, had a wonderful knack for explaining the simplest things in such a way that nobody could possibly understand them.

• • •

The end of the second series signaled the departure of Michael Bentine. Creative differences were cited. He and Spike were seeing eye-to-eye less and less. According to Secombe, "Only when Michael Bentine left did *The Goon Show* really begin—really take shape." It was also becoming legendary, not only with the average bright Briton, but with the next generation of satirists, comics, and puckish intellectuals.

For instance, the physician-turned-comedian-turned-avante-garde-opera-and-theater-director Jonathan Miller remains a dedicated fan. "*The Goon Show* really is the best thing Sellers ever did," Miller declares. "He did some films that are interesting, and of course *Dr. Strangelove* has some nice jokes, but I think the characters that everyone in England remembers, and will remember all their lives, were from *The Goon Show*. At its best it was as good as Lewis Carroll."

Does the director of such works as Leoš Janáček's *Katya Kabanova* at the Metropolitan Opera really think that *The Goon Show* is art? Dr. Miller is insistent: "Unless it's printed, people don't think it's literature, but actually, at its best, *The Goon Show* is on a par with *Alice in Wonderland*. I don't think people have registered the importance of Milligan's imagination; Milligan is an important writer.

"It's a series of pastiches of English boys' literature of the '20s and '30s, which they grew up on—*The Lives of the Bengal Lancers* and that sort of thing. People in England of my age, people in their fifties, can still speak to each other in very detailed *Goon Show* voices—particularly Bluebottle and Bloodnok and Grytpype-Thynne." Miller proceeds to prove the point.

"There's a session between Bluebottle and that sort of Mortimer Snerd–like figure called Eccles. They're soldiers in a trench, and Bluebottle says, [in perfect imitation of Bluebottle's nasal squeal] 'What time is it, Eccles?' Eccles says [again in impeccable imitation], 'I don' know, but I'll tell you sumthun'—last night a very kind gen'leman wrote down the time on a piece of paper for me.' And Bluebottle says, 'Show me that. Hey! This piece of paper is not working!'

"It's such a brilliant, *logical* joke, that. Carroll would have given his eyeteeth to have made a joke of that quality.

"These characters are a brilliant gallery of British social life. That wonderful character Sellers plays—Major Bloodnok, a sort of drunken, gin-shaken, shortly-to-be-cashiered English major living on the northwest frontier and afflicted, obviously all the time, with catastrophic attacks of Indian diarrhea." Dr. Miller can't help but launch into another routine from memory: " 'Meanwhile, in the smallest and coldest room in the fort on the northwest frontier, Major Bloodnok is experiencing difficulties.' And then you hear this wonderful *pppffoooosh*. [Bloodnok's huffing voice:] 'Oh, it goes right through you, you know—I'll never eat Bombay duck again!'

"I don't know if that comes across to Americans," he admits with a touch of scolding. "You Americans get very prudish about lavatory jokes. You think they're infantile. I think it's far more infantile when you *don't* laugh at them."

John Lennon, too, found it all precisely, gloriously English and expressed concern that others just wouldn't get it: "I was twelve when the *Goon Show* first hit. Sixteen when they finished with me. Their humor was the only proof that the *world* was insane. . . . What it means to Americans I can't imagine (apart from a rumored few fanatics). As they say in Tibet, 'You had to be there.' "

• • •

The third series began recording in November 1952. Bentine's departure and Eton's arrival were not enough to dispel all the tension. Geldray tells of the time a young BBC underling rushed up to him and breathlessly reported the day's gossip: He'd heard that Spike had just charged over to

Peter's house with a gun. "Yeah? So what else is new?" was Geldray's response.

In late December, Spike actually suffered the nervous breakdown.

Always high strung, on the brink, too many thoughts in his head and many of them unhygienic, Spike crashed. The pressure of weekly creation—and the success it was bringing him—pushed him over the edge. He was hospitalized and ended up missing a total of twelve shows—nearly half the third series, though he began contributing scripts after only a few tentative weeks of recovery. Madness was the point, after all.

• • •

In 1953, Peter made his phonographic recording debut under the production of George Martin, who went on to produce the Beatles. His first single, released by Parlophone, was a skit called "Jakka and the Flying Saucers"—a Chipmunk-voiced boy, Jakka, and his doughnut-shaped dog, Dunker, both from Venus, embark on a quest for the Golden Cheese.

Martin once called it "probably the worst-selling record that Parlophone ever made."

But Peter was undaunted; "Jakka and the Flying Saucers" was followed by many more successful records in the 1950s alone, including the singles "Dipso Calypso" (1955), "Any Old Iron" (1957), and a rather sick rendition of the detested "My Old Dutch" (1959), the song Peg made him perform as an infant in white tie and tails. These 45s and 78s performed substantially better in the marketplace than "Jakka and the Flying Saucers."

Around this time Peter suffered a disappointment of a more personal nature. Max Geldray reports that Sellers had gone to see the French comedian Jacques Tati's most recent film, *M. Hulot's Holiday* and was tremendously impressed—so much so that he wrote a fan letter to Tati, who replied with a casual invitation to Peter to visit him some time. Peter left immediately for France.

He returned deeply let down. Tati spent most of their time together lecturing Peter on the subject of comedy. As Sellers told Geldray, "All he did was talk to me about how great he is." Years later, Tati wrote his own fan letter to Peter after seeing one his pictures. Peter didn't bother to reply.

• • •

The Super Secret Service (1953), released in late summer to little notice, works much better than either *Penny Points to Paradise* or *Down Among the*

Z Men, perhaps because it's too short to require much in the way of plot or structure. A 24-minute comedy scripted by Spike and Larry Stephens, the film begins with Sellers, a cigarette hanging out of his mouth and a thin mustache gracing his lip, opening a door into a bleak film-noir office. He frantically reaches into his trenchcoat pocket for a gun. Unable to find it, he waves sheepishly at the camera and backs out of the room. The credits roll.

In the film, Milligan and Stephens's music hall absurdism takes the place of *Z Men*'s misguided conventionality:

GRAHAM STARK: The phone is ringing.
PETER SELLERS: Then answer it!
STARK: But we haven't got a phone.

When the phone is located—it has been filed under *T* in the filing cabinet—Sellers answers it, but only after putting on a wig to disguise himself.

A gun battle ensues—in the top drawer of the desk. Smoke comes pouring out to the sound of bullets.

A rock comes crashing through the window. There's a note attached:

STARK: What does it say?
SELLERS: Fred Smith, window repairer.
STARK: I wonder what he charges?
[Second rock]
SELLERS: Three shillings and fifty pence.

Enter Miss Jones. It's Anne, coming out of Peter's enforced retirement long enough to put on a big black beard:

PETER: What are you trying to hide?
ANNE: This! (She pulls off the beard to reveal a goatee.)

And suddenly, for no reason, the comedy grinds to a halt in order to give the Ray Ellington Quartet a chance to perform a jazzy version of "Teddy Bears Picnic."

• • •

Thanks to Peter's extended family, Highgate, where Peter and Anne were living, was turning into a neighborhood version of the Grafton Arms, a place where Goons and their friends could spend even more time together when they weren't actually working as a team. "We became friends early," Max Geldray says, "because we lived rather close. Peter had a cousin who was a real estate man, and he heard of a bunch of new apartments being built in Highgate. Peter called me and said, 'My cousin tells me there are several apartments available there. Are you interested?' That's how we all came to live in Highgate—all meaning Spike Milligan and Ray Ellington [and Geldray and Sellers]. Actually Ray and I lived in the same apartment building. Peter lived around the corner."

He was sticking to the familiar neighborhoods of his youth but enjoying them with money. He had good friends, a beautiful wife, and his mother was nearby. He might even have felt a wave of contentment once in a while.

But one day he called Peg on the telephone: "I'm at Bedford at the railway station. I'm feeling so low I'm going to end it all. I'm going to jump in front of a train." Rushing to save him, just as she'd always done, Mother found him sitting alone on a bench, staring into an abyss only he could see.

• • •

Happy families may all be alike—since there are so few of them it's difficult to tell—but as countless dysfunctional family memoirs so repetitively prove, unhappy families are similar, too. Marital tantrums sound the same. So do crying children. Peter Sellers's family was no exception.

Wally Stott took a benign view of Peter's marriage to Anne, a perspective made possible by the relative distance from which he viewed it: "Sometimes I'd be at parties at Peter's house. They were always very enjoyable affairs. There'd always be music we both liked. His wife, Anne, was a very lovely lady, and a great hostess." (Years after his professional association with Peter ended, Wally Stott became Angela Morley. Spike Milligan commented with a mean sort of affection for his old friend: "He has now had a sex change. I don't know why. When he undresses he still looks like Wally Stott. I think when Secombe undressed at night he looked like Wally Stott. Peter didn't. When he undressed at night he looked like Diana Dors." When I spoke with Angela Morley, I asked her how she wished to be identified in this book, and she replied, "It's a judgment you'll have to make and I'll have to accept." My judgment is to attribute her quotes to Wally

Stott, since he was the person with whom Peter Sellers worked on *The Goon Show*, and to thank Angela Morley for them in the acknowledgments.)

Anne was putting up a good front. In private, it was she who bore the brunt of Peter's mercurial moods, the bleak stretches of silence as well as the hot rages, his tendency to grow bored with their living arrangements and insist that they go someplace else. "We did move a lot," she notes. "I'm not quite sure why. I guess he got sick of wherever we were. I guess we lived in about [long pause] oh, I can't think how many. . . . About eight different houses, I guess." Her mother-in-law barely spoke to her, which, come to think of it, was probably for the best.

Anne understood Peter. She knew that he was erratic in predictable ways. He would buy a car on a whim—a used Jaguar here, a used Rolls there—and sell it equally whimsically, usually at a loss, and buy another. He piled up more and more photographic equipment and turned the kitchen into a darkroom, where his chemicals took precedence over her milk and eggs, thereby rendering the sink unusable. He was making more money than he'd ever seen, but so drastically had he always overspent his income that his accountant, Bill Wills, once attempted to put him on a severe allowance—£12 per week. Peter inevitably exceeded it, and rather than raise the rate, Wills gave up, leaving Peter to spend as freely as he wished.

Anne wanted children. She thought they might stabilize the marriage. And so it was in this rickety domestic context that in July 1953, Anne Sellers announced that she was pregnant again. Peter responded joyously. He went out and bought a £300 electric train set and began playing with it in earnest.

• • •

As cherished radio stars with bills to pay, Peter, Spike, and Harry were periodically obliged to leave London, head out to the various shires, and adapt recorded Goon broadcast comedy into live music hall routines. The more successful Peter became, the less willing he was to do it. Since he'd been holding provincial audiences in contempt since his squalid vaudeville infancy with his grandmother's traveling water tank, his growing fame and fortune in the mid-1950s carried with it a lingering, ever-souring wrath. Late in his life, Peter described with unbridled contempt the Goons' audiences outside London. They were Goonlike, he said, but in the worst possible sense: "You're usually telling jokes to a crowd of people with two-thousandths of an inch of forehead." In Peter's increasingly lofty view, it was one thing to act like a moron but quite another to perform for one. When he looked out through the footlights at his audiences he saw a vision of hell.

Still, apart from having to face the dreaded Cro-Magnons of the hinterlands, the regularized camaraderie of *The Goon Show* gave Peter immense pleasure, as did the lasting comic art he was creating with his friends. That several Goons and associates lived in more or less the same neighborhood of North London wasn't simply due to Peter's family real estate connection; having close friends close at hand was important to Peter. He enjoyed fellowship.

When asked about his *Goon Show* years after they were long gone, his answer was inevitably a variation on a simple declarative statement: "It was the happiest time in my life professionally." Beloved by its creators and its fans alike, the program provided steady employment, national fame, and bizarre comedy in equal measure. Peter craved all three.

Sellers wasn't exactly the star of the show, but he was certainly the most vocally gifted Goon, and as a result the United Kingdom experienced a rising tide of impressionists of the impressionist. Listeners loved to do Peter's many voices themselves—their flattery was sincere—and Sellers imitators began popping up all over the country. Wally Stott tells of his experience in the mid-fifties when he learned, surreally, to fly a plane: "My instructor used to give me my lessons in Peter Sellers's voices. One lesson he'd be Bloodnok, another lesson he'd be Bluebottle."

Stott fondly remembers Peter's upbeat mood in the recording studio on Sundays: "Peter used to do a lot of clownish things. For instance, we used to warm up the audience before the show started. Harry would sing, and we would play. And Peter would go around the back of the studio and play the timpani, and put on a real show doing it. You know how timpanists, years ago, used to turn handles to tune them? Peter used to give a terrific impression of one of the old-time timpani players—playing it, listening to it, and darting his hand over it tightening the taps. And then one of the sound effects men would fire a blank—it was really crazy." Peter may not have succeeded entirely in finding himself by clowning for an ever-growing public, but he was trying.

"There were quarrels from time to time," Wally Stott admits. "I don't think Harry was ever involved in those things. They were between Peter and Spike. I never knew what they were about, but there would be certain weeks when I'd realize that all was not well." But the Sunday recording sessions were generally merry—at least when Spike wasn't suffering one of his spells—so much so that rumors of on-air drunkenness began to surface. Max Geldray dismisses these reports as absolutely false, though he does acknowledge that the Goons sometimes seized the opportunity afforded by Geldray's harmonica interlude to swig a little brandy out of milk bottles. It was a smuggler's trick. Wouldn't you know it? The BBC banned alcohol on the premises.

• • •

Goon art was evolving. Under Peter Eton's supervision, the show's structure really began to cohere in the fourth series (1953–54), though Spike and Larry Stephens still weren't developing single story lines for the duration of each half hour. But by the fifth series (1954–55), with scripts by Milligan and Eric Sykes, each episode began to feature a self-contained plot, albeit in a Milliganesque way. These plots, such as they were, might be steered as much by the sound of the words as by character motivation or narrative drive—hence the subsequent comparisons to Carroll and James Joyce.

And they were often bleak. Modernist disaster abounded. In "The Phantom Head-Shaver (of Brighton)," for instance, the charming seaside resort is thrown into chaos by a goofy terror: a lightning-fast, hair-obsessed criminal wielding a razorblade. The story makes no sense, but it's a story, and its governing principle is that no one is ever safe. The episode features the shrieking Prunella Dirt (Sellers), whose husband is rendered bald by the eponymous villain; the broadly Jewish Judge Schnorrer (Sellers); Major Bloodnok (Sellers); Professor Crun (Sellers); and Willium, a dopey window cleaner (Sellers).

And it was rude. British humor, even on the BBC, was even less culturally sensitive than American comedy was at the time. "The Phantom Head-Shaver" episode features this breathtaking introductory remark: "Tonight's broadcast comes to you from an Arab Stench–Recuperating Centre in Stoke Poges."

"Hitler—*there* was a painter for you." A Peter Sellers World War II joke.

Spike's longtime assistant and editor Norma Farnes has observed that each of the Goons had suffered military service during World War II, and it was this direct experience of the armed forces, not to mention their experience of the war itself, that made them so skeptical of authority. They were also morbid by nature. In an episode called "The Dreaded Batter Pudding Hurler (of Bexhill-on-Sea)," Seagoon and Crun are standing on a beach during a blackout. Crun insists that no Nazi could never see "a little match being struck," so Seagoon strikes one. They're instantly hit by an exploding shell. "Any questions?" Seagoon asks. "Yes," Crun responds. "Where are my legs?"

Wally Stott ties one of the Goons' ruder, lewder jokes directly to the war: "Sometimes there was material that the boys tried to get away with, which the BBC wouldn't allow. There was a lot of British-Army coarse language that they tried to get through. I mean, *there was a character called Hugh Jampton!*"

The American interviewer falls silent. "You don't understand that? Well, Hampton is a crude word for penis. So Hugh Jampton would be a very big one, wouldn't it? Of course anybody who'd been through the war in Britain would know."

• • •

On the home front, Michael Peter Anthony Sellers was born on April 2, 1954. He was a cute baby with his mother's light complexion and twinkling eyes. They called him Pooh.

Now Peter had a son to go with the train set, and Anne had a real infant to go with her husband. Peg was overjoyed. She was Anne's first visitor at the hospital, the arrival of Pooh having reduced her to grand-motherliness.

• • •

Peter began filming another movie. Even after *Much Binding in the Marsh* and other postwar radio comedies had left the airwaves, British cinema still produced war-inspired comedy-dramas and even outright farces, as did Hollywood. The Boulting brothers, Roy and John, featured Gene Kelly in *Crest of the Wave* (1954); Billy Wilder had William Holden in *Stalag 17* (1953); and John Ford showcased James Cagney in *What Price Glory?* (1952). Peter Sellers's next film, *Orders Are Orders* (1954), is part of the same cycle, though it lands on the far side of *Francis Goes to West Point* (1952).

Filmed at Beaconsfield Studios (and no, there are no reports of Peter having tried to impress the front gate by signing in as the Fifth Earl), and released in the autumn, *Orders Are Orders* is a military farce in which an American film company overruns a British army camp in an attempt to film a B-grade, ray-gun–filled sci-fi movie on the grounds. Despite his increasing fame as a Goon, Peter is far from the top of the cast, a position occupied jointly by Margot Grahame, Brian Reece, and Raymond Huntley. Peter plays the subservient but graft-grabbing Private Goffin. Looking purposely dumpy, he's stuck with an ill-fitting white valet jacket that pulls severely at the bottom button. Corrupt but ineptly so, Goffin takes a conspiratorial attitude with the brash Hollywood director, who wants to pay somebody off to get the camp's cooperation. This is not high comedy. At the vulgar moment when Goffin first encounters the glamour-puss starlet tagging along with the production he actually licks his lips.

The highlight of this eminently inexpensive exercise is the preposterous fifties Martian Girl costuming employed to outfit the outerspace invaders. Complete with flapping antennae and bodices that resemble Jantzen swimsuits, they're irresistible getups, especially when Peter ends up in one. His is composed of a sequined, V-shaped top that looks like two gaudy beauty-contest sashes meeting in the middle. It's paired with a short black skirt. At one point Peter runs onto the makeshift sci-fi set in a little cardboard spaceship powered, like Fred Flintstone's car, with his feet. The rest of the film is of no interest. Even at Peter Sellers's bottom-rung position in British cinema, the material was beneath him.

• • •

Peter's omnidextrous voice was still his best asset, and one day it reached the ears of the European production head of Columbia Pictures. Mike Frankovich was in his car on the way to the airport and, to kill time, he tuned into the BBC. At the end of the radio play that happened to be on, Frankovich was stunned to hear the announcer say, "All the characters were played by Peter Sellers."

"We were doing *Fire Over Africa* with Maureen O'Hara at the time," Frankovich told the Hollywood gossip columnist Sheilah Graham some years later. "I needed English and American voices of all classes. When I returned to London, I called Peter and asked him to do the seven voices and paid him £250 for the lot." Disembodied movie voices were a fine sideline. According to Peter, by the time he did the voices in *Fire Over Africa*—and *he* always claimed that there were *seventeen*, not seven, and that they were all individuated Spaniards—he'd performed four voices for the sound track of John Huston's *Beat the Devil* (1953), including that of the film's star, Humphrey Bogart, who'd suffered tooth damage in a car accident and couldn't provide some of his own dialogue. He also went on to perform his chestnut Churchill in the opening moments of *The Man Who Never Was* (1956), not to mention a drunk, a newsreel announcer, a taxi driver, and a couple of crones later in the film.

Peter also performed a more bizarre audio cameo, uncredited, in a Joan Collins South Seas epic called *Our Girl Friday* (1954). He's the voice of a shrieking cockatoo:

Sadie Patch (Collins) is on a ship somewhere in the Pacific. There's a shipwreck. Everybody piles into a lifeboat, but, in sight of shore, it sinks. Sadie is washed onto the beach, and, with her back to the camera, she removes her clothes to let them dry in the sun. She's startled by a cockatoo and turns around. In short, Joan Collins takes her shirt off and Peter Sellers screams.

• • •

Just as he was assuming responsibility as the father of a newborn son, Peter's professional life was becoming a whirlwind. *The Goon Show*'s fifth series began recording on the last Sunday in September and continued nearly every week for the next twenty-five weeks. He did guest spots on the BBC television show *And So to Bentley* (starring Dick Bentley). And on November 1, Peter performed for Elizabeth II. The *Royal Variety Show* was certainly prestigious; it brought Peter into the company of the show's headliners, Noel Coward and Bob Hope.

Peter, Spike, and Harry continued to tour. Their acts couldn't use the words *Goon Show* in the title, since the BBC owned the copyright, but audiences all over Britain knew precisely who they'd come to see and why. Pleasing provincial audiences was even more of a strain, however, and not only for Peter. In December 1954, Spike once again reached the end of his rope, this time literally.

They were doing a mock-acrobatic act in Coventry. Billed as "Les Trois Charleys," Peter, Spike, and Harry wore gold headbands and flaming red capes. The audience was already confused by the three comedians' scatter-shot antics, but when Milligan appeared alone onstage and proceeded to blow a series of off-key trumpet solos, the audience rebelled with catcalls. Spike responded by clomping down to the edge of the stage and shouting, "You hate me, don't you?!" The audience roared back its unanimous affirmation. And with that they Coventrated him.

Spike ran to his dressing room and locked himself in. Harry and Peter, knowing Spike well, understood that he might well be killing himself. They broke down the door and found Spike putting the noose around his neck.

For Peter, this incident was the last straw in an ugly pile that had been growing in size since he was three, and so he decided to quit doing music hall shows. It wasn't just Spike's suicidal state that convinced him. These tours were simply too grueling, too awful and demeaning. But he still had a contractual obligation in Coventry to fulfill, and thus he had a chance to effect vengeance.

The morning after Spike's episode—they saved him, he continued writing and acting, somebody finally invented Lithium, and decades later he took it—Peter bought one of the *Goon Show* conductor's records (*Wally Stott's Christmas Melodies*) along with a record player, and that afternoon, at a reduced-price matinee for an elderly crowd, he appeared onstage clad in an oversized leopardskin leotard. He put the record on the record player, stood there, and played three songs straight through, not saying a word. At the end of each song, he led the audience in a round of hearty applause and then he left the stage.

Strangely, the audience appreciated the joke and applauded happily when Peter's essentially Dadaist routine concluded. The theater management was not nearly as entertained, however, and a furious manager challenged Peter on the basis of the "as known" clause. He had "performed"— no one disputed that—but not "as known."

"I'm going into films," the fed up comedian told his agent. "Not as a sideline, but all the way. This life is too bloody impossible. It'll kill me if I don't get out now."

Peter Sellers was safely back in London in late December 1954, appearing at the Palladium in a stylish riff on Mother Goose. Written by Phil Park and Eric Sykes, the comedy was a top-notch production—the antithesis of "Les Trois Charleys," with its headbands and capes and trumpets. The director was Val Parnell, a fixture of West End theater, and in fact, the production was officially billed as *Val Parnell's Seventh Magnificent Christmas Pantomime, "Mother Goose."* Erté codesigned the costumes. There was a Goose, a Vulture, a Bailiff, and a Policeman. There was a Sammy, a Donald, and the Pauline Grant Ballet. There was an evil Squire, too; that was Peter.

The actor-comedian Max Bygraves, who played Sammy, reports that Sellers couldn't help but depart from the script and improvise throughout the show's run. On one particular night, Bygraves well recalls, the evil Squire departed from the family-safe script, slipped without warning into Groucho Marx, and blurted, "Lady Dicker, that's ridiculous!"

Mother Goose—grumpy Richard Hearne in drag—was not amused by Peter's filthy joke, and immediately after the curtain fell she gave the management a piece of her fairy-tale mind. When the sympathetic Bygraves showed up at Peter's dressing room the next day, he found Peter in tears. Val Parnell himself had scolded the errant Peter, telling him that if he continued veering so luridly off script he'd never work again.

This was a relatively empty threat, since Parnell didn't control British radio, television, or film. But Peter seems thereafter to have stuck to the dialogue he'd originally been given—only for the duration of *Mother Goose,* of course, for by the end of March 1955, when the show closed (after 156 performances, usually two a day), he was once again free to exercise his dazzling improvisational skills.

But there was yet another new constraint. In late December 1954, toward the end of the *Goon Show* episode called "Ye Bandit of Sherwood Forest," Maid Marian (Charlotte Mitchell, one of the rare female guests) suddenly squealed, "Oh! There's someone crawling under the table! What are you doing under there, sir?"

"I'm looking for a telegram," a familiar politician's voice intoned. The studio audience thundered its approval, and from that moment forward Peter Sellers was officially forbidden to impersonate Winston Churchill on the British Broadcasting Corporation's airwaves.

• • •

In February 1955, Peter and Anne bought their first house, a mock-Tudor in Muswell Hill, a neighborhood just north of Highgate. North London was still his orbit, though he was moving progressively farther away from the center of town. But the more significant turning point that year occurred on film. After appearing in the small role of a police constable in *John and Julie* (1955; two cheeping children make their way to London to see the coronation of Elizabeth II), Peter made his first great movie, *The Ladykillers* (1955), for his first great director, Alexander Mackendrick, who cast him in support of the first great star Peter was able to study at close range.

"I first worked with him on *The Ladykillers,*" Sir Alec Guinness recalled in one of his last interviews. "He was not difficult at all—certainly not in those days. He was cast by Sandy Mackendrick, who knew him already. He was always very courteous to me; we got on very well. I mostly remember him having some kind of recording machine into which he would do imitations of people."

Long before his stellar appearances in international blockbusters—*The Bridge on the River Kwai* (1957), *Lawrence of Arabia* (1962), *Doctor Zhivago* (1965), *Star Wars* (1977), *The Empire Strikes Back* (1980), *Return of the Jedi* (1983), *A Passage to India* (1984)—Alec Guinness was a titan of British theater and cinema, and Peter admired him immensely. Guinness subsumed himself to an unparalleled degree into the roles he played. He was an apparently blank screen onto which he projected dazzlingly variegated characters. In the single year of 1951 Guinness did remarkable star turns in both *Oliver Twist,* as an especially vicious hook-nosed Fagin, and *The Lavender Hill Mob,* as the bland bank employee who casually steals £1 million. But it was in the great Ealing Studios comedy *Kind Hearts and Coronets* (1949) that Guinness gave his showiest chameleonic performance—that of all eight members of the titled d'Ascoyne family who are systematically bumped off by a distant relative, the ninth in line for the dukedom: Ascoyne d'Ascoyne, Henry d'Ascoyne, Canon d'Ascoyne, Admiral d'Ascoyne, General d'Ascoyne, Lady Agatha d'Ascoyne. . . .

The titan invited the nervous novice to lunch before *The Ladykillers* began filming in the summer of 1955. Sir Alec was not simply being kind when he spoke of the Peter Sellers he knew then. They *did* get along well at the time. After all, they had something in common. As Peter told Max Geldray afterward, "You cannot believe how quiet this man is. He's shy! He's got a switch inside. He turns it on, and another person pops up."

The Ladykillers was the Ealing Studio's last great comedy, a film both of the studio and *against* the studio. Ealing's longtime head, Michael Balcon, had envisioned and created a dogmatically British cinema—films that were homegrown, popular, and inconceivable in any other national film industry. Under Balcon's supervision, the best Ealing directors—Mackendrick among them—developed a style so consistent that by the mid-1950s it had become formulaic: An identifiably British setting (a city block in London, an island in the Hebrides, a manor house in the country) turns out to be populated by crazed eccentrics, or hurled into chaos by some fantastic event, or both. Surface realism meets absurdity—a biting comment on the kingdom.

But with *The Ladykillers*, Mackendrick set out to satirize not only British society but Ealing's own internal culture as well. In *The Ladykillers*, the familiar British setting represented the very studio in which Mackendrick worked: Mackendrick himself was the chief eccentric, who, in this case, was so defeated by Balcon's enforced conventionality that he left Ealing after finishing the film.

The Ladykillers concerns an elderly, Victorian-throwback widow, Mrs. Wilberforce (Katie Johnson). She seems sweet enough at first glance as she walks down a residential London street, but at the steps of a police station she looks into a baby carriage and causes the baby to shriek in terror. The infant's wail is predictive. In the course of the comedy Mrs. Wilberforce reveals herself to be so profoundly irritating that garroting her, knifing her, and shooting her become increasingly desirable outcomes in the minds of both characters and audiences alike.

She takes in a lodger, Professor Marcus (Guinness, wearing hideous rat-like teeth), who uses his upstairs rooms to plan a heist with four henchmen:

a jovial, well-spoken major (Cecil Parker), a dopey, sentimental boxer called One-Round (Danny Green), a frightening thug dressed all in black (Herbert Lom), and a Teddy Boy named Harry (Peter). (The British historian Arthur Marwick defines the Teddy Boy as "the first nationally recognized figure representative of youth's detachment from the rest of society and representative of the fact that for the first time working-class youth could take the initiative." The name comes from the Edwardian-style suits the boys wore as a kind of uniform; they got the idea from upper-class spivs of the late 1940s.) The thieves tell Mrs. Wilberforce that they are members of an amateur string quintet and incessantly play a single piece—Boccherini's String Quintet in E Major—on a record player to disguise their criminal planning sessions.

When casting calls began in the spring, Dennis Selinger arranged for Peter to meet with Mackendrick and the film's associate producer, Seth Holt—but not for the role of Harry. They wanted Peter to read One-Round. It wasn't a particularly successful audition. As Mackendrick told Selinger, "Frankly, we can't see him with a broken nose and a cauliflower ear."

Holt, however, had the inspiration of casting Peter instead as Harry—the role for which Mackendrick had originally considered Richard Attenborough. Peter may have ended up playing another role or two in *The Ladykillers* as well; both Guinness's and Mackendrick's biographers insist that Peter provided the voices of Mrs. Wilberforce's two parrots.

Birds aside, Peter could certainly produce a flawless working-class Teddy Boy voice, but his casting in *The Ladykillers* caused him great anxiety nonetheless. This strange, morbid satire might bomb; his film career might be scuttled; he was terrified of failure. Michael Balcon later described him as being "desperately anxious" while shooting his scenes: "He kept asking: 'Is it all right? Am I any good?' "

Mackendrick's painstaking directing style, combined with the sheer length of time it took to shoot in three-strip Technicolor, resulted in multiple takes of almost every scene. Peter was used to cheaper productions, of which the one-take, two-week *Penny Points to Paradise* was only the most extreme example. And he was quite unnerved by the careful and methodical Mackendrick's demand that he—and Guinness, and Katie Johnson, and everybody else—play the same scene over and over again in front of fully loaded, softly humming cameras. Mackendrick simply wanted to use the best of a variety of takes; Peter kept assuming that something had gone wrong each time, but he never could tell what it was.

From Peter's perspective, Alec Guinness was a soothing influence as well as a generous performer with whom he could share a scene. During the production of *The Ladykillers*, Guinness offered Peter a piece of advice: "Don't ever let the press know anything about your private life." Peter told the press later that Guinness had been "patient enough to listen to me for hours as I spoke about my problems and aspirations."

Peter also claimed that Guinness was so impressed with his performance that he sent a note to a prominent English film critic, Cecil Wilson: "If you want a hot tip for the future," Guinness is said to have written, "put your money on Peter Sellers."

But in private, Guinness grew concerned about Sellers's influence on him. According to the critic Kenneth Tynan, during the production of *The Ladykillers*, and for a long time thereafter, Peter "sought Guinness's advice at every opportunity, so assiduously that Guinness began to be worried, and even to suspect that his own personality was being absorbed by some process of osmosis into that of Sellers."

A dogged apprentice and a paranoid master: Sellers's relationship with Guinness played perfectly into the film. Like so many of his performances, Guinness's rendition of Professor Marcus is one of exquisite gestures and exacting timing: an insinuating tilt of the head, a jaunty hip jiggle to the tune of the string quintet, all with an air of suspicion toward everyone around him. Sellers's Harry is much less flamboyant. Peter lets his face and body go absolutely slack when Harry listens to Professor Marcus's instructions. Enthralled to the point of stupefaction, Harry is a stylish Teddy Boy, but not a particularly smart or hammy one.

Mrs. Wilberforce inadvertently ruins the criminals' scheme from the start, but the old bat's suspicions are aroused only after she closes the front door too soon on One-Round, who, with the strap of his cello case stuck in the door, gives a hard yank and money flies out, all over the street. She has got to be killed:

MARCUS: It ought to look like an accident.
HARRY: (with a dawning inspiration) How about suicide?! (The other crooks gaze in amazement at his stupidity while Harry eagerly moistens his lips.) Get her to write a note, you know? "I just couldn't

stand it no more, signed Mrs. Wilberforce," and then somebody goes down and hangs her! (He jerks enthusiastically on his own black Teddy Boy tie.)

But one by one the men kill each other instead. Mrs. Wilberforce survives. Because the police know she's batty, she gets to keep all the money for herself. Peter's Harry meets his end in a farcical chase during which he emits pipsqueaky sounds of panic until his final line: "Where's your sense of humor, One-Round?" at which point One-Round clobbers him to death with a plank.

• • •

"He struck me as a very charming, chirpy little spiv with a big car—a red Bentley—prominently parked every morning," Herbert Lom says, looking back on his first film with Peter Sellers. "He was very nice. We struck up a friendship." Lom makes a particular point about working with Peter. As an actor, Lom declares, Peter "was very generous," meaning that he didn't find ways of upstaging his colleagues, stealing their thunder with distracting tics and gestures of his own.

There were offscreen pranks. Lom, his fellow actors, and some members of the crew couldn't help but notice Peter's ostentatious devotion to the big red Bentley, so they thought they'd pull a little joke at his expense by painting a long scratch on the side of the car. Peter reacted poorly. But the fact that it turned out to be washable paint led him to wreak vengeance in harmless, practical-joke kind. A few days later, Lom smelled something fishy on the way home from a day of shooting. Peter "had pinned a kipper at the bottom of my engine, which started frying every time the engine got hot."

All the while, as Sir Alec remembered, Peter had been playing with his recorder. As the production neared its end in late summer, he showed up with his own limited-edition work of audio art—a spoof trailer for *The Ladykillers* in which Peter played not only all the central characters' roles but also the voice of Sandy Mackendrick giving directions. He handed out the recordings as gifts, and they were a hit. Danny Green was amused to hear himself trying out important line readings ("I'm stayin' with *Ma! I'm* stayin' with Ma! I'm *stayin'* with Ma!"). Guinness, Lom, and Cecil Parker were respectfully skewered as well. So was Katie Johnson. "It sounded exactly like all of us," Herbert Lom declares, though other more critical listeners felt that Peter's rendition of Mrs. Wilberforce bore a discomfiting similarity to Bluebottle.

It was then that Peter presented his critique of Mackendrick. Assuming a neutral narrator voice, Peter announced that listeners would now be offered "a brief glimpse of the brilliant technique of Alexander Mackendrick, director." The clapper boy (Peter) barks, "Scene 5, take *73!*" whereupon Peter, in blithering imitation of Peter, emits a string of rapid-fire gibberish, to which Mackendrick (Peter) responds, "Er, Peter—Peter—that's, er . . . that's very good. We'll do another."

• • •

Herbert Lom remembers of Peter that "at the end of the film he came to me and said if I could help him get another film part. And he obviously wasn't putting it on. He meant it. And *I* meant it when I said, 'You won't need my help.' "

The Ladykillers was released in December to rave if rather less than perceptive reviews: "The most stylish, inventive, and funniest British comedy of the year"; "captivating"; "accomplished and polished"; "lots of laughs"; "wonderfully funny."

Typically, it took years before British film scholars pointed out what the reviewers had missed at the time. Neil Sinyard sees in *The Ladykillers* an "elderly, paralyzed, hallucinatory, hidebound England"; Roy Armes calls it "a black and surreal masterpiece." Charles Barr reads the film marvelously as a political allegory: the gang of thieves as the postwar Labor government, who mask their radical plan to redistribute wealth by a cover of familiar, recorded classical music: "Their success is undermined by two factors, interacting: their own internecine quarrels, and the startling, paralyzing charisma of the 'natural' governing class."

After *The Ladykillers*, Alexander Mackendrick left Ealing—and England—and moved to Hollywood, where he made the beautifully rancid *The Sweet Smell of Success* (1957) and was fired from his next two pictures. He didn't make another movie for six years.

Peter, meanwhile, found himself with no other film offers and turned instead to television.

• • •

While watching TV one evening in December 1955, Peter found himself unusually entertained, so the following day he placed a call to the show's director. As Richard Lester later reported the conversation, "A voice said, 'You don't know me, but I saw your show last night. Either that was the worst show that British television has so far produced, or I think you're onto something.' " Sellers and Lester met, quickly hit it off, and decided to make TV's answer to *The Goon Show*. It would not be the radio Goons televised. It would be Goonavision, a radical rethinking of visual comedy in the video age.

Idiot Weekly, Price 2d premiered on February 24, 1956. (*2d* is two pence, or tuppence.) Notably, *Idiot Weekly* didn't appear on the BBC; it was produced independently by Associated-Rediffusion and broadcast on the less hidebound ITV. Still, ITV had its limits. *Idiot Weekly* wasn't broadcast outside of greater London, the obvious fear being that Peter's nemeses—the no-brow miners up North—weren't sophisticated enough to handle the show's avant-garde humor.

Peter was the star of the series, his most consistent character being the editor of a sleazy Victorian tabloid, the headlines of which served as lead-ins to comedy skits featuring Sellers, Spike, and Eric Sykes, along with Valentine Dyall, Graham Stark, Kenneth Connor, and Max Geldray. Spike Milligan wrote the scripts, along with a stabilizing—and very large—backup team that included Sykes, John Antrobus, Brad Ashton, Dick Barry, Dave Freeman, Ray Galton, John Junkin, Eric Merriman, Terry Nation, Lew Schwarz, Alan Simpson, and Johnny Speight. The comedy wasn't simply manic and self-reflexive like *The Goon Show*. It was *visually* so, with purposely strange and ultramodern camerawork to match the vocal and narrative jokes.

There was, in addition, a severe but vitalizing risk involved. *Idiot Weekly* was broadcast *live*.

"The one thing we tried to do," Lester later explained, "was to push the rather narrow bounds of television comedy. Spike and Peter were anxious not to fall into those traps." What they wanted instead was "to produce material which was as visually anarchic and stimulating as their verbal work had been." As with *The Goon Show*, Milligan was what Lester calls "the creative force," Peter "the performer." "I think Peter envied—in the best sense—Spike's need to create. Peter was a wonderful adapter of other people's ideas. He honed them and made them into something infinitely better than what they could have been. But in terms of raw creation, certainly, Spike was the creator of almost all the ideas that came up."

Idiot Weekly, Price 2d ran for its allotted six weeks, whereupon a follow-up series, *A Show Called Fred*, blasted onscreen on five successive Wednes-days in May. It too, was recorded live from A-R's studios at Wembley. Peter's name was now above the title: "Peter Sellers in *A Show Called Fred*." Spike, having made it through the creation of *Idiot Weekly* without going unhinged, now retained full control of the writing; the backup team was dropped. Still, *A Show Called Fred*'s broadcast range continued to be lim-ited to Greater London.

Spike himself was productive; at this point it was only his writing that was unquestionably deranged, but it was deranged in an especially novel and exciting way. And it proved to be popular, striking a chord with the urbane public lucky enough to have been granted access to it. (Michael Balcon was right: England *is* a land of surface realism dotted with secretly crazed eccentrics.) To say that *A Show Called Fred* embraced the still rela-tively new medium of television fully is too mild a claim. It was *Laugh-In* and *Monty Python* a decade ahead.

One show featured a Dr. Jekyll and Mr. Hyde routine: Peter appears onscreen mixing potions in test tubes and declaring that he wishes to re-move all his evil and leave only the good. He sloshes it down; the camera swings wildly back and forth; the image goes drastically in and out of focus. Peter reappears with ghastly makeup. "It went wrong! I'm evil!" He rushes to Hyde Park, attacks a woman, drags her into the bushes, and flings a rubber dummy around. The woman returns, delighted. "Oh you kinky thing!" Back at the lab, Dr. Jekyll asks his assistant (Graham Stark) to drive him home. Stark places a steering wheel against Peter's forehead and steers him out.

Several years later, the *New York Times* asked Sellers the obvious ques-tion: Why Fred? Peter's response: "You can ruin *anything* with 'Fred.' Sup-pose somebody shows you a painting. 'Oh,' he says, 'isn't it beautiful—it's a Rembrandt!' 'Beautiful!,' you say. Then you look a bit closer and you see it's signed 'Fred Rembrandt.' It's no good. You can't take it seriously if it's by Fred Rembrandt."

But it *was* good, and everybody knew it—Spike and Peter, Richard Lester, Associated-Rediffusion, and ITV. Peter, who had originally been signed to do *Idiot Weekly* at £100 pounds per program was given a raise, to £500.

In one of *A Show Called Fred*'s most celebrated incidents, Milligan wrote a sketch in which Sellers would play *Richard III*—not the character of Richard III, but *all* the major parts—dressed, madeup, and speaking precisely as Laurence Olivier. Milligan's idea was to invite Olivier himself to end the scene as a lone sentinel on the battlements; having heard Sellers's rendition, Olivier would simply shake his head in grief. Unfortunately, nobody had the nerve to approach Olivier himself, who, when told of it later, claimed to be disappointed not to have been asked. In any event, Peter played it all utterly straight, especially the part of Richard.

The pace began to pick up, as did the mania. After *Fred* came *Son of Fred*. And *The Goon Show* entered its seventh series.

Son of Fred ran from September 17 through November 5, 1956, eight programs in all, and with it, Peter and Spike's disjointed proto-postmodernist video went national. Because of its father's success, *Son of Fred* could now be seen in the Midlands and the North. The billing also changed and lengthened: "Peter Sellers in *Son of Fred* by Spike Milligan." Spike, who limited himself mainly to walk-on roles, began aiming instead for an even sparer, starker comedy style.

An "Idiot's Postbag" sequence:

We see a simple ship set—with a back-projection tracking shot of trains.

Peter is wearing a Nazi uniform—just the jacket. He's got on pajama bottoms as pants.

A mountaineer writes in with a question from the Alps. We see him hanging on the side of a cliff. He asks Peter what to do. Peter advises him to take the only course of action an experienced mountaineer could take under the circumstances: "Fall off." The mountaineer thanks Peter, lets go, and plunges to his death.

Max Geldray strolls through the set with his harmonica. A black man in a hut appears with a violin. Max, playing "Anything Goes," wanders out to the street, hails a cab, hops in, and rides away. He ends up in a field and gets carried away on a stretcher.

Sellers turns up at a Lost and Found department looking for his mate—someone he misplaced on the London tube. Behind the counter there's a body with a tag on its toe. But no, that's not his friend. Sellers, wearing an oversized hat that sits on his ears, then lies down on a slab himself, along with Spike and Graham Stark. They each await someone to claim them.

Son of Fred, episode four:

Peter, wearing tiny black tights, attempts to bang a giant gong to open the show. (It's a farcical parody of the great Rank Organization film logo, the British equivalent of the MGM lion.)

Two musicians prepare to walk backward around the world while playing sousaphones.

A skit set in nineteenth century France: Sellers, playing a character named Monte Carlo, effects a broad and ridiculous French accent until the chateau walls, which have obviously been made of fabric all along, are lifted up to reveal a large television camera. Peter addresses the camera in a British accent until someone throws a sheet over it to enable Peter to resume speaking French. An unrelated technician runs onscreen and speaks to the *other* camera—the one that's actually filming. Suddenly there's music—the old Gang Show chestnut, "We're Riding Along on the Crest of a Wave"—at which point the chateau backdrop flies up and everybody launches into a music hall routine.

Max Geldray begins playing "Lady Be Good."

Cut to Spike's mouth, in extreme close-up, yammering nonsense syllables.

Cut to Max Geldray, who attempts to finish "Lady Be Good."

Cut to Peter playing a squirt bottle, squirting in time to "Lady Be Good."

Michael Palin, interviewed about *The Goon Show*, responded by saying that "*The Goon Show* didn't attempt to make any sense," and that "the influence of *The Goon Show* on *me* was that when it came to *Python*, we could write whatever we wanted." But it was *A Show Called Fred* and *Son of Fred* that were *Monty Python*'s real precursors. They were visually anarchic as well as verbally brilliant and mentally abnormal.

And they *really* made no sense.

Other programs featured such things as an underwater violin recital. A meeting between someone called Fred Nurk and his son's headmaster—that one ended with a meaningless waltz. There were parody commercials: one here for "Footo, the Patent Book Exploder"; one there for Muc, a detergent that chopped down trees.

One (possibly apocryphal) *Fred* story involved a location shoot at a zoo, where unemployed actors were supposed to serve as understudies for animals on the animals' days off. Graham Stark is said to have jumped into the sea lions' tank and had great fun until one of the sea lions became aroused by the smell of his crotch. Stark appears to have survived the episode intact, but there were other tensions all around. Just before filming a *Fred*, Peter suffered a severe anxiety attack and attempted to alleviate it with half a bottle of brandy. He managed to speak his lines perfectly without slurring a word; it was his reaction time that suffered. The show was running eight minutes over schedule, which forced Dick Lester to cut the final sketch— not that anybody in the audience could tell the difference.

On another program Sellers and Stark were to sit on a park bench and enjoy an absurd conversation, gradually coming to realize that they are caught in a dream. The question was, whose dream was it? Lester planned to reveal the answer by tilting the camera down to a St. Bernard asleep under the bench. Rehearsals went fantastically well; the dog was a pro. But during the live performance it stood up and attempted to leave. It was leashed. With increasing annoyance, the dog began dragging scenery to the floor, including Sellers and Stark. Lester, frantic in the control booth, pleaded to the broadcast technicians to yank the show off the air. "We can't," was their reply. Lester had no choice. "Tell them to keep going! Tell them to ad-lib!" Sellers and Stark, evidently more professional than the dog, did exactly that—not that anyone in the audience could tell the difference.

Apart from his anxiety attack, Sellers's offscreen emotional state was relatively normal, especially in comparison to Milligan, who is said by this point to have been sedated much of the time. The combination of Milligan's tenuous emotional state and the increasingly radical absurdity of his comedy style led ITV to grow more and more nervous during the run of *Son of Fred,* and at the end of eight weeks the executives pulled the plug. There were no plans to spawn *Fred*'s grandchild. As for Spike, he had to wait eight years before returning to British television with *Milligan's Wake.*

• • •

Peter and Spike returned to the movies. Together with their friend Dick Emery, Peter and Spike filmed a half-hour comedy quickie at the Merton Park Studios in deepest southwest London. *The Case of the Mukkinese Battle Horn,* scripted by the film's producers with help from Spike, Peter, and Larry Stephens, was directed by Joseph Sterling, but more important, it was filmed (as the title sequence tells us) "in the wonder of SchizophrenoScope, the new split-screen."

Compared to any of the *Freds* it's tame stuff, but *The Case of the Mukkinese Battle Horn* does have its moments. Peter plays a trenchcoat and mustache–clad Scotland Yard inspector investigating the theft of the rare eponymous instrument, a twisted contraption said to be the only one in existence except for the identical twin kept in the storage room. Spike is his assistant, Brown, and the night watchman, White; White is Eccles under another name. Emery is the museum's curator:

> EMERY: We had a robbery last night.
> SELLERS: A robbery? Anything stolen?

Back at Scotland Yard, a rock comes crashing through the window. There's a note attached, etc.

Henry Crun shows up as the doddering owner of a pawn shop; Minnie shrieks offscreen. A much more fetching Peter turns up lounging on a chaise under a heavily pomaded platinum wig and a satin smoking jacket, languidly drawing from a cigarette holder. Sir Jervis Fruit was hardly the first screaming queen in Peter's repertoire; footage of an early cabaret performance shows him mincing hand on hip across the stage. And one historian of gay images in British culture claims that Sellers performed these flaming faggot bits on a routine basis and that at least one gay audience member was so offended by it that he stood up in the middle of the sketch and told Peter to stop it.

What's striking about Sir Jervis Fruit, though, is that while he makes Quentin Crisp look like a rugby player, Peter invests him with the same core dignity he lends all of his most flamboyant creations. He *believes* in Fruit. There's no contempt or derision. Like Crystal Jollibottom, Sir Jervis would be a delightful tablemate at a dinner party. The same can't be said, say, for Spike's moronic Eccles, who, toward the end of *The Case of the Mukkinese Battle Horn*, gets the chance to perform the Dance of the Seven Veils in drag before a captivated Peter. It is an unnerving spectacle.

• • •

Because Peter's star was rising higher and higher, he was booked to appear on any number of television specials: *The Billy Cotton Band Show*, *Six Five Special*, *Don't Spare the Horses*, the third of three specials called *Secombe Here!*, and others. He was supposed to be on *Jack Benny in London*, too. He was great in rehearsals. In fact, he may have been a little too great, for Benny took the show's producer aside and told him that he thought Peter's line deliveries and timing were so similar to his own that Peter's appearance would be detrimental to the show as a whole, and so, perhaps, they should let him go.

As the comedian Steve Allen points out in regard to this incident, Benny and Sellers "were not at all alike in their natural manner of speech." Perhaps Benny felt Sellers was upstaging him. Either that or Peter's routine included a devilish impersonation of Benny, and Benny felt that one of him was enough on his own British television special. In any event, they paid off Peter's contract and sent him home in disappointment.

For Peter, the rejection stung, but it didn't hurt his chances in the industry. Far from it. Peter starred in two of his *own* television specials that year, both called *Eric Sykes Presents Peter Sellers.*

• • •

The Goon Show's seventh series began in October, but even before it finished in March 1957, Peter had done *yet another* television series, not to mention his first appearance on North American TV. Because his contract with Associated-Rediffusion required four short television series and he'd done only three, he was obliged to star in one more despite Spike's departure after *Son of Fred.* With Richard Lester having moved on to other work as well, he called on his friend and former Goonmate Michael Bentine. Bentine's quarrels, after all, had been with Spike, not Peter. Bentine, in turn, brought in the Australian writer-performer David Nettheim, whom he'd met in Australia while working on the radio series *Three's a Crowd.* But this time there would be no confusion or dispute as to Bentine's creative role: On this show he was to be billed as "Creator."

The result was *Yes, It's the Cathode-Ray Tube Show!*, which enjoyed its surreal run on ITV from February 11 through March 18, 1957, six programs in all. It was *Fred*-like, but in a Bentine way: this time, the surreality was such that the show's very title disintegrated over the course of the series. In a conceit worthy of both Tristan Tzara and Yoko Ono, one word fell off the title each week. By the last program it was a show called *Yes.*

• • •

About this time, Peter took a brief trip to North America, his first. His journey to Toronto owed to his appearance on Canadian Broadcasting Corporation's *Chrysler Show.* He was booked to do his *Richard III* bit; Graham Stark accompanied him as the Duke of Clarence. For whatever reason, the show itself terrified Peter.

As Stark describes the scene in his memoirs, "large, well-dressed, cigar-toting Chrysler executives nervously prowled behind the cameras" all day during rehearsals, and Peter became increasingly upset. Moments before filming the scene, he looked at himself, all wigged and behumped, in his dressing room mirror and said in the voice of Laurence Olivier, "Now is the winter of an absolute bleeding disaster." But as usual, when he actually performed the scene before a laughing audience he was fine.

• • •

Peter continued to appear in film comedy shorts in the twenty-minute to half-hour range. Even more than *Mukkinese Battle Horn*, these were steps backward in terms of artistic adventure, but they provided exposure, they occupied his mind, and they paid.

Dearth of a Salesman, from A.B.-Pathé, was released in early summer. Hector Dimwittie (Sellers) attempts to become the best salesman in Britain, tries vainly to sell toilet supplies and moves quickly on to washing machines and tape recorders, suffering all the while the gross indignity of a too-successful brother-in-law. "Peter Sellers works hard," *Today's Cinema* opined; "handy footage appeal"—in other words, there was enough celluloid to keep the audience awake before the feature began. *Insomnia Is Good for You*, running roughly the same length, was released shortly thereafter. Typically for the businessman culture of the fifties, it featured salesman Hector again, now unable to sleep. "A normal, lazy, married man," is how the film describes the newly successful Hector. His boss has de-manded a meeting on Monday morning for reasons Hector can't fathom. Unable to stop spinning fantasies of his boss's fierce temper, Hector fails to sleep for sixty-two hours. Unlike the avant-garde comedy Peter did with Spike or Michael Bentine, the material practically writes itself, to its det-riment. Hector tries to remember cherished verse; he can't. He worries about his job; that he can do. And, in the end, the reason for the meeting? His boss wants him to take a client out for a night on the town. "Falls very flat," *Monthly Film Bulletin* scoffed.

And there was *Cold Comfort*, from C. M. George Film Productions. *Today's Cinema*'s review, in toto: "Gentle thumbnail lecture on how to catch a cold and keep it. Radio star Peter Sellars (*sic*) illustrates it, mainly in pajamas, and the homely domestic touches will strike a responsive chord anywhere."

This was all very well as far as it went, but it hadn't gone nearly far enough for Peter. Nightclubs, cabarets, radio, stage, television, big roles in short films, short roles in big films, and one sizable role in a masterpiece. Peter Sellers saw himself as stuck.

He had his toys, his cars, his friends, his wife, his son. He had his mother.

What he felt was lack.

PART TWO

IN WONDERLAND

1957–64

―――――――

" 'Curiouser and curiouser!' cried Alice,"
as she finds herself growing to enormous proportions
after having simply followed the directions given to her.
She eats the cake, grows larger and larger,
and discovers that she is unhappier than ever.
Soon she is swimming in a pool of her own tears.

Peter Sellers's cinematic stock rose again in 1957, paradoxically in a film called *The Smallest Show on Earth* (1957), in which he plays a loyal if drunken film projectionist. The film's director, Basil Dearden, had been one of Ealing's most prolific—twenty-one films in fifteen years, the most commercially successful of which was the 1950 drama *The Blue Lamp*, which caused a great stir thanks to its radical portrayal of British law enforcement. (For once the copper *wasn't* a bungling boob.) But like Alexander Mackendrick, Dearden had had enough of Michael Balcon's regimentation at Ealing, and by 1957 he'd left the studio. He made *The Smallest Show on Earth*, a surprisingly bitter comedy, for British Lion.

The story: Matt Spenser and his wife, Jean, inherit a movie theater in the North. They're a cute 1950s English couple—a pretty, sharp-chinned blonde cheerfully married to a beefcake husband. She's good-natured, a great gal; he's a little dim but not without a certain magnetism, a British Tab Hunter with lovehandles and a slightly higher IQ. A screwball couple updated to the 1950s, Matt and Jean are played by Bill Travers and Virginia McKenna, who went on to star in the wildlife movie that inspired the Oscar-winning song "Born Free" (1966).

They're looped when they arrive at their destination, so when they see the town's theater, the Grand—a streamline-Moderne, quasi-fascist affair with a uniformed doorman and a crowd of eager patrons—they naturally assume it's theirs. It's not. Theirs is the decrepit Bijou, a Babylonian-Baroque-Revival heap under the train tracks.

Margaret Rutherford is the ticket seller, Mrs. Fazackalee, except that she sells no tickets.

Peter Sellers, as the weary projectionist, Mr. Quill, drinks:

> MR. QUILL: (all but overcome with emotion) Well, uh, Mr. Spenser, it's like this 'ere. I would like you 'a know that I, well, I appreciate what you said, and what you're tryin' 'a do. And believe me, I don't say this lightly—I am absolutely determined that I won't take another drop! Not another drop I won't touch, I won't!
> MRS. FAZACKALEE: I don't think you may realize, Mr. Spenser, what a big sacrifice this may mean for Mr. Quill.

Basil Dearden may enjoy a reputation in Britain for a certain liberalism in his social problem dramas—after this comedy he made *Violent Playground* (juvenile delinquency, 1958), *Sapphire* (racism, 1959), and *Victim* (homosexuality, 1961)—but *The Smallest Show on Earth* bears a strikingly antipopulist contempt for movie audiences. Patrons of the Bijou, after the Spensers get it up and running, are comprised of a bunch of cruel rubes, teenage makeout artists, and a whore. At the same time, Dearden isn't above sweetening his nasty streak with easy sentimentality when Sellers's Mr. Quill projects a silent melodrama to an audience of two—Mrs. Fazackalee and Old Tom, the usher (Bernard Miles):

Mr. Quill (describing the movie to the Spensers): "Old film. Classic, you might say. I've saved 'em for years, bits of 'em. We used to run 'em like this in the old days, but, not for years we haven't done it. Now it seems like old times once more."

But the look on Sellers's face saves it, an expression of meditative warmth. To his great credit as a dramatic actor-in-training, Peter learned in *The Smallest Show on Earth* how to subvert maudlin dialogue by photogenically sustaining silence.

• • •

Peter cut and released his third single record, "Any Old Iron," with "Boiled Bananas and Carrots" on the flip side. A banjo-strumming, incomprehensibly fast-talking novelty song, "Any Old Iron," made it onto the British pop charts and stayed there for eleven weeks in the autumn. It even rose briefly into the Top Twenty.

His reputation kept growing and, inexorably, he won his first costarring role—as a faux-Scottish extortion victim in the black comedy *The Naked Truth* (1957). Written by Michael Pertwee and directed by Mario Zampi for the Rank Organization, *The Naked Truth* traces several prominent citizens' attempts to avoid, stifle, and finally snuff the unctuous editor of a *Confidential*-like scandal sheet. Terry-Thomas, with whom Peter shared top billing, is a philandering lord, about to be exposed. Peter is a thickly brogued television star, beloved by his elderly audience and a slumlord on the side.

With a studio audience in place and the cameras rolling, an enthusiastic announcer heralds his appearance: "The star of the show, the man who made it all possible! The jack of all faces! The king of kindness! And the ace of good hearts, *'Wee Sonny' MacGregor!*" Enter a dimple-grinning Peter, literally jumping onstage in a roaring plaid kilt, a matching plaid banner on his shoulder held in place by a pin, a pair of equally screaming kneesocks, and an awfully frilly shirt. He's the Liberace of Brigadoon:

> WEE SONNY: (Squeak of pleasure, gasp, grin and . . .) A great big welcome t' all th' old folk an' the bonny young lad's 'n lassi's! I can't tell the difference, you know! (giggle).

Wee Sonny is about as Scottish as Peter himself, a fact Sellers reveals by pushing his brogue just a step too far. The blackmailing editor (Dennis Price) pays him a slimy visit and lets Wee Sonny know that while he doesn't much care about the fake accent, he's fascinated by the chance to reveal to the TV star's aged fans the famous owner of a dismal old people's ghetto in Eastditch. Soon thereafter, a guest on Sonny's show mentions that he hails from Eastditch and begins to describe the wretched place in detail. Wee Sonny loses control. It makes the papers. ("Sonny Faded Out—Shouts at Aged Contestant. Overcome by heat, says producer.") Sonny responds with nominally more control by planning to kill the blackmailer under one of the many identities the "jack of all faces" believes he's able to assume: "*I* couldn't. But someone else might! Any one of a thousand characters that I can create and then destroy, *just like that!*" Wee Sonny gets carried away: "Murder by a figment of my imagination!"

Sonny's valet (Kenneth Griffith), tethered more tightly to reality, tells him that the scheme is doomed to failure—not because it's immoral, but because Wee Sonny is a dreadful actor.

• • •

Terry-Thomas recalled in his memoirs that Peter, whom he had known since the Grafton Arms days, had run into him one day early in his career and began complaining about a part he'd been asked to play (one Terry-Thomas doesn't identify): "The trouble about my role," Peter told him, "is that they wanted an actor with a Cockney accent. To me this is devastating because I've spent five years trying to lose my Cockney twang." "He had lost it so successfully," Terry-Thomas went on to write, that "by the time we made *The Naked Truth* he confided to me one day, 'I've come to the part of the film which is scaring me to death. I'm supposed to use my own accent. *And I haven't got one.*' "

But Peter never had a Cockney twang to begin with; not everyone in London grows up sounding like Michael Caine in *Alfie* (1966). And since adolescence he could imitate any accent at all, practically at will. Although Terry-Thomas had no reason to realize it, what Peter was actually confessing was his sense of self—one that was depleted on the one hand and mutantly reduplicating on the other, a multiple emptiness he was trying to fill by turning it into a point of conversation.

Terry-Thomas did sense another kind of trouble brewing. Peter was no longer the eager-to-please novice granted the chance to appear alongside Alec Guinness and grateful just to be there. Now that he was sharing top billing on *The Naked Truth*, Peter Sellers was getting a bit touchy.

He "made one of his 'protests' during shooting," Terry-Thomas writes. "He turned to Mario Zampi and shouted, 'The way you are making this film is ridiculous. You can't direct! I know much more about the camera than you do. I'll give you one more take and then I'm off.' Mario didn't reply. He stood there, shocked."

Characteristically, others had an easier time of it. "I was pleased to meet him," Kenneth Griffith says. "Didn't know much about him, but he was very pleased to meet me. And from that day to this—with one exception—he was an unshiftable friend to me. And as he became very influential, he was a great help to me."

However, even a friend as loyal and loving as Griffith adds, "He was notoriously treacherous. Of course, he was in a powerless mental and emotional state. He was a manic-depressive, and, well, yes—I have sympathy for people. I understood Sellers. Very complicated, you know. He was pretty well inarticulate as himself."

• • •

The loyalty of Peter Sellers's closest friends remains seemingly boundless. They loved him. And they still do. "Anne was a very nice woman," Griffith reflected recently. "*Of course* he had lovely women. Anne was a nice woman, and that's what he was like to me."

Peter could be friendly to total strangers. "One day I was at a cinema in Hampstead," the director Joseph McGrath remembers, "and Peter Sellers was standing there as I came out. And I had just seen him in the film, so I went up to him and said, 'You're Peter Sellers, and I claim the reward.' And he said, 'Who are you?' and I told him who I was. He said, 'What do you do?' I said, 'Well, I'm an art student.' He said, 'Let's go and have a cup of tea.' "

A few years went by, and McGrath became a television director. "I got his home phone number, and telephoned him, and he said, 'Who are you?' I said, 'McGrath—Joe McGrath.' He said, 'I remember you. You've made it, and without my help." They remained extremely friendly—again, with one notable exception—for the rest of Peter's life.

"I had had surgery on my leg," Max Geldray reports. (*The Goon Show*, of course, was still running to national acclaim and amusement.) "Harry Secombe started calling everybody and telling them I was in the hospital. Harry sent me flowers and fruit—typical of him—and I had telegrams from people. When Peter heard about it, he immediately came over and saw all the flowers and said 'My God, I'm so *stupid*.' He was very angry that he hadn't sent things first.

"I'm sitting there not able to walk. He said, 'What do you want?' I said, 'Peter, I can't go anywhere. *I can't walk*.' He said, 'I have a new car!'

"That meant absolutely nothing to me, since he had a new car once a week. 'It's a new Rover, and you've got to see it! I have to take you for a ride!' So he carried me, physically, bodily, into the car. We drove away. We went for a five-minute drive and stopped. He said, 'Just sit there. I'll be back.'

"After a *long* time sitting there, I see him coming down the street with another guy who was carrying a lot of packages. He said, 'That's yours.' What it was I had no idea. We drove back home, he carried me inside, and there was a whole new sound system.

"I said, 'Peter, I *have* a sound system. I don't *need* one.' He said, 'Yes, you do. This is a *newer* system.' "

Things were always important to Peter Sellers. What he missed by lacking a stable or even single self he tried to make up with possessions. Like Charles Foster Kane, he collected himself by collecting buyable objects—cars, cameras, stereo systems, toys, radios, recorders, expensive suits—things that proved to himself something so fleeting that he inevitably had to buy something else as soon as possible. Buying and giving was Peter's way of expressing love. Empty and needy, he bestowed what he wanted—to himself as well as to his friends and family.

"He was impatient if he wanted something," Geldray says. "He was definitely an 'I want it *now*' kind of person. There used to be a saying—we all said it: '*You've got to have it.*' The whole cast of *The Goon Show* said it, but it came from him: '*You've got to have it!*'

"There was a Ford Zephyr, an English car, that had won the Monte Carlo rally. I got a call from him: 'Did you hear? The Ford Zephyr won the Monte Carlo rally!' " Geldray told Peter that he'd already ordered one from a dealer they both knew. "I had ordered the car, and it was going to take a long time because it was a very popular car. Peter said, '*I've got to have it.*' To make a long story short, he had it two or three months before I got mine, because *he* went crazy. *He had to have it!*

"He said 'Let's go to the car show.' So he, and Anne, and I went. All of a sudden, Anne and I see him talking to the Bentley people. Anne said, 'Uh-oh.' I saw it from afar, this Bentley, and to me it looked like it sagged in the middle. It obviously didn't, but it appeared to. I said to Anne, 'You know, I don't think I like that car. It looks like it's sagging in the middle.' So she goes over to him and says, 'Peter, Max thinks it sags in the middle.' He said, 'What? Oh. Okay.' He said to the salesman, 'Never mind,' and he walked away. All I had to do was say something negative, and he would immediately act upon it.

"However, several weeks later he had a Rolls-Royce."

But as Wally Stott kindly reflects, "He *was* fond of all those things, but there was no harm in that. I hate to believe that there was any harm in Peter. He was a very likeable person."

Anne was always the first to acknowledge her husband's likability, but for her, marriage to Peter Sellers "was like living on the edge of a volcano." On October 16, 1957, she got burned. That was the night she gave birth to their daughter.

Sarah Jane Sellers always had her mother, but beginning in a literal way at the instant of her birth and continuing metaphorically throughout her life, Peter simply wasn't there. On that particular night he simply *had* to see Judy Garland open at the Palladium.

• • •

By 1958, Peter, Anne, Michael, Sarah and a horde of stuffed animals from Harrods were living in a large white stucco house on Oakleigh Avenue in the fashionable, even-further-north village of Whetstone. It featured a lovely bay window overlooking a large terraced garden. Peter called it "St. Fred's" and had a sign painted for the front gate to announce it. As he'd explained, "You can ruin *anything* with 'Fred.'"

Michael, on the brink of four, was the titular owner of an electric car set, a pair of walkie-talkies, a number of radios, and a vast army of toy soldiers, but, as Michael later noted of his father's playtime needs, "Only when he grew tired of playing with them himself was I permitted to touch them." One evening, Peter spent several hours setting up opposing toy battalions for combat. Michael made the mistake of staging the engagement the following day when Peter was out of the house. It was a glorious battle with lots of dead bodies, but it paled in comparison to the rather more unequal clash that occurred when Peter returned home. Today we call it child abuse.

The children's first nanny was named Frieda Heinlein. The kids loved her. Peter called her a "German swine" and fired her. Nanny Clarke arrived. Peter became so enraged by something she said that he stormed out of the house, drove to London, checked into a club, called Anne, shouted something about "that bloody nanny," returned home, and picked up the nearest carving knife. Awakening Nanny Clarke with shouts of "I'll kill you, you cow," Peter plunged the knife into her bedroom door, which split. Quick-thinking but not as nimble as she might have been, Nanny Clarke hurled herself out the window, crawled to the house next door, and ended up in the hospital with a sprained ankle. Frieda Heinlein returned.

• • •

As abusive a parent as Peter could be at times, he wasn't without affection toward his children. He loved them to the extent that he was capable of love. Blame Peg, of course. She made him what he was. But blame Peter, too. A rotten mother doesn't absolve her son's rotten fathering.

Home movie footage shows Peter playing with a grinning Michael on a swing set in the yard at St. Fred's. Another has him helping toddler Sarah learn to walk. Still another features Michael, resplendent in a plaid playsuit, examining Peter's newest car. This little vignette is clearly staged, although the child star remains quite unaware of the fact. Peter, in voice over, plays the role of a showroom car salesman: "Try the driving position!" he cries as customer Michael climbs in—"I'm sure you'll find it *Ab-So-Lute-Ly* First Class!" Then: "I'm going inside now to see to the projector, so I'll see you in just a few moments. Jolly good luck!"

It's cute to outsiders, but Sarah Sellers, in retrospect, finds this sort of thing to be painful to watch. "There's not really very much just 'natural' footage of us playing or anything," she notes. "It's all staged. It's all telling us exactly what to do, and when to laugh, and *'Be happy!'* and *'Enjoy yourself! Have a good time!'* "

Peter liked to drive Michael and Sarah down to London for a stroll in the zoo on Sunday mornings. Of course, being Peter, he followed up by taking them to lunch at the Ritz or the Savoy. Like everything else, much depended on his mood.

One particular Sunday, Peter was driving his brand-new red Bentley Continental. Michael Sellers claims that Peter's other luxury cars had been previously owned, which helps explain how Peter afforded an unending slew of top-of-the-line luxury automobiles before he was pulling in the extraordinary income necessary to sustain such a habit. The Bentley Continental, however, was unblemished by other hands. It featured handmade fittings, cost £9,000, and was the trophy of trophies. Peter adored it.

A barrage of pebbles hit the car during a family drive. Chips appeared on the bright, shiny surface. Helpfully, Michael took it upon himself to fix them. He found touch-up paint in the garage and, with a child's logic, painted a long stripe down the length of the car to make sure he'd covered every nick.

Peter screamed when he saw his disfigured Bentley Continental. Then he grabbed his son and dragged him upstairs, whipped him with a belt and sent him to bed hungry, took away all of his toys, and didn't give them back for several months. "I thought he was going to kill him," Spike Milligan said.

As totalitarian as Peg could be, hers was a tyranny of baby's-breath-sucking love. She is never said to have hit her son and, given what *has* been said, it's impossible to imagine. Rather than striking, she pampered. Peter's rage toward Michael, uncontrollable and bordering on psychosis, was clearly of a different order, in one sense the flip side of Peg's indulgence. Peter had a violent streak even as a child, as the incident involving him shoving his auntie into the roaring fireplace well demonstrates. And because Peg abhorred disciplining him for such outbursts of physical fury, he grew into manhood without several of the key inhibitions that sustain civilization, let alone a healthy family life. He excused himself anything. After all, he was Peter Sellers.

• • •

The Peter Sellers Show, a comedy special written by Eric Sykes, aired on ITV in early February. *The April 8th Show (Seven Days Early)* appeared two months later on the BBC; Peter starred, with support from Graham Stark and David Lodge. There was a record, too—"The Best of Sellers."

The Goon Show's eighth series had been running since September 1957. In March 1958, an episode called "Tiddlywinks" aired. It was based on the real-life match that had occurred on March 2 between the Cambridge University tiddlywinks team on one side and the three Goons and Graham Stark on the other. The college boys had originally thrown their challenge to the Duke of Edinburgh, but the Duke, knowing of his son's admiration for Sellers, Milligan, and Secombe, gallantly nominated them as his stand-ins. Although they did have the last laugh with their broadcast, the Goons lost the match itself by a lopsided score of 120 to 50.

But Peter Sellers had other winks to tiddle. He was making movies, superindustriously—two completed in 1958, another two started in 1958 and finished in 1959, three started and finished in 1959, and two started in 1959 and released in 1960.

He was working steadily (to say the least) and earning good money, and he still believed—with Dennis Selinger assenting—that he needed as much exposure as possible. Does it matter if some of these movies aren't masterpieces?

Returning Peter to the drab territory of *Orders Are Orders, Up the Creek* (1958), directed by Val Guest, is a comedy about the British Navy. It's both rum and bum. Having fired a homemade rocket through the bathroom window of an admiral (Wilfrid Hyde-White)—it homed in on a sudden rush of water—Lt. Fairweather (David Tomlinson) is exiled to a command in "the mothball fleet," specifically H.M.S. *Berkeley.* The ship is virtually dry-docked in Suffolk, and in the absence of a commanding officer, the

Berkeley's shady bo's'n, Chief Petty Officer Doherty (Peter), has turned it into a money-making operation for himself and the ship's skeleton crew. Sellers' bo's'n is an Anglicized Sgt. Bilko from *The Phil Silvers Show* (which was then in its third hit season on American television). With Peter's nasal, fast-talking Doherty keeping the books, the sailors tend chickens on deck, pigs in the cabins; they sell the eggs and bacon to the townspeople. They wash laundry in the boiler and deliver it directly to customers' doors. There's rum-running involved. And pork pies. Doherty has requisitioned paint, presumably for the Berkeley, and none of it remains:

FAIRWEATHER: Do you mean to tell me that you sold that, too?
DOHERTY: Well, we couldn't very well *give* government property away.

Peter declined to appear in Val Guest's hastily filmed sequel, *Further Up the Creek* (also 1958); they replaced him with Frankie Howerd. But he did show up for *tom thumb* (1958), based on the tale by the Brothers Grimm. A rustic and his wife, granted three wishes by the beautiful Queen of the Forest, waste them on two meaningless requests involving a lengthy sausage that grows on the rustic's nose. After using up the third wish to make the wiener disappear, they're granted one extra: teenage Russ Tamblyn wearing an off-the-shoulder pea leaf. He shall be their son. Only he's two inches long. Tall. Whichever.

The lithe and virile boy dances with animated cartoons and claymation animals, and all is well in his childhood until his father takes him near the Black Swamp, "an evil place where horrid birds and animals live." That's where Peter and Terry-Thomas come in. Peter's done up in a fat suit and heavy black fur. Terry wears a domed Zeppo Marx hat. "I like you," says Terry to the father. "So do I," says Peter, leaning in close with a vocal insinuation entirely lacking in Terry's previous line delivery. "I don't like the looks of those fellows," says Dad after the villains leave. "I thought they were kind of nice," says Russ.

Peter, affecting a bizarre gypso-Fagin accent, plays a total dolt, Terry as well, though somewhat less so. They decide to bump Tom off by taking him to the edge of the swamp, tossing a coin in, and telling Tom to go chase it. Tom skips happily into the swamp and promptly falls into the muck. Unfortunately, he's saved by the Queen of the Forest and another hour of the film ensues, but it ends happily after a character named Woody teaches Tom how to kiss a girl. It was the 1950s, after all.

Up the Creek was released on November 11, 1958, *tom thumb* on December 24. But by then Peter was back on the BBC with *The Goon Show*'s ninth series, and oh, yes, he had also been starring for four months in a West End play.

• • •

A year earlier, the producer Robert L. Joseph had been talking to Alec Guinness about starring as an Arabian sultan in George Tabori's comedy *Brouhaha*; Peter Brooks was supposed to direct. By July 1957, that plan had fallen apart, but in July 1958, the play opened. Peter Hall directed. Peter Sellers starred.

As Anne Sellers noted, Peter had long been nursing a not-so-secret desire to add theater to radio, television, film, cabaret, and music hall. Tabori's thin farce, entirely dependent on the ridiculous Sultan of Huwaiyat, provided the perfect vehicle:

Huwaiyat has fallen on hard times. To extract foreign aid from both the Americans and the Soviets, the Sultan concocts a revolution.

By signing on to *Brouhaha*, Peter took the risk (to reap the glory) of making his legitimate-theatrical debut in a play in which he'd be onstage almost all the time. There would be touches of slapstick and lots of costume and personality and accent changes, and he'd be given relatively free rein to improvise dialogue and bits of comedy business at will. All of this came with a price, of course. For an actor, *any* role onstage, especially on Broadway or the West End, demands an extraordinary commitment of time and energy. Still, Peter took on the challenge and the work, agreeing to appear in *Brouhaha* for at least seven months, all the while continuing his radio and film careers. In addition to the regular evening performances of *Brouhaha* there would be two shows on Saturday night as well as a Thursday matinee.

After previewing in Brighton for three weeks, *Brouhaha* opened in London. From its printing presses 3,000 miles away, the *New York Times* was delighted. Dateline London, August 27: "Gales of laughter greeted George Tabori's new comedy *Brouhaha*, which opened at the Aldwych Theatre tonight. It left the newspaper reviewers indulgently tickled, too. But the laughter and the warm newspaper notices were more for the players, particularly the star, Peter Sellers, than for the play."

It hadn't been an easy road to opening night. For one thing, Peter decided he didn't like one of the young actors and refused to rehearse with him. Then, at the dress rehearsal, he declined to provide the proper cue lines. "I can't stay," Peter Hall confided to a cast member, "because if I lose my temper with Peter, he'll walk out and close the play." So the director left the theater rather than argue with the star.

Much, if not all, was forgiven after opening night, when *Brouhaha* proved to be a hit, though not all the reviews were quite as glowing as the *Times* correspondent led his readers to believe. One English critic snorted that *Brouhaha* "will appeal only to addicts of the type of humor served up by the Marx Bros.," a remark that was apparently meant to be an insult. Another commented that "a mildly absurd initial situation is put through the mill of verbal and situating extravagance: deliberate irrelevance, banality, wild quasi-improvised pantomime twist it and turn it, inflate it only to prick the bubble." As for Peter, the critic wrote, "calculated inconsequence and a kind of dynamic helplessness are mother's milk to him. Tall, plump and dark, he also revealed a personality of enormous kindliness and charm."

The Daily Mail was more abrupt: "Brou, but not enough haha."

Still London scribes did tend to agree that *Brouhaha*'s success depended entirely on Peter, and that he more than carried it off in his appealing, gleeful, manic, multipersonality way. In the trial scene, for instance, Peter played judge, counsel, and prisoner. The judge turned up at one point in a garbage can.

Advance ticket sales were brisk enough that even on opening night British theater wags were already mulling over the most obvious risk of taking the show to New York: "Careful casting would likely be needed for a Broadway presentation, because the comedy has been re-written and tailored to suit the particular requirements of Sellers."

In other words, Sellers's *Brouhaha* was radically open to improvisation. On the night of October 16, Peter got carried away, waltzed off the stage, and fell into the orchestra pit. He pulled Hermione Harvey (playing Mrs. Alma Exegis Diddle) right along with him. The audience thought it was hilarious, but when they saw Peter's face contorting in agony they fell into silence. Sellers's leg was badly cut. Harvey suffered bruises as well. Peter, still a trouper, made an effort to go on with the show but simply couldn't manage it, and his understudy finished the performance. Anne, who was in the audience that night, thought at first that the whole thing was just a new bit—a little extreme, perhaps, but given Peter's tendency to depart from the script, not entirely without precedent. "But when I went round to the dressing room poor Peter was lying there saying some very unfunny things." She whisked him home in their latest Rolls-Royce.

"I found Peter a great joy to work with, wholly generous and wonderfully inventive," the actor Leo McKern recalled of his experiences with Peter in *Brouhaha*. (McKern played Tyepkin, the Soviet envoy, but he also appeared with Peter in four films.) "Innovation and continual invention was essential to keep him interested, and the straitjacket of conventional reproduction was not for him." These inventions not only included ad-libs and funny if irrelevant accents. Peter also found it personally amusing to stroll up to the footlights and engage in conversation—albeit one-sided—with the audience. Peter Hall once commented on what it was like to direct him: "It was one of the most amazing and terrible experiences of my life, because one of the things about working in the theater is that you have to repeat what you do. . . . Peter couldn't bear doing it again and again."

"I went to see him in it," Alec Guinness noted. "It was pretty lousy. Sellers knew I was in the stalls. Suddenly, in the middle of a speech, he came down to the footlights and saluted and said, 'That's to you, Captain Guinness!' The audience had no idea what he was talking about."

McKern remembered that one night Peter's inventions got the best of him after he showed up for the performance absolutely drunk. It was, in McKern's description, "after some kind of reception or other." Actually, it was after a party thrown in honor of Alec Guinness's knighthood. Peter had stopped by on his way to the Aldwych. Beaujolais flowed, much of it into Peter's glass. Kenneth Tynan picks up the tale: "He arrived at the theater beamingly tight and admitted as much to the audience; 'I am sloshed,' he said, and offered refunds to those who wanted them. Few did, and he went on to give a striking, if bizarre, performance."

Unfortunately, it wasn't just a single night's worth of Beaujolais that was talking. By the first week of December, having appeared in *Brouhaha* steadily for five months—not to mention the fact that he was already shooting his next picture, in which he starred as three different characters, the male lead and two supporting roles—Peter had grown sick of the theater. He casually mentioned this fact to the press.

"Very bored" were the precise words Peter chose to describe his experience as the star of a West End hit. He went on to add that he was only giving "about two good performances a week" and was thinking about leaving the show.

Brouhaha's presenters, the International Playwright's Theatre, Ltd., were most displeased by this interview, having put up with Sellers's lack of theatrical discipline all along. Dennis Selinger later said that he "used to get two or three phone calls a week from the management, saying 'Come down here, he's done something terrible.'" This time it was different, though. Peter had gone public.

The firm quickly issued a multipronged statement: Peter Sellers had signed a run-of-the-play contract for *Brouhaha*; Peter Sellers, under the terms of his contract, could give four-weeks notice beginning in February 1959; Peter Sellers had not given, and at that time was not in a position to give, four-weeks notice to end his participation in *Brouhaha*; and, finally, Peter Sellers's contract stated that "he shall appear at all performances and perform . . . in a diligent and painstaking manner and shall play the part as directed by the manager."

Peter Sellers was contrite, at least in public. "What I meant," he told the press, who were only just beginning to sniff the first wisps of an aroma that promised to ripen over the years, "was what any West End actor will tell you—that you are only at your best two nights a week. You do your best every night, but it doesn't always come over."

He gave notice on February 1 and the show closed four weeks later.

Peter Hall, who had accommodated as best he could his one-time-only star's tendency to make unscheduled entrances whenever he was fatigued by the nightly routine of stage acting, described Peter in retrospect: "He was as good an actor as Alec Guinness, as good an actor as Laurence Olivier. And he had the ability to identify completely with another person—to get physically and mentally and emotionally into their skin. Where does that come from? I have no idea. Is it a curse? Often.

"It's not enough in this business to have talent," Hall continued, knowing the end of the story. "You have to have talent to handle the talent, and that, I think, Peter did not have. I think he was a genius. And I think his perfectionism made him extremely neurotic, extremely selfish."

Hall, who was later knighted, believes that a director can only throw up his hands in the face of such a psyche. Many other directors would find themselves in the same situation in the years to come.

"I mean, I'm sure the play or the film was always about *him* in his view. It's no good arguing with that."

Walter Shenson, the London-based head of European publicity for Columbia Pictures, ran into Tyrone Power on the street one day in
1958. Power mentioned the novel he happened to be reading at the time
and recommended it to Shenson, who read it, bought the film rights, and
thereby turned himself into an independent producer. *The Mouse That
Roared* (1959) was his first picture.

There was something odd about Peter Sellers's interest in signing onto
this particular production. Having never produced a film in his life, Walter
Shenson was not exactly in the top ranks of the profession when he approached Sellers through Dennis Selinger. But as Shenson recalled, "Peter
said he wanted to meet me. The first thing he said to me was, 'Are you a
producer?' I said, 'Well, if I make this picture I'll be a producer.'

"What I found out later was that the clairvoyant he used to talk to
every morning had said to him—something rather obvious to Peter Sellers—'An American producer is going to ask you to be in a film.' I don't
even think he'd read the script yet when he wanted to meet me, because
the first question he said to me was, 'Are you a producer?' He could see I
was an American."

The clairvoyant in question was Maurice Woodruff, a nationally syndicated columnist of the old Jeanne Dixon school. In short, Woodruff was
a showman and a fraud. Peter began to rely on him.

Peter had been superstitious since at least his teens. Later on, he added
a bit of paranoia; his postwar girlfriend Hilda Parkin states that he used to
insist "that 'mad mullahs' haunted him whenever he slept in a certain four-
poster bed in one of my relatives' homes in Peterborough." Now he turned
to a syndicated soothsayer.

"He would live, die, and breathe by Maurice Woodruff," the director

Bryan Forbes declares. "He wouldn't take a foot outside the house unless he'd spoken to Maurice." Woodruff had seen his mark.

In Graham Stark's view, Woodruff "clung like a leech."

• • •

The Mouse That Roared is a satirical comedy. The Grand Duchy of Fenwick has fallen on hard times. To extract foreign aid from the Americans, the Prime Minister concocts a war with the United States. The express purpose is to lose immediately and reap thereafter the benefits of Marshall Plan–like foreign aid.

At first, Shenson only considered Peter for the role of Tully Bascombe, the bland and well-meaning gamekeeper who leads the Fenwick forces against the United States—and wins. But another Columbia executive mentioned the idea of Peter playing two supporting roles as well, and despite Peter's later claim that he resisted the notion, he told Shenson at the time that he knew he could play all three: Tully; Prime Minister Mountjoy, a goateed aristocrat; and the Grand Duchess Gloriana XII, a full-figured regent. As it happened, Sellers was *least* comfortable playing Tully, the role he'd originally been offered and the most lifelike of the three: "I don't quite have a handle on the leading guy," he confessed, "but we'll come up with something."

Whether because of the original benevolent augury or simple good will, Peter caused no trouble during the production of *The Mouse That Roared*. "He got along with everybody," Walter Shenson said. "I think he liked the idea of working for Americans." Peter's costar, Jean Seberg, later told a reporter that "to work with him is to love him. He's angelic."

The film's director, Jack Arnold, described him in somewhat more detail: "Peter was a marvelous improvisational actor, brilliant if you got him on the first take. The second take would be good, but after the third take he could be really awful. If he had to repeat the same words too many times they became meaningless. But it was such a joy to work with Peter because he was such an inspired actor. Sometimes he would literally knock me off my feet. I'd fall down convulsed with laughter."

With Peter having to rush back to the Aldwych nearly every evening to star in *Brouhaha*, filming of *The Mouse That Roared* began in mid-October with three weeks on location in Surrey and on the Channel coast. The production moved on to Shepperton sound stages on November 10. Despite the general goodwill on the set, Arnold described the first day of shooting as being somewhat tense, owing to the seemingly countless takes it took Jean Seberg to get her lines right. Seberg was used to being directed, at times to the point of browbeating, by Otto Preminger, for whom she had starred in two dramas, *Saint Joan* and *Bonjour Tristesse* (both 1957). (Seberg was only seventeen when Preminger cast her in *Saint Joan*, her first film.) *The Mouse That Roared*, however, was a comedy, the director wasn't a tyrant, and Seberg was consequently cut adrift from her method. According to Arnold, "By take twenty-five Peter didn't know what he was saying either. He was just spouting gibberish. I could see he was really getting crazy."

Seberg's need for multiple takes aside, Peter's schedule was purely grueling—especially after *The Goon Show*'s ninth series began recording in November—so much so that he actually hired an ambulance to whisk him away from each day's shooting of *The Mouse That Roared* to his evening's performance in *Brouhaha*. It was much better than a limousine or any of his cars. He could lie down.

A bit simplistic but still very funny, *The Mouse That Roared* did well enough at the box office in England, but it was much more widely popular in the States, probably because its satire struck a more genial note with the benefactors of American foreign relations largesse than it did with the recipients. And while Peter gives one great and two good performances in the film, he hadn't yet achieved the kind of direct, natural rapport with the camera that eventually made him a superstar. Tully is the weakest of the three for exactly that reason; agreeable blandness barely registers on celluloid unless the actor is a technical genius. The two caricatures, Mountjoy and Gloriana, required much less skill because they were built on excess.

Gloriana XII remains one of Peter Sellers's greatest creations. With a bust too large and a voice too deep, she's Margaret Rutherford with testes.

Tully pleasantly introduces her to his American captives:

TULLY: Your Grace, uh, this is General Snippet—he's a rear general.
SNIPPET: I warn you, Madam, I know the Geneva Convention by heart!
GLORIANA: Oh, how nice! You must recite it to me some evening. I'll
   play the harpsichord!

A few years later, Shenson asked Peter if he'd be interested in starring in the sequel, *Mouse on the Moon* (1963). Sellers was by that point an international star, so he rather loftily turned Shenson down. In fact, by that point Peter had stated in public that he never liked *The Mouse That Roared* to begin with. Shenson ended up replacing him with two other actors— Ron Moody and, yes, Margaret Rutherford. (Moody played Mountjoy; there was no Tully.)

But Peter did suggest a director for the picture: Richard Lester. "Who's he?" Shenson asked. "He's another American—you met him at my house at my Christmas party." Lester did end up directing *Mouse on the Moon* for Shenson, after which the producer-director team went on to make *A Hard Day's Night* (1964).

• • •

One summer day Peter took his new Paillard Bolex 16mm movie camera into an open field at the end of Totteridge Lane in North London and shot some footage of Spike acting up. Dick Lester added some stuff, and the film ended up getting nominated for an Oscar.

The Running Jumping & Standing Still Film (1959) was a game played by buddies—a way of having fun for about £70. Graham Stark pitched in, along with his girlfriend, Audrey (who later became his wife). Joe McGrath did the titles. Bruce Lacey, a props manager at Granada Television, managed to come up with some props. Johnny Vyvyan and David Lodge appeared, as did the comic Mario Fabrizi.

Milligan missed the second day of shooting, which occurred some time after the initial shoot. Bitterness resulted.

Spike: "Most of the jokes in it are mine. I wrote the jokes, and I directed part of it. Then I had to go to Australia, and I left the film with Peter, and Peter gave it to Dick Lester to edit. And he did something I would never do. He put music on it in the background—what for I don't know. Some kind of saxophone player. . . ."

Lester insists on the other hand that "it was written in equal parts by Peter, Spike, and myself."

"We shot only one take for any gag," Lester explains. "When we got the rushes, we took them to Peter's house the next Sunday to edit in his study. The editing, which was really just topping and tailing, took two hours," a process that occurred on a minimal editing machine perched on one of Peter's drums in the attic of St. Fred's. ("Topping and tailing" refers to the process of removing the first and last frames of a piece of film footage and leaving the usable center.) "Every gag we shot, every piece of film that we shot, is in the finished film. We showed it to our wives by projecting it onto the wall in the living room.

"We never had any plan to distribute it when we made it," Lester claims. "We were just friends who wanted to make a film to enjoy ourselves." Nevertheless, the "just friends" were hungry, ambitious filmmakers. Peter quickly screened it for Herbert Kretzmer, the London television reviewer and fan of the *Freds*, who told him "You've got to show this around," a supportive but redundant piece of advice, since that was what Peter was already doing.

They transferred their 16mm home movie to 35mm, had it sepia-toned ("daguerreotype pigment made from condensed yak's breath," according to Sellers), and got it into the Edinburgh Film Festival. A scout from the San Francisco Film Festival saw it, and the next thing anyone knew it was nominated for an Academy Award.

The category was Short Subject (Live Action). And since Peter was credited as the film's producer, if *The Running Jumping & Standing Still Film* won the Oscar, the little man, naked and golden, would be his.

They were up against a French effort, *The Golden Fish*, produced by Jacques Cousteau: An Asian boy watches an old, big-nosed man wearing a long black coat and beard, win a beautiful goldfish. It swiftly hides from the evil old man under a rock. After breaking the boy's milk bottle, the old man gives him a coin. The boy places a bet on the goldfish and wins. The Jew winds up with a crummy minnow. Obviously more heartwarming than *The Running Jumping & Standing Still Film*, *The Golden Fish* won.

• • •

In America, Frank Sinatra had had a hit album in 1955 called *Songs for Swingin' Lovers*. In England in 1959, Peter Sellers recorded one of his own: *Songs for Swingin' Sellers*. Sinatra's album cover featured a dancing couple beaming into each other's eyes. Peter's featured a tree on the trunk of which hangs a wanted poster with Peter's mug on it; from a high limb hangs a corpse wearing cowboy boots and spurs.

The album begins with a pseudo-Sinatra, an impersonation that even Peter Sellers could not do. *Speaking* as Sinatra might have been possible; duplicating that literally inimitable singing voice was not, so a crooner named Matt Monro was hired for the equivalent of about $50. Monro is credited on the album as Fred Flange.

The actress-comedienne Irene Handl recorded several of the cuts with

Peter, including one that skewers BBC radio talk shows. But the highlights are Peter's sniveling, ham-ridden rendition of "My Old Dutch," the song his mother forced him to perform onstage in white tie and tails at age two, a fact that might explain why the contemporary version has a distinctly nasty edge. Then there's a certain Mr. Banerjee's production of *My Fair Lady*:

> MR. BANERJEE: I am walking through the marketplace one day at Maharacheekee, which is near Bombay, and I am walking by there, and I am saying to my friend, who is with me, "Look! There! Over there is a beautiful and untouchable girl!" And I am saying to her, "Come with me, my dear—I will make you touchable!"

Mr. Banerjee then sings a tabla and cymbals–filled version of Lerner and Loewe's charming, already-a-chestnut song, "Would That Not Be Lovely" ("warm face, warm hands, warm foot").

Songs for Swingin' Sellers ends with "Peter Sellers Sings George Gershwin." It goes like this: (chord) "George Ge-ersh-win!"

• • •

In September 1959, the British Prime Minister Harold Macmillan traveled to Balmoral to ask that Parliament be dissolved. Elizabeth II, always a gracious hostess, entertained her guest by showing a movie—*I'm All Right, Jack* (1959), starring Peter Sellers.

A social satire that reveals the one characteristic common to all the classes in Britain—strident self-interest—*I'm All Right, Jack* brought Peter such acclaim that the force of his performance successfully distorted the satire. As conceived, written, and directed, the film is a bitter attack on postwar British industrial paralysis, the class-based antagonism, particular to the 1950s, that the historian Arthur Marwick calls Britain's "industrial cold war." But as performed by Peter, Fred Kite, the martinet chief shop steward at the armament factory Missiles, Ltd., is so commanding a figure of contempt and blame that all the other characters' corruption or daftness fades away, leaving *I'm All Right, Jack* to seem like a scathing denunciation of lazy, overpaid, communist-sympathizing trade unions.

Peter himself didn't find the Conservatives' landslide victory in the fall of 1959 a complete coincidence to his film's extraordinary popularity: "I heard the Tories liked it. It probably did more good to them than it did to Labor."

Ironically, Peter didn't want to do the film at all. It wasn't because he didn't approve of the film's politics, which never seem to have crossed his mind. ("I don't vote," he later said. "Never have. There are things about the Tories I like, and things about the Socialists. I suppose the ideal would be some kind of Communism, but not Soviet Communism, so what could I vote for?") It was because he didn't think his part was funny.

He later claimed to have been offered the role after playing on the director John Boulting's cricket team in a charity match, but there was a bit more struggle behind it. As Roy Boulting, the film's producer, describes Peter's response to the offer: "He read it. And he didn't want to do it. So we asked him, 'Why, Peter?' He said, 'Where are the laughs? Where does one get a laugh?' We had to explain to him as best we could that we didn't regard him as a Goon for this film—that he was going to be playing a real character."

Peter grew more interested in the role, but he was also attracted by the complete package the Boultings were offering. In January 1959, Peter and the Boultings announced their new five-picture nonexclusive deal. (A nonexclusive deal permits an actor to appear in other producers' films.) "It's worth £100,000," Peter declared; an American newspaper put the figure at $280,000. *I'm All Right, Jack* would be the first made under the new terms. "For an actor," Peter explained, "a term contract is a bit like a marriage. You've got to have confidence in your partner."

• • •

I'm All Right, Jack was not Peter's first picture with the Boultings. In 1958, he'd filmed a supporting role—Terry-Thomas was the lead—in a weak foreign-policy satire called *Carlton-Browne of the F.O.* (1959), though that film had not yet been released when *I'm All Right, Jack* began shooting in January. Terry-Thomas plays the title character, the bungling head of an obscure subsection of the Foreign Office. He's sent to the remote and ridiculous island nation of Gaillardia, a former colony granted the privileges of self-government fifty years before, but nobody in either Britain or Gaillardia has yet been informed of the decision. Peter plays the slimy Amphibulos, who sounds disconcertingly like a Greek waiter.

Gaillardia is a mix of burro-driven carts, unbearable heat, assassinations, and a Baroque palace enjoyed by its handsome, young, British-educated,

British-looking king (fine-featured Ian Bannen under brownish makeup). The rest of Gaillardia is treated to fairly harsh satire, though the conquering Britons are scarcely more competent. Peter, clad in a rumpled, ever-damp, and ill-fitting white cotton suit, and wearing boot-black hair and a matching droopy mustache, provides a precise blend of obsequiousness and contamination as the king's greasy-palmed minister. His best moment in the film is a simple one: Conferring on the Gaillardian crisis on a beach with Carlton-Browne while being fanned and rubbed by two nubile native girls, Amphibulos, who has been lying on his back, rolls himself over (with some labor) and says, gesturing toward a nipple, "Over heeere, dar-leeng."

According to Roy Boulting, *I'm All Right, Jack*'s Fred Kite was based on the Electricians Trades Union shop steward at another studio: "He was a very funny little man—unintentionally funny, but he was funny." Peter, who took the Boultings' word for it that his role would certainly pull laughs if performed realistically, received confirmation when the Shepperton Studios Works Committee, which represented the various filmmaking trade unions, showed up on the set to watch the filming of one of Peter's earliest scenes. They recognized Fred Kite's type immediately and, according to Roy Boulting, reacted all too well during a red-light-flashing, camera-rolling take: "They burst into laughter, which they couldn't contain. I saw the change in Peter's face. He hadn't thought it was funny himself, but now he knew. It *was* funny." Thanks to Peter's skill, Fred Kite was also poignant. As the critic Raymond Durgnat has noted, "There is something sadly sympathetic about his pig-headed notions." Maxine Ventham, who chairs the lively Peter Sellers Appreciation Society (Spike Milligan, patron; David Lodge, president; HRH the Prince of Wales, honorary member) notes that this "sadly sympathetic" effect derives mainly from Peter's sensitive, vulnerable eyes: "Fred Kite is betrayed by them," Ventham rightly declares.

Spike Milligan, of course, took a contrarian view of the film's politics: "He was heavily pressurized by the Boultings, through the writing, to become this character, because the Boultings were violently against trade unions. And they used this as the spearhead of their attack: Peter Sellers representing something that they hated. He ended up making a very great film for them."

The sarcastic title *I'm All Right, Jack* refers to the Boultings' original satirical target, the money-grubbing, every-class-for-itself attitude the filmmakers ascribe to all of England in the 1950s. (As David Tomlinson's Lieutenant Fairweather explains to the admiral in *Up the Creek*, "To put it in the Queen's English, 'You scratch my back, and we'll scratch yours, Jack.' ") The film begins with a pre-credits sequence. Sir John Kennaway, an old white-haired man, sleeps peacefully in a deserted clubroom. The camera tracks slowly forward. A servant appears and informs Sir John that the Germans have surrendered—that World War II is over at last. Crowds are shouting in triumph outside the window; Sir John barely registers the news. "Look hard," a bland voice over intones, "for this is the last we shall see of Sir John," who rises from his club chair and totters out of the room— "a solid block in an edifice of what seems to be an ordered and stable society. There he goes, on his way out." There is another reason to look hard at Sir John. He's Peter, all but hidden under bleached hair and a prosthetic nose.

After a rock-and-roll credits sequence featuring the title song, we meet the protagonist of *I'm All Right, Jack*—Stanley Windrush (Ian Carmichael), Sir John's well-named symbolic heir, a man whose class would have entitled him to the same clubby, do-nothing life had a catastrophic world war not provided the working class with some political muscle. Stanley's father has blithely withdrawn to a nudist camp. Stanley, though, feels the need to earn a living. Too bad he's incompetent at everything but reading the *Times*. Interviews and training programs at a variety of industries (soap, candy, corsets) having failed miserably, Stanley lands at Missiles, Ltd. It's a setup: Stanley's aristocratic Uncle Bertie (Dennis Price), in collusion with the equally corrupt but bourgeois-born Sidney De Vere Cox (Richard Attenborough), knowingly sends the idiotic Stanley into Bertie's munitions factory in order to muck everything up. The reason: so that Missiles, Ltd., won't be able to fulfill its new Arab-contracted munitions order, thereby forcing the contract to go—at a higher price, naturally—to Cox's own company, of which Bertie, of course, is a hidden partner.

With his sparkling smile and utter ineptitude, Stanley is perfect for the job. He instantly arouses the workers' suspicions, and they call in Fred Kite, the shop steward. Kite marches into the office of Major Hitchcock (Terry-Thomas), the personnel manager, and in a complicated, dead-on accent Peter hadn't employed before—a Cockney base overlaid with semieducated pretension and its carry-along insecurity—Kite demands that Stanley be sacked: "In permi'in' him to drive one of them trucks, I would say the management is willfully je-ro-podizing the safety of its employees!" Hitchcock quickly agrees, but when he mentions that Stanley has been sent into the factory by the Labor Exchange, Kite, who sees himself as the embodiment of labor, instantly demands that Stanley *not* be sacked: "We do not—

and cannot!—accept the principle that incompetence justifies dismissal. That is victim-I-zation!"

Kite takes Stanley in as his lodger and suggests that he read some Lenin. "I see from your particulars," he tells his perplexed guest, "you was at college in Oxford. I was up there meself. I was at the Baliol summer school in 1946. Very good toast and preserves they give you at tea time, as you probably know." Kite's English-heimish wife (the marvelous Irene Handl), and his voluptuous daughter, Cynthia (Liz Fraser), welcome him with open arms—particularly Cynthia. She quickly whisks poor Stanley away to a necking session in a garbage dump.

By the end, Stanley has succeeded in driving all of British industry to its knees by causing a national labor strike. He becomes a national hero, briefly, and eventually exposes the various scam artists on a televised debate led by Malcolm Muggeridge (playing himself), only to find that the keystones of British power are not so easily dislodged. Told by a judge to acknowledge his own mental illness, Stanley withdraws to the nudist camp.

The film's editor, Anthony Harvey, believes that Peter's performance in *I'm All Right, Jack* is due in large measure to his trust in John Boulting, who "had the most wonderful rapport with Peter, I think, of all the directors" for whom Harvey witnessed Peter performing. (This is quite a claim, for Harvey went on to edit *Lolita* and *Dr. Strangelove*, among other films.)

Ian Carmichael, who plays Stanley, found Peter both easy to work with and companionable in their off-hours. "During *I'm All Right, Jack* he seemed to get on terribly well with everybody. He was a very amusing man. He could be amusing sitting in his chair in the studio waiting for takes. He was *always* amusing. I like peace and quiet when I'm working; I don't like to be distracted by a lot of loose gossip. But Peter was very light and frothy with everybody all the time. Of course it all changed later.

"He was a zany sort of chap in many ways. He would have great fun with a tape recorder, and he had great fun in sort of recording things and conversations with you. Also, he played the ukulele, singing songs into his microphone and then playing them back at different speeds. That gave him enormous pleasure.

"He had a cinema in the attic in his house, where he had a 16mm projector," Carmichael recalls. "And a couple of times he said, 'Come and have a meal on Saturday night and see a film. What would you like to see?' "

(Anne has a rather different memory of St. Fred's: "a house with cameras, lights, and lots and lots of cable all over the place. And drawers and cupboards full of cable, and plugs and lamps, and everything.")

Carmichael continues: "He had a set of drums there, too. [But] his main fixation really was motor cars. He used to change his cars about as often as he changed his socks." Still, Peter liked to give others gifts as well as himself. "He was very generous with his money," Carmichael points out. "His makeup man was Stuart Freeborn, and as the picture was coming to an end, he bought him a real top-of-the-range tape recorder with huge speakers and everything—the Rolls Royce of tape recorders."

There was some tension involving Terry-Thomas, however: "Peter hated a lot of takes. I mean, he would [want to] print the first and second take if possible and not go on. He thought that by every take his performance diminished. He had a bit of a problem with Terry-Thomas because Terry had a problem with lines. I'd been with Terry when he'd gone through thirty and thirty-five takes." With Carmichael's comments in mind one can't help but notice that Anthony Harvey has edited Peter and Terry's first scene together in such a way that the two actors are mostly in separate shots, and that when they do appear onscreen together, Terry is for the most part sitting behind his desk listening to Peter rather than delivering any lines himself. Those moments are handled in medium shot from a different angle.

Liz Fraser, who played Kite's daughter, had troubles of a different sort: "I do remember some scenes—and I don't mean film scenes—that he and I had, and which I tried to extricate myself from. In retrospect he wasn't so much a nasty man as a childish one."

• • •

At home during the holiday season each year, Peter and Anne set up a classic Christmas negativity scene. At 1 P.M. on Christmas Day, a full holiday luncheon was served to the kids and Anne's parents, who, according to Michael, "would have to vacate the house" by 5 P.M., at which time Peg and Bill arrived for an equally elaborate Christmas dinner. Peg, by this point, was smoking two packs a day and drinking heavily, even to the point of hiding fifths of gin under the mattress. Whenever she greeted Michael and Sarah, she kissed and hugged them both. The trouble was, these fierce displays of grandmotherly love often lasted for ten minutes at a time.

Anne and Peter had begun to argue. A lot. When they fought, Peter tended to grab Anne's left hand, pry her wedding ring off her finger, and throw it in whatever direction was handiest. One flew out of a Paris window.

Then the Sellers family moved into a twenty-room Elizabethan estate after Peter nearly torched St. Fred's.

The move to Chipperfield had been planned, of course. One can scarcely trade in a fire-damaged fake Tudor for a much larger real one— one of England's legendary stately homes, a seven-acre park, a tennis court, a swimming pool, paddocks, and two Tudor barns—without some advance planning. In fact, Peter had sold St. Fred's by early November 1959, though he and Anne and the children were still living in it, when he decided to throw a party on Guy Fawkes Day. (On November 5, 1605, thirteen profoundly aggrieved Roman Catholics attempted to blow up Parliament in an attempt to launch a Helter Skelter–like uprising against King James I and the Anglican church. The conspirators got as far as loading thirty-six barrels of gunpowder into a cellar under the House of Lords, but at nearly the last minute the plot was foiled. Guy Fawkes, one of the conspirators, was in the cellar when the king's soldiers burst in. He was tortured and killed, of course, and ever since, Guy Fawkes Day has been celebrated each year by British pyromaniacs, though it remains unclear whether they are honoring Guy's death or his urge to blow up the government.)

Wally Stott was one of the horrified guests: "I had nearly bought Peter's house! I paid a deposit on it, but after we were in escrow I decided I didn't want to buy it. It was a long way from the center of London—it was on the outer fringe, and I'd always lived in town. So I backed out. After that [Peter's friend, the actor] Alfred Marks bought it. But Peter was still living in it for a short time, because his new house wasn't finished.

"During this time, November 5 came around. On Guy Fawkes Day there are always a lot of fireworks and bonfires. Peter loved fireworks—this was the very, very childish element in him, like the walkie-talkies and the cars—and of course he had to have fireworks. He got some of his friends around, and they were letting off rockets in the garden. Peter's living room had a big plate glass door that opened onto the garden, and on the inside he had his Arriflex movie camera on a tripod, and he was taking movies of the fireworks. There was a rogue firework, which instead of going up went straight at the house, into the living room, and set fire to it. It caused tremendous destruction. I thought, 'My gosh, that could have been *my* house!' "

• • •

"I wanted a place I could walk around without crossing any streets. It is a very civilized exile," Peter said of his new £17,500 estate. Twenty-three miles north-northwest of London on the border of Hertford and Buckingham, Chipperfield was magnificently excessive. "You've bought bleeding Buckingham Palace!" Graham Stark exclaimed on his first visit. Peter also paid for the staff to match. As Anne later described the array, "We had three gardeners, two dailies, a nanny, a nanny for Peter—his dresser, Harry—a cook, and a butler."

Peter had bought the place on impulse. "We saw this advert in the Sunday *Times* for this manor house in Chipperfield," Anne remembers. "So we went out to have a look at it, and Peter decided, there and then, *he had to have it.*"

It was at Chipperfield, says Anne, that the marriage "really turned sour."

It didn't start off that way, according to Michael, who has described his life as being "comparatively happy at this time. I think Sarah and I had both learned how to fade into the landscape." By the expression "at this time," Michael seems to be referring to a period of several months.

At both St. Fred's and Chipperfield, Peter tended to bring pets home. Hamsters. Goldfish. Kittens. Puppies (two Labradors, a cocker spaniel, a pair of white Maltese terriers). Guinea pigs. Rabbits. The trouble was, he almost always gave them away at the first provocation. Except for the terriers, who stayed for a while, a single poorly timed bark or puddle and out the animal went.

There was a parrot, too. Peg, cleverly, taught it to say "Bollocks." Peter, reactively, became enraged the first time "Henry" swore at him and immediately forced Anne to call Peg and insist that his mother keep and care for the bird herself. That Anne had to place the call is itself notable, since Peter called his mother at least once a day and usually more often. But despite the fact that it was phrased as Anne's demand and not Peter's, Peg complied. She took Henry and fed it nothing but the best seed until Henry swooped down on her one day as she lay naked in her bathtub and began pecking. At that point Peg dispatched Henry on a hastily arranged, one-way trip to its birthplace.

• • •

In 1960, after all the receipts were totaled, *I'm All Right, Jack* turned out to be the biggest box office hit in Britain. British Lion hadn't given the film a larger-than-usual advertising budget, but word of mouth had made it an initial success, and its sheer longevity did the rest. The only region in the United Kingdom in which this industrial satire didn't work was the working-class mining districts of Wales; the characterization of the union steward may be blamed.

In London, however, the film was a smash. *I'm All Right, Jack* ran for seventeen weeks at Studio One, and it was an art-house hit in New York as well, breaking all house records at the Guild Theater, where it ran for over four months. *The Observer's* film critic declared in her end-of-year wrap-up that "Peter Sellers's performance in *I'm All Right, Jack* is the best piece of acting in any British picture." The British Academy of Film and Television Arts (which was then called the Society of Film and Television Arts) agreed. When it named its nominees for Best British Actor, among them were Laurence Olivier (for *The Devil's Disciple*) and Richard Burton (for *Look Back in Anger*).

Peter won.

NINE

A grayed, haunted Peter wanders toward the camera in the opening sequence of *The Battle of the Sexes* (1959). "Every war produces its hero"—the narrator announces—"the man with that little extra something that other men haven't got. The superman."

When Peter learned that the writer-producer Monja Danischewsky had adapted James Thurber's satirical short story "The Catbird Seat," transposing the action across the Atlantic to Scotland, he told Danischewsky that he wanted to play the lead—the mild-mannered clerk-turned-would-be-killer. *The Battle of the Sexes* was written, cast, and filmed before *I'm All Right, Jack*'s blockbuster release made Peter a bona-fide movie star, and as a consequence Sellers's casting wasn't as easy as one might assume in retrospect. According to Danischewsky, "it was a fight at that time to get the finance people to agree that he was a big enough name for the budget." Peter's financial connections helped; Danischewsky credited Sellers for being "a tower of practical help to me as a producer, for he found for me two 'angels' for the end money." (Danischewsky doesn't specify the angelic capitalists' identities.)

Danischewsky found Peter to be a dependable actor, qualifying his praise with a few sympathetic, sensible observations: "He's really an absolute sweetie to work with. Terribly sensitive. An easily hurt man—but desperately. Once he knows you're on his side he'll do anything on earth for you."

Filmed on location in Edinburgh and at the Beaconsfield studios in London, *The Battle of the Sexes* concerns the intrusion of heartless modernity and grotesque feminism into the staid House of Macpherson, makers of fine Scottish woolens. Peter is Mr. Martin, a teetotaling, nonsmoking clerk of indeterminate age. Sellers plays him purposefully vaguely. With his air of resilient beatenness, Mr. Martin could be anywhere from forty to seventy-five. Upon the death of Old Macpherson, the company falls into the inept hands of the son—Robert Morley in a Lane Bryant kilt. The British-educated (and therefore, as his dying father says, "soft") heir, true to form, swiftly hires a lady efficiency expert, a brassy American divorcee (Constance Cummings), who wreaks havoc with new time clocks, metal filing cabinets, and a confident insistence that the House of Macpherson forgo sheep for synthetics. Mrs. Barrows speaks in italics: "And as for those *weavers*, well, I mean they can just *draw* their *pensions* and *take* to their *caves*, that's how much you need *them*." Mr. Martin concludes that he must murder her.

It's a remarkable performance on Peter's part, because he lets his audience notice, but only barely, Mr. Martin's transformation from obedient functionary to noble killer: A well-timed dart of the eyes when Mrs. Barrows speaks. A touch of sarcasm, mild almost to the point of imperceptibility. (Mrs. Barrows demands a time and motion survey; Mr. Martin responds: "We've plenty of time here, Mrs. Barrows, but there's not a great deal of motion.") The film would play better today if it weren't for the gleaming, distracting misogyny of the late 1950s, of which poor Constance Cummings is the shrill vehicle.

Mr. Martin's abortive murder of Mrs. Barrows in her kitchen, said to be mainly improvised while shooting, is one of Peter Sellers's classic comedy sequences: the hand on the butcher knife, the knife hesitatingly put back in the drawer, the decisive reaching into the drawer when Mrs. Barrows turns her back, the ensuing attempt to stab her to death with a wire whisk. But in comparison to the rest of the film, the key sequence comes off as strangely canned. Because it's the climactic set piece, the laughs depend not only on Sellers's having prepared the ground in all of his previous scenes but also on the director's sense of timing. Peter's performance is superb throughout; Charles Crichton's direction isn't quite up to the task in the key sequence. Still, Peter's plunging the knife into Mrs. Barrows's wooden door strikes a rivetingly autobiographical note. Luckily for Peter, contemporary audiences had no way of knowing it.

● ● ●

His increasing fame brought him into stellar company—and a small controversy. In early January, the British Film Institute set up a lecture series to be held at the National Film Theatre. The proposed guest speakers were an unusual trio: Ivor Montagu, the filmmaker, theorist, associate of both Sergei Eisenstein and Alfred Hitchcock, and winner of the Lenin Peace

Prize of 1959; Peter Sellers, the movie star; and Leni Riefenstahl, Hitler's in-house director, the cinema's most talented fascist.

Montagu, who hadn't won the Lenin Prize for nothing, fired off a letter denouncing Riefenstahl. Sellers fired off one of his own denouncing Montagu for denouncing Riefenstahl. The BFI tacitly denounced Riefenstahl by rescinding its own invitation to her, though it used parts of Sellers's letter to Montagu in its press release announcing the denouncing: "Miss Riefenstahl has presumably been invited to lecture because of her outstanding talents as a filmmaker," Peter had written. "Alongside her contributions to the art of filmmaking, our efforts, if I may say so, Mr. Montagu, appear very puny indeed."

At the end of the month was a more notable milestone. On Thursday, January 28, 1960, nine years' and ten series' worth of *Goon Show*s drew to a close. The series was still immensely popular, but it had played itself out, and, for the time being, at least, it was time for the threesome to say farewell to one another. In "The Last Smoking Seagoon," the worn and torn but still farcical Milligan, Secombe, and Sellers gamely worked their way through one of Spike's lesser works, the tale of Nicotine Neddie's attempt to quit smoking. Milligan and Secombe were famous, but Sellers was now a flashy star, a fact acknowledged in the final show:

(*Sound of screeching limousine*)
SECOMBE: Heavens! A ninety-five-foot-long motor car covered in mink! It must be Peter Sellers!
SELLERS: No, he hasn't heard of this one yet.

Crun and Min, Grytpype-Thynne and Moriarty, Bloodnok—Peter's key antiheroic characters all turned up for the last hurrah, along with an unnamed Hindu man who carries on an incomprehensible shipboard conversation with Eccles. The saga ends with Ned blowing himself up while smoking a ninety-foot-long cigarette, landing in the hospital, and running off screaming amid the unscripted laughter of his fellow Goons. "Yes, that was the last *Goon Show*," the particularly weary-sounding announcer Wallace Greenslade says in the final seconds of the program. "Bye, now."

• • •

Life at Chipperfield, as with Peter's life as a whole, was alternately social and amusing, isolated and strange. Given the immensity of the place, Peter was now able to vanish completely into his photographic and filmmaking hideout, Peter's answer to a Cold War bomb shelter. According to Anne, he "actually had a whole wing with a darkroom and a little cinema." Michael was carted off daily to whatever private school Peter had installed him in— he himself attributes the decisions to his father—and nannies took care of Sarah. Peter was often in London filming, or recording, or broadcasting. Anne was increasingly secluded.

At the same time, Peter loved having his friends come for an afternoon, or evening, or two, or three. He was at heart much more comfortable being a friend than a husband and father. David Lodge was such a frequent guest that he kept a stash of supplies at Chipperfield: "There was a toothbrush and pajamas there all the time, and a razor. I was unmarried and spent most of my time there when I wasn't working." Max Geldray was also a regular: "He used to call me a lot—very often in my voice. He would ask me to come over and play. This was one of the phrases that he used—'Will you come over and play?' Like two kids—'come and play.' It meant he had gotten two tape recorders. He would borrow them from stores, or he would buy them, and he would give them back, and he would buy something different. It meant photography, different cameras, not liking this camera and going to get another one. It meant a three- or four-day weekend."

Peter's mood-driven sociability was genuine. He was intensely loyal to his friends, and he loved having them around, but his affability was becoming faintly spiced with a sense of lordliness that crept into his personality to go along with the real estate. He was telling the press that he wanted to maintain a certain distance from his new neighbors: "As a matter of fact, I'm trying to build a legend that I'm a mad actor who rides a black mare across the fields at night with a hook on my hand. Then maybe they'll leave me alone." But David Lodge describes a rather different Peter: "Being the squire of Chipperfield, he behaved like the squire of Chipperfield, certainly when he was in front of the people of the village."

Picture a piece of home movie footage of a snowball fight between Anne, Peter, David, and the two kids. It's a domestic scene that could have been played out in any family's backyard in wintertime. As recorded on celluloid, Chipperfield on that day looks like a landscape of fun, family, and friendship. The subjects, running and laughing, dodge icy cannonfire and pitch return volleys, all in good nature. Like snapshots, home movies catch a certain truth. But Anne, in a few words, hits at a deeper fact about life at the manor—something the amateur director wasn't able to capture in his images: "I never knew what we were doing there. I'm not sure that Peter ever knew what we were doing there either."

· · ·

By 1960, the British and American press were industriously setting up a competition of the sort no one can possibly win:

"There have been rumors (unsubstantiated) that he wants to do an Alec Guinness."

"He may even be crowding his idol, Sir Alec Guinness, with his mixed bag of characterizations and multiple roles."

"There's no doubt about it—Alec Guinness stands in clear peril of losing his eminent position as Britain's most distinguished film comedian."

Peter himself played it up: "I work from the voice inward—probably from being in radio—instead of going for the physical characteristics first. Then I figure out what they're going to look like. Guinness, who of course is wonderful, works from the body outward and plans every movement in advance. I play a scene the way I feel it." And: "Alec likes to use technique to work out just what he will do before he starts. I use technique too but I have to get into the part—feel it from the inside, you know. I think that's why his characters sometimes seem cool, if not cold."

It was in this context that Peter ignored the advice of his close friends and made the decision to appear as a ruthless criminal mastermind in John Guillermin's Brit noir, *Never Let Go* (1960). Like Guinness, he'd already played multiple characters in the same film, and he could do practically any voice he wished, but he was remaining, after all, just a comedy star, albeit the greatest in the United Kingdom. As such he considered his art "puny." Heavy drama beckoned. *Never Let Go* was not going to be funny on any level, and Peter's character—the car-thieving, girlfriend-slapping, murderous Lionel Meadows—appealed to his sense of challenge. He would actually be *doing* the Guinness if the now-retired Major Bloodnok and Bluebottle turned himself into an unremittingly vicious thug.

Shooting began at Beaconsfield in late November 1959. The story is bleak and simple: A failing salesman (Richard Todd) leaves his office one day to find that his car is stolen. His life unravels, and his obsession with finding the car consumes him. He traces the theft first to the young punk who actually pinched it (the heartthrob Adam Faith), and then to Lionel Meadows (Peter) and his chippie girlfriend, Jackie, played by the nubile Carol White.

According to White, Peter started out as an avuncular figure: "When I stepped in front of the cameras at Beaconsfield, my self-confidence deserted me. Peter Sellers saw me wobbling like a jelly and quickly came to the rescue. He cracked jokes and went into his 'Ying tong iddle I po' routine, my moment of anxiety passed, and we were soon whistling through the takes." White also reports that her mother and Peter quickly developed a friendship. Their discussion centering on dieting techniques, Peter was soon wearing pink plastic sweat bags under his clothes, convinced that pounds of fat were melting away every day.

His attitude toward Carol White shifted as shooting progressed. It remained warmly protective, but the tone darkened. Everyone involved with *Never Let Go* knew that the two hottest youths in the cast, White and Faith, were privately conducting themselves in the manner expected of hot youths, and Peter grew jealous—so much so that when he had to slap White's face in one scene he really whapped her hard with his palm. For whatever reason, the director, John Guillermin, ordered about a dozen takes of the action.

Characteristically, Peter soon appeared, contrite and amorous, at the door of White's dressing room. Yes, he confessed, he had indeed become insanely jealous of Adam Faith. "I was sleeping with Adam," White observes in her memoirs, "and there was superstar Peter Sellers telling me that I filled his every dream." White decided, as she puts it, to play "one man off against the other."

The two of them were rehearsing one day in Peter's dressing room—a noirishly threatening bedroom scene, as it happened. But in the dressing room it was romantic comedy, Sellers-style: Peter began his conquest by doing a series of Goon voices and followed through by delivering all of his gangster lines in the voice of an Italian gigolo. The method worked, though there was some assistance from two factors beyond Peter's control: "He had helped me through my brief spell of insecurity and I felt I owed him something." Also, Carol White adds, "I liked the fact that most men wanted to make love to me and I had gotten over being raped."

By the time they filmed their scene, in which Meadows menaces Jackie into bed, they'd had each other offscreen as well, and they continued to do so over the next few weeks of shooting.

The unusually active Carol then proceeded to launch an affair with the *other* leading man, Richard Todd. Never having given up Adam Faith during her affair with Peter, she was quite the star of the offscreen show:

"During the last two weeks of shooting *Never Let Go* I enjoyed my triangle of lovers. When filming was over, Peter Sellers returned to his wife and our secret adventure was over."

"The fact that her mother was on the set a lot I always found very suspicious," John Guillermin observes. "When the mother's there it doesn't mean that the daughter's innocent. It means the opposite."

• • •

"He was very loyal to his friends from the radio days," says John Guillermin. That's how David Lodge ended up playing Lionel Meadows's henchman in *Never Let Go*. "Peter introduced me to David, and we cast him." (Lodge went on to marry Guillermin's sister, Lyn.) "We had a very funny scene on that film," Guillermin declares unexpectedly, given *Never Let Go*'s utter lack of comedy. "Peter and David had a history of inside jokes, mostly on Peter's side. He had an absolutely manic sense of humor—a wonderful, crazy humor that suddenly exploded, and he'd be helpless with laughter. So there was a line of David's—it was a very dramatic moment, they're in the garage, and David runs in and says, 'The police are outside!' For some reason, this line absolutely dissolved Peter. *Every time*, David ran in, full of terror, and said it, and Peter exploded with laughter. We got *one* take in—the laughter started about a second after the last mod [audio signal], and we managed to print it."

There was mirth during the shooting, but none during the accounting after the film's release. Despite Sellers's enormous popularity at the time, *Never Let Go* was neither a commercial nor critical success. "Now that this so unnecessary film has been made," wrote the reviewer for the *New York Times*, "will Mr. Sellers please go and do something precisely the opposite?" Says Guillermin, "Box-office-wise it didn't do anything like his comedies, so for him it wasn't lucrative." Peter never played a thoroughly unsympathetic character again.

Peter's rendition of a gangster is rather successful nevertheless. Lionel Meadows gave him a chance to channel some real rage, especially during the scene in which he slams Adam Faith's hand in a desk drawer. Perhaps it's the knowledge of Peter's more famous roles that gets in the way, but one gets the slightest sense that he's impersonating a movie thug rather than *being* the thug in the movie, a tendency the camera can't help but register. Drawing his lips back in an intimidating, mirthless grin, and speaking in a nasal twang derived from old Jimmy Cagney movies, Peter seems just a little bit adrift as he tries to be despicable. It's as though he simply didn't have it in him to be so unbendingly cruel onscreen.

According to Michael Sellers, however, Peter immersed himself in *Never Let Go* so thoroughly during the production that he returned to Chipperfield every night as Lionel Meadows, savagery and all. Peter acknowledged that his inability to shake his adoptive thug persona was hard on Anne: "I was sort of edgy with her while we made that film." Michael goes a few steps further: "He was abusive and violent and we became terrified of him."

One can hardly fail to note that bringing Lionel Meadows home with him was not wholly a Method-acting technique on Peter's part, since he'd clearly been able to break character whenever he and Carol White were alone together in one of their dressing rooms. According to Guillermin, Peter's Method didn't even extend to the set, where it belonged. The director does add, however, that "he was unto himself quite a bit. Peter wasn't that relaxed, as it were."

Still, the unparalleled viciousness of his character in *Never Let Go* gave Peter Sellers an excuse, however unconscious, to vent even more wrath than usual at home with his family. One evening, for example, he came home from the studio, made some phone calls, turned on Anne, screamed "What the bloody hell is the matter with you," and threw a vase at her, after which he destroyed a bathroom towel bar and some pictures in the dressing room. On another evening he tried to bean her with a bottle of milk. She called David Lodge and begged him to drive over quickly and help calm Peter down. Lodge, a staunch friend to both of them, obliged.

• • •

Peter was big in New York in late April 1960, when he made his second trip across the Atlantic. *The Mouse That Roared* had just closed after its phenomenal twenty-six-week run at the Guild. ("Wow!" "Smash!" *Variety* applauded.) *The Battle of the Sexes* was opening; *I'm All Right, Jack* took *Mouse*'s place at the Guild. American newspapers were full of lavish profiles of Peter, not to mention helpful observations about the United Kingdom— clarifications meant to explain quaint customs. For example, in regard to *The Battle of the Sexes*, the *New York Times* declared that "the scene has been moved to Scotland because kilts are comical."

Peter traveled first class on Air France, with dining service courtesy of

Maxim's, and he took along his trustworthy companion Graham Stark. They were greeted at Kennedy Airport (then called Idlewild) by a fleet of Cadillac limousines and whisked to the Hampshire House on Central Park South, where Peter nabbed the penthouse. A bevy of blue-suited film executives occupied the other cars, and when the entourage arrived at the hotel, Peter overheard one of them place a phone call with a one-line message: "The property has arrived."

Fame could be demeaning. "The property has arrived" was a line he never forgot.

When Peter wasn't being hustled to and from interviews and parties, the actor Jules Munshin was taking him out on the town. Munshin, who had appeared with Peter in *Brouhaha*, was blown away when they arrived at Sardi's and were presented with an A-list table. "Pete, you bastard," Munshin blurted, "*I* never got this table before." Munshin pointed to a man in the outer-Yukon-like back corner. Peter recognized the Scarecrow from *The Wizard of Oz* (1939). "Yeah, Ray Bolger," Munshin said. "He ain't got what you got. He ain't got four pictures playin' on Broadway. Come to think of it, he ain't got no picture playin' anywhere." Peter had bested the Scarecrow. Gossip columnists were swarming around him. Having imitated Americans since childhood, he was now a star among them. The evening was a complete success.

The next morning, one of the many public relations people hovering around Peter shrieked with joy when she picked up one of the New York papers: "Leonard Lyons gave you four inches!"

• • •

Peter's nightlife was glittering. Peter appeared with Jack Paar on his popular late-night talk show. Kenneth Tynan interviewed him and introduced him to Mike Nichols and Elaine May, who in turn introduced him to Kay Thompson. (Tynan later noted that the meeting between Nichols and Sellers had been more or less a disaster; neither understood the other's sense of humor.) The film brass introduced him to Walter Reade, the immensely wealthy owner of a film distribution and exhibition company, who hosted Peter and Graham at a drunken bash at his Long Island estate. Peter also met James Thurber at a party thrown in celebration of the New York premiere of *The Battle of the Sexes*. Thurber told Monja Danischewsky a few days later that they'd "had a fine time together," but that Peter was "being driven crazy by the New York pressure." This was a feeling Peter never really overcame. Despite his subsequent global travels over the next two decades, Sellers spent little time in New York.

The two Englishmen returned to London in first-class cabins on the *Queen Elizabeth*.

• • •

Two-Way Stretch (1960) is a light and unpretentious diversion, a sympathetic critic's way of saying it isn't very good. Three con-artist convicts (Peter Sellers, David Lodge, and Bernard Cribbins) plot a diamond heist from their prison cell with the help of a visiting fake vicar (Wilfrid Hyde-White), their old partner in crime. A comic neo-Nazi guard named Crout (Lionel Jeffries) tries to foil the scheme. Everybody loses.

The comedienne (and associate Goon from the Grafton Arms) Beryl Reid, who plays a small role in the film, later said that because Peter "was so inventive himself, he probably couldn't understand that a director couldn't keep up with his mind. That's the thing—that his mind went at such a rate when he was inventing characters that a director had to be talked into it." While Reid's remarks are undoubtedly true, their context is peculiar because Peter employs such restraint with Dodger Lane, his character in *Two-Way Stretch*, that the director Robert Day probably didn't have to be talked into very much. Reid went on to note, though, that Peter's inventions in *Two-Way Stretch* didn't stop at his own character: "He used to give me rather dirty lines to say, because I always looked as though I didn't know what they meant."

Dodger Lane speaks in a most muted Cockney. It's one of Peter's least showy and therefore most generous performances, since he consistently throws attention away from himself in order to showcase Lodge and Cribbins. It's lanky Lionel Jeffries who produces the only outrageous voice in *Two-Way Stretch*—a barking squeak, evidently the result of the figurative crowbar that Crout harbors up his fascistic rear. Perhaps it's this funny voice that Peter resented when he began bickering with Jeffries during the production. Settling into the exasperated groove that would define much of the rest of his career, Peter was annoyed at Jeffries's insistence on long rehearsals, while Jeffries, who responded precisely as many of Peter's fellow actors would over the next twenty years, was irritated at Peter's distaste for any rehearsals at all. It wasn't a particularly happy shoot, but it wasn't a disaster, either. And it was scarcely the last time that the dull ache of filming a Peter Sellers comedy wasn't justified by the final result.

• • •

Lena Horne was playing at the Savoy, an excellent occasion for Anne and Peter and some friends to spend a luxe night on the town. Anne wore a beautiful hand-embroidered dress. Their friends thought she looked smashing, so much so that by the time they got home Peter was in such a white rage of jealousy that he physically ripped it off of her and shredded it.

After almost ten years of marriage, the word *divorce* began to be used with some frequency in the halls and rooms of Chipperfield, even as he began earnestly to confine Anne to the house. Shopping trips were cause for the third degree. From whatever studio at which he happened to be filming, Peter would place two, three, four telephone calls to Anne every day, just to check her whereabouts. When she mentioned to him one evening that she'd like to get out of the house a bit more, Peter destroyed everything in sight—porcelains, a Chippendale chair, bookcases. He also threatened to kill her, but he didn't follow through. He beat her up instead. Today, the intake desks of women's shelters accept wives and girlfriends with fewer bruises than Anne sustained.

Another day, a small flock of doves nested under one of Chipperfield's many gables. They cooed. So Peter brought out his double-barreled shotgun and massacred them.

• • •

When Peter was first approached to appear as an Indian doctor in an adaptation of a George Bernard Shaw satire, he was decidedly underwhelmed despite the potential acquisition of a literary pedigree. *The Millionairess* (1960) simply didn't interest him. Then they told him who his costar would be: Sophia Loren, the most unearthly beauty in all cinema. He accepted the role.

A high fee helped as well. Carried away by Peter Sellers's exponentially increasing popularity, the agent Leonard Urry (representing the producer, Dimitri de Grunwald) is said by Terry-Thomas to have made Sellers an offer of £85,000. Terry, who was a friend of Urry's, asked Urry why on earth he'd offered so much. Urry answered, "I only offered what I thought was a fair price." Terry then told Urry that he could probably have gotten Peter for £50,000, since he, Terry, knew "exactly what Peter had been earning up to then. After that his price soared." It certainly did, though Alexander Walker reports that Sellers actually *was* paid a flat fee of £50,000, "of which £17,000 went to Wolf Mankowitz" as part of the formation of the production company he and Mankowitz were trying to put together at the time. (As a point of comparison and a measure of their relative statures at the time, Sophia got $200,000 and a percentage of the profits.)

The film was to be directed by the respected Anthony Asquith, produced by de Grunwald and distributed, they all hoped, by Twentieth Century-Fox, though Fox executives tried to talk de Grunwald out of Sophia Loren in favor of Ava Gardner. De Grunwald had been friendly with Peter for several years already. Some time earlier, in fact, he'd taken Peter to a Russian nightclub in Paris. The émigré producer was dazzled by Peter's disarming nature as a changeling: "We'd only been there two minutes when Peter became one hundred times more Russian than I am—and I'm very Russian. He went absolutely wild—nostalgic, sentimental, gay, tragic, romantic—*everything* a Russian is. The gypsies came over to our table, and Peter sang with them and cried during all the sad songs, and in half an hour he was dancing madly all over the place and smashing empty vodka glasses against the wall."

Now they wanted him to be the love interest in a lavish Sophia Loren comedy. And so he did it. In Technicolor.

• • •

Sophia's arrival in London, on a boat train from Paris, was heralded long in advance; the press was primed. On the day of the event, the producers threw a party for the express purpose of recording the meeting of Europe's most voluptuous star with Britain's funniest comic, both set to star in a gown-filled but artistically respectable top-of-the-line motion picture.

Sophia was on one side of the ballroom, glorious; Peter, armed with flowers and champagne, was on the other, a nervous wreck. "I don't normally act with a romantic glamorous woman," he told a fellow guest. "You'd be scared, too. She's a lot different from Harry Secombe."

The moment had to happen, though—the press were getting itchy—and when it did it was forced and stilted. Only after the photographers demanded it did Peter provide Sophia with a kiss on the cheek. Later that evening, when he got home, Anne asked him what she was like; "Ugly, with spots," he said.

• • •

Filming began. In an early scene in *The Millionairess*, Peter's character, the selfless Dr. Kabir, minister to the wretched of the earth, rubs lotion on the naked back of the world's richest and most beautiful woman. By the time Anthony Asquith called "cut," Peter was wildly in love.

Starring with Sophia Loren in a romantic comedy appealed so greatly to Peter because by 1960 he wanted to be someone he never imagined he could be: a romantic lead. *The Millionairess* provided the flip side of Lionel Meadows in *Never Let Go*. "I was there at the time," his friend Bryan Forbes declares. "It stemmed from the moment he opened a paper and it said, 'Mastroianni—Peter Sellers with Sex Appeal.' And that plunged him into a deep sorrow and angst and he immediately went on a crash diet and changed his whole personality. He was a fat boy struggling to get out." Richard Lester puts it even more bluntly: "Once he was on the yogurt, things began to alter."

Peter himself once remarked on his own metamorphosis: "I fell in love with Sophia, and when I took a look at myself in the mirror I felt sick."

Having had enough of the pink plastic wrap, Peter went on a diet of hard-boiled eggs and oranges. He'd already had his teeth capped.

As private affairs go, this one was public. Observing him on the set, Anthony Asquith said, "He looks like a boy with a pinup in his bedroom." Peter took Sophia out to the elegant Fu Tong restaurant in Kensington, where he taught her the intricacies of Cockney rhyming slang. His friends began to hear stories of a rather more intimate nature. Graham Stark recalls the would-be private incidents Peter excitedly related to him: "I was given details of furtive meetings, of passion in the dressing room and even awkward (I would have thought totally impossible) gymnastics in the back seats of parked cars. I got it all. It was, to say the least, embarrassing."

Peter's family heard about it, too, since he would come home from the day's shooting and report on Sophia's every move in infatuated detail. One day she'd treat him badly, the next day she'd be charming, and Anne, Michael, and baby Sarah would be treated to it all over dinner. Oblivious to the role his family ought to have played in his life—that of his family—he shared with them his unbridled enthusiasm for his costar, the stupefying bombshell from Rome. Anne offers a simple explanation for her husband's behavior: "He treated me as his mother: I should allow him to do whatever he wanted to do."

He brought Sophia to Chipperfield, first for a large catered party in her honor, then for smaller gatherings. At one of them she played Ping-Pong with Michael, who didn't like her very much. After all, even a child could plainly see what she was doing to his father and what he was doing to himself and his family.

Anne recalls that Peter "brought her to the house quite often, usually with her husband, Carlo Ponti, and she was absolutely stunning and extremely charming. I didn't take much notice at first when he told me he was in love with her. But then he'd be lying in bed and say her spirit was coming into the room."

• • •

One Saturday night during the production of *The Millionairess* £750,000 worth of Sophia's jewels were stolen from the house in which she was staying in Hertfordshire. The police summoned Pierre Rouve, one of the producers of the film, to the studio on Sunday, and he stayed there dealing with the ensuing media turmoil and legal complications all the way through until Monday morning, at which point Sophia arrived on schedule in her Rolls Royce promptly at 7 A.M., ready for the day's work. Everyone knew how upset she was—the jewelry was uninsured—but according to Rouve she was a complete professional and "carried on as though nothing had happened." But, Rouve continues, "Later that morning somebody else's nerves cracked—Peter Sellers's. He fainted and had to be taken to the hospital."

Asquith and his team spent the rest of the day taking close-ups of Sophia, who, despite the trauma she had just suffered, never looks anything short of magnificent in the final cut. But Peter, when released from the hospital, didn't go back to the studio, nor did he return home. He went to Asprey and bought his love a £750 bracelet with which to begin her new collection.

• • •

Sophia had a bodyguard named Basilio. Peter described him years later: "He was a sort of watchdog. . . . He said to me, 'When the husband he finds out about this there will be trouble!' "

But the question lingers unanswered to this day: What exactly did Carlo Ponti have to find out about? Some of Sellers's friends, Spike Milligan among them, believed his stories at the time and swore that he and Sophia Loren enjoyed a torrid affair during the filming of *The Millionairess*. Others, like Graham Stark, think it was all in Peter's head.

Dimitri de Grunwald: "There is nothing that will convince me that Sophia returned his passion with anything more than the mutually narcissistic feelings such stars go in for when the limelight is on them, and the romantic content of the film may have helped. . . . The nice way of describing her attitude is to say that she was kind to him. The other way is to say that her attitude gave him greater hope than was warranted."

Someone else involved with *The Millionairess* has another theory: "I've always felt that Sophia is one of those actresses who need to feel that their leading men love them before they can give a good performance. Peter had no experience playing romantic roles. He misread the signals and developed a delusion."

Sophia herself said, some years later: "I was very close to him—as much as I could be. But love is something else. He is really a great, great friend. We have built up a fine relationship over the years and I think that is rare for a man and a woman, when the woman is married to someone else."

Anne: "I don't know to this day whether he had an affair with her. Nobody does."

• • •

More important than the precise whereabouts of Peter's penis during the production of *The Millionairess* was the effect that his emotional arousal had on his wife and children. According to Michael, he was already out of control when he confessed to Anne, who remembers the scene vividly: Peter "came in and straightened his shoulders like a politician about to make a major speech in the House of Commons and said, as though he had rehearsed the line all the way home from the studios, 'Anne, I've got to tell you that I've fallen madly in love with Sophia Loren.' "

Despite her comment that she "didn't take much notice at first" when Peter told her that he was in love with someone else, according to Graham Stark Anne packed her bags and showed up that very night at the Starks' door, asking if she could stay in their guest room. She wasn't in tears. She was in a rage, one that was made all the more fiery by the characteristic restraint with which she expressed it. "The bastard only told me because he couldn't be bothered to have a bad conscience," she told Graham.

"We had some terrible rows over it," Anne does acknowledge. "One of them lasted fifteen hours." But as Stark remembers it, Peter almost immediately began showing up at the Starks' house asking for permission to take Anne out for the evening. He was all very proper and polite, so much so that the Starks felt as though they'd become Anne's parents.

Of course Peter was contrite. That Anne had left *him* was what mattered, and it mattered because it hurt. Hurting could make him sweet. After a week or so Anne moved back to Chipperfield.

Still, according to Michael, his mother spent many of the ensuing nights in one of the guest rooms rather than the bedroom she once shared with her husband. She had good reason to keep a distance. As Michael describes his father at the time, "At home he became a crazed, manic figure." One night was extra-special: "He hauled me from my bed at 3 A.M. 'Do you think I should divorce your mummy?' "

• • •

If *The Millionairess* were a comic masterpiece, all the sordid behind-the-scenes turmoil might have served some lofty aesthetic purpose. But as it turned out, Peter's agony of love was largely for naught. Sophia did not end up leaving Carlo Ponti for him, nor was *The Millionairess* one of Peter's better films. It's an extravagant but dull (for lack of a better word) affair. Sophia's costumes are dazzling, her unnatural beauty even more so, her performance hammy. Shaw's wit can be brittle, which may not be a bad thing, but in this case—or at least in Wolf Mankowitz's adaptation—it's impossible to accept without the lingering odor of smut. Why would a pious Muslim doctor who has devoted his life to the poor consent, even at the end, to spend the rest of his life with the world's most spoiled and cutthroat heiress, other than to finally get his hands on her gigantic breasts? There's just something fundamentally filthy about it. The closing scene, in which the heiress and the doctor finally declare their love and share a moon-lit dance on a terrace, is lush but inane. *The Millionairess* did only so-so at the box office.

And yet Peter's performance is extraordinary. His earlier Indian routines on *The Goon Show* and on comedy records were funny because they were so broad; Dr. Kabir is funny—*when* he is funny, that is—because of Peter's technical restraint. At times, in fact, there's no comedy to speak of in the performance. In a pivotal scene, Sophia's character, Epiphania, shows up at Dr. Kabir's clinic having bought it and all the surrounding land in a gesture of spoiled meanness and callous intimidation. She then strips down to an eye-popping black corset, stockings, and garters. Dr. Kabir loses his temper.

The idea of Peter Sellers as an enraged Indian doctor seems, of course, to be inherently hilarious, but in point of fact Dr. Kabir's breakdown isn't comical at all, nor is it meant to be, at least from the perspective of the performer. Dr. Kabir is genuinely appalled at her arrogance, and for good reason. There's also a touch of defensiveness, owing to his awareness of her attractiveness to him. His pitch rises slightly; he gesticulates, but only to a point; and suddenly he begins speaking rapidly in his own language. Dr. Kabir is not a caricature, and whatever authentic emotion *The Millionairess* projects is due to what the camera's cool lens recorded, as it often did, as Peter Sellers's innate humanity.

• • •

The end of shooting *The Millionairess* scarcely dampened Peter's ardor. Sophia left for Rome.

He followed.

"After the film was finished he'd phone her all over the place and go off to Italy to try to see her," says Anne. Michael recalls Peter's telephone conversations with Sophia occurring no matter whether his wife or children were in earshot. "I love you, darling," Peter would say, and say, and say again, his children overhearing all of it.

Sophia returned to London for a few days to record a song with Peter, "Goodness Gracious Me," as publicity for the film: A patient (Sophia) describes to her Indian doctor (Peter) her heart's peculiar response to a certain man. His chief response, initially placid but increasingly excited, is the song's title. With its bouncy, jingly tune and spoken lyrics, it's basically a novelty record. But although *The Millionairess* itself wasn't a hit, the song— which was deemed too frivolous for inclusion as title music in a George Bernard Shaw film—appeared on the best-selling charts in November 1960, and stayed there for fourteen weeks, peaking at number four.

Carlo Ponti accompanied his wife to London on the "Goodness Gracious Me" trip, but Mr. Loren's presence didn't seem to affect Peter one way or the other. As he saw it, she would leave Carlo, he would leave Anne, and then he and Sophia would be free.

Implausibly, the whole thing didn't blow up in anyone's face—at least not at the time. Peter, Sophia, and Carlo all remained friendly, and in fact Peter was a guest in their home for many years. As further publicity for *The Millionairess*, Peter and Sophia recorded three other songs for inclusion on an entire album, *Peter Sellers and Sophia Loren*, released late in 1960 by

EMI. "Bangers and Mash," like "Goodness Gracious Me," was a novelty hit—it's a mostly spoken menu battle between an English WWII veteran and his Neapolitan war bride. He craves the eponymous sausages; she insists on tagliatelle, all to the tune of a jaunty military fife-and-trumpet background. The song reached number twenty-two on the pop charts in January 1961.

The other two songs they recorded together were "I Fell in Love with an Englishman" and "Fare Thee Well."

• • •

Early in 1960, before their collaboration on *The Millionairess*, Peter and Wolf Mankowitz decided to form their own production company, Sellers-Mankowitz Productions, Ltd. In March, before their own deal with each other had been signed, they announced a distribution deal with Continental to produce, in Britain, two out of three of the following projects: *Memoirs of a Cross-Eyed Man*, *My Old Man's a Dustman*, and *The Man Who Corrupted America*. (Continental was already set to distribute *Battle of the Sexes* in the United States.) *Memoirs of a Cross-Eyed Man* seems to have been the most likely of the projects to be produced; it was the story of an everyday kind of fellow who falls in love with a movie star. They considered Shirley MacLaine for the role.

The writer Peter Evans once described the producer-screenwriter with whom Peter tried to form a business: "Mankowitz is a phlegmatic, cultivated East End Jew whose bulk lends his look of supine disdain a threatening authority. His face, even in repose, seems a network of subtle sneers." "I have found in Wolf a person who really understands me," Peter said. A portrait of Daniel Mendoza was to be their logo.

By summer, however, Mankowitz was becoming annoyed with the slow pace of his negotiations with Peter, or, better, the slow pace with which Peter conducted his side of the negotiations. "I can't understand why Peter's and my contracts with one another are taking so long to draw up," he wrote to Bill Wills.

Mankowitz scheduled a meeting on August 30 with some financiers who were almost ready to back the company to the tune of £124,000. That morning, Peter sent him a letter, delivered by hand, in which he told Mankowitz that the deal was off; Peter had decided to keep his focus on acting. Mankowitz was thus forced to show up at the meeting and tell the financiers, "I think you should put your money back in your pockets." Peter had

closed his letter by calling Mankowitz "muzzel," a Yiddish term of endear-
ment. Mankowitz didn't feel especially endearing in return.

Peter then proceeded to shoot his now-former friend in the back. Mankowitz, Sellers told the press, "is a very strange person with so many things
on his mind. He should concentrate more on one thing, like screenwriting,
and leave the impresario business alone."

As for himself, Peter had a different employment option in mind that
year, or so he said. Beyond the constant onslaught of cars, Peter also purchased a life-size mechanical elephant. One could ride atop it on its howdah.
Peter was captivated. To him, the peculiar contraption represented a sort
of safety net for his career: "I was thinking of things I could fall back on—it
was a security if I ever failed," he told the *Observer*. Apparently he believed
that advertisers would flock to it for use in product promotion.

"Peter's not a genius," Spike Milligan declared in 1960. "He's something more. He's a freak."

• • •

The movie star took a reporter on a tour of Chipperfield, which the star
had filled with antiques. He proudly pointed out the remarkable early Victorian (as he put it) "commode": "You must admit they disguised them
well." With the "Emperor Waltz" playing on the high-end hi-fi, the Sellerses' butler silently walked in and poured tea while Peter told the reporter
that he had owned fifty-two cars in the last six years. Presents for friends,
toys for the kids, clothes, cameras, pets, collectibles, cars, more cars, all the
result of deepening despair.

Stardom demanded upkeep. Peter enjoyed some of it. There were film
premieres at which to show his face, charity events, theater openings, parties. At the Royal Film Show at London's Empire Cinema in 1959, he and
Anne celebrated in the company of Queen Elizabeth the Queen Mother,
Princess Margaret, Maurice Chevalier, Alec Guinness, and Lauren Bacall.
At the Lord Taverners' Ball the following year, he mingled with Prince
Philip, if a prince can be said to mingle. He nabbed the Film Actor of 1960
award at the Variety Club. At the 1961 Evening Standard Drama awards
(held in January 1962), he presented the award for Best Musical to the
antic masterminds of *Beyond the Fringe*—Peter Cook, Dudley Moore, Alan
Bennett, and Jonathan Miller. The Queen herself showed up at the Odeon,
Leicester Square, in March 1962, along with Princess Margaret, Claudia
Cardinale, Yul Brynner, Pat Boone, Leslie Caron and her husband Peter

Hall, Peter Finch, and Melina Mercouri. Peter enjoyed a few moments of conversation with the queen in the theater's foyer.

Personality profiles were appearing at a furious pace. "In relaxed moments he has a slightly bewildered look, like an awakening owl," was one truly great observation.

And to Peter Sellers's eventual peril, he repeatedly ignored the advice Alec Guinness had given him during the production of *The Ladykillers*: "Don't ever let the press know anything about your private life." Indeed, Peter came up with a strategy to solve the problem. Killing two birds with a single stone, he began to tell the world he had no personality at all: "In myself I have nothing to offer as a personality. But as soon as I can get into some character I'm away. I use the characters to protect myself, as a shield—like getting into a hut and saying 'nobody can see me.' " And, "As far as I'm aware, I have no personality of my own whatsoever. That is, I have no personality to offer the public. I have nothing to project."

The press took the bait. Peter Sellers, wrote one of the many critics to follow Peter's lead over the years, "possesses one rare distinction—that of total anonymity."

• • •

Around this time, Peter's friend Herbert Kretzmer described him more closely, more sympathetically, and consequently more tragically:

"He is the most successful actor since Olivier and Guinness. He enjoys a riotous acclaim clear across the world. He has more money than he can spend in his lifetime—and the endless promise of more. . . . Yet Peter Sellers is one of the saddest, most self-tortured men I have ever known. Here is a man almost devoid of any capacity to sit back and enjoy the riches his genius has produced. There is certainly no more complex personality in the whole spectrum of British show business."

"I can't explain myself, I'm afraid, sir," said Alice,
"because I'm not myself, you see."

In January 1961, Peter found himself in need of a new driver. Bert Mortimer had been Cary Grant's chauffeur when Grant was in England, but Cary was spending more time in Hollywood and Bert was looking for work. First Peter tried him out on Peg. When that worked out, he took Bert for himself.

"I was a bit concerned because I'd heard that staff came and went like turning on the tap and running water," Bert later observed. "But we prevailed. And everything turned out fine." Until the end.

Bert Mortimer became Peter's primary caregiver. Driving, fetching, emotional-crisis management, delivering messages Peter wanted to avoid delivering himself, cleaning up dog shit deposited in the back seat of a Rolls Royce. Mortimer performed many tasks. Says Bryan Forbes, "Peter built him up into a legend. He became known as 'The Great Bert.' "

Peter also hired a new secretary. Naturally, Peter believed that every fan letter required a personal reply. Hattie Stevenson wrote them. She, too, came to clean up messes.

• • •

Only Two Can Play (1962) might have served as the title of a memoir devoted to the waning years of Peter's marriage, but in fact it's fictional. Based on Kingsley Amis's novel *That Uncertain Feeling*, it concerns a dapper Welsh librarian, a lady's man with a wife and two kids who can't help but have an affair with a gorgeous, wealthy, foreign-born woman, herself a serial adulterer. The British novelist Thomas Wiseman once wrote perceptively about Peter's ongoing tendency to play out the blunt facts of his own interiority in the roles he chose to play for the public. *Only Two Can Play*, Wiseman declared, was yet another "ingenious form of psychological buck-passing."

Scripted by Bryan Forbes and directed by Sidney Gilliat for the Boult-ings, *Only Two Can Play* is one of Peter's lowest-key films, a muted look at a conventional marriage and its vicissitudes. It's Sellers at his most un-derstated. The performance seems effortless, and the film is fascinating.

Only Two Can Play's production team knew what they were getting with Peter Sellers. Forbes had known Sellers since the war, when they'd appeared together in *Stars in Battledress* along with Sgts. Harry Secombe and Terry-Thomas and Lt. Roger Moore. Forbes had always enjoyed Sell-ers's company, and as they rose in the world of British entertainment they became even closer friends. Sidney Gilliat had cowritten Hitchcock's *The Lady Vanishes* (1938)—the other two screenwriters were Frank Launder and Alma Reville, Hitchcock's wife; Gilliat went on to produce many films with Launder, among them *The Smallest Show on Earth*, with Peter as the drunken projectionist. In short, Forbes, Gilliat, and the Boultings were all seasoned to Peter Sellers—a funny if mercurial friend, an exceptionally skilled actor with star power and a prickly nature.

Forbes finished his script in April 1960, after which casting began. The beautiful Mai Zetterling was chosen for the bombshell role, Virginia Mas-kell for the plainer, warmer wife. Peter's friend Kenneth Griffith took the role of the other librarian, the one with whom Peter vies for a promotion. (The bombshell, whose husband chairs the library board, uses this potential promotion as leverage to get Peter's character into the sack.) Graham Stark came along, too; his was the small role of a dirty-minded library patron clad in an even filthier raincoat.

Griffith had experienced Peter's preparatory method before: "On a film job—*always*, I think—he'd agree to do it, he would sign the contract, and then inevitably he would say, 'Kenny, I can't do it, I can't.' On this occa-sion, he said to me about three weeks before we started filming, 'Kenny, I can't be a Welshman. I can't do it. I'm sorry, because I would like to have done it with you.' He was serious. So I said to him, 'Look, Pete, why don't we go down to Wales right away and I'll introduce you to a number of Welshmen who, I think, could be like the character you're playing.'

" 'That's a good idea.' "

Bert whisked them to Wales in a Rolls. First Griffith introduced Peter to his friend the poet (and crony of Dylan Thomas) John Ormond, but

Peter wasn't especially inspired. "The next one on my list was John Pike, a close friend of mine who was a newsreel cameraman. The moment Sellers saw Pike all his problems were over. A brilliant impersonation of John Pike is what you're seeing." (Griffith digresses: "John was sent by the BBC to the war in Vietnam. The effect over there. . . . He had a nervous breakdown. Killed him. Drink.")

• • •

A few weeks later, with shooting about to commence, Sellers and Griffith returned to Wales, this time along with the rest of the company. There was an immediate flap over the hotel.

"He expected me to stay wherever he stayed, which I didn't mind," says Griffith. "Swansea was the town they got. They've got pretty substantial hotels there now—it's changed. [Then] it was just tidied up from the wreckage after the war and that was about it. The best hotel was the hotel at the railway station. That's where we were both going to stay. Suddenly I could hear some disagreement between Sellers and the manageress. He said, 'Mr. Griffith and I can't stay here.' She said, 'Why not?' He said, 'It's claustrophobic.' So he drags *me* in and he says, 'Kenny we can't stay here—I'm not going to *let* you stay here. We'll go down and see Launder and Gilliat and tell them.'

"I didn't want to. He had money in the film—he was helping to finance it—so it was easy for him. But I, you know, I'm not fussy, and I remember trying to hide behind him. He said [to Launder and Gilliat], 'Kenny and I—we can't stay there,' and I said, 'Oh, shit.' And indeed, we moved out to a seaside hotel at Porthcawl [about fifteen miles down the coast to the east]. It was a real old boardinghouse, but he liked it."

Kingsley Amis put it more curtly in his *Memoirs*: Peter "buggered off down the coast to Porthcawl and what proved to be a measurably worse hotel."

Then came the costar crisis. It occurred quite early in the shoot. Virginia Maskell had filmed but a single scene, when:

Roy Boulting: "[Peter] was on vacation making *Only Two Can Play*, and he had as his wife in the film a young actress called Virginia Maskell. Her talent had already been noted by the critics, and I think she had a very promising future. Well, for whatever reason—and I have my own suspicion as to what the reason was—Peter Sellers took agin' her."

Sidney Gilliat: "Peter rang me up at the hotel and said, 'That girl is no good. She must go. She must go *at once*. And you must cast somebody else.' Just like that. I said, 'I won't do anything of the kind.' 'Why not?' 'Well, you've got to be fair to the girl to begin with. She's only played one scene, and that consisted of taking a milk bottle out.' "

Peter took the matter to the heads of the studio.

Roy Boulting: "He phoned John and myself and said, 'Look, this girl is worse than useless. She will ruin the film. Will you get on to Sidney Gilliat and tell him that he must recast another actress immediately!' " Boulting, who had worked with Maskell on another film (*Happy Is the Bride*, 1958), refused to do it. "We had to very gently tell Peter that he should get on with his acting and leave the judgment of performance to his director," he later explained.

Sidney Gilliat finishes the story: "Rather ironically, she was nominated by the British film academy as Best Actress, and Peter wasn't nominated for anything."

During the filming, Peter took his harmless revenge not against Maskell but against the Boultings—not in person, of course, but behind their backs. Kenneth Griffith was in on the private joke: "Now, in the morning to get to work I would sit with Peter in the back of the Rolls, which was driven by Bert. It was at least a thirty-minute journey into Swansea. Peter wouldn't know how to talk about this, that, or the other, or he could be stumbling, or he could be depressed . . . *but suddenly it's John Boulting talking!* If you didn't look you wouldn't know it wasn't John Boulting. Now [the Boultings were] very, very broad, general, not very intelligent but very well educated, and Peter would speak to me as John, using John's vocabulary and John's point of view, none of which had anything to do with Sellers. It was hoped that I would reply as Roy. Which I did."

The impersonations hardly stopped with the Boulting brothers. Peter enjoyed playing with people.

Griffith: "He said at the end of one day, 'Kenny—you being Welsh, you know the best restaurants here in Swansea.' I said, 'I don't really, Pete— I don't spend much time here.' And then I remembered a very simple little lino'd-floor Chinese restaurant and I thought the food was good there. 'Oh,' he said, 'That's a good idea. I like Chinese food.'

"So we got Bert and the Rolls and we went there. It was little, very clean, very nice, but not even any Chinese nonsense hanging about—just a little place with Chinese food. We got seated there, Bert, Peter and I, and in came two big steelworkers, youngsters, big thugs—oh, they might have been miners—but they were big tough Welsh guys with their girlfriends, and you could hear everything that anyone said, and one of the girls said, 'Hey—those two are on telly. *Peter Sellers! On telly!*' One of the fellows said, 'Don't be bloody daft, what do you mean "on telly"?' She said, 'Who in the hell do *you* think they are?'

"Anyway, he got up and trundled over to us and says, 'Yeah, my girlfriend is bloody daft, she says you two are on telly. Peter Sellers!' Sellers answered him with a Welsh accent: 'Oh no, no, no, no,' he said, 'no, Mr. Jones here and myself are on the staff of the steelworks, no, no, no. Come to think of it,' he said—*I* was thinking, 'Shit, let's run away!,' and there he was, *playing!*—'no, no, come to think of it, when the Queen opened the big wing at the steelworks, well, Mr. Jones here and myself were present, and though I didn't have the privilege of seeing it myself we have been told that when the camera tracked along we were distinctly seen.'

"He bought it. He trundled back to his table: 'Yeah, yeah, I told you—bloody nonsense. They're both with the steelworks.' "

• • •

Peter and Kingsley Amis, who was there for at least some of the production, successfully embarrassed themselves in the eyes of the cast and crew with an ongoing contest of dirty wit; it was a battle of obscene jokes between two able warriors, but their spectators were merely disgusted at the competition. Moreover, Amis himself was under the impression that it was Griffith's own coaching that helped Sellers find his Welsh voice, and the novelist had a strangely ambivalent response to what he heard: "Partly to my chagrin, the result of this, or what Sellers made of it, was unimprovable, the precisely accurate local-university Welsh-English!" Amis was rather pleased with *Only Two Can Play* and credited Sellers with much of the success.

Necessarily, Peter came on to Mai Zetterling during the shoot, but she gently but firmly fended him off in favor of her husband. Still, she offers a sympathetic assessment of her costar in retrospect: "He was a very insecure man, and a very frightened man who felt very small, and unloved, and ugly, and all that kind of thing. With all the success he had it's very difficult for the public to understand."

• • •

In March 1962, Launder and Gilliat announced their new film production—an adaptation of Aubrey Menen's *The Fig Tree* starring Peter Sellers. The plan was soon scuttled and they never worked with each other again.

The break may have occurred because there was a financial issue after *Only Two Can Play* was completed but before it was released. As Graham Stark puts it, "Peter took such a dislike to it that he sold out his share of the profits." According to Roy Boulting, after Peter saw the final cut, "He was despondent, he had no faith in it, in fact he really hated it." The Boultings are said to have paid him £17,500 for his share; the film turned out to be such a hit that Peter's share alone eventually earned over £120,000.

• • •

Even before Vladimir Nabokov published his novel, *Lolita*, in 1955, the casting of Peter Sellers as Quilty in Stanley Kubrick's 1962 film adaptation had suggested itself fantastically in the novelist's own handwritten manuscript. Humbert Humbert describes the preteen object of his passion, the fire of his loins, his sin, his soul: "the Lolita of the strident voice and the rich brown hair—of the bangs and the swirls at the sides and the curls at the back, and the sticky hot neck, and the vulgar vocabulary—'revolting,' 'super,' 'luscious,' 'goon,' 'drip'—*that* Lolita, *my* Lolita." Humbert proceeds to lose Lolita to Quilty; Nabokov always appreciated a cosmic joke.

In 1958, Kubrick and his associate, James B. Harris, placed a telephone call to the Production Code office in Hollywood. They were thinking about buying the rights to *Lolita*, they said, and they were wondering how the boys at the Code would react to the idea. Geoffrey Shurlock, the longtime head of the office, responded: "I suggested that the subject matter, an elderly man having an affair with a twelve-year-old girl, would probably fall into the area of sex perversion." But by 1960, the dark and dynamic Kubrick— who in the meantime had tossed off *Spartacus* (1960)—had actually succeeded in convincing Shurlock that the film would not in fact violate the Code. Kubrick's argument was specious but effective: Young girls could legally marry in certain Appalachian states, and what was legal could not be immoral. Kubrick also had history on his side; enforcement of the Code was becoming increasingly lax and dismissable.

With Shurlock's provisional green light, Kubrick struck a deal with Nabokov to write the screenplay, the erudite author being represented by Swifty Lazar. Nabokov turned in a draft in June. It was four hundred pages long. Kubrick responded by telling the novelist that such a picture would run for seven hours. "You couldn't make it," James Harris once said; "you couldn't *lift* it." Nabokov turned in a shorter version in September, but Harris, uncredited, ended up revising it, leaving Nabokov to comment later that, for him, watching *Lolita* was like "a scenic drive as perceived by the horizontal passenger of an ambulance."

For the role of the pervert Humbert, a series of stellar men were approached: James Mason (couldn't schedule it); Laurence Olivier (sorry, no); David Niven (yes, but then no); Cary Grant ("I have too much respect for the movie industry to do a picture like that"). But then, suddenly, James Mason became available after all. His wife and friends had helped to change his mind, and luckily so. Humbert Humbert is one of Mason's most delicately wrought performances.

Despite its Hollywood-based director and producer and New York financiers, *Lolita*'s production took place in England. Harris explains: "We wanted to keep a very low profile during the shooting of that film. Everybody seemed to be interested in *how* we were going to do *Lolita*, and *what* was going to be in terms of censorship, and *what did the girl look like* . . . We felt that if we just got away from Hollywood and got to England, a place where we spoke the language, we could keep a much lower profile." But it was financial considerations that actually drove the decision. To attract foreign film productions, the United Kingdom was offering filmmakers the ability to write off substantial expenses if four out of five of the cast and crew were subjects of the queen.

Peter counted. "The word was that this guy was just terrific," Harris later said. "It caused us to feel lucky if we could get him. It turned out that Peter had an availability—but not much, because he was so busy going from one picture to another. If we could shoot his part in the picture on fourteen consecutive days, he could work us in." Shooting began in late November 1960, at Elstree.

For the role of Lolita's mother, Kubrick cast Shelley Winters, the undisputed queen of poignant tawdriness. In 1951, for instance, she invited audiences to cheer Montgomery Clift on in his goal of killing her in *A Place in the Sun*. (It requires extraordinary skill to achieve that degree of contempt.) For Lolita herself, Kubrick signed an unknown, Sue Lyon, after Nabokov nixed Tuesday Weld. Peter was necessarily captivated by the girl, but even *he* knew she was off limits. Still, at a party at James Mason's house during the production, Mason's wife was fascinated to see Peter spending most of the evening lying on his back, Michelangelo-like but on the floor, snapping photos of the sexy fifteen-year-old.

Like the making of so many great films, the construction of *Lolita* was a matter of methodically creating nuanced art among gargantuan egos. Mason, the star of the picture (not to mention the star of Max Ophuls's *Caught*, 1949; George Cukor's *A Star Is Born*, 1954; Nicholas Ray's *Bigger than Life*, 1956; and many other films) was not at all happy at the way Kubrick fawned over him—meaning Peter. According to Mason, Kubrick "was so besotted with the genius of Peter Sellers that he seemed never to have enough of him." Mason was right. Sellers and Kubrick harmonized in a way that rarely occurred between Peter and his directors. They shared the same macabre sensibility. They bonded.

At the time, as James B. Harris recalls, Peter was particularly social as far as Kubrick and Harris were concerned: "Every Sunday we used to go out to Chipperfield and visit with Peter and Annie and all his friends. The Boulting brothers were there, and Graham Stark, and David Lodge. It became sort of a ritual." It also seems to have helped drive a wedge between Peter and the rest of the cast.

During rehearsals, Kubrick suggested that his actors pretend to have forgotten the lines they had just meticulously memorized—except for Peter, who'd been told not to worry about his scripted dialogue at all. Instead, Kubrick announced, Peter should do what Peter did best: Make things up on the spur of the moment. Cues be damned—let it fly! Mason was annoyed, but he didn't blame his costar: "You could not fault Peter Sellers. He was the only one allowed, or rather encouraged, to improvise his entire performance. The rest of us improvised only during rehearsals, then incorporated any departures from the original script that had seemed particularly effective." Kubrick's artistic instinct was right on target. With Sellers given free rein, Quilty became even more unpredictable and terrifying.

But ironically, and comically, they were *all* speaking dialogue that was written by Harris but continued to be credited to Nabokov, an extraordinarily pedantic author who, when he turned in his essays to *The Saturday Review*, forbade the magazine's copy editors from altering a single comma.

Mason also offered a strange and unexpected detail in his autobiography: "Sellers told us that he did not enjoy improvising." Mason tried to explain the remark: "I think that he was referring to the occasional necessity to think on his feet when giving a live performance. He was painstaking and meticulous in preparation." This is a generous but unconvincing clarification. One has no doubt that Peter told his colleagues that he didn't like to improvise. This was, after all, a man who told people he'd descended from Disraeli, and no doubt he believed what he said at the time. But what Peter expected to achieve from the remark nevertheless remains obscure. The only sense one can make of it is that Peter seems to have been developing an even greater need to confound—to prove to people who didn't know him very well that, in fact, they didn't know him at all.

• • •

With Shelley Winters, Peter found himself back in the baffling, excruciating land of Terry-Thomas and Jean Seberg. To his total horror, he discovered that Miss Winters tended to use a director's calls for "camera!" and "action!" as the most convenient time in which to memorize her lines. Anthony Harvey faced the problem later in the editing room. "When we were shooting *Lolita*, Peter had a scene with Shelley Winters," Harvey says. (Their only scene together, it's set at Lolita's high school dance, where the blowsy Charlotte reminds Quilty that she and the vague roue had screwed the year before.) "Stanley Kubrick made about sixty-five takes. Shelley didn't know any of her lines at all. The first few takes, Peter was absolutely brilliant. And as it progressed, Shelley began to learn her lines, and Peter totally blew them, so that by take thirty-eight, or forty-eight, or whatever it was, when I got back to the cutting room, I had to cut take two of Peter and take forty of Shelley together." (It's a sequence of over-the-shoulder shot/reverse shots. When Peter delivers his lines and listens to Shelley's responses, Shelley's lips can't be seen forming her exact words and vice versa.)

Harvey concurs with James Mason on the subject of Peter's relationship with Kubrick, though without Mason's tinge of jealousy: "They had great respect for one another and had a marvelous rapport." As for Peter himself, says Harvey, "I liked him a lot, but he was a totally haunted fellow."

Kubrick was even more abrupt in one of his descriptions of Peter Sellers: "There is no such person."

• • •

"He was the only actor I knew who could really improvise," Kubrick once wrote. "Improvisation is something useful in rehearsal, to explore a role. But most actors, when they improvise, stray into a sort of repetitive hodgepodge which leads them down a dead end, while Sellers, by contrast—even when he wasn't on form—after a time fell into the spirit of the character and just took off. It was miraculous." The critic Janet Maslin once put it equally well: "Sellers could bring a musician's improvisatory sense to a role, teasing and stretching a character until it took off in the free-flowing slip of a jazz riff."

But it took work, not only for Sellers but for Kubrick, who painstakingly had to lift his star out of his typical morning funk. "He would usually arrive walking very slowly and staring morosely," Kubrick told Alexander Walker. "As the work progressed, he would begin to respond to something or other in the scene, his mood would visibly brighten, and we would begin to have fun. . . . On many of these occasions, I think, Peter reached what can only be described as a state of comic ecstasy."

Lolita builds the tortured skill Kubrick saw in Peter Sellers into its essential nature. The film begins with Humbert wandering through a decimated, Xanadu-like mansion—the Kane, not the Khan—full of empty bottles and glasses, cigarette stubs, torn paper, breakage, furniture covered with rumpled sheets. One of the sheets rustles. Peter's head slumps out:

HUMBERT: Are you Quilty?
QUILTY: (in broad Long Island tones): No, I'm Spartacus. Ya come ta free the slaves er somethin'?

He drapes the sheet over his shoulder like a toga. He's hungover. And still drunk. Slurred words spill out: "Lissen lissen le's have a game a li'l lovely game of Roman Ping-Pong like two civilized senators." (He picks up a paddle and ball and hits one across the table at the mystified, appalled, murderous Humbert.) "Roman ping?" (Silence from Humbert, who fails to hit it back.) "You're s'posed to say 'Roman pong!' "

Quilty adjourns to a chair and a leftover drink into which an anonymous partygoer has stubbed out an old smoke. *"Quilty!"* barks Humbert in exasperation. "I want you to concentrate. *You're going to die.* Try and understand what is happening to you. . . . Think of what you did, Quilty, and think of what is happening to you *now*."

At which Quilty turns into a frontier spinster: "Heh heh! Say, tha's a, tha's a *durlin'* little gun you got there! Tha's a *durlin'* li'l thing! How much a guy like you want for a *durlin'* li'l gun like that?" As written, Quilty is what a later generation would call Humbert Humbert's worst nightmare, but that phrase fails to capture the fact that even Humbert's unconscious could never conjure up the black anarchy of a Goon.

At the close of the scene Quilty stumbles up the stairs and hides behind a massive portrait of an elegant woman. Humbert shoots it up. "Oh, that hurt," says Quilty.

An extended flashback follows, extending all the way to the film's penultimate scene: Humbert arrives in mild Ramsdale, sees his nymphet sunbathing in the backyard of a possible lodging, and immediately moves in. Humbert marries the little sexpot's mother, Charlotte, in order to remain close to the girl. Charlotte gets run over by a car. Humbert begins sleeping with Lolita and travels with her around the country, all the while being pursued by Lolita's wraithlike suitor, Quilty, with whom she ultimately vanishes.

In the novel, Quilty appears as in a haze. Nabokov inscribes him mainly in shadow form—wordplay, oblique references, appearances in absentia. In the film, he's more present, but in nebulous, desultory ways. Peter Sellers is his perfect embodiment.

He turns up at the high school dance wearing a pair of black-rimmed glasses—the kind that became a standard feature of Peter's own early-sixties look—and performs a finger-snapping, eyebrow-arched Latin-lover dance with an evil-looking mystery woman (Vivian Darkbloom—an anagram of her creator). Only after Charlotte prompts him by whispering the details of their afternoon tryst in his ear does Quilty remember, whereupon a chipmunky beam dawns: "Did I do that? Did I? . . . Yes, really great fun, lissen, lissen, didn't you, didn't you have a daughter? Didn't you have a daughter with a lovely name? Yeah, a lovely—what was it now?—a lovely lyrical lilting name like, uh—"

"Lolita!" Charlotte cries.

"Lolita, that's right! Diminutive of Dolores, the tears and the roses. . . ."

Charlotte is thrilled. Overcome with excitement, she proclaims: "Wednesday she's going to have a cavity filled by your Uncle Ivor!"

Later, after Charlotte's messy demise, Quilty accosts Humbert on the porch of an old hotel. At once insinuating, nervous, bold, tic-y, sly, and fast-talking, Peter's Quilty threatens the paranoid Humbert by his evershifting and inexplicable demeanor, not to mention by his very presence, which is more or less an absence, since Humbert has no idea who this man is or what he wants.

In another scene, Humbert arrives at home and turns on the light. There sits Peter: "Good eev'neeng, Doktor Humbardtz!"

Peter/Quilty has now turned into Dr. Zemf, "ze Beardsley High school zychiatrist." With hair greased back and yet another of Peter's cherished paste-on mustaches gracing his upper lip, the horrifying doctor describes the troubled schoolgirl and her various neurotic symptoms: Lolita, he notes, "chews gum, vehemently! All ze time she is chewing zis gum!" And she "has private jokes of her own, vich no one understands so they can't enjoy them mit her!"

Backstage at Lolita's play, *The Hunted Enchanters* (by Claire Quilty), Quilty is seen fingering his camera and asking for film. But the anonymous midnight caller in a still later scene is the one who really lets loose Humbert's paranoia: "Uh, Professor, uh, tell me something—uh, with all this traveling around you do, uh, you don't get much time to, uh, see a psychiatrist, uh, regularly, is that right?" It's Quilty's (ab)normal voice, but now it's disembodied, and all the creepier for it.

Near the end, Lolita, poor, worn, Quilty-free, and pregnant by the happy nobody to whom she is now married, writes to Humbert asking for money to bail her out of debt. Humbert, not having seen or heard from her since she took off with Quilty, tracks her down in her slummy house. After fending off his pathetic advances, Lolita explains her original attraction to Quilty. There's an eerie ring to her words, and not only because she has screwed her own stepfather and he's the stepfather in question:

"He wasn't like you and me," she explains to Humbert. "He wasn't a normal person. He was a genius. He had a kind of, um, beautiful Japanese-Oriental philosophy of life." In her description of Quilty, one catches another fleeting glimpse of the comic cosmic.

• • •

With great fanfare and an excellent tagline—"How did they ever make a movie of *Lolita?*"—the film was released in the United States on June 13, 1962, a year and a half after Peter shot his scenes. Notices were mixed. "Whenever Sellers leaves, the life of the picture leaves with him," *Time* opined. This was a most unfair assessment—Mason, Winters, and Lyon are all superb—but it gives some indication of the impression Peter was making at the time, not only on film screens, but in the buzzing press. *Lolita's* reputation has grown considerably since then.

In January 1963, the important pre-Oscar jockeying season began with the Academy of Motion Picture Arts and Sciences announcing Peter's eligibility in the Best Actor category. For two reasons, James B. Harris tried to convince the Academy to shift Sellers into the Best Supporting Actor list. For one thing, Harris obviously wanted to avoid a head-to-head competition between Sellers and Mason. For another, Sellers had appeared in only thirty-four minutes of the 154-minute *Lolita*. But the Academy refused to budge. If Peter Sellers was to be nominated at all, it would be in the category of Best Actor. Harris was, in his own word, "flabbergasted." Sellers was originally signed simply to do a cameo appearance, Harris told the press, but "then we decided to take advantage of his name." This, he explained, was the reason Sellers received star billing.

The nominations themselves rendered the matter moot, for neither Sellers nor Mason was tapped for Best Actor. Gregory Peck won for *To Kill a Mockingbird* (1962). *Lolita*'s sole nomination was for its adapted screenplay—Vladimir Nabokov was honored for writing words he hadn't written, but it didn't matter, because he lost to Horton Foote for *To Kill a Mockingbird*.

• • •

On June 11, 1962, with *Lolita* on the brink of release, Peter Sellers addressed the University Indian Society at Cambridge. "I hope you did not all think I was going to be funny," he announced, "because I am a uniquely unfunny person. I usually climb into a corner." Bob Hope took a different point of view during the production of Peter's next picture—Hope and Crosby's *The Road to Hong Kong* (1962), in which Peter, uncredited, appeared in a five-minute cameo as a crank Indian neurologist. "Get rid of this man," Hope had declared during the production. "He's too funny."

However amusing Hope found Sellers, the scene itself is singly unpleasant. In this, the seventh and final *Road to . . .* comedy (Bob and Bing had already trekked to Singapore, Zanzibar, Morocco, Utopia, Rio, and Bali), Bob loses his memory in a freak flying contraption accident, so Bing hustles him to "the most highly respected neurologist in India." It's Peter replaying Dr. Kabir as ghastly parody.

The dark-faced doctor examines Hope and groans repeatedly. "What is it, doctor?" Bing asks with alarm. "Terrible heartburn," Peter replies. "Put too much curry in my cornflakes."

He then shines a light in Bob's ear and tosses off his only good line in the now-trademarked Indian accent: "I'm looking in here—goodness gracious me!"

• • •

It was inevitable. He wanted to direct.

And so, *Mr. Topaze* (1961). Of course he also had to star.

Mr. Topaze came and went and never returned. The film currently exists in one print stored deep in the archives of the British Film Institute, its once-bright colors having faded to a nearly uniform shade of sick pink.

Based on Marcel Pagnol's play *Topaze*, the film, a satirical comedy, traces the rise of Auguste Topaze (Sellers) from shy schoolteacher to corrupt business magnate. At first, Auguste is a saintly figure, teaching his young charges by day and, after school, taking on the task of private tutor to a familiar-looking young boy (Michael Sellers). "Money does not buy happiness," he tells his students; "money is the trial of friendship." He is rewarded for his moralism by getting fired. A wealthy couple (Herbert Lom and Nadia Gray) hires him to run a dummy corporation for them, but he proves to be so proficient at corrupt business practices that he takes over the company, becomes a millionaire, and seizes the couple's chateau. At the end, one of his old schoolteacher colleagues leads a group of boys past the magnificent residence. The self-satisfied Topaze tells his old friend that he's come to accept the criminal nature of the business world; he's had to accept it, he says, since everything he has done since he left teaching is punishable by law.

"Has your money bought you happiness?" the friend asks.

And Topaze replies: "Has it bought me happiness?" He smiles and gestures to the grand chateau behind him. "It's buying it now."

The friend leaves Topaze standing alone on the terrace. Directing himself, Peter films this sardonic conclusion in extreme long shot, dwarfing himself on the vast CinemaScope screen.

He seemed upbeat during the production. His fee was substantial, £75,000 for directing and starring. "What I am really hoping for is that I will be able to achieve sufficient success as a director to give up acting entirely," he told a reporter. "I writhe when I see myself on the screen. I'm such a dreadful clumsy hulking image. I say to myself, 'Why doesn't he get off? Why doesn't he get off?' I mean I look like such an idiot. Some fat awkward thing dredged up from some third-rate drama company. I must stop thinking about it, otherwise I shan't be able to go on working."

His friend Kenneth Tynan was writing a profile of him at the time, so

Peter invited him to watch some dailies. Sellers's response to himself was quite different then:

"Observing himself in the rushes, Sellers seemed to be watching a total stranger. 'Look at that idiot!' he would cry when Topaze bumped into something; or 'Poor bastard!' during a scene of edgy flirtation. And he would laugh, merrily and musically, shaking his head like a man at once baffled and amused by the behavior of someone he had never met."

Billie Whitelaw, who played Topaze's love interest early in the film, found Sellers very easy to work with, and in fact she stresses the point in her memoirs in a self-evident effort to correct Sellers's postmortem reputation as nothing more than a buffoonish crank. Herbert Lom agrees: "We worked easily together. It was all charming and easy and natural."

Still, looking back on his single experience of being directed by Peter, Herbert Lom declares simply that "he was not a director. He wasn't particularly interested in directing. Why he directed I wouldn't know."

Lom goes on to explain that Sellers wasn't inattentive to his fellow actors, he just didn't perform any of the many other responsibilities of a film director: "He certainly tried to help us in acting the parts. He was one of the actors—he never really figured as the director. He was a colleague who helped us plan the scenes. I have no particular memories of him as an inspiring or irritating director. He was just Peter Sellers."

Lom makes a point of the fact that there wasn't anybody else taking on the tasks Peter wasn't carrying out. Peter was the director in name only, but according to Lom there was no de facto supervisor to back him up: "Probably *nobody* directed us. That's why the picture, if I remember, didn't really turn out to be anything worth talking about—because we probably had no director."

Mr. Topaze isn't bad; it just isn't good. Despite its bitter tone, it's dull. "Judgment on his directing powers must be reserved until he can handle a subject without the extra headache of acting," was *Variety*'s critique, and because Peter was directing himself, "His personal performance has suffered some." The critic was also troubled by the cruelty of the subject matter; the "quiet comedy" of a shy schoolteacher erupted into "an uncomfortably brittle, snide drama." That *Mr. Topaze* is not a feel-good comedy is inherent to the material. What's notable is that Sellers didn't play up this intrinsic acerbity more; the problem with *Mr. Topaze* is its blandness.

The film's tepid reception was a very personal disappointment to Peter—so much so that he barely talked again about *Mr. Topaze*. Soon thereafter he called Spike Milligan and suggested they bring back *The Goon Show*. In his later years he actually insisted that he'd never directed a movie in his life.

He was growing bitter. "Criticism should be done by critics," Peter declared in September 1961, "and a critic should have some training and some love for the medium he is discussing. But these days, gossip-columnist training seems to be enough qualification. I suppose an ability to stand on your feet through interminable cocktail parties and swig interminable gins in between devouring masses of fried prawns may just possibly help you to understand and appreciate what a director is getting at, but for the life of me I can't see how."

ELEVEN

Peter didn't bother to ask his wife when he put Chipperfield up for sale near the end of 1961. He didn't even tell his mother. A *Daily Mail* reporter called Peg for confirmation after hearing the rumor. "I'm sure it can't be right," Mother stated with authority. "Peter rings me up nearly every night for a mother-and-son heart-to-heart. And he hasn't mentioned anything about moving."

According to Sigmund Freud, the key to a healthy personality is the tolerance of contradiction, but Peter's ability to sustain drastic paradox offers a twist to the theory. At times, at least, *he* seemed to tolerate his radical contradictions rather well; it was those around him who couldn't handle the strain. More and more, Peter's mind functioned like two geological fault lines grinding inexorably against each other, all part of nature. It was nearby residents who felt the rumblings and lived in fear.

A case in point: With the sale of Chipperfield, Peter believed, or wanted to believe, that by leading his wife and two children out of one more house and into still another, he was acting in *their* interests. For him, changing addresses again would engender a sense of stability. "One tries to create roots," he explained. "It's vital for the children." It's incidents like this that lead the great Sellers fan Dimitris Verionis to offer an astonishingly acute observation: "Peter was never a double-dealer. He was straight in his reactions—instinctive and sometimes brutally innocent."

So with the cruel guilelessness of the spoiled child he always was, Peter Sellers impulsively bought a seven-year, £31,000 lease on a vast penthouse apartment overlooking Hampstead Heath. As Graham Stark puts it, "He couldn't have done anything worse."

While the apartment was being renovated, the Sellerses moved into a fourteenth-floor suite at the Carlton Tower hotel in Belgravia. Stark recalls the bitter litter of Christmas 1961. Covering the floor of the suite were scads of unopened holiday presents that had been given, nominally, to Michael and Sarah. Many of them had been trod into a trampled mess. It was not the result of a lightning-like Peter tantrum. These children's gifts were British film producers' way of currying the movie star's favor. And the kids, being kids, simply stopped unwrapping them out of sheer boredom with all the obsequious plenitude. After that they stomped the rest to death.

• • •

"At the moment I've got a South African architect working on my new flat in Hampstead," Peter told *Playboy*. It was affecting his personality: "I tend to speak in a South African accent all the time."

The designer, Ted Levy, was hauling his clients out of the Tudor era by way of a preciously masculine, Euro-Beverly Hills style—High Sixties early in the decade. The Hampstead apartment was large, polished, and very rich—five bedrooms, three bathrooms, and a fully equipped recording studio. Many of the rooms were fully paneled in opulent, garnet-dark rosewood. No hoi-polloi drapes here; Levy designed the windows to be covered by moveable leather panels.

Anne worked closely with the architect. "They kind of overruled me, always around, the two of them buying wallpaper and wood and stuff," Peter later complained. Michael Sellers reports that it was Peter who convinced Anne to take Ted along on the shopping trips, it was Peter who "encouraged Ted to take Mum out for lunch," and it was Peter who suddenly turned on his interior designer one day and "ordered Ted to take my mother away." "I don't want her!" Peter shouted.

What with Peter and Anne's affectionate hand-holding and public solicitousness, all of Peter's pecking of Anne's cheek when the couple and Levy were together (two captivating performances by actors, after all), it was only when Peter broke down and shrieked at him that Ted Levy finally comprehended that his clients' marriage was a sour charade.

• • •

Peter went off to Paris to film John Guillermin's adaptation of Jean Anouilh's play *The Waltz of the Toreadors* (1962). A period-piece costume comedy scripted by Wolf Mankowitz, it's *Millionairess*-like in its grand oversizing of a small satirical idea. The beautiful French actress Dany Robin takes the Sophia role, with the requisite breathtaking costumes and hats. Peter, instead of playing a low-key Indian doctor, reverts to Bloodnok for his characterization of the aging general who pursues his old flame (Dany) in the face of his equally aging and shrewish wife (Margaret Leighton). Owing to the requirements of the script, however *this* Bloodnok is a satyr in a fat suit, and the effect is a little jarring.

"Wolf Mankowitz was a friend of mine, and Wolf wrote the script in about two weeks, and we made the picture," says John Guillermin. It wasn't easy, and it didn't turn out well, especially from Guillermin's perspective. The director maintains his respect for Peter Sellers, however, as many directors continue to do despite the troubles they faced with him. "Based on the scores of people I've worked with over the years, I think Peter was an outstanding artist who worked in a very eccentric and curious way. It's rare that you find people who come out of radio and adapt to the screen successfully. To me, he was unique in that sense.

"Whether or not he was taking lessons from Stanislavsky, he had an instinct that was totally Method. The very fact that he started with an actorly tangible, the voice, and then built from it—that's a very sound way of going about it."

Kenneth Griffith provides another colorful description of Peter's approach to performing. "Once we discussed acting," Griffith says, "and we came to the agreement that what we were both trying to achieve was a mushroom in its prime—beautiful rounded top, stem, febrile roots. *I* always started from the febrile roots, built up, and finished, I hoped, with a polished clear top. *He* started with the top—because he *saw* it. But it would be very wrong to say that's where he stopped. He wasn't just a brilliant impersonator. He worked from the top down—to what made that top tick."

Guillermin continues: "In *Toreadors* he started with the voice—it was a neighbor of his, an old boy in his sixties, a retired Army man. Once he got the voice, his whole body followed. But when I said, 'Okay, it's terrific, Peter, but now we've got to talk about the makeup,' he said, 'I don't want any makeup.'

" 'Don't worry about it, John,' he said. He didn't want to have to come to the studio two hours early and have a lot of stuff put on his face. He played the whole part with very, very little makeup—extraordinary, actually, because his skin is quite smooth, and yet he does convey very well the feeling of a man in his late sixties."

The strain of his disintegrating marriage took its toll during filming, but it's difficult to pin down whether Peter's shattered emotional state was due to his collapsing marriage or whether the marriage collapsed owing to

Peter's mental deterioration. "Peter was breaking down into tears now and again," Guillermin recalls. "In fact, the scene when he's about to commit suicide—he gets a revolver and he's going to blow his brains out—was a very bad day for Peter. He said, 'I can't work.' I finally persuaded him to just sit down at the desk. He was in tears, but it worked for the scene, which we shot. That was one of the tragic moments. He was tortured. A very complicated man."

Waltz of the Toreadors was widely critiqued for being a kind of pratfall-ridden bowdlerization of Anouilh's play. Guillermin himself agrees. "The film was fucked up by the producers," he declares. "They wanted to make a slapstick comedy. And they ruined a wonderful scene that Anouilh wrote for his play and I shot. It was a long take—a whole reel, ten minutes—of Peter and Maggie Leighton in their quarters, and they tear each other apart."

But Guillermin did not have the right of final cut. "I was thrown off the editing of the film," he says, still bitter. "They brought in a yes man, and they intercut it with a light comedy scene of Dany Robin and John Fraser larking about in the fields. There were doves fluttering about! They intercut Peter and Maggie's scene three or four or five times, and it totally took the heart out of the film."

Because Peter had such high expectations of his own talent, gripped by idealized goals that were thus impossible to achieve, he was increasingly struck by deep depression after seeing his films. "The whole thing looks terrible, amateurish, bad," he told a British reporter after seeing *Waltz of the Toreadors*. "And you want to pack it all in and look round quickly for a means of employment. Suicide? No, not that. But who can you talk to? Who'd understand your problem?"

But of course there were multiple Peters. He was elated when he won the Best Actor award at the San Sebastian Film Festival for *Waltz of the Toreadors*. His press agent, Theo Cowan, found him to be "like a ten-year-old, going about with four cameras slung around his neck, taking thousands of snaps. . . . His great joy was to mingle with the crowds outside the hotel where the stars were staying and do what he called 'seeing myself go in.' "

• • •

During the filming of *Waltz of the Toreadors*, the distance between Paris and London hardly mattered as far as Peter's marriage was concerned, since fighting and begging could continue by long-distance telephone. David

Lodge tells of Peter sitting in his trailer one day stewing over his most recent argument with Anne. "Everyone cooled their heels outside, including the cavalry horses needed for the scene." With his marriage in tatters, the mercurial star was being even more so; the film's producer, Julian Wintle, "went out of his mind as the costs climbed hourly." Eventually Peter handed Lodge a vast pile of pennies and told him to call Anne on his behalf and apologize.

Lodge did so. Anne refused to accept remorse by proxy.

As Lodge reports, "I couldn't tell Peter that in his state of mind. So I reported back, 'She says she'll talk to you tonight, so get on with your work now.' "

Graham and Audrey Stark joined him for a weekend at the Raphael hotel, where Peter was staying during the production, and the three of them spent some time with Dany Robin. By that point, Peter's heart had taken the predictable turn: "I'm in love with her, and she's in love with me," he confided to Graham. The fact of Dany Robin's marriage was no deterrence. After dinner one evening, they all adjourned to one of the suites for coffee and conversation. Peter had to take a phone call, at which point Robin whispered to the Starks (in Graham's rendition of her charmingly broken English), "Please, I beg you, do not leave me alone wiz Petair. 'E is so sweet, but such a leetle boy. 'E think 'e love me. 'E think I love im. *Merde!*"

It was only after Peter returned from Paris that Anne told him that she planned to move out. This was Peter's cue to announce that he'd slept with Anne's best friend.

• • •

He acted out.

"Peter used Mike as a punching bag," says Anne Sellers Levy in retrospect, adding that she "drank more than I've ever done in my life," alcohol in her case being a material form of denial, a way for a mother to cope with the regularized abuse of her children.

When she told him that she was leaving him, Peter "wrecked the entire living room. I was sitting in a big chair trying to protect my head with my hands. Have you ever seen a child lose its temper and go berserk and pick up things and throw them? Imagine that on a grown-up scale in a very beautiful living room."

Threats were employed. One night he proposed to jump off the terrace. Dangerous acts occurred. At one point he tried to strangle her. But Anne had had enough of the melodrama and knew precisely what to do to stop it. With his fingers clenched around her neck, she calmly told him just to go ahead and do it, so of course he stopped.

Peter was in New York when Anne moved out. "It was a very cowardly way of doing it," she confesses, "but I'd never have got out otherwise." With the two kids being cared for by Frieda Heinlein, she paused long enough in the garden to tell Michael that she was going to stay with her mother for a while, and "please look after Sarah for me, won't you?" and with that she departed.

• • •

There were threats to assassinate Ted.

"Ted Levy has destroyed my life!" Peter yelled to the children. "He has taken your mother away from me! I'll kill him! I'll kill him!"

When Peter showed up at Ted's place at two in the morning and began banging on the door, Ted considered the possibility that he might actually follow through. According to Levy, "He wore an expression of hate, anger, and frustration, the like of which I'd never seen on the face of any human being before. . . . Suddenly he looked up and offered me a cigarette."

• • •

One day while Anne was staying at her parents' house, Peter appeared, behaving, as Anne describes him, "very peculiarly." He acted as though he'd never met her mother; he seemed not to know who she was. Believing him to be either drunk or deranged, she decided she'd better drive him home, but when they got back to the penthouse, Peter announced, "You're not leaving" and locked her in. When it became clear to her that pleading wasn't going to help, she telephoned the family doctor and asked to be saved. The physician showed up, sedatives in hand, and put Peter to bed. Anne left again.

For a while she returned on weekends to spend time with Michael and Sarah, who remained briefly under what passed for Peter's care. Later she took the kids during the week and Peter had them on Saturdays and Sundays. Eventually she got full custody. "In a way I was lucky," Anne says, "because he did spend a lot of time in America, so as the children got older they were hardly with him at all. He wasn't really interested in their schooling or how they thought or their welfare." His moving Michael from school to school was a form of abusive whimsy rather than a concerned attempt to rectify an ongoing problem with the boy's education or behavior.

After a period of fully justifiable bitterness, Sarah Sellers tries to see the best in her father: "I think he had an idea of how he'd like family life to be, but he couldn't really live up to it. So we'd come along and be with him—but once we were there he didn't really know what to do with us."

• • •

Alone and miserable, Peter brooded. The dependable Bert Mortimer grew fearful. "He was so isolated and lonely that I got scared for his safety. He would sit in the penthouse—'my bloody palace,' he'd call it—and threaten to tear 'Ted Levy's Teutonic look' apart. 'Overmasculine—it's just not me,' he'd say."

The director Robert Parrish and his wife, Kathleen, stopped in to visit Peter shortly after Anne left him. He had, says Kathleen Parrish, "lots of toys," one of which was a new electric organ, which he began to play. Taking their cue, the Parrishes began to make a big fuss over it, at which point Peter abruptly stopped playing. "Isn't this bullshit?" he said.

Michael Sellers saw a more intimate despair. He remembers his father muttering. "Who would want me? Who would want me?"

Well, Laurence Olivier, for one.

"Larry asked me to play Lear at the Chichester Festival," said Peter to the journalist Roderick Mann. "It's one of the great parts," he explained. "And Larry said, 'You'd be good, Peter. You must do it. The best Lears have nearly always been new to Shakespeare.'

"But I turned it down. It was too big a risk. In my heart I hadn't the confidence, and that's the place you've got to have it. I'm always seeking perfection, and that makes me difficult to live with. I'm sure it's a nagging thing."

• • •

A less risky choice, and so a less exciting one, *The Dock Brief* (1962) is a sad comedy, a courtroom drama that is played out almost entirely in the minds of a pathetic defendant (Richard Attenborough) and his inept lawyer (Peter). Based on John Mortimer's play, the film takes place in a prison holding cell, with several flashbacks and flash-forwards breaking up the deliberate claustrophobia. Wilfrid Morgenhall, the barrister assigned to the hopeless case of Herbert Fowle, uses his creative intellect to imagine ways of getting his client off the hook; the client, meanwhile, is a pitiful sap who did, indeed, kill his indefatigably laughing wife (Beryl Reid, in flashback). David Lodge plays, of all things, a lodger; the twist is that Fowle kills his wife not because she launched an affair with the lodger but because she didn't.

As always, Peter required a vocal hook into his character. Mortimer dined with him just before shooting began and found Peter to be "desperately uncertain" about his performance of Morgenhall. Then a plate of cockles arrived at their table. Memories flowed; the little mollusks cast Peter into a disastrous lost-time reverie of a youthful visit to Morecambe on the Lancashire coast. The cockles, Mortimer was horrified to witness, "brought a faded north-country accent and the suggestion of a scrappy mustache. He felt he had been thrown the lifeline of a voice and work could begin."

Mortimer was appalled because the character he'd written was not from the North, did not speak with a Lancashire twang, and bore no scrappy mustache. "It took a great deal of patience and tact by the director, James Hill, to undo the effect of the cockles." (There *is* a mustache on Morgenhall's lip, but it's a trim, linear number tinged with gray.)

Mortimer also claims that Peter told him that he feared for his safety. The Mafia was after him. Sophia.

• • •

Work might have provided some steadiness, but it did not. It was merely constant.

In *The Wrong Arm of the Law* (1962), Peter played opposite Nanette Newman, the glamorous, almond-eyed wife of Peter's war buddy, Bryan Forbes. "I want to marry Nanette," Peter confided to Forbes one day. Taking Forbes aside, he admitted to his old friend that he hadn't broached the subject with Nanette herself, but his attitude on this point was one of forthright honesty. He wanted to clear it with Bryan first; it was a matter of fair play.

"The scene had taken on the characteristics of a Pinter play," Forbes later wrote. "But I knew it would be a mistake to appear outraged or to mock him: that was not the way to handle Peter." So Forbes simply proceeded with the conversation, adopting the same patient, solicitous tone that Peter was employing. Bryan Forbes was one of those who sympathized with Peter's nature: "He was so patently sincere and desperate to do the right thing according to his unique code of ethics."

FORBES: Of course there's the children to take into account.

SELLERS: You'd always be able to see them. . . . You're not angry, are you?

When Nanette Newman learned of her imminent divorce and remarriage, she gently convinced Peter that *any* intimate relationship with him was impossible, let alone marriage. According to Forbes, "On two occasions he bought a gun and threatened suicide, and both times Nanette somehow calmed him and talked him out of it."

And remarkably, work continued. In *The Wrong Arm of the Law*, Peter greets us as a couturier wearing a smoking jacket collared in silver quilt; he's also adorned with a precise, thin mustache and a pronounced French accent. "Exquiseet! Byeautiful!" Monsieur Jules cries as he flounces a bride-to-be's poofy net veil. "I weesh you every 'appiness," he purrs as he kisses the bride's hand in a manner *très Continental*, "and my felicitations to the, uh [his eyebrows arch], *greum*." Monsieur Jules swiftly devolves into lower-class London when the buyers leave. The fashion house is a front; he's actually the criminal "Pearly" Gates.

The cops are onto him. An officer played by Lionel Jeffries conveys the news in a scene of dueling accents:

JEFFRIES: Well gor bilmey, it's "Pearly" Gates!

SELLERS: I'm delighted to meet you, but there mus' be some meestek! My nem is Sharls Jewlz.

JEFFRIES: Oh don't gimme that. When I took you in in 1948 you was "Pearly" Gates, an' "Pearly" Gates you'll always be.

SELLERS: Inspecteur, 1948 was a long time ageu. Theengs shenge.

JEFFRIES: Look, mite, jus' 'cause you sell a few women's frocks in the West End it does not mean to say that things change.

SELLERS: [Enraged, and thus reverting to Pearly-speak]: I do not sell "women's frocks" in the West End. I sell *gowns, mite*."

The Wrong Arm of the Law opened in the United Kingdom in March 1963, and in New York the following month. What's most curious about the film is not its gimmick (because a rival gang of Australian crooks dresses up as cops and steals from "Pearly," "Pearly" teams up with the real cops), nor the fact that the film was cowritten by several of the writers of *Idiot Weekly, Price 2d* (Ray Galton, Alan Simpson, and John Antrobus), but this:

At this point in his career, Peter was attracting directors of the stature of Stanley Kubrick, not to mention the Boultings and Anthony Asquith, and still he ended up taking on another role in a another small-scale movie made by a competent but undistinguished director (Cliff Owen).

Why wasn't an actor of Peter's caliber more discerning? For one thing, he liked money. He certainly wasn't born to it, and he enjoyed his wealth. But financial desire (to the unsympathetic, the word would be *greed*) seems secondary to the emotional gratification he seized from the roles into which he threw himself. Work was essential, it was sport; work was a necessary distraction, *it was simply what he did.* Performing filled him in a way the rest of the world could not. Without constant filming and recording, Peter Sellers was simply unable to stand it.

• • •

Naturally, he found his way to Hollywood. After *Waltz of the Toreadors* opened in London in mid-April, Peter embarked on his first trip to Los Angeles, with a weeklong stopover in New York on the way. There was also a brief side trip to Washington.

In New York, he received his many supplicant flacks and hacks in a Hampshire House suite. He had much to report. Larry had offered him the Shakespeare role, after all; his car collection made its prolix appearance; he had no personality of his own; he was quite boring, really; and so on. He was a heavy smoker, readers learned. His cigarettes were described as "oversized," the normal length apparently not able to provide the necessary jolt. And he told the *New York Times* of his experiences in Burma during World War II: "As a corporal I had the completely unglamorous job of arming up fighter planes with shells and bombs." *A corporal?* When Peter Sellers was in Burma—briefly—he was drumming and telling jokes.

With *Lolita* about to open, Peter announced to the public that he wasn't happy with it. And he was particularly nervous about how his American accent would come off to Americans.

But he seemed giddy with the imminent prospect of Tinseltown: "I can't wait to see Hollywood! It may sound a bit silly, but I almost feel I'd like to have an autograph book along." He actually did take one.

• • •

On Friday, April 27, at the annual black-tie White House Press Dinner at Washington's Sheraton-Park Hotel, Peter Sellers of North London and

Ilfracombe met John F. Kennedy of the White House and Hyannisport as well as Harold Macmillan of 10 Downing Street. Kennedy and Sellers impressed each other; Macmillan's response remains less clear.

Benny Goodman, Elliott Reid, Bob Fosse and Gwen Verdon (who performed bits from *Damn Yankees*), and Peter provided the evening's entertainment. Among the fifteen hundred guests were Vice President Lyndon Johnson, Chief Justice Earl Warren, seven Cabinet members, the entire White House press corps, and enough British reporters to cover any little scandal that might helpfully occur. Elliott Reid did his impersonation of Kennedy. Peter began by announcing that he never consciously tried to be funny, after which he did a hilarious impression of Macmillan.

Responding with characteristic warmth and laughter, Kennedy, who had recently ripped into the American steel industry for raising prices, said of Sellers and Reid (whose impersonation consisted of Kennedy ripping into the steel industry), "I've arranged for them to appear next week on the U.S. Steel Hour." Kennedy then clarified the issue for the crowd: "Actually, I didn't do it. Bobby did it."

But with Peter's Macmillan imitation, the British press got its scandal. It was not newsworthy for an American comedian to mimic his president's distinctive Bostonian accent; everyone in America was doing it. And Kennedy, as his friend and aide Ted Sorensen recalls, "loved to laugh." But a British half-Jew mocking his conservative prime minister's patrician voice—to the prime minister's face—was apparently unconscionable. Hungrily, British newspaper reporters forced Peter to justify himself.

In the first place, he said, *they* had asked *him*. "The Office of the prime minister called me in London," Peter explained under pressure, "and I told them they wanted Mort Sahl. I'm no stand-up comic. They insisted, and I finally agreed to do five minutes of mild political joking, on the condition I could have my picture taken with the leaders.

"*He* was on home ground," Peter said, referring to Elliott Reid. "And he knew already how much the President enjoyed his take-off." Sellers went on to explain that he'd met Macmillan at the reception before the dinner and that Macmillan told him to go ahead and do it. "Don't forget," the prime minister told the comedian—"No holds barred." "So I barred no holds," said Peter. "And Mr. Macmillan took it as sportingly as President Kennedy took the Elliott Reid skit." If only the British press had been as sporting.

For his part, JFK told Sellers that he'd loved several of his films, though

Sellers didn't want to bring up the subject of *Lolita*'s looming release, apparently for fear of offending Kennedy by mentioning a sex story.

• • •

Three days later Peter Sellers was in Hollywood, lunching with an MGM executive on the Culver City lot in the afternoon and dining with the director Billy Wilder in Beverly Hills at Chasens that night.

Offers were already pouring in. For example, they wanted him for *Peter Pan*. George Cukor would direct.

If it hadn't been for his body, about which he could only do so much, Peter Sellers would not have made a bad Peter Pan. But in this proposed production the role of Peter was to go to Audrey Hepburn, with Peter as Captain Hook. Hayley Mills would be Wendy.

As with most business in Hollywood, there was a lot of buzz and very little action, and Peter found it frustrating. "I know it's exciting to have an idea," he told a reporter some months later, "but it's more exciting to have a screenplay. Take *Peter Pan*. All I've ever done is to say I like the idea of playing Captain Hook, but I've never even seen a script, and everybody seems to think it's all set up. And it isn't."

It turned out to be the fault of the Great Ormond Street Hospital for Sick Children in disharmonious concert with the Walt Disney Company. Peter Pan's creator, the playwright James Barrie, had left the rights to the play to the hospital. Disney wished to make the film on its own terms. Thus did Sick Children wage war against the mouse, and by the fall of 1962 the project was in full collapse.

• • •

Billy Wilder had more luck than George Cukor. At first.

Producers were practically dumping scripts on Peter's doorstep during his stay in Hollywood, but very few of them caught his attention. Wilder's idea did, however, as did Wilder himself. It was to be an adultery comedy, and it would be directed by the acerbic and blazingly funny writer-director of such films as *Double Indemnity* (1944), *The Lost Weekend* (1945), *Sunset Boulevard* (1950), and *Some Like It Hot* (1959). The costars Wilder managed to mention were also enticing. If he accepted the role, Peter was told, he might be playing opposite Marilyn Monroe, Frank Sinatra, and Shirley MacLaine.

Wilder's films generally bore a bitter edge with raunchy undertones, but by the early 1960s, with the Production Code seemingly in full retreat, Wilder was itching to push things a little further. In the new film he was thinking about making, Peter would play an insanely jealous husband. Sinatra would be a Sinatra-like star who gets headaches if he doesn't get laid once a day. MacLaine would be Peter's long-suffering wife. Marilyn would be the local hooker. Irresistible.

The movie wouldn't be filmed right away, however; the as yet untitled comedy wouldn't go before the cameras for at least another year.

Other directors, writers, and producers could scarcely compete with the package of Wilder, Monroe, Sinatra, and MacLaine. Peter turned down twenty-seven other film roles in the first week he spent in Hollywood.

But there was one other idea that interested him: *Ulysses.*

This was neither a joke nor a fabrication: Peter Sellers wanted to play Leopold Bloom. Jerry Wald would produce the picture, Jack Cardiff would direct it. "Bloom could be the ultimate in characterization," Peter told Hedda Hopper. "I have great faith in Jack Cardiff's intuition and good taste, and he can do it if anyone can." Unfortunately, Jerry Wald died of a heart attack two months later.

Peter was upbeat about his trip, but there was a dark foreshadowing. "I shall enjoy working in Hollywood," he told the British scribes upon his return to London, "but I could never *live* there."

• • •

Even in the context of Peter Sellers's previously frenetic work schedule and tension-filled private life, 1962 was ridiculous. The year his marriage collapsed and he was jettisoned out on his own for virtually the first time in his life (David Lodge and others shepherded him through the war), *six* of his films played in the United States: *Only Two Can Play* (which opened in March), *Mr. Topaze* (May), *Lolita* (June), *Road to Hong Kong* (June), *Waltz of the Toreadors* (August), and *Trial and Error* (November). These were accompanied by the personal interlude of Peter and Anne officially announcing their separation in July.

He had an overly spacious den-like penthouse in Hampstead and an office on Panton Street in Soho. He had Bert, Hattie, and two children he saw less and less. He had his cars, the charlatan psychic Maurice Woodruff, a lot of publicity, and an enormous amount of money. He became so depressed that Bert Mortimer, fearing for his boss's life, moved into the penthouse to be at his side all the time. As Bert recalls it, Bryan Forbes and

Nanette Newman used to come over and "hold his hands as he went to sleep."

Forbes is succinct: "In many cases, Peter was, uh, slightly mad, shall we say?"

• • •

Peter was back in New York at the end of September and continued to be starstruck. "Peter Sellers, who claimed to have always 'dreamed' of knowing me, finally arranged a meeting," Myrna Loy wrote in her autobiography. "He took me to Peter Duchin's opening at the Maisonette [at the St. Regis hotel], where he was rather shy and as full of wonder about my career as any fan. He even asked for an autographed picture."

But Peter was himself a star trying to navigate a course toward international superstardom, and the split between shyness and celebrity was becoming nearly impossible for him to sustain. The fault lines scraped more noticeably.

He was getting tired of being hammered by British journalists, who, then as now, enjoyed the moist sensation of blood on their fangs. "The more success you have," he complained, "the more people want to have a go at you in the press. And I just haven't got the confidence to shrug off what is said about me." He was making £150,000 a year, but money itself didn't seem to help.

To be more precise, Peter's wealth didn't help his emotional state. It did, however, aid Harold Pinter. In December, Elizabeth Taylor, Richard Burton, Noel Coward, Leslie Caron, and Peter Sellers announced that they were among the unlikely financiers of Pinter's *The Caretaker* (1962).

Peter spent money on less flashy causes as well. According to Bert Mortimer, he liked to prowl London's parks at night looking for homeless people. When he found an appropriate one, he'd stuff a £5 note in his pocket. Bert witnessed these transactions: "You'd see the man flinch back, thinking he was going to be hit, then fish out the note and stare in utter disbelief at it."

Nothing was simple. For Peter, this type of generosity came at a price. As Kenneth Tynan reported, "Sellers is a self-accusing man who incessantly ponders ethical questions. Once, driving home from the studio, he saw a ragged old woman standing on a street corner, and ordered his car to stop. 'I got out and gave her some money, without telling her who I was. And then, just as I was getting back into the car, I heard myself thinking, "This'll do me good later. This'll make God like me."

" ' "That's wrecked it," I said to myself. "That's absolutely wrecked it." ' "

There was some degree of paranoia involved in Peter's erratic behavior. Peter himself labeled it "intuition."

Roy Boulting remembers that Peter "would keep you up half the night on the telephone, then when you yawned out of sheer fatigue, it would be interpreted as an unfriendly attitude. It got to be a killer, his 'intuition.' "

Maurice Woodruff played right into it, and so, surprisingly, did Dennis Selinger—in secret collaboration with the quack Woodruff. As Selinger later told it, "Maurice used to phone me and say, 'Peter's coming. Is there anything you want me to tell him? Should I say 'yes' or 'no'?" Selinger was only too happy to oblige. This way, *everyone* was happy: Woodruff's bogus predictions turned out to be sound, Peter made responsible career choices, and Selinger got his cut.

• • •

Bill Sellers died in October. He was sixty-two.

"My father died following three coronary attacks," Peter later said, "but it was trouble with his prostate that killed him."

Echoing just about everyone else who knew him, two of Bill's nephews describe their uncle as a shadow man who "wouldn't say boo to a goose." What gives Dick Ray and Ray Marks's observations about their uncle their bite is their follow-up contention: that this was Peter's essential nature as well—half of it, anyway.

According to Dick Ray, Peter took after both of his parents—the aggressive, performing mother and the quiet and aloof father. But then, says Ray, "the minute the camera stopped he'd go back to himself again—"

Ray Marks finishes the sentence: ". . . to Bill Sellers."

• • •

Peter Sellers was asked that year what he saw when he looked into a mirror. His answer: "Someone who has never grown up, a wild sentimentalist, capable of great heights and black, black depths—a person who has no real voice of his own. I'm like a mike—I have no set sound of my own. I pick it up from my surroundings."

And this: "I don't know who Peter Sellers is, except that he's the one who gets paid."

By the end of 1962, Peter had successfully created for himself a public persona based on blank peculiarity. The automobile fixation had become a journalistic cliché, but once in a while Peter would touch on something authentic when discussing his lists of cars. There were two factors behind his obsessive buying and selling of automobiles, he announced: "One is a search for perfection in a machine; the other stems from a great sense of depression at being unable to supply what I know I should be able to deliver." He was himself the best sports car, the finest Rolls, the silkiest limousine, endlessly nicked by a siege of pebbles. Beyond, or behind, or in some way circling around the escalating nuttiness, Peter Sellers did know himself. Sometimes.

But, he immediately declared, everything had just changed.

"*Now* I've finally got what I want," he swore. It was a Bristol 407.

"It's perfect! I didn't know such a car existed! The Bentley Continental wasn't bad for room, for speed. But the 407 combines *everything*."

M eanwhile, in Hollywood, the screenwriter Maurice Richlin was shopping for a collaborator. He approached Blake Edwards. "I have an
idea about a detective who is trying to catch a jewel thief who is having an
affair with his wife," Richlin announced to the director of *Breakfast at
Tiffany's* (1961) and *Days of Wine and Roses* (1962). Together they carved
out a script that featured a variety of gimmicks: two glamorous women, an
urbane leading man, a piece of early sixties vealcake, fashionable European
locales, and a wondrous gem with a tiny flaw. If one looked at it closely,
the jewel would seem to have embedded deep within it the distinct image
of an animal. The director knew one thing for certain: *The Pink Panther*
(1964) would be a perfect vehicle for David Niven.

By late October 1962, casting was completed, financing had been secured from the Mirisch Company, the independent production company
that made such critical and commercial hits as *Some Like It Hot* (1959) and
The Apartment (1960)—both by Billy Wilder—and shooting was ready to
commence at the Cinecittà soundstages in Rome. Niven would be the sophisticated thief, Robert Wagner his handsome playboy nephew. Claudia
Cardinale would be Princess Darla, the owner of the jewel, a curvaceous
but nevertheless deposed ruler of a necessarily vague Eastern sovereignty.
The detective's wife, who would be having the affair with the thief, would
be the striking, one-named Capucine. The detective would be Peter Ustinov. (Brigitte Bardot once claimed to have been offered one of the two
babe roles but turned it down. Ava Gardner may also have been sought,
hired, and swiftly replaced because of her excessive demands.)

Edwards and his team flew to Rome, and Ustinov changed his mind.
He didn't want to be Inspector Clouseau after all. That he waited until
three days before principal photography began wasn't very nice. Blake Edwards was "ready to kill."

"At the very last minute—we were in Rome, we were set to shoot the following Monday, it was Friday—Ustinov said, 'I can't do the movie.' We all said, 'Is there somebody we can recast?' I couldn't think of anybody at that time who could do that sort of thing. [The agent] Freddie Fields said, 'I've got an actor who has a window. You've got to do him in four weeks.' " (Dennis Selinger was not Peter's only agent; he had several working in tandem.) "All I could think of was *I'm All Right, Jack.* In desperation, I said, 'Let's go. We've got to do *something.*' He got off the plane in Rome, we got in the car, drove back from the airport, [and] by the time we got to the hotel Clouseau was born."

Peter himself later claimed to have turned down *The Pink Panther* originally because he hadn't liked the part—"I didn't want anything to do with it"—after which Edwards offered the role to Ustinov. But this account is doubtful. Graham Stark recounts Peter's glee upon landing the part of Clouseau at the eleventh hour: "When he got the first *Panther*, he rang me up like a child—'I've got five weeks in Rome . . . and I'm getting £90,000!' "

• • •

Panther lore abounds. Jacques Clouseau's name is said to have been inspired by the director Henri Georges Clouzot, his demeanor by the maladroit M. Hulot in Jacques Tati's comedies. But there's also the story of Peter, on the airplane to Rome, fishing a book of matches out of his pocket and instantly basing the comportment of his new character on the hero depicted thereon—the mustachioed Capt. Matthew Webb, who, in 1875, had become the first man to swim the English Channel. It makes a good anecdote, but it's not especially convincing, since Peter had been a sucker for a fake mustache since he was a teenager in Ilfracombe.

As for the accent, despite Peter's having done Frenchmen at least since 1945, Blake Edwards declares that it was really *his* invention: "I ran into a French concierge who talked liked this. And he did it for me. And I said, 'We've gotta do it.' "

A better genesis story comes from Max Geldray, who remains convinced that Peter, on the suggestion of Michael Bentine, based Inspector Jacques Clouseau on one of Princess Margaret's hairdressers.

Shooting on *The Pink Panther* commenced on Monday, November 12, 1962, and in a certain sense it continued sporadically for the next sixteen years. And of course it was Sellers rather than Niven who emerged upon the film's release as the key to its charm and popularity. Peter used to claim, not without a certain accuracy, that Clouseau became such a hero because of the character's bedrock dignity in the face of his own buffoonishness. He was specifically reminded of his own teenage years and the loss of his virginity:

"When I was making *The Pink Panther* and playing the accident-prone Inspector Clouseau for the first time, I remembered the embarrassment I'd suffered struggling out of my nightwear so that I could get on with satisfying my barely containable passion. It made a good gag and consolidated the conviction I had about Clouseau that, in all circumstances, whatever boob he'd made, the man must keep his dignity—which gave him a certain pathetic charm that the girls found seductive. It all went back to the frustrations I suffered as a result of a lack of priorities in love-making." Still, one must never forget that Clouseau is first and foremost a moron, and that audiences all over the globe love to laugh at anyone so fiercely idiotic.

Peter took to the role, but then he usually took to the roles he played to an alarming extent. While filming a *Pink Panther* scene on location, an onlooker accosted him. "Aren't you Peter Sellers?" the man asked, to which Peter replied, "Not today."

The Pink Panther's plot, like those of *The Goon Show*, is more or less irrelevant. It concerns a gentleman thief (Niven), whose partner in love and crime (Capucine) happens to be the wife of a hapless Parisian detective (Sellers). A fine gem goes missing in Rome. It belongs to Princess Darla (Claudia Cardinale). She wants it back. The gentleman thief's playboy nephew (Robert Wagner) romances the inspector's wife as well. Everyone goes to Cortina.

What makes *The Pink Panther* work is Edwards's comic style and tone, which is given its most acute embodiment by Peter. Like Spike Milligan, Edwards finds comedy to be profoundly painful, and Peter generally agreed. Edwards had worked with Leo McCarey early in his career, and he credits McCarey—the director of such comedies as *Ruggles of Red Gap* (1935) and *The Awful Truth* (1937)—for teaching him the essential truth that humor can hurt. McCarey had a knack for extending tension-provoking comedy routines way past the audience's initial discomfort. "He called it 'breaking the pain barrier,' " Edwards recalls. Peter Sellers's Inspector Jacques Clouseau may be the pain barrier's apotheosis.

At the same time, Peter's performance in *The Pink Panther* is remarkably restrained. His accent is pronounced but not asinine, his physical comedy likewise. That would come later.

• • •

The Mirisch Company, in association with United Artists, didn't open *The Pink Panther* until February and March 1964 (in Britain and the United States, respectively), whereupon *Time* dismissed it, citing its "pervasive air of desperation," as though Edwards and Sellers's joint comedy style wasn't consciously based on cold despair. "Some of Sellers's sight gags are funny," the critic wrote, "but not funny enough." "A so-so comedy" sniffed the critic for *Cue*. But the Hollywood trade paper *Variety* pegged it correctly: "A vintage record of the farcical Sellers at his peak."

Looking back on it, Robert Wagner attributes Sellers's performance to his disruptive interior life. Sellers was able to achieve so much variety in his art because, as Wagner puts it, he "had such a circus going on within his head."

Blake Edwards is even more succinct: "I think he lived a great part of his life in hell."

• • •

Peter Sellers was at the top of his game, his fame, his taste in projects, and his luck, and he was visibly miserable much of the time, so through the guidance of Harry Secombe, he sought spiritual advice from a priest.

The sanest and best-natured Goon, Secombe was active in the Actors' Church Union and, seeing his old friend in increasing distress, made a point of introducing Peter to Canon John Hester. This priest's particular ministry was to men and women whose shifting identities earned them their daily bread, and still, Peter Sellers presented a special case. "Peter never really settled, and he seemed aware that this was a real problem," Hester later said, referring to Sellers's spiritual life more than to his locale. "He was never baptized, and a lot of our sessions were about the possibility of this happening." (That a Jew would not have been baptized ought to go without saying, so Hester, in his restrained Anglican way, left it unsaid that Peter considered converting to Christianity.)

"He never came very near to settling on any single manifestation of faith," Hester continued. "He was looking in all sorts of directions, just as if he were playing with one of those cameras of his." The baptism failed to occur, then or ever—though another equally sacred Roman Catholic ritual later did—and Peter continued on his unsteady course, ceaselessly seeking and unable to rest.

Peter's theological beliefs resembled his relationships with women. He was a spiritual compulsive whose piety carried with it an attendant poison, the latter bringing about another upsurge of the former. "He made great demands," Peter's priest acknowledged. "Having been your best friend, he could then turn on you and be quite vile. I have some letters from him which are really beastly. He would stab you in the back and then be very penitent."

• • •

He craved the spiritual strength he lacked, and he thought the same should apply to his money. To be "financially impregnable"—that was Peter's goal in the material world.

"If one has money one should spend it wisely," Peter told the Hollywood columnist Sidney Skolsky. "There are things that give me pleasure, and it's only fair to me to lavish them on myself. After all, I've earned the money. I didn't steal it, though a lot of people who have seen my pictures may think so."

He told another eager interviewer, "And only seven years ago, I practically had less pounds in the bank than I had in my body. I got rich by working hard and *not* following Socrates's advice. 'Know thyself.' I couldn't follow it even if I wanted to."

By 1963, he was earning an annual income of £150,000. In order to manage it to its best advantage, his accountant Bill Wills tried once again to enforce an allowance: Wills began doling out Peter's spending money in £20,000 installments, the rest to be stashed in a Swiss account. It was the same system as the £12 per week Wills had given Peter in the old days, but as though on cue, Peter rendered the matter moot by purchasing a seventy-five-foot, £75,000, custom-built yacht. (An American newspaper valued the yacht at $215,000.)

A string of new apartment rentals also cut into Peter's balance sheet. These flats were not for Peter himself but rather for a string of girlfriends. He scarcely wanted to *live* with these young women, after all, but he felt he owed them something for their trouble, and housing seemed a fair trade.

The task of finding and renting these flats fell to Hattie Stevenson. The leases she produced for Peter's signature were inevitably longer than the relationships themselves, some of which lasted but a night or two. There was no pause in this trajectory, no relief, but Peter's luck remained uncanny, for his state of mind, now in constant crisis, found itself coinciding with a film about the end of all human life.

• • •

Stanley Kubrick nursed a morbid interest in thermonuclear war, and like most sane people, he personalized it. In the late 1950s, when he was living on East 10th Street in New York, he well understood that his apartment was located in the heart of one of the world's top three bombing targets, so he contemplated a move to Australia, an unlikely ground zero. Kubrick's fascination with global immolation was further amplified by a novel he considered adapting for the screen. Written by an ex-RAF officer and spy who had become active in the Campaign for Nuclear Disarmament, Peter George's *Red Alert* was the tale of a U.S. Army general who, consumed by suicidal depression, dispatches forty bombers to destroy the Soviet Union. It was not a funny book. (Peter George published *Red Alert* under the pseudonym Peter Bryant; he titled an earlier version *Two Hours to Doom*.)

Kubrick initially worked with George to develop a screenplay, but as he brooded on the basic scenario, his creative intelligence drew him from doomsday thriller to satire. One night, he and his producer, James B. Harris, just couldn't help themselves: they dreamt up comedy scenes involving the practicalities of humanity's annihilation. Kubrick himself described a bit of business from their improvisational game: "What would happen in the War Room if everybody's hungry and they want the guy from the deli to come in and a waiter with an apron around him takes the sandwich order?"

Peter George (who committed suicide in 1966 at the age of forty-one) failed to see the humor. So Kubrick asked the cartoonist and playwright Jules Feiffer to take up the script, but that collaboration didn't go very far either. "My idea of an anti-nuclear satire and Stanley's were miles apart," Feiffer said later.

In December 1962, Kubrick told the *New York Times* that he and Harris were hard at work on a project with a nuclear theme and that Peter Sellers would star. Sellers, he said, would play "an American college professor who rises to power in sex and politics by becoming a nuclear wise man." They planned to shoot the film mostly on location "here in the East and elsewhere this September." Their new film would have a very long title:

Dr. Strangelove, or: How I Learned to Stop Worrying and Love the Bomb (1964).

The *Times* account seemed simple enough, but behind the scenes it was a more complicated series of deals, breakups, and pleas that brought *Dr. Strangelove* into being. Harris and Kubrick's deal for *Lolita*, which they had forged with Ray Stark and Seven Arts, entailed a commitment from Harris-Kubrick for another film for Seven Arts. But Harris, having worked with Kubrick on *The Killing* (1956), *Paths of Glory* (1957), and *Lolita* by that point, decided to make a break with his colleague and strike out on his own, and the collapse of the partnership brought with it artistic as well as business consequences. It had been Harris who had (re)written the screenplay for *Lolita* in addition to producing the film, and it had been Harris whose like-minded imagination had instigated Kubrick's tilt toward comedy for the nuclear disaster project. And now, with Harris-Kubrick dissolving, the Seven Arts production connection disappeared as well. Columbia Pictures took over *Dr. Strangelove*.

Peter Sellers ended up helping to solve both the artistic and the business problems, though not without putting Kubrick into a bit of a pique in the process. The aesthetic solution occurred because someone had given Peter a copy of a strange and flamboyant novel called *The Magic Christian* by the American writer Terry Southern. (Whether that someone was the satirist Jonathan Miller or the novelist Henry Green is disputed.) Peter, flush with excitement over finding a kindred worldview, began doling out copies as gifts to all of his friends. Kubrick was one of the recipients. Columbia Pictures, meanwhile, was certain that *Lolita* succeeded not because of Stanley Kubrick or James Mason or the film's provocative topic, but because of Peter Sellers and his many masks, and when the studio assumed financial control of *Dr. Strangelove*, it stipulated that Peter not only star in the film but also that he appear in multiple roles. Kubrick got along well with Peter, but he was still annoyed at front-office interference in a decision he considered his alone. "What we are dealing with is film by fiat, film by frenzy!" he fumed.

Terry Southern, meanwhile, had learned that Peter had given a copy of *The Magic Christian* to Kubrick and suggested to his friend George Plimpton, editor of the *Paris Review*, that he, Southern, write a profile of Kubrick for the journal. Or *Atlantic Monthly*. Or maybe *Esquire*. . . . It was an enticing proposal—a great, hip writer profiling a great, hip director, and all three magazines expressed interest. *Esquire* ultimately assigned the piece.

Southern's first interview with Kubrick began on a more or less standard track. But then, as Southern described it, "Somehow or other we get into this rather heavy rap—about *death*, and *infinity*, and *the origin of time*—you know the sort of thing. We never got through with the interview." Something much better than a celebrity profile took its place: "We met a few times, had a few laughs and some groovy rap . . . and then about three months later he called from London and asked me to come over and work on *Strangelove*." Southern said that Kubrick "had thought of the story as 'a straightforward melodrama' until . . . he 'woke up and realized that nuclear war was too outrageous, too fantastic to be treated in any conventional manner.' He said he could only see it now as 'some kind of hideous joke.' "

Complicating matters was the fact that Peter refused to leave England for the duration of the production. Whether it was because of the tension of his divorce, which was finalized in March, or his latest affair—with the British actress and former child star Janette Scott—the result was that Peter wouldn't budge out of Britain. Kubrick thus felt he had to go begging. He's said to have shown up late at night in the lobby of Peter's Hampstead apartment building, where he would simply wait for Peter to arrive from his nights on the town, whereupon the director would spend the early hours of the morning cajoling the partied-out movie star. Peter succumbed to the pressure, in addition to the million dollars (a most significant raise) and the promise to film at Shepperton. Peter also wangled himself a luxury suite in town at the Dorchester for the duration of the shoot. He liked to stay in town after work.

"To me it's like having three different great actors," Kubrick said in response to a *Queen* magazine reporter's question about why he cast Sellers in multiple roles. But there was supposed to have been a fourth and maybe, if one believes Peter, even a fifth. Originally, Sellers was signed to play the President of the United States, Merkin Muffley; the British Group Captain Lionel Mandrake; the eponymous nuclear physicist; and Major T. J. "King" Kong, the whooping Texan who eventually straddles an atom bomb like a broncobuster at the end of the film. But in Sellers's own account, he "was going to do them *all!*"

"Stanley was convinced I could. I could do no wrong, you see. Some days Stanley used to be sitting outside my front door saying, 'What about Buck Schmuck Turgidson [the role played by George C. Scott]? You've *got* to play Buck Schmuck!' And I'd say, 'I physically can't do it! I don't like the role anyway, Stan. And I'll try to do the [Kong] thing, but, I mean, I think that's *enough.*' "

But there was a problem with Kong, too—one that made little sense at the time and makes even less in retrospect. The world's greatest mimic found himself unable to produce the twangy drawl of a Texan. It just wasn't happening.

Because of Peter's long-standing need for a vocal model on which to hang his performance, Kubrick assigned a genuine Texan—Terry Southern, of Alvarado, Johnson County—the task of making a recording of Kong's dialogue. Some time elapsed before Kubrick convinced Peter to listen to the tape, but Sellers eventually appeared for the requested hearing at Kubrick's offices at Shepperton. At that point it was Kubrick's turn to become nutty. When Peter "finally did show up," Southern later wrote, "he had with him the latest state-of-the-art portable tape recorder, specially designed for learning languages. Its ultrasensitive earphones were so oversized they resembled some kind of eccentric hat or space headgear. From the office [Kubrick and Southern] would see Sellers pacing between the lilac bushes, script in hand, his face tiny and obscured beneath his earphones. Kubrick found it a disturbing image. 'Is he kidding?' he said. 'That's exactly the sort of thing that would bring some British heat down for weirdness.'

"I laughed," Southern continued, "but he wasn't joking. He phoned the production manager, Victor Lyndon, right away. 'Listen, Victor,' I heard him say, 'you'd better check out Pete and those earphones. He may be stressing. . . . Well, I think he ought to cool it with the earphones. Yeah, it looks like he's trying to ridicule the BBC or something, know what I'm saying? All we need is to get shut down for a crazy stunt like that. Jesus Christ!' " (In point of fact, Victor Lyndon was the associate producer of *Dr. Strangelove*; Clifton Brandon was the production manager.)

Peter *tried* to do the accent. According to Southern, the first day of shooting consisted of one of Kong's B-52 bomber scenes, and Kubrick was pleased with the results of Peter's performance. But the next day, Kubrick took a phone call from Victor Lyndon. Bad news. Peter had slipped while getting out of a Buick in front of an Indian restaurant on King's Road. A sprained ankle was theorized.

Peter returned to the set that afternoon and filming resumed without incident, but after breaking for tea, Kubrick suddenly altered the shooting schedule. Without warning, he told Peter to climb down two separate ladders into the belly of the plane. Southern witnessed: "Sellers negotiated the first, but coming down the second, at about the fourth rung from the bottom, one of his legs abruptly buckled, and he tumbled and sprawled, in obvious pain, on the unforgiving bomb-bay floor."

The next day Victor Lyndon was once again the bearer of bad tidings. Peter had not only seen his doctor, he'd made his injury known to the men who mattered: "The completion bond people know about Peter's injury and the physical demands of the Major Kong role," Lyndon reported. "They say they'll pull out if he plays the part."

It wasn't as though Peter would actually have had to fall very far, but it was apparently *too* far for the fearful Peter, the prop bomb being poised about ten feet off the floor. "He didn't fancy dropping out on the bomb" is Bert Mortimer's explanation. Hattie Stevenson goes further: "It was *not* a broken ankle, but he still insisted on getting put in a plaster cast so he could get out of the part."

Diagnostics aside, Kubrick needed an actor on short notice. It has been reported that Kubrick approached John Wayne and that Wayne instantly refused. Terry Southern's companion, Gail Gerber, recalls that Southern himself proposed the fat *Bonanza* cowboy, Dan Blocker, who also found *Dr. Strangelove* to be too left-leaning for his taste. Slim Pickens had no such political qualms and, so, at the end of the film, it is Pickens who literally goes down in film history by descending deliriously on the bomb that destroys the planet. But then Pickens became a problem for Peter. Hattie Stevenson claims that Sellers "was infuriated, really frightfully angry that Slim Pickens played the part so well in the end."

• • •

As though a satire about bombing all of humanity to death wasn't grue-some enough, Kubrick brought in as a technical consultant the photogra-pher Weegee, who was known for having taken stark, emotionally charged photographs of an estimated five thousand murder scenes over the course of his grim career. Named Usher Fellig at birth, Weegee moved with his family to New York at the age of ten; officials at Ellis Island changed his name to Arthur. As a photographer, he seemed to be clairvoyant in terms of knowing where crimes had been committed; Weegee often arrived on the scene before the police. Hence his nickname (inspired by the Ouija board). Officially, Weegee's technical consultations involved *Dr. Strange-love*'s periodically harsh, crime-scene–like black-and-white cinematogra-phy, but because he had an unusual accent—German overlaid with New

York, all with a nasal, slightly strangled, back-of-the-throat quality—he inadvertently provided technical assistance for the film's star as well.

"*I vas psychic!,*" Weegee told Peter on the set one day—a conversation Peter was taping for research purposes. "I vould go to a moidah before it vas committed!" Peter's vocal model for Strangelove was Weegee, whom Sellers pushed further into parody.

(Contemporary audiences sometimes assume that Strangelove's accent was based at least in part on Henry Kissinger's, but although Kissinger was one of Kennedy's security advisors, he was not a public figure when *Dr. Strangelove* was made. Kubrick himself denied the association: "I think this is slightly unfair to Kissinger. . . . It was certainly unintentional. Neither Peter nor I had ever seen Kissinger before the film was shot.")

• • •

Principal photography began in January 1963.

"He was harder to reach," Kubrick said of Peter, comparing his friend's demeanor on the set of *Dr. Strangelove* to the already unusual actor with whom he'd made *Lolita*. Sellers would arrive in the morning in what one of Kubrick's biographers, John Baxter, calls a "near-torpor, saying very little, looking depressed, tired, and ill. Only when Kubrick began to set up the cameras—of which he always used at least three for any Sellers scene—did he begin to revive. By the afternoon, coaxed by Kubrick, he would have hit his stride."

"Kubrick is a god as far as I am concerned," Sellers said later.

As with *Lolita*, Kubrick began the making of *Dr. Strangelove* by giving Peter free rein to improvise. Kubrick would then pick out what he liked and build the film accordingly. During one take of a scene with Strangelove, for example, Sellers, without warning, shot his arm in the air and shouted "Heil Hitler!" Sellers recalled the moment: "One day Stanley suggested that I should wear a black glove, which would look rather sinister on a man in a wheelchair. 'Maybe he had some injury in a nuclear experiment of some sort,' Kubrick said. So I put on the black glove and looked at the arm and I suddenly thought, 'Hey, that's a storm-trooper's arm.' So instead of leaving it there looking malignant I gave the arm a life of its own. That arm hated the rest of the body for having made a compromise. That arm was a Nazi."

"I don't think he made up a whole scene that didn't already exist," Kubrick reported, "but he did a bit of embroidery. In the famous phone call to the Russian premier, for instance, he may have added the rueful line, 'Well, how do you think *I* feel, Dimitri?' "

Some of Peter's inventions didn't work, and Kubrick nipped them in the bud. For instance, Peter originally played the obscenely named Merkin Muffley as a limp-wristed clown with a nasal inhaler. That was Peter's inspiration; Kubrick's was to have Muffley rise into place in the War Room on a hydraulic lift. But between the lift and the nasal spray, the cast and crew laughed so hard that Kubrick couldn't get a usable take. Apart from the fact that this single bit wasted an entire afternoon, Kubrick didn't like the broadness of Sellers's performance in it. In the director's vision of the character, Muffley should have been the only sane person in the room, and so the lift and the inhaler were cut and the scene reworked. This time, an American political figure did strongly influence the characterization: Muffley is a parody of Adlai Stevenson, a bland intellectual nominally in command of a gang of military madmen.

Peter embraced the new Muffley so fully that Hattie Stevenson couldn't even identify her own boss under his makeup: "I shall never forget while he was making *Dr. Strangelove*, he asked me to pop down to the studios with some letters. I walked onto the set—the very lavish one they had when he was playing the bald-headed president—they had just broken for lunch—and I walked straight past him. Having worked for him for two or three years, I didn't even recognize him."

The War Room set to which Stevenson refers was designed by Ken Adam, the art director responsible for the looks of such disparate but equally eye-catching films as *Around the World in 80 Days* (1956), *Curse of the Demon* (1957), and *Dr. No* (1962). Adam supervised its construction in Shepperton's Stage B: Twelve-hundred square meters of polished black flooring; a massive circular table, also black; a demonic halo of a chandelier suspended above the table; and a looming map of the world, with tiny lightbulbs representing centers of human population. Complementing Adam's design were the actors' dark, nearly identical military costumes (plus Muffley's *schvach* dark suit), all made in wool. Unseen by the spectator are the felt overshoes everyone wore to protect Adam's immaculate jet-black floor. It was all very warm.

The War Room is graced by banquet tables full of food, including a seemingly endless parade of custard pies. In Kubrick's vision, this was the way the world would end, not only with a bang but with slapstick. The original concluding scene of *Dr. Strangelove*:

With all hope lost, Strangelove, having fallen out of his wheelchair, rolls around on the lustrous black floor while President Muffley demands a search of the Soviet Ambassador DeSadesky's body cavities—"in view of the tininess of your equipment." "The seven bodily orifices!" Buck Turgidson cries, whereupon George C. Scott points directly at the camera—it's a point-of-view shot taken from DeSadesky's perspective. Buck ducks, causing the President of the United States to be struck by a pie. Muffley collapses into Turgidson's arms, a modern Pietà.

Turgidson: "Mr. President! Mr. President! [No response.] Gentlemen, our beloved president has just been infamously struck down by a pie in the prime of life! Are we going to let that happen? *Massive retaliation!*"

In jittery fast-motion, everyone in the War Room begins to hurl cream pies, all to the tune of hopped-up silent-movie music. Great globs of white custard cover the floor; Buck skids on it. The huge round chandelier swings as men climb on top of the conference table. Kubrick includes a tracking shot of a line of men ending with Buck atop somebody's shoulders; you can see him stuff a handful of pie into his mouth between throws. A subsequent master shot of the room makes the brilliantly lit table look like a boxing ring.

Suddenly, a gunshot. It's Strangelove firing into the air. Kubrick cuts to a high angle shot. Strangelove: "Gentlemen! Ve must stop zis childish game! There is verk—*verk!*—to do!"

Kubrick then cuts to a high angle shot of a physically recovered but mentally stricken Muffley sitting on the floor opposite De Sadesky amid a lunar landscape of custard, craters, and crust. Drenched in it, they're happily building meringue mudpies and sandcastles. Kubrick cranes down to floor level to watch them play at closer range; the president destroys his own castle.

Strangelove speaks: "Zis is regretable, but I think their minds have snepped from the strain!" Peter bites down on every word: "Perhaps they Vill Heff To Be In-Stit-Utiona-Lized!" Buck Turgidson responds by calling for a three-cheer salute to Strangelove, at which point Kubrick brings Vera Lynn onto the sound track. She's singing the World War II chestnut "We'll Meet Again."

• • •

George C. Scott later claimed that they'd "shot a thousand pies a day for a week"; one of Kubrick's biographers, Vincent LoBrutto, doubles both figures. Terry Southern remembered it differently: "The studio representatives, who were skeptical of the scene all along, had been excruciatingly clear about the matter: 'We're talkin' one take. One take and you're outta here, even if you only got shit in the can!' "

Whatever actually occurred, it didn't matter, because Kubrick cut the sequence. "It was too farcical and not consistent with the satiric tone of the rest of the film," he later explained.

Southern believed that this was because the characters were enjoying themselves too much: "He [Kubrick] believed that watching people have fun is never funny." (Even in the final cut of *Dr. Strangelove*, Peter Bull, who plays De Sadesky, cracks up onscreen during one of Peter's gestures. Bull remains embarrassed about his inability to keep a straight face, "grinning in an obvious and inane way. [It] makes me blush to think of it.")

As far as the custard pie sequence is concerned, Kubrick was right; it doesn't work. History also intervened in the cutting of the legendary, supposedly lost sequence. (It exists in the archives of the British Film Institute.) Test screenings of *Dr. Strangelove, or: How I Learned to Stop Worrying and Love the Bomb* were conducted in late November 1963. Given the artistic failure of the sequence, the question of whether it took the assassination of President Kennedy to cause the sequence to be deleted is irrelevant.

• • •

With *Dr. Strangelove*, Peter Sellers achieved genius once again. His three characters are variegated, complex, and refined. He effaces himself as an actor, but not completely; he invites his audience to appreciate his performance as a stylistic tour de force, but he doesn't issue the invitation hammily. He lets his characters speak for themselves, and yet they do so with Sellers's unique panache.

He gives Mandrake that slight British slack-jaw quality, ending each of his sentences with his mouth left slightly agape, perhaps in expectation of receiving a further command that would require a dutiful response. He's got the unflappable politesse of a seasoned British military officer, one who, facing atomic holocaust, responds in unflappable kind. He is above all an Englishman.

Muffley is an unnaturally placid, somewhat indigestive-looking middle-aged man with a flat, indistinguishable American accent and little hair. He's intelligent—perhaps too much so for the job. The nasal inhaler routine is reduced to a faint sniffle, which Muffley dabs methodically with a hanky. One of the most remarkable aspects of the performance is that Kubrick's camera keeps catching Muffley with an eerily neutral expression on his face. It's not Sellers in plain repose; it's a precisely studied lack of affect, the elimination of emotion without the simultaneous expulsion of intellect.

Time ticks by, but Muffley remains on his imperturbable course. He's on the phone with Kisoff, the Soviet premier:

"Fine, I can hear you now, Dimitri—clear and plain and coming through fine. I'm coming through fine, too, then? Fine. Well then, as you say, we're both coming through fine. Good. Well then it's good that you're fine and, and I'm fine. I agree with you. It's great to be fine. [At this point even Muffley grows a bit frustrated and launches into a slightly sickly sing-song tone in an attempt to steer the drunken Kisoff to the matter at hand.] Well then Dimitri. You know how we've always talked about something going wrong with the bomb? [Pause.] The bomb, Dimitri. [Pause.] The *hydrogen* bomb."

But it's the grimace-grinning Strangelove who steals the show, for obvious reasons. Beyond his ghastly German accent, which transcends imitation no matter how often it has been imitated, Peter Sellers achieves pure grotesquerie on the level of physicality and intelligence combined. With his persistent baring of teeth while holding his lips rigid, Strangelove's mouth is a leering, terrifying rictus, and everything that comes out of it is infected. With a high-pitched nasality, he spits nothing but contempt for the self-evidently lower-functioning brains of his so-called peers in the War Room. And yet he cannot master his own right arm, which flails or goes rigid on its own schedule. He bites it; it keeps coming. It tries to strangle him. At one point it drops to the side, seemingly lifeless, at which point he begins frantically beating on it with his left hand, attempting beyond all reason to revive the monstrous thing—an improvised gesture.

It is this that causes Peter Bull, standing to Peter's right, to break out into unrestrained laughter. Kubrick found Peter's raw spontaneity more important than a background actor's giggle, so he used that take rather than reshooting it.

· · ·

Dr. Strangelove ends with a miracle. Peter, as the brilliant but decrepit Strangelove, a technical genius but not a whole man, rises out of his wheelchair and hobbles stiffly across the shiny floor. It's shot low-angle, like an aggrandizing ad for a crippled children's hospital, except, of course, that the angle is aggrandizing a madman and the world is blowing up.

"Mein Fuehrer! *I can walk!*" Cue Vera Lynne as a montage of mushroom clouds fills the screen.

THIRTEEN

"How do you know I'm mad?" said Alice.
"You must be," said the Cat,
"or you wouldn't have come here."

The Hollywood gossip columnist and former actress Hedda Hopper had several items to report about Peter Sellers in 1963. Sarah and Michael had accompanied him on a trip to Hollywood in early summer, and he'd taken them to all three of the region's major amusement parks—Disneyland, Marineland, and Knott's Berry Farm. "The recently divorced Peter took out some glamour girls at night," Hopper noted, "but he says it's nothing serious." Peter had become quite the swinging single, and he finally had the body to go with the image. He weighed 158 pounds, down from his all-time high of 210.

On the professional front, Hopper and others reported that a *second* Billy Wilder project had found its way onto Peter Sellers's horizon. Wilder had purchased the rights to the Sherlock Holmes characters from the estate of Arthur Conan Doyle, the scribes revealed, and he planned to write and direct a new Holmes film. Peter O'Toole was to be Sherlock, Peter Sellers Watson.

He recorded a new comedy album, *Fool Britannia*, with Anthony Newley and Joan Collins; it was a warped-from-the-headlines satire of the Profumo sex scandal—involving John Profumo, the British Secretary of State for War; Eugene Ivanov, the Soviet Assistant Naval Attaché and spy; and Christine Keeler, the showgirl they shared—that rocked Britain that year.

The *Telegoons* arrived on British television in the fall of 1963—a puppet version of the radio series, with Peter, Harry, and Secombe providing the voices.

The director Jules Dassin offered him the lead role in his lavish heist comedy *Topkapi*, but when Peter learned that Maximilian Schell was being considered for the picture as well, he turned Dassin down. It makes little sense, but Schell and Sophia had costarred in a film already, and that apparently made Peter's participation in *Topkapi* impossible. So Peter Ustinov took the role.

Robert Aldrich considered making a film version of *Brouhaha*, of all things—with Peter, perhaps needless to say, in the leading role—but production delays on Aldrich's *Hush, Hush, Sweet Charlotte* stalled the project permanently.

The comedy writer S. J. Perelman met with Peter and Harvey Orkin, one of his several agents; Perelman tried to persuade Peter to play all of the major roles in a film version of his play *The Beauty Part*—Bert Lahr had played them onstage—but Peter seems not to have been interested, and the film was never made.

And the entertainment writer Joe Hyams told Elke Sommer that he had struck a deal with Peter to write his life story. But the deal fell apart and the book was never written.

• • •

In addition to the Los Angeles trip, Peter spirited his kids away on flash vacations, making up his mind suddenly and tearing into whatever new locale he'd chosen with a frenzy. As Bert Mortimer rather too colorfully put it, "for the first few days he'd rape the place."

Bert was given the job of taking family pictures, but Peter would soon grow bored and go off on his own, leaving the children in the care of Bert and Hattie. "He wanted the photos to establish that he'd had children," said Bert, "and was capable of playing the father to them the way fathers are supposed to do. The sad thing was, children really didn't interest him at all."

With Peter out of town so often, the task of accompanying Peg on shopping trips in her brand new Bentley fell to Hattie Stevenson. "Go and spend what you like, my darling," Peter told his mother, and "have it all charged to me." Off Peg went.

"I'm Peter Sellers's mother," she would proclaim upon entering any given shop. "And I want *the best*."

• • •

In the Boultings' *Heavens Above* (1963), Peg's son played a priest.

The Rev. John Smallwood (Peter) is appointed to the position of vicar at Holy Trinity in the parish of Orbiston Parva, a factory town dominated by the Despards, an old industrialist family. (They make "Tranquilax," a popular sedative, stimulant, and laxative.) He pays visits to the locals to discuss the residents' spiritual lives and finds that they have none. His first sermon is direct on this point: "This town is full of people who call themselves 'Christian,' but from what I've seen of it, I wouldn't mind taking a bet there aren't enough *real* Christians about to feed one decent lion." While constructing his character, Sellers once said, he stood in front of a mirror and suddenly realized that he was Brother Cornelius, his old teacher at St. Aloysius: "The Jewish boy knows his catechism better than the rest of you!"

A squatter camp spreads its dingy self just outside the windows of the Tranquilax offices; Irene Handl plays the queen of the dump. At Smallwood's behest, the squatters move—to the grounds of the church. To the entrenched vestry's dismay, he brings in a black man, a Caribbean immigrant, as the new vicar's warden. He piles outrage upon outrage, and yet the vicar begins to have an effect upon Lady Despard, who, seeing the light of mercy and charity for the first time in her life, abruptly spurs the establishment of a church food bank. But like Ian Carmichael's character in *I'm All Right, Jack*, Smallwood only succeeds in provoking chaos.

As it happens, they've got the wrong John Smallwood; the real one (Ian Carmichael), shows up later, suitably complacent and patrician.

Peter's is a muted performance—priestly sincerity dusted with a thin veneer of a skilled actor's sardonic calculation, a balanced response on Sellers's part to what is at its Boulting-brothers core a cynical social comedy. Once again, the Boultings gently rib the rich, including the Church, and save their bitter wrath to shower on the ignorant poor. Then again, when the good people of Orbison Parva beat the Rev. Smallwood to a pulp at the end of *Heaven's Above*, the crowd does appear to cross all class lines.

• • •

The World of Henry Orient (1964) took Peter back to New York for several weeks of shooting in July and August 1963. Written by Nunnally Johnson and his daughter, Nora Johnson, and directed by George Roy Hill, *Henry Orient* concerns a pianist, not of the highest rank, and his absurd encounters with two Upper East Side schoolgirls (played by Tippy Walker and Merrie Spaeth), who find him dreamy. Budgeted at $2 million, *The World of Henry*

Orient was, according to the *Times*, the most expensive movie ever filmed in New York.

Johnson, a longtime Hollywood screenwriter, was unhappy with Peter's casting as Henry; Johnson wanted Rex Harrison. According to George Roy Hill, the filmmakers had Oscar Levant in mind as the model for Henry, but that's most unfair to Levant, who was extraordinarily witty, urbane, and depressed, whereas Henry Orient is an unadulterated fool whose erotic interest lies in some unseen guy's neurotic wife (Paula Prentiss). In any event, Peter concocted one of his most bizarre voices for Henry. As he described it, "He has a dreadful Brooklynese accent, but in an attempt to appear cultured and charming, he hides it with a phony French accent." One critic described the result as "a cross between Rocky Graziano, Liberace, and Charles Boyer," an assessment that lands not far off the mark. ("Shut the door" comes out "Shu' de doerr.") Adding to the voice's complexity is its instability; Henry keeps slipping out of it, and as such he's one of Peter's most openly fragmented creations.

(Just to note: Nunnally Johnson's credits include the adaptation of John Steinbeck's novel *The Grapes of Wrath*, 1940, for John Ford; Fritz Lang's *The Woman in the Window*, 1944; and *The Three Faces of Eve*, 1959, which he directed. George Roy Hill went on to direct such hits as *Butch Cassidy and the Sundance Kid*, 1969, and *The Sting*, 1973. And Oscar Levant was not from Brooklyn; he was from Pittsburgh.)

Nora Johnson's initial reaction to Peter's performance was to be "jarred to the roots," though when she saw *Henry Orient* again many years later, she was "no longer jarred . . . it had somehow blended like old wine."

• • •

During a location shoot on East 64th Street, the cameras and klieg lights drew a crowd. A New York City cop grew so weary of the many bystanders asking him what they were filming that he told one, "*Guadalcanal Diary*, lady."

For the most part, Peter remained serenely above the fray in his trailer drinking vodka and tonics and waiting to be called. He took the opportunity to show off his wardrobe for a reporter: the bright red lining of Orient's houndstooth jacket, his gold karate pants, his opera cape, his blue, custom-made Tillinger shirts with the initials HO embroidered on the cuffs. "This role will do great things for my image," Peter remarked.

Although Sellers brings star power to *The World of Henry Orient*, his role is surprisingly small. The Johnsons' script originally contained a strange coda: Henry ends up playing the piano in a whorehouse. It had been written, in Nunnally Johnson's words, in case "more exposure was needed to keep Sellers happy." But George Roy Hill excised it from the script before filming even began. But even *with* the coda the film would still have belonged to the two girls; the primary story would have remained theirs. Henry himself provides only a subplot.

Still, perhaps as part of the predictable backlash against a prolific star, many reviewers made a point of claiming that Merrie Spaeth and Tippy Walker "steal" the film away from Peter, who, owing to the script itself, had already ceded it to them. What with his accent and disagreeable character, it's a strange, high stakes–gambling performance on Peter's part, a fact the director didn't seem to respect enough. George Roy Hill told the press when the film was released in February 1964, that "Sellers, for all his experience, actually comes off second best now and then due to these two kids," an attitude that scarcely endeared him to Peter, who flatly refused to work with him ever again.

• • •

Peter's offscreen life during the production of *The World of Henry Orient* featured its own sad little comedy or two. Shortly after arriving in New York, Peter received a fan letter. It was from a blond girl. She enclosed a close-up of herself along with her note, and Peter quickly contacted her and invited her to join him.

Peter accompanied Bert and Hattie to the airport to pick her up, but just before she stepped off the plane he made sure to hide himself behind a pillar so he could give the thumbs-up (or -down) signal to his factotums. The fat girl emerged and was instantly vetoed.

He couldn't very well send her back on the next plane, could he? So Bert and Hattie took her to a hotel in midtown Manhattan—though emphatically *not* the Plaza, which was where *he* was staying. They kept her sequestered there for a few days before telling her that, really, she might think about shedding a few pounds before meeting Mr. Sellers. Then Peter telephoned her himself and advised her of what he considered to be an acceptable weight, all this while attempting—and failing—to romance his happily married costar, Angela Lansbury, who plays the mother of one of the girls.

For three weeks he kept the girl waiting and dieting. Supposedly she lost thirty pounds, at which point Peter presented her with an engagement ring—in absentia, of course. Eventually he grew bored with the situation and sent the girl home, richer and thinner, never having met her face to face.

Of much more interest were the contestants in the Miss Universe pageant held in Miami Beach, where Peter served as one of the judges. Indeed, the playboy Sellers appeared to be turning the judging of beauty contests into something of a sustained hobby; a few months later he worked the Miss World pageant at the Lyceum Ballroom in London.

• • •

He bought another estate—Brookfield, located in Elstead, Surrey. (Surrey is just southwest of London.) It was his first adult home south of London; even with the out-there Chipperfield, Peter kept his geographical bearings secure. Apart from the fact that the Hampstead penthouse obviously had been contaminated by Ted Levy, Peter simply felt the familiar urge for newness. This time, it took the form of a fifteenth-century redbrick house with stone floors, lead-latticed windows, and thick-beamed ceilings. In place of Hampstead's rosewood walls and leather-paneled window treatments came inglenooks. There was a lake, some paddocks, and a walled garden. There were several barns, one of which Peter turned into a gymnasium in one part and a movie theater with a retractable screen in the other. In the yard he kept a donkey. Its name was Fred.

Peter was thirty-eight. He weighed less than ever, smoked three packs of cigarettes a day, and popped a variety of prescription drugs to combat frequent insomnia and depression. "I was getting into the pill area in a big way," he later admitted. At the time, the movie star described his experience of life starkly: "ghostly and unreal" were the words he used.

• • •

Peter Sellers was always going to be the star of *A Shot in the Dark* (1964), but Clouseau, surprisingly, was something of an afterthought. The Mirisch brothers—Harold, Walter, and Marvin—owned the rights to Harry Kurnitz's one-set, dialogue-heavy stage play, which was itself an adaptation of a French play by Marcel Achard. With *The Pink Panther* safely in the can after a smooth production, they signed Peter to play the lead—a French magistrate leading a pretrial murder investigation. Anatole Litvak would direct.

But Peter found Litvak to be uninspiring, as have many film critics over the years, and he threatened to quit. (To be fair to Litvak, he did direct some good pictures in his long and commercially successful career, among them *Sorry, Wrong Number* and *The Snake Pit*, both released in 1948.) So to keep their star happy, the Mirisches fired Litvak and brought in Blake Edwards, who already had a multifilm contract with their company. Edwards then hired a new writer, William Peter Blatty, and together they turned *A Shot in the Dark* into a Clouseau comedy. In the process, two actors dropped out—Walter Matthau and, of all people, Sophia Loren.

And yet, despite all the preproduction commotion, *A Shot in the Dark* turned out to be a much finer film than *The Pink Panther*. On the narrative level, the stakes are higher. People die. And they die just as Clouseau's level of competence sinks even lower. From the fluid, carefully orchestrated pre-credits sequence to the equally calibrated interrogation scene at the end, *A Shot in the Dark* is one of the richest, most fully realized films of Peter's career.

Elke Sommer is Maria Gambrelli, the maid accused of shooting the chauffeur. George Sanders is Maria's employer, Benjamin Ballon. For the role of Chief Inspector Dreyfus, whom Clouseau's incompetence drives insane, Edwards chose Herbert Lom. And as was often the case, Peter suggested his best friends for two of the smaller roles: Graham Stark would be Clouseau's laconic assistant, Hercule, and David Lodge would show up briefly as a gardener. Shooting took place between November 1963 and January 1964 at Shepperton, and once again, Peter got the best suite at the Dorchester for the duration of the production as part of his lucrative deal.

A Shot in the Dark presents the first roll-out of Clouseau's many signature disguises, none of which works for the purpose of disguising him; he's the easily identifiable balloon seller standing outside the jail when Maria Gambrelli is released from custody. When she's released a second time, there's Toulouse-Lautrec kneeling on the sidewalk. In similar fashion, *A Shot in the Dark*'s broad physical comedy only barely disguises the fact that, like *The Goon Show*, the movie is an essentially philosophical enterprise. The film historians Peter Lehman and William Luhr get it right when they point out that "reason is likely to be not a guiding light but a Judas goat" in the *Pink Panther* films. Clouseau, they write, "exudes logical disconnectedness," a paradox that calls into question the basic assumptions of civilization. For these clever critics, Clouseau is a ceaselessly disintegrating protagonist, a character much more in synch with the absurdity of late twentieth-century life than anyone else. That's how he's able to continue functioning in the face of an unending series of calamities.

As an example of what Lehman and Luhr call Clouseau's merely "vestigial" rationality, they cite the sequence from *A Shot in the Dark* in which "instead of walking through a doorway, he walks behind the door into a wall [and] attempts to regain the dignity he never had by declaring that the architect should be investigated."

The servant Maurice, responding to Maria Gambrelli's claim of innocence, utters the word "ridiculous." This sets Clouseau off. It is *he* who is necessarily the arbiter of postmodern incoherence:

"*I* will decide what is ridiculous! I believe everything. I believe nothing. I suspect everyone, and I suspect no one. I gather the facts"—he is examining a jar of cold cream at close range and places it to his nose—"I examine the clues"—his nose emerges with a white tip, and—"Before you know it, the case is seulved."

Told by Maria Gambrelli that he should get out of his wet clothes because he'll catch his death of pneumonia—he has made his entrance by falling into a fountain—Clouseau responds with resignation: "Yes, I probably will. But it's all part of life's rich pageant, you know." (Many years later, this line inspired the title of an R.E.M. album.)

Soon afterward, he sets his trenchcoat on fire. "Your coat!" Maria cries. "Yes," says Clouseau, "it *is* my coat."

He trails her to a rustic summer camp. Despite the fact that everyone he sees is completely undressed, Clouseau cannot comprehend what he sees and must be specifically instructed by a guitar-strumming naked man, "This is a nudist colony!" (The naked man is played by Peter's friend Bryan Forbes, credited pseudonymously as "Turk Thrust.") Clouseau jumps backward in shock and alarm. "A *nudist* colony?!" he cries, appalled. He emerges a few moments later stark naked, holding the guitar as his fig leaf, and immediately encounters an absurd nudist orchestra absurdly playing "Theme from *A Shot in the Dark*" by Henry Mancini.

Moments later, language itself loses its logical foundation and devolves into a series of Goon-like sounds when Clouseau comes upon what he sees as a slumbering nudist. Maria calls to him from the bushes:

"That's Dudu!"
"Dudu?"
"She's dead!"

"Dead? Dudu?"

Then he faints.

• • •

To say that Clouseau illustrates the modern human condition is also to say that he is a jackass, an imbecile beyond either hope or contempt. Chief Inspector Dreyfus proceeds to lose his mind under the threat to rationality that Clouseau's brainless anarchy represents. Dreyfus is correct in his response:

> DREYFUS (agitated): Are you saying that this man—the man Maria Gambrelli is protecting, her former lover—killed eight people because he was jealous?!
>
> CLOUSEAU (calm): Insanely jealous.
>
> DREYFUS: So jealous he made it look like Maria Gambrelli was the murderer?!
>
> CLOUSEAU: He's a madman. A psychotic.
>
> DREYFUS: (increasingly agitated) What about the maid? Was he jealous of her, too? He strangled her!
>
> CLOUSEAU: (calm) It's possible that his intended victim was a man and he made a mistake.
>
> DREYFUS: *A mistake?! In a nudist camp?! Idiot! Nincompoop! Lunatic!*

By the end of the film Dreyfus is on the ground, dementedly biting Clouseau's ankles. It is the "lunatic" Clouseau who survives unscathed.

Clouseau's improbable durability also reveals itself when, in the dim light of Clouseau's apartment, the door handle turns. An Asian man enters, dressed all in black. He sneaks into Clouseau's bedroom and, with a piercing shriek, leaps upon the supine detective and begins to strangle him. A desperate fight ensues until the phone rings. The intruder answers it: "Inspector Clouseau's residence."

The job of Clouseau's valet, Cato, includes karate attacks sprung on his boss without warning, the nominal goal being to keep Clouseau's barely functioning physical coordination from collapsing entirely. Burt Kwouk was the nimble young actor Edwards cast in the role. "Cato is a physically very agile human being," Kwouk says today. "In those days, so was Burt Kwouk." Asked about the development of what was to become a recurring character,

Kwouk cuts right through it: "Cato did what Clouseau told him. And Burt Kwouk did what Blake Edwards told him."

Kwouk takes a similarly clear-eyed perspective toward Peter: "Complex people are very difficult to understand. That's about the size of it, really." He continues: "Hardly anybody has the same perception of Peter Sellers; hardly any of us saw every facet of him. Possibly only his mother ever saw that. I mean, there's the view that there was *no* Peter Sellers—there was just all those characters—[but] that's just a facile way of putting it." Kwouk is onto something. Some sociologists consider the self to be relatively stable; postmodernists see it not as *it* at all, but *them*—provisional, relational selves dependent on circumstance and changeable over time. Sellers was ahead of the curve on this; postmodern theory is a late twentieth-century construct. As Kwouk puts it, "Like everybody, we present different faces to different people. People in different areas see different angles, different sides of us, and therefore have different perceptions of us. In Peter's case it was exaggerated.

"He was very complex—*more* complex than most people," Kwouk concludes. "This is part of the fascination with the man—twenty years after his death. Very few actors are still interesting twenty years after they die. Most of them aren't interesting while they're alive."

A Shot in the Dark builds to a crucial interrogation scene in which, in radical violation of detective genre convention, reason loses. Chaos reigns, and language slips away. Clouseau mentions to Ballon the fact that his fingerprints have been found inside a closet:

BALLON: Why not? It's my house. I've often been in that closet.
CLOUSEAU: For what reason?
BALLON: The last time was moths.
CLOUSEAU: Meuths?
BALLON: *Moths*.
CLOUSEAU: Yes, *meuths*.

It's infectious. Ballon can't help but reply: "Maria was complaining of *meuths*," after which he winces, perplexed.

Blake Edwards later recalled the difficulty of shooting that scene in particular: "One person would start laughing, then someone else. Sellers was the worst. Finally, I put some money in the center of the room and said, 'I don't care who it is that breaks up, they have to match the pot.' I'll

"But We'd Much Rather Be with the Boys": The Gang Show camping it up in Germany, 1945. (Peter is standing, far right, David Lodge far left.) COURTESY OF DAVID LODGE.

Peter Sellers, RAF: In occupied Germany, 1946.
COURTESY OF DAVID LODGE.

"Britain's answer to Gene Krupa": A promotional photo for Peter's drumming act, circa 1947.
COURTESY OF DAVID LODGE.

Three Goons in a Row: Harry Secombe, Peter Sellers, and Spike Milligan.

Teddy Boy: Peter as street tough in *The Ladykillers*.

Family Man: Peter, Anne, Michael, and newborn Sarah, 1957.

Creatures from the Black Swamp: Peter and Terry-Thomas have their way with Russ Tamblyn in *tom thumb*.

Her Grace: Peter as the Grand Duchess Gloriana XII in *The Mouse that Roared*.
COURTESY OF PHOTOFEST.

Man with a Movie Camera: Peter, in costume as Fred Kite, on the set of *I'm All Right, Jack.*

Bangers and Mash?: Peter and Sophia in a publicity shot for *The Millionairess.*
COURTESY OF PHOTOFEST.

Directing Himself: Peter as the schoolteacher-turned-millionaire in *Mr. Topaze.*

A Difficult Client: Peter and Richard "Dickie" Attenborough in *The Dock Brief*.

"Good Evening, Dr. Humbardtz": Dr. Zemf (Peter, left) pays a visit to Humbert (James Mason, right) in *Lolita*.

Getting Reacquainted: Claire Quilty (Peter) has to be reminded of his fling with Charlotte Haze (Shelley Winters, right) while a bored Vivian Darkbloom (Marianne Stone, left) looks the other way in *Lolita*.

The British Officer: Sellers as Group Captain Lionel Mandrake in *Dr. Strangelove.* COURTESY OF THE ACADEMY OF MOTION PICTURE ARTS AND SCIENCES.

Welcome to Hollywood: Peter enjoys reading one of the scripts he was offered during his first trip to Tinseltown. COURTESY OF THE ACADEMY OF MOTION PICTURE ARTS AND SCIENCES.

The American President: Sellers as Merkin Muffley in *Dr. Strangelove.* COURTESY OF THE ACADEMY OF MOTION PICTURE ARTS AND SCIENCES.

The German Nuclear Physicist: Sellers as the eponymous antihero in *Dr. Strangelove.*

Camaraderie: Peter Sellers (as Inspector Clouseau) and his friend Graham Stark (as Clouseau's assistant, Hercule Lajoy) in *A Shot in the Dark.* COURTESY OF THE ACADEMY OF MOTION PICTURE ARTS AND SCIENCES.

Private Moment, Public-Style: Peter and Britt Ekland announce their engagement in a conference room at Heathrow Airport in February 1964. The bride-to-be is wearing what she later described as "a second-hand, moth-eaten leopard skin coat."

Paranoid: Henry Orient (Peter) peeps through the blinds in *The World of Henry Orient.*

Sailing: Peter and Michael Sellers take a boat trip on the Hudson River during a visit to New York.

The One that Got Away: Peter enjoys an apparently relaxed moment with his costars Dean Martin and Cliff Osmond on the set of Billy Wilder's *Kiss Me, Stupid.* COURTESY OF PHOTOFEST.

Hollywood Immortality: With Britt kneeling by his side, Peter puts his hands in wet cement at Grauman's Chinese Theater less than two months after suffering a series of nearly fatal heart attacks in 1964.

"I Like Thighs": Sellers as the demented Dr. Fritz Fassbender in *What's New, Pussycat?*

Disaster Royale: Robert Parrish (left), Ursula Andress, and Peter Sellers go over one of the many scripts of *Casino Royale.* COURTESY OF MRS. ROBERT PARRISH.

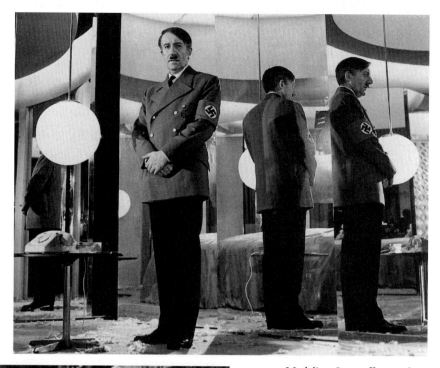

Modeling: In an effort to please Vesper (Ursula Andress), Evelyn Tremble (Peter) poses as Hitler in *Casino Royale*. COURTESY OF THE ACADEMY OF MOTION PICTURE ARTS AND SCIENCES.

When in Rome: Britt and Peter show off to Michael Sellers's apparent humiliation in a publicity shot for *After the Fox.*

Pulled from Both Ends: Britt, Victoria, and Peter enjoy a domestic moment during the production of *After the Fox* in Rome, but given the parents' later battles over the child, the pose proved to be ironic. COURTESY OF PHOTOFEST.

Still Speaking: Peter, in makeup as Hrundi V. Bakshri, discusses an idea with his director, Blake Edwards, on the set of *The Party*.

Learning from the Master: Ravi Shankar teaches Peter how to play the sitar for his role in *The Party*.

Tune In, Turn On, Wear Wig: Peter and Leigh Taylor-Young in a publicity shot for *I Love You, Alice B. Toklas!*

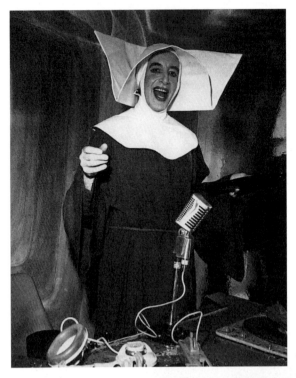

"I'm Peg!": According to Peter, he looked exactly like his mother in this brief scene in *The Magic Christian.* COURTESY OF PHOTOFEST.

In London: Peter Sellers, Terry Southern, and Ringo Starr take a stroll during the production of *The Magic Christian.* PHOTOGRAPH BY WILLIAM CLAXTON/COURTESY OF DPM.

In His Element: Peter taking a snapshot of Terry Southern, who took this snapshot. COURTESY OF NILE SOUTHERN.

The Big Question: Princess Margaret visits the set of *The Magic Christian*. COURTESY OF PHOTOFEST.

Wife Number Three, Meet Wife Number Two: Miranda Quarry, Peter, and Britt Ekland. COURTESY OF PHOTOFEST.

The Look of Love?: Peter and Goldie Hawn on the set of *There's a Girl in My Soup*.

A Lasting Friendship: David Lodge and Peter Sellers take a break during the production of *Hoffman*. COURTESY OF DAVID LODGE.

"Can't Help Lovin' That Man": Peter and Liza, engaged to be married. COURTESY OF PHOTOFEST.

Titi: Peter on the go with Christina Wachtmeister. AP/WIDE WORLD PHOTOS.

Sidney Wang: Peter in full makeup in *Murder by Death.*

He's Got a Hunch: Sellers as Jacques Clouseau disguised as Quasimodo in *The Pink Panther Strikes Again.*

Signs of Stress: An older if not wiser-looking Peter Sellers as Chief Inspector Clouseau in *The Revenge of the Pink Panther.*
COURTESY OF THE ACADEMY OF MOTION PICTURE ARTS AND SCIENCES.

One More Try: Peter and his fourth wife, Lynne Frederick. COURTESY OF THE ACADEMY OF MOTION PICTURE ARTS AND SCIENCES.

"**All Is Well in the Garden**": Peter and Shirley MacLaine in *Being There*.

always remember this because George Sanders was in the scene, and he's someone who usually just did his role and went to sleep. He didn't get actively involved. But when Sellers started using these words—a 'meuth' in the closet, a 'beump' on the head—Sanders fell down and wept like a cocker spaniel."

But all was not mirth. By the end of the shoot, Edwards and Sellers had stopped speaking. Their communication consisted of little notes slipped underneath each other's door. Each man was experienced; each knew comedy; each had precise ideas; each was neurotic and disturbed. After all, Edwards's nickname is "Blackie"—not a diminutive of Blake, but a reference to one of his most frequent moods. In retrospect, it seems inevitable that because Sellers and Edwards shared a kind of communal personality, at a certain point they would necessarily cease to communicate.

• • •

Offscreen, Peter Sellers was earnestly repeating himself. "He asked me to marry him, believe it or not," Elke Sommer says, "even though no physicality, *nothing* had passed between us.

"I think he was just desperate to marry. I said, 'Peter, I like you very much as a person, but I don't *love* you.' He said, 'But that'll come.'

"I always got the feeling of a very lonely man who would do practically anything to have somebody who was his."

Moving along to his next target, in early February 1964, Peter, still ensconced in his Dorchester suite, sent Bert around to a young starlet's room to issue a dinner invitation by proxy. Perhaps the girl would consent to having some photographs taken as well, Bert asked. She would. Britt-Marie Eklund, a twenty-one-year-old pouty-lipped blond, had just arrived in London courtesy of Twentieth Century-Fox, which had cast her in a new action-adventure film, *Guns at Batasi* (1964), in the process forcing her to shorten her name to Britt Ekland. Thanks to the studio's publicity machine, London's playboy elite was already in the know about her arrival. Michael Caine had issued an invitation but hadn't called back yet as he'd promised to do, so Britt was free to join Peter, who by that point had started in on the room-service sweet and sour pork. He took some photos of Britt after dinner, after which they drove by limousine to see *The Pink Panther*, returning afterward to the Dorchester, where Peter and Britt capped their night with caviar, champagne, and Peter's new toy, marijuana. Over the next few days he sent flowers, took her to Trader Vic's, where they shared a drink with a floating gardenia; gave her a diamond and gold brooch from Asprey; and bought her a dachshund. Before the week was over, she flew to New York on *Guns at Batasi* business, but he called her often during her brief stay in America. In one call, he mentioned some news: "I've told everyone in London we're going to marry. Is that all right by you?" Britt flew back to London. After her plane landed at Heathrow at 7:40 A.M., one of the many aggressive journalists who had congregated for the event shouted, "Where's your engagement ring, Britt?" whereupon Peter pulled her into a nearby broom closet and presented her with a triple-banded Victorian ring (emeralds, diamonds, rubies) he'd picked up at Garrards. They emerged from the closet for a photo op and got married the following Wednesday.

The wedding took place in Surrey at the Guildford registry office, which Peter's wedding planner had transfigured into what Britt later called "a chamber of spiritual beauty." There were fifty burning candles and bowls and bowls of lilacs and roses, creamy white and pink. The bride wore a Norman Hartnell gown. Peter had chosen the designer; Hartnell also happened to make dresses for the queen. Draped across Britt's shoulders was a $15,000 black mink coat, her wedding present from the groom. (A red Lotus sports car had served as an engagement gift.) Peter wore a simple blue suit and overcoat.

David Lodge and Graham Stark were Peter's best men for the brief ceremony. There were only a handful of guests, but fifteen hundred fans reportedly cramped themselves around the front of the building as an icy wind blew snow in their faces. The newspapers were ecstatic: "They outdid the Beatles fans in their shrieks. . . . Babies were abandoned in their prams on the lawns!"

It was an unusual day for Michael and Sarah Sellers. "I was at boarding school," says Michael. "I was told to get my stuff together because I was going out for the day. But nobody told me [for] what. The driver picked me up and said it was because Father was getting married." Sarah adds, "We didn't actually get to go to the wedding ceremony, which I remember I would have liked to have done."

At least they made it to the reception at Brookfield.

• • •

Peter insisted that Maurice Woodruff had predicted the whole thing. Someone with the initials B.E. would have a great influence in his life, Peter repeated. He had told Elke Sommer the news during the production of *A Shot in the Dark*. That B.E. also stood for Blake Edwards was of no concern. . . . Peter had no idea that his psychic was in collusion with his agent.

Peter was smitten as only Peter could be, and Britt gave him very good reason to be so. Charming, young, fresh, and willing, she also happened to be mind-bogglingly beautiful. "Darling," he said to her at one point early on, "you're so unspoiled, so pristine, and so very *dishy*." Bert Mortimer, who saw Peter in his blackest moments, later said that he "had never seen him so happy. . . . It made life a lot easier for everybody around him." Peter's mother, on the other hand, wasn't impressed. Peg showed up at her son's wedding this time, but behind Britt's back she tended to call Peter's sweet young bride "the bleeding Nazi."

Four days after the wedding Peter flew to Los Angeles and checked into the Beverly Hills Hotel and Bungalows. He was there to film *Kiss Me, Stupid*, Billy Wilder's feel-bad comedy about a nebbish Nevada husband and the fantastic jealousy he sports over his pretty blond wife. Sinatra was out, Dean Martin was in. Monroe was out, Kim Novak in. Shirley MacLaine was out, Felicia Farr (who was married to Jack Lemmon) was in.

Britt stayed in London to begin filming *Guns at Batasi* with Richard Attenborough and John Leyton. David Lodge and Graham Stark both had roles in the film, so naturally Peter asked them to spy on Britt and report back to him any suspicious behavior.

Capucine threw a party for him on February 25. Blake Edwards was there; so were Jack Lemmon and Felicia Farr, Billy and Audrey Wilder, the director William Wyler, and Swifty Lazar.

Peter taped *The Steve Allen Show* on March 20 and brought the house down. "It was a very interesting period in my life," Peter said in response to Allen's question about *The Goon Show*. "I worked with a very brilliant colleague called Spike Milligan, who wrote the show. Who unfortunately is in a mental home at the moment. [Laughter.] No. He gets a bit under the weather. [Laughter.] But anyway. . . ."

Allen asked him what he called his mother-in-law: "Well, I think the English have quite a good way out of it. They just say 'Hallo!' [Laughter.] But Britt's mother is called Mai-Britt, and I call Britt *my* Britt, you see, because she belongs to me."

After keeping Allen unusually entertained and playing drums with the band on "Honeysuckle Rose" (complete with a show-stopping solo), Peter finished off his appearance with an extended improvisation in which he placed a prank call to Scotland Yard. (This was not Peter's invention. Random phone calls were a standard routine on *The Steve Allen Show*; Jerry Lewis, Mel Brooks, Johnny Carson, and Jack Lemmon had each placed one during their guest appearances on the show.)

Given the American premiere of *The Pink Panther*, the L.A. papers were also full of Peter:

"I don't enjoy playing multiple parts at all. I know Alec Guinness doesn't either. But they do have a sort of showcase value."

"I feel I'm the only one who really knows basically that I'm a phony and eventually it will all be found out."

"Only my children have given me any real happiness. What is wrong with me? What am I looking for?"

Meanwhile, Peter's spies not having anything to report, he proceeded to grill Britt over the phone. What scenes did she film that day? Who with? Did she have to kiss him? "Britt, just *tell* me."

He sent telegrams. On March 10, he sent five. "Ying," read the first. "Tong," read the second.

"Iddle."

"I."

"Po. Love, Bluebottle."

He also wrote letters. In one, he described having just attended a screening of *The Great Escape* (1963): "I was getting deeply engrossed when somebody said, 'Who's that fellow?' Someone else said, 'That's John Leyton.' I thought, 'John Leyton? He's in the film that my Britt's doing. She kissed him. Oh, but that's nothing, that's just acting.' Then I thought of something an actor once said to me, that he always had to become involved with the women he worked with, otherwise it didn't look real enough. The thought of this made me break out into a cold sweat and want to be sick.

"I've depressed myself getting into a state like this. I really am an idiot. They say all comedians are sad. I wonder if that's true? Still, I'm not really a comedian. I don't know what I am."

Under the barrage of Peter's phone calls, Britt took a break from filming. She left London for Los Angeles on March 24. Peter was overjoyed to see her. They lunched in his dressing room and dined at hotspots like La Scala or the Bistro. She met Peter's friends—Cary Grant, Steve McQueen, Shirley MacLaine, Capucine, "R. J." Wagner, Goldie Hawn.

Peter had rented a marbled mansion in Beverly Hills for the duration of *Kiss Me, Stupid*. Home movie footage of the house, which was located just off Sunset Boulevard in Beverly Hills, reveals, along with the obligatory swimming pool, a monochromatic, showy, haute-L.A. style: white front doors, white marble walls, white marble floors, white dining table, white chairs. . . . By the time Britt arrived Peter had already outfitted it with a closet's worth of clothes for her. Michael and Sarah appeared soon thereafter for another trip to Disneyland.

The trouble was, Britt had not even come close to completing her scenes in *Guns at Batasi*, and on March 31, Fox filed a $4.5 million suit against her for breach of contract. The studio named Peter as well. By a strange coincidence, the house he had rented in Beverly Hills was owned by Spyros Skouras, the head of Twentieth Century-Fox, though the landlord decided not to intervene in Peter's domestic life. A little later, Peter Sellers countersued for $4 million, but his case was dismissed, and he ended up paying Fox $60,200 to compensate the studio for the celluloid containing images of Britt.

John Guillermin was *Guns at Batasi*'s under-the-gun director. "Peter was desperately unhappy, you know, and was talking to Britt all the time on the phone. She left the picture after two weeks. She was inexperienced. She hadn't done much, and I don't think if she'd had more experience she'd have left. We got Mia Farrow to do the role and had to reshoot a couple of weeks of it. Dickie Attenborough was not pleased. I saw Peter after that— it didn't leave any scars." Britt herself was later embarrassed by the episode: "I knew in my heart I was doing the wrong thing. I just knew it. But I wasn't my own woman in those days. So I went."

She was captivated by him—his magnetism, his fame, and his potent love for her were a dazzling combination. To say that he was controlling is obvious; more to the point is that Britt loved him.

Peter, of course, was resolute that she had every right to leave the picture. "The only thing my wife ever signed was Darryl F. Zanuck's autograph book," he declared.

• • •

Kiss Me, Stupid, for which Peter was to be paid $250,000 plus a percentage of the profits, was only the first picture Wilder planned to make with Peter; *Sherlock Holmes* was the second. Obviously the director had high hopes for him. But the actual, day-to-day experience of shooting a film together revealed that these two brilliant filmmakers had radically different work habits and personal styles. Wilder liked to share meals with his stars; he enjoyed the camaraderie of collaborative filmmaking, as long as no actor dared alter a single word of the scripts he so carefully crafted with his writing partner, I. A. L. Diamond. Peter had lunch in his dressing room, and improvisation was his stock in trade. The hyper and gregarious Wilder enjoyed commanding a wildly open set. His friends; his chic wife, Audrey; his chic wife's friends; visitors from out of town. . . . The doors of *Kiss Me, Stupid*'s soundstage at the Goldwyn studio were thrown wide. Peter preferred to film in relative privacy. Audrey Wilder, a quick-witted pistol and former big-band singer who, by this point, had become one of Hollywood's foremost social leaders, characteristically has something to say about Peter, too: "He queered his pitch with *me* when he didn't show up for a dinner we were giving for him at the apartment. I was *real* mad."

Sellers later described the atmosphere of *Kiss Me, Stupid*: "I used to go down to the set with Billy Wilder, and find a Cooks Tour of hangers-on and sightseers standing off the set in my line of vision. Friends and relatives of people in the front office come to kibitz. When I told Billy I couldn't work with that crowd there, he said, 'Be like Jack Lemmon. Whenever he starts a scene he shuts his eyes and says to himself, "It's magic time" and then forgets everything else.' " Peter found it difficult to forget everything else. The idea of completing the picture began to gnaw at him.

Then came the sty.

According to Jack Lemmon, Sellers was plagued that week by "a massive sty" on his right eye. Sheilah Graham reported that he'd missed at least one day of filming because of it. Lemmon also noticed that Peter "looked as if he were approaching nervous exhaustion." He was tired, anxious, irritated. He could do bits of physical business that pleased his writer-director, but he couldn't change a single word of the dialogue. The sty was a clinically hysterical reaction—a bodily manifestation of what Peter felt inside.

On Friday, April 3, Wilder and Sellers filmed the scene in which Orville gives a piano lesson to a child while growing increasingly convinced that his wife, played by Felicia Farr, is (as Wilder put it) "doing it" with the milkman. Standing on the sidelines along with Peter's costars Dean Martin, Kim Novak, Felicia Farr, and Cliff Osmond, Britt watched her husband perform for the first time. She was amazed by his extraordinary talent and spark. So were the others, including Wilder himself, who, despite his experience as a director, couldn't help but break out into unrestrained laughter during Peter's takes.

"And then he did not show up on Monday," Billy Wilder declared from a distance of thirty-five years. "He had borrowed some money from me because he wanted to take his kids to Disneyland. He was at Disneyland! That's the last I saw of him, giving him the money. It was two or three hundred dollars."

• • •

There is a funny but foreboding exchange in *The World of Henry Orient* between the difficult Henry and his earnest manager, Sidney (John Fiedler). "Henry!" Sidney pleads. "You've got to remember you're not Van Cliburn! Now if Van Cliburn misses a rehearsal, he's still Van Cliburn, and nobody says, 'Throw the bum out!' " But Henry is having his hair done at the moment and is too busy admiring his own head in a handheld mirror to concern himself with the warning. "I tried 'a phone 'em," he mumbles.

In 1964, Peter's profound misfortune was that he *was* Van Cliburn. On that incontrovertible basis, he believed he could do as he pleased. In fact, if comparisons are to be drawn, Peter Sellers was better than Van Cliburn. He was more famous. And he made more money. And ironically, despite years of outrageous behavior and eccentricity and periodically debilitating despair, Peter Sellers ended up remaining far longer on the klieg-lit world stage than Van Cliburn.

• • •

He was worried about his body. As Britt describes it, Peter "believed that the essence of his masculinity relied on his ardor as a lover. He was always searching for what he liked to term as the 'ultimate' orgasm, and when he discovered that amyl nitrate assisted his physical endurance the tiny capsules of chemical became almost a routine component of our nightly love-making pattern." So on Monday, April 6, after forgoing the tension-provoking sound stages of *Kiss Me, Stupid* for VIP treatment at the Magic Kingdom, Peter and Britt put the kids to sleep and went to bed, inhaled some poppers, made love with their hearts racing, and afterward opened a bottle of champagne, which spilled all over the sheets. They were changing them when Peter reached for his chest. "Get me some brandy—quickly," he said.

When Britt returned to the bedroom she found Peter lying in the damp bed.

"I know what it is. I've had a heart attack. Phone the doctor."

Dr. Rex Kennamer, physician to the stars, arrived very shortly, gave Peter a sedative, and told Britt to take him to Cedars of Lebanon Hospital in the morning. Kennamer wasn't alarmed enough to call an ambulance on the spot, but he did decide to cancel his trip to New York, where he was to join his other patients Elizabeth Taylor and Richard Burton for the opening of *Hamlet*.

In the morning they did as they were told. Peter checked into Cedars of Lebanon. Britt told the kids he just had "a bit of a cold." A hospital spokesman told the press it was a myocardial infarction. Peter rested comfortably in his private room.

Reporters and entertainment columnists in Hollywood covered the story, of course—it's always exciting when a thirty-eight-year-old international superstar suffers a mild heart attack—but British papers were quite a bit more breathless. The *Daily Express* rushed to report that Peter phoned "director William Wyler" from his hospital bed to say that he was sick.

Then, at 4:32 A.M. on April 8, 1964, Peter Sellers's heart stopped beating and stayed off. It had had enough.

PART THREE

THROUGH THE LOOKING GLASS

1964–80

FOURTEEN

"*That* was *a narrow escape!*" *said Alice, a good deal frightened
at the sudden change, but very glad to find herself still in
existence.*

Think of a whole area of blackness. Then imagine an arm—a bare arm,
but a very strong arm, pulling you. And this arm says, in its own way,
'I won't let you go, I won't let you go.' I held on to this arm, and I knew
that as long as I had that arm, I wouldn't die."

A doctor pounded on Peter's chest, and the heart began to beat.

Some hours later, a boy recovering from open-heart surgery in the
intensive care unit cried for his mother. Peter suggested that the child be
wheeled next to him, whereupon he distracted the child with a Cockney
song: "I was walking down the Strand with a banana in my hand . . ." The
boy began to laugh, Britt began to cry, and Peter suddenly stopped
breathing. In came the doctors, who revived him again.

The heart stopped at least eight times during the next two days, only
to be startled back to life each time. Up, down, starting, stopping, all to
the tune of jolts from a defibrillator. It was a *Goon Show* routine. "You've
deaded him," Bluebottle used to say.

In England, a national icon seemed about to die, and TV tributes were
already in production. "It was uncanny," Ian Carmichael reports. "He was
on life support in the Cedars of Lebanon Hospital, and a television station
called. They were preparing an obituary program for that night. They said,
'We've got Spike Milligan, we've got this, we've got that, we've got the
others all standing by to come in if necessary, but we would like you to be
link man, and we've got to rehearse you to get the links right, so will you
come in this afternoon and run them with us?' I said, 'Yes, okay.' So I went
in and was handed this script, and it started off, 'Today the _____'

—the date was left blank—'at the Cedars of Lebanon Hospital in California, Peter Sellers died.' It was terrifying to have to do this. I knew the man was still alive. As I left the corridors of power in that television station, I got the feeling that if he didn't die, for the executives it would be the ruination of a bloody good show."

The doctors installed a pacemaker. Peter himself described it: "Two electrodes were sewn in the tissue on each side of my sternum. Doctors watching my heart graph on an oscilloscope knew exactly how it was functioning. If my heart stopped, a warning buzzer sounded, an oscilloscope flashed a report, and an electrical stimulus was sent through the wires directly to my heart to start it up again." (This pacemaker was an earlier, rarer, and obviously more cumbersome version of the tiny, fully-implanted device in widespread use today.)

By 7 A.M. on Thursday morning, the crisis was over. Alert, cheerful, and propped relatively upright with pillows, Peter told the hospital staff that he was worried about his appearance, so they gave him a shave and combed his hair. By Friday morning Peter was off the critical list, Rediffusion Television had lost their special, and Billy Wilder had replaced him with Ray Walston in *Kiss Me, Stupid*.

Britt Ekland, who had kept a near-constant vigil at the hospital, found herself the object of morbid curiosity and fashion scrutiny. The press duly reported that Peter's twenty-one-year-old bride of less than two months had arrived at Cedars of Lebanon on Friday morning cutting a "wistful figure" in a tailored blue-green suit. Forced by circumstances into a brief news conference that day, she thanked Dr. Kennamer; the chief of cardiology, Dr. Clarence Agress; and a senior resident physician, Dr. Robert Coblin, for saving her husband's life. What she didn't mention was that Peter, for whom work was life, was already insisting on talking to his agents and managers and accountants and had to be sedated.

• • •

Peter Sellers's deaths in April 1964 were by far the most adult experiences he had ever had, with the possible exception of facing hostile audiences as a stand-up comedian. Involuntary though coronaries are, they evidence more maturity than did Peter's two marriages, in which he often behaved like a child, or his forays into fatherhood, his love for his children being solipsistic and abstract. Dying changed him.

The doctors told him that he'd suffered no discernable mental deterioration despite the lack of oxygen to the brain when his heart kept stopping. Peter himself wasn't so sure.

"He told me that he wasn't afraid of dying after that," David Lodge declares. "Obviously it did have something to do with his way of life, with his attitude. It did affect him. I'm not saying he was mental, but it mentally affected him."

Harry Secombe agreed: "Perhaps he realized his own mortality then and decided to make the most of life before it happened again. That could have been some of the reason behind his behavior afterward."

The Goons, of course, took a jocular approach to Peter's health crisis. Secombe claimed that "when he was getting better, Spike and I sent him a wire saying 'You swine! We had you heavily insured.' "

Peter and Britt necessarily had to cancel their appearance at the Oscars party Harold Mirisch planned to throw in their honor on April 13. In fact, Peter remained at Cedars of Lebanon for a solid month, only making his exit, in a wheelchair, on May 7. The crowd of reporters and photographers swarming around outside the hospital noted that he was wearing a yellow T-shirt, jeans, and a blue-denim jacket. He was also chewing gum. Peter said very little on his way to the waiting ambulance that took him back to the rented mansion, but he did toss off one good line: "When you come out of the hospital, you want to look as nonchalant as possible."

His recovery was quiet and uneventful over the next four weeks, and on June 3, he was ready for his first public appearance. With Britt at his side, he stuck his hands and shoes in wet cement at Grauman's Chinese Theater on Hollywood Boulevard. Privately, he also ventured out to a Santa Monica apartment to pay a visit to an aging star he had long admired. He signed Stan Laurel's guest book "To Dear Stan—with my greatest admiration. Peter Sellers, June 1964."

On June 7, Peter and Britt ended their catastrophic trip to Hollywood and flew back to London; they were accompanied by a British physician who had flown to California specifically to be at Peter's side for the duration of his flight home.

• • •

A week and a half later, from the apparently safe distance of 5,500 miles, Peter casually mentioned to Alexander Walker of the *Evening Standard* that, in his opinion, the Hollywood studios "give you every creature comfort except the satisfaction of being able to get the best work out of yourself."

He didn't like all the hangers-on who had crowded around the *Kiss Me, Stupid* soundstages, he said. He hadn't had a good time in L.A.

It was a mild interview, but it hit a nerve back in Hollywood. Billy Wilder, Dean Martin, Kim Novak, and Felicia Farr sent him a terse and testy wire: "Talk about unprofessional rat finks."

The following day, Peter announced that he had officially dropped out of Wilder's proposed Sherlock Holmes film. "I'm surprised they should be so sensitive," he commented. "I made my criticisms in public and in America and I only told the truth." He also defined the expression *rat fink* for the British: "someone who says something you don't like."

He issued a statement in *Variety* the following week—a full-page ad titled "Open Letter from Peter Sellers": "There appears to be a feeling getting around in Hollywood that I am an ungrateful limey or rat fink or whatever, who has been abusing everything Hollywood behind its back. I must take this opportunity to correct this impression categorically." Peter proceeded to thank the doctors and staff of Cedars of Lebanon, the Mirisch brothers, his friends at the Goldwyn Studios, and all the fans who sent him cards and letters. "I didn't go to Hollywood to be ill," he continued. "I went there to work, and found regrettably that the creative side in me couldn't accept the sort of conditions under which work had to be carried out. . . . The atmosphere is wrong for me."

Billy Wilder wasn't sympathetic. "Heart attack?" he once remarked about Peter. "You have to have a heart before you can have an attack."

• • •

Peter's convalescence in England was relatively serene. Mostly he and Britt stayed at Brookfield, but one weekend they were among the guests at Testbourne, the home of Jocelyn Stevens, the editor of *Queen* magazine. Others included Evelyn de Rothschild and Peter's increasingly good friends Princess Margaret and her husband, Lord Snowdon.

Their friendship had been sparked by Alec Guinness. "I was the one who . . ." Guinness said before changing his mind about the direction his sentence should take. "I spent the day with Princess Margaret and Lord Snowdon's sister and her husband, with whom Margaret was staying. I said, 'You know, Mum, there's someone who you ought to meet—Peter Sellers.' She hadn't met him yet. I read in the papers about a month later that they had become very friendly. [Later] I went to call at Kensington Palace. I was returning some photographs to Lord Snowdon; Peter turned up after dinner."

In February, during the brief period of his engagement to Britt, Peter had managed to find time to introduce his fiancée to the princess and her husband, who himself had found time that week to conduct a photo shoot at Kensington Palace with Peter's braless bride-to-be. Now they could spend more than a few hours together, and, sociably, Peter organized a comedy routine and filmed it. Peter began the act by doing impersonations and, as Stevens later described them, "getting them deliberately wrong, so that we all groaned. Then, of course, he produced this perfect version of Margaret."

Footage of the escapade also reveals Margaret playing along with another of Peter's stunts—a tasteful version of something he, Spike, and Richard Lester might have thought up for *Idiot's Weekly, Price 2d*. Standing in front of a makeshift theatrical curtain, Peter announces that for his next trick he is going to do an impression of Princess Margaret. He darts behind the curtain, and, after a pause, Margaret herself comes out and takes a bow. It was a relatively intimate goof between friends, one of whom happened to be royal—a good-natured amusement on a weekend afternoon.

In another bit, Snowdon, in trenchcoat and hat, played what turned out to be a cross-dressing gangster sidekick to a gun-wielding, eventually-mincing Peter. But it's "Riding Along on the Crest of a Wave" that best captures the spirit of Peter's royal friendships. There's the queen's sister in a stylish black dress, gamely hopping up and down and waving her arms over her head in a line of mock WWII soldier-chorines.

There's something poignant about this footage. As the British writer Alan Franks has observed, Peter's intense need to photograph, film, and tape record the day-to-day events of his life was essentially a tragic enterprise, "a device for fixing into place the otherwise transient moment. It was as though he was trying to inject some permanence into a life which he knew was condemned to flit from role to role, home to home, wife to wife." That this particular home movie starred Princess Margaret meant only that Peter had risen higher than he had ever dreamed. What hadn't changed was that Peter still tried, with his latest technological toys, to keep his evanescent soul from evaporating completely.

• • •

By that point, Britt was pregnant.

Not only had they started having sex while still in Los Angeles. They began immediately after his return from the hospital. An especially dog-matic home-care nurse had insisted on following doctor's orders by remaining at Peter's side constantly. Peter and Britt couldn't even go to bed together without Peter's nurse remaining in the room with them, so the only place the couple could have a bit of sexual privacy was under a blast of running water in the shower. They begged the doctor to tell the nurse to back off, and soon after she moved to a nearby bedroom at night, Britt found herself in what passed for a family way.

They told very few people. But near the end of the summer, during a brief trip to Costa Brava, Britt took an unexpected call from a British gossip columnist, who asked her to confirm the rumor that she was carrying Peter's baby.

Britt's marriage with Peter was, like Anne's with Peter—and everyone's, for that matter—punctuated by moments of tension and argument. But despite witnessing her husband's irrational jealousy during their first weeks of matrimony, Britt once claimed not to have noticed anything truly out of the ordinary about his behavior until later that summer: "The first time I felt it was not normal was when Hugh Hefner called and said 'We have nude photographs of Britt, but we feel that you are such a wonderful photographer, so why don't you take some photographs of her?' I said, 'But Peter, I have never, *ever* posed for nude photographs.' Peter said, 'If Hugh Hefner says you have, you have.' There was nothing I could say or do."

Ekland was even more shocked and hurt when Peter suggested during one of their escalating fights that she abort the fetus. Britt sought the help of Bryan Forbes and Nanette Newman, who talked him out of it. With his quicksilver mood swings, he soon stopped mentioning abortion as a solution and began referring to an idea he claimed to have learned from Stanley Kubrick. There was an African tribe, Kubrick supposedly told Peter, a tribe that blended ancient ritual with modern Western medical practices and believed that the best and healthiest babies were produced only when a pregnant woman was strapped into a chair and placed in an oxygen tent. He suggested that Britt try it. According to Britt, only an increasing stream of calls from his agents and managers distracted him enough that he never forced her to go through with it.

• • •

Before his ill-fated trip to Los Angeles, Peter had formed a new production company with a filmmaker of great experience. John Bryan was a former art director (Anthony Asquith's *Pygmalion*, 1938, among others), and production designer (including David Lean's *Great Expectations*, 1946, for which he won an Oscar, and *Becket*, 1964, with Peter O'Toole and Richard Burton, for which he won a BAFTA award). Bryan was also a producer, two of whose better known films starred Alec Guinness: *The Card* (1952) and *The Horse's Mouth* (1958).

Calling their company Brookfield, Sellers and Bryan were quite active in terms of planning. Between March and October 1964, Brookfield announced five film projects that were in various stages of preproduction. First was *The Borrowers*, which was to be written by the screenwriter Jay Presson based on May Norton's children's book about a family of minuscule people who lived under the floorboards of somebody's country home. They announced this one in March, before Peter's heart attacks. In April, with Peter still in his hospital bed, Brookfield pledged to do a film version of *Oliver!*, Lionel Bart's hit musical based on *Oliver Twist*, with Peter as Fagin. Then came *My Favorite Comrade*, written by Maurice Richlin; that, too, was announced with Peter still recuperating at Cedars of Lebanon. Next came *Don Quixote*, with Peter (both ironically and not) in the title role. In October *Maggie May* was added to the roster; it was based on a West End play.

With characteristic enthusiasm and verve for work, Peter explained why he wanted to become a producer. "I love this medium so much," he said, "I thought it might be ideal if and when I begin to slip in popularity as an actor. And there's such a dearth of really good acting material—so much bad stuff. My hospitalization was a time of reflection for me."

As far as playing Fagin was concerned, Peter was acutely conscious of the material's inherent racism. What had been acceptable to Dickens and his readers in the late 1830s was no longer so in the mid-1960s, especially not to Jews. There had been some uproar when Alec Guinness played the role in David Lean's 1948 drama, the first production since the Holocaust; this time, the *New York Times* reported, it would be different: "From the start, [Sellers] said he would play Fagin simply as an old rogue. After all, he argued, he was part-Jewish himself and would not be a party to any hint of anti-Semitism."

But the question of how Peter would play Fagin in *Oliver!* was permanently tabled because Sellers and Bryan weren't allowed to make the film. A legal dispute with a rival production company ended badly for Brookfield. As it turned out, Ron Moody played Fagin in *Oliver!* (1968),

The Borrowers was eventually produced as a made-for-television movie in 1973, and *My Favorite Comrade*, *Don Quixote*, and *Maggie May* were never made at all.

In late October, Peter went before the cameras for the first time since his last day on the set of *Kiss Me, Stupid*. It was charity work. He agreed to spend four days in New York shooting a United Nations–sponsored plea for world peace called *Carol for Another Christmas* (1965). The project did boast a prestige director, Joseph L. Mankiewicz, who made the brilliant comedy of theater ill-manners, *All About Eve* (1950), among other fine films. But Peter agreed to appear in *Carol for Another Christmas*, he told the press, because Adlai Stevenson had asked him personally. Also, he said, "After an illness like this, you wonder if you can work again." The possibility of brain damage nagged at him. He worried about whether he could even remember dialogue any more, so he thought he'd start back to work with something small.

They paid him $350, total, and chauffeured him each of the four days of filming from his suite at the Regency to the studio, which was actually a converted hangar at Long Island's Roosevelt Field. Peter's American fans were anxious to see him, and a number of them showed up clamoring at the gate. *Newsweek* rather cruelly reported the excitement at the old airport: " 'We want Pete! We want Pete!,' shrieked the gaggle of middle-aged, fruit-hatted females outside the studio fence. 'Come on out, Pete!,' they shouted, clutching at the wire like frenzied monkeys."

Carol for Another Christmas was a relatively low-budget, made-for-television, post–atomic holocaust parable with good intentions and a (mostly) reputable cast: Sterling Hayden, Eva Marie Saint, Ben Gazzara, Richard Harris, Peter Fonda, and Steve Lawrence (who played the Ghost of Christmas Past). The script was by *The Twilight Zone*'s Rod Serling, who provided even more arch irony than usual—so much so that it verged on clairvoyance. Peter played the head of a band of fanatical individualists. "The Individual Me's" have survived a devastating atomic bomb blast only to devote their lives to eliminating everyone else—except, of course, for the perfect Me, who would be allowed to live. Clad in a gaudy Wild West show outfit complete with a ten-gallon hat emblazoned with the word "Me" in sequins, Peter's charismatic character addresses his cult: "If we let them seep in here from down yonder and cross river—if we let these do-gooders, these bleeding hearts, propagate their insidious doctrine of involvement among us—then my dear friends, my beloved Me's" [dramatic pause] "we's in trouble." His eyes glistening with the thrill of control, the greatest Me continues: "We must carry our glorious philosophy through to its glorious culmination! So that in the end, with enterprise and determination, the world and everything in it will belong to one individual Me! And that will be the ultimate! The absolute ultimate!"

The heart attack survivor then breezed out of New York and returned to London, where, on October 29, he and Britt accompanied Princess Margaret and Lord Snowdon to the Variety Club of Great Britain's Royal Gala performance, the beneficiary of which was the National Society for the Prevention of Cruelty to Children. The event was a circus, literally. As one of the highlights, a group of children had to lie very still on the ground while an elephant stepped over them. A few days later, Peter flew to Paris and began shooting his next feature film.

• • •

What's New Pussycat?'s opening credits are historic. In lurid, squiggly cartoon script, the typographic equivalent of sixties' paisley, they read: "Charles K. Feldman / presents / Peter Sellers / Peter O'Toole / Romy Schneider / Capucine / Paula Prentiss / and introducing Woody Allen."

What's New Pussycat? was the former television writer and diffident stand-up comic Allen's first appearance on film as well as being his first screenplay. Characteristically, it was all about sex and the mind. O'Toole plays Michael James, the disturbed editor of a fashion magazine. Michael considers himself to be sexually compulsive, so he seeks the aid of a Viennese psychiatrist, Dr. Fritz Fassbender—Peter Sellers in a Prince Valiant wig and maroon velvet suit. "My job is a lecher's dream," Michael confesses during their first session. Dr. Fassbender leans in very close, his interest more than piqued. Very soon he takes Michael's place on the couch and confides with a rutting tone, "I like thighs. Do you like thighs?"

Romy Schneider is Michael's long-suffering girlfriend; Capucine, Prentiss, and Allen are ancillary neurotics.

Sellers had been friendly with O'Toole for some years. "I introduced those two," says the actor Kenneth Griffith. "O'Toole wanted to meet Sellers, and he wanted to meet him right away. Peter was going to see a play at the Duchess Theater, I think, so he said 'Well, if it's today, it will have to be when I come out of the theater.'" Then, says Griffith, "a strange thing happened. The play ended, and all the people came out, and there was no Sellers. As I recall it, he was virtually hiding inside. There was great unease about meeting O'Toole. We went to a restaurant in Chelsea, which had just shut because it was rather late at night. They said, 'Oh, we just shut, Mr. Griffith.' I said, 'I've got a couple of friends outside—have a peek.' They opened up quick. It was a great evening. I remember Sellers helping with the cooking."

"We were totally comfortable together," O'Toole once said of Peter. "Not cozy—it was far from cozy. It was sometimes downright edgy, but it was the sharp edginess of stimulation and exploration. I found myself completely eaten up by Pete's personality."

Siân Phillips, who was married to O'Toole at the time, recalls that Sellers's casting in *What's New Pussycat?* was problematic from a financial standpoint, since his heart attacks had rendered him uninsurable. "O'Toole, out of the kindness of his heart, said, 'No, I must, must, *must* have Peter Sellers.' " The result was that Charlie Feldman, the film's producer, essentially self-insured Peter by casting him without outside indemnification. Siân Phillips goes on: "Sellers insisted on top billing, and O'Toole said, 'Oh, give it to him.' I thought that was ungrateful, actually. I didn't think it was very chic." Feldman, on the other hand, told United Artists' Arthur Krim that "O'Toole had insisted on flipping a coin to decide whether he or Sellers should get first billing, [and] Sellers won the toss-up." Whatever the circumstances, Peter Sellers's name did come first.

Peter's doctors, meanwhile, were insisting that he not go beyond a five-hour working day. To ease Peter's mind even further, Feldman had sent the film's young director, Clive Donner (who had directed *The Caretaker*, among other films) to meet with Peter the day before he was to leave for New York to shoot *Carol for Another Christmas*. Donner reassured the justifiably worried Peter that he wouldn't exceed Peter's relatively light schedule and that the production itself would be as relaxed as possible.

Shooting began on November 2. During the production, Peter and Britt stayed in a suite at the Plaza-Athenée. "I mustn't get into any arguments while filming," Peter told the columnist Roderick Mann. "It'll make me too nervous. I just have to shut up and walk away." But, he added, referring jocularly to his fellow filmmakers, "In six months' time I can tell them all what I think of them, the swine!"

He was still discussing matters of the spirit with Cannon John Hester and, at least from Hester's perspective, preparing to convert to Christianity.

They met once a week at the Plaza-Athenée and talked about God. Ursula Andress, clad in leopardskin or cheetah, sometimes joined in. According to Hester, Peter was especially intrigued by the story of Jesus walking on water.

• • •

Woody Allen remains a great admirer of Peter Sellers's talent: "Sellers goes to the deep core of what's funny," he said fairly recently. "His funniness was the funniness of genius. What he had to offer was clearly gold."

But Peter's genius came at price. Allen found the task of actually working with Peter to be strenuous. Peter O'Toole was no help, either. With *What's New, Pussycat?*, the first-time actor and screenwriter found himself rudely belittled by the great Dr. Strangelove and his good friend Lawrence of Arabia.

"Woody," Siân Phillips sighs. "They upset Woody Allen on the set— they were not nice to him. They used to rewrite the script every day, and Sellers was very supercilious with him. 'We are way beyond rehearsing, you know. I'll be in my dressing room.' There was a lot of pulling rank. Woody got so neurotic he wouldn't even come out of his bedroom."

"Met the cast in person today," Allen wrote in his diary, which he later published as publicity for the film. "Sellers and I eyed one another carefully. I think he senses in me a threat to his current position as cinema's leading funnyman. I tried to make him feel at ease and I think I succeeded. He seemed more preoccupied with his wife than with my ideas."

Sellers and O'Toole indeed began to tinker with Allen's script. Tinkering soon turned into wholesale reworking. "Scenes have been taken away from Woody and . . . reworked and repolished by Sellers and O'Toole," Charles Feldman reported on December 2. "I spent the last three days with Woody getting a new Bateau Mouche scene, then I spent endless time with Sellers getting him to approve it." In addition, Sellers thoroughly rewrote the scene in which Dr. Fassbender and Michael muse drunkenly in a lonely bar:

MICHAEL: (drunk) I need help.
FRITZ: (drunk) Don't mention dat verd to me—"*help*." Dat is vat I need—dat *help*, oh God, how I need dat ting! (Confidingly:) You know I am in love vit a patient? (Broadcasting:) *I am in love vit a patient!* (Casually:) Ya got a minute?

Then Peter wrote—and Donner shot—three entirely new scenes that weren't in Allen's original script at all. This was no longer on the level of spontaneous improvisation.

• • •

"You'll like zis group analyzis," Dr. Fassbender tells Michael early in the film. "It's a real *frrreak* show! If it gets dull ve sing songs!"

Clive Donner, asked how Fassbender's character was developed, responded that "it evolved a little from discussions we had, but that was Peter's idea. He would keep coming up with ideas, and I'd say, 'Are you sure, Peter?' And he'd say, 'Don't worry, it'll be all right. . . .' The character was trying to be young again—trying to be a mod to keep up with it all. It's a search for youth."

At Michael's first group session, Peter as Fassbender slaps his hands together and rubs them expectantly as the camera tracks back from a close-up. "And now, group! Whose e-*mo*-zhen'l problems shall we discuss today?" "Me! Me! Me! Mine! Me!" they all shriek. "I've been coming here ten months and we haven't discussed my problem *once* yet," one woman complains, but Dr. Fassbender offers no apologies. "Well," he replies, bored and irritated, "perhaps if you'd be kind enough to tell us what your problem is then ve could all have a go at dis-gussing it or something." A little later, a chubby patient acts out physically by attacking Michael for no apparent reason. Dr. Fassbender, outraged, calls him a "great fat Moby Dick" and, launching into song—"Ven it's *spring time* in Vi-*en-na*"—begins whipping him across the back with a bouquet of flowers.

Dr. Fassbender's lust-object patient, Renée (Capucine), paces the room while rattling off a lengthy speech, which ends, "You see, I can't help it. I'm a physical woman! I feel guilty about it, but I come from a family of acute nymphomaniacs. That includes my father and my two brothers." Dr. Fassbender (visibly aroused): "Vhy don't ve all take off our clothes, it's so modern. . . ."

But it is Liz (Paula Prentiss), the suicidal stripper, who takes it furthest. Profoundly unstable, she explains her "semi-virgin" status to Michael— "Here I'm a virgin, in America I'm not"—and suddenly announces, "I feel faint. Would you excuse me for a minute? I'm going into the bathroom to take an overdose of sleeping pills."

"I thought she was joking," Michael tells the doctor summoned to revive her. "It was all poems and 'Don't touch me'. . . ."

After her second suicide attempt (sparked by Michael's having told her that no, he didn't love her), the physician responding to the call presents her with a commemorative watch: "Mademoiselle, the boys of the Emergency Suicide Board voted you this gold watch for unusual devotion."

• • •

With the strange and disturbing production of *What's New Pussycat?* finally winding down just before Christmas and nobody having died, Charlie Feldman parceled out holiday gifts to the cast and principal crew—Hermes cigarette boxes all around. Peter had already received his own special present from Feldman two weeks earlier—a new red Rolls Royce Silver Cloud III.

Feldman had been growing worried about two things in particular: Peter was far exceeding his contractual obligations on *What's New Pussycat?* by working longer hours than required and by substantially rewriting the script without additional compensation. He was also showing signs of depression. Feldman, telling United Artists that he had been anticipating problems and thought he'd found a way to circumvent them, voluntarily offered Sellers a new car to keep him happy. "His enthusiasm thereafter was incredible and he has worked like a dog since," Feldman reported.

The Rolls was not Peter's first choice. He had originally suggested a new Ferrari Superfast. But they couldn't get one in time, so he settled on the cheaper Silver Cloud, which was available right away.

He had to have it.

• • •

"She looks just like her father!" Britt wrote to Charlie Feldman, thanking him for the congratulatory flowers he had sent to the proud parents of a baby girl. "As you can imagine, Peter and I are just thrilled with her!"

Victoria Sellers was born on January 20, 1965, at the Welbeck Street Clinic in London. Her parents had moved into the Dorchester after their return from Paris, specifically to be close to the clinic. "When my water went and I felt the first pangs," Britt reports, "Sellers whisked me from the hotel to the clinic in a flash. My suitcase was already packed."

Then Peter made his exit: "Unceremoniously he dumped me on the steps of the clinic and promptly disappeared without so much as taking one step inside the door." Whatever the cause of this, his second birthing abandonment—fear, revulsion, somebody's opening night at an exclusive club?—Peter once again proved unable to support his wife emotionally, particularly when she expected it.

But in the morning, with his daughter safely born, Peter was "proud as punch." After scooping the tiny girl up in his arms, he was overcome by joy. "Thank God she is safely here," he said.

• • •

They were not destined to be a stay-at-home family, and swinging London in 1965 was not a stay-at-home kind of place. With Victoria only a few weeks old, Peter and Britt left her in the care of her nurse, where she was to remain through much of her childhood, and turned up at the Cool Elephant, a private nightclub, to hear a performance by Mel Torme. Princess Margaret joined them. The comedian Dudley Moore was there, too; he got up on stage at one point and played the piano for Mel. London being essentially a small town of hipsters, mods, models, international stars, and the Beatles, all of whom knew one another, it was not surprising that relationships were becoming notoriously intertwined. Also present at the Cool Elephant that night were David Frost and his girlfriend, who happened to be Peter's ex-girlfriend, Janette Scott, who happened later to marry Mel Torme.

The jet set was, in a word, flying. In April, Peter and Britt skipped over to Blue Harbor, Jamaica, where they visited Noel Coward. ("Peter Sellers and his wife came over to lunch the other day and were sweet," Coward wrote in his diary.) They were back in London in time for the queen's thirty-ninth birthday bash, hosted by Princess Margaret at Kensington Palace. The evening began with everyone—Elizabeth, Philip, Margaret, Snowdon, Peter, Michael Bentine, and Harry Secombe—attending a performance of *Son of Oblomov*, a West End comedy starring Spike Milligan. The actor Peter Eyre remembers that particular night all too well:

"Basically, the play was Spike Milligan humiliating a lot of actors, of which I was the youngest. (It was a straight play, but it began to go wrong in rehearsals. They didn't know what to do, so they began adding gags.) On the Queen's birthday, the Royal Family all came to the theater. Princess Margaret and Snowdon brought Peter Sellers along, and he did a sort of double act from the stalls with Spike Milligan on the stage." The other performers, including Eyre, found themselves upstaged not only by the show's erratic star but by a member of the audience. Eyre resented it, though the audience itself seems to have been delighted. Still, Eyre may have a point: "I thought that Milligan was, like most comedians, totally selfish. Comedians want it to be just them and the audience. They don't want other people."

• • •

Peter and Britt were traveling in a closed circle of celebrities and growing rather used to hanging out with the royals. One of Peter's young fans used to call him at the office. Hattie Stevenson remembers answering the phone and finding the teenage Prince Charles on the line: "You'd suddenly get the heir-apparent on the other end of the phone talking Bluebottle at you." Charles was a guest at Peter's estate, Brookfield, as well.

And the royals reciprocated. Peter and Britt were invited to Windsor Castle to go pheasant shooting, an occasion that provided Peter with the opportunity to outfit himself with a new £1,200 Purdy 12-bore shotgun and a fine hunting costume topped by a deerstalker. With practice, Peter wasn't a bad shot. It was thrilling to watch birds drop out of the sky at his instigation, and the congratulations of Princes Philip and Charles didn't hurt either. Peter and Britt also enjoyed teatime with Elizabeth II. The queen arranged the cups and saucers; Britt discussed Sweden; Phillip, Peter, Margaret, Tony, Charles, Princess Anne, and the Duke and Duchess of Kent put their two pence in. After tea was finished, they all played charades.

They were hanging out with the Beatles, too. George Harrison became a particularly good friend to Peter over the next few years; they shared an interest in Eastern religions. At first, Peter's fame was such that even the Fab Four were daunted by him. "We met him at numerous parties and different things," Harrison later said, "but at that time we were more in awe of him because of our childhoods and the Goons. We just loved the Goons. It was the greatest thing we'd ever heard. I remember thinking that we'd met all these film stars and presidents and kings and queens. . . . But there were very few people who really impressed me." Peter Sellers was one who did.

When the Beatles won two Grammy awards that year—Best New Artist(s) and Best Vocal Performance by a Group (for "A Hard Day's Night")—it was Peter who presented it to them in a videotaped sequence. John, Paul, George, and Ringo could not attend the proceedings in person because they were in London filming *Help*, 1965, with Richard Lester.

After Sellers gave the Beatles their awards, John Lennon responded Goonishly by launching into a speech in nonsense French; the others fol-

lowed suit, and the whole thing ended up slipping into "It's a Long Way
to Tipperary."

• • •

Although Peter had filmed his scenes in *Dr. Strangelove* two years earlier,
the film was still very much in the news in the spring of 1965. It had been
Columbia's biggest hit of 1964, pulling in the then-sizable sum of $5 mil-
lion in the United States alone. Now it was up for four Oscars, all in top
categories: Best Actor (Peter), Best Director (Kubrick), Best Screenplay
Based on Material from Another Medium (Kubrick, Southern, and
George), and Best Picture.

It lost all four.

My Fair Lady was named Best Picture, *Becket* Best Screenplay, George
Cukor Best Director (for *My Fair Lady*), and Rex Harrison Best Actor (also
for *My Fair Lady*).

Dr. Strangelove fared better at the BAFTA gala, where it won the
BAFTA Film Award, the award for Best British Film, and the award for
Best Film from Any Source.

Peter, however, lost again in the category of Best Actor—to none other
than Richard Attenborough for *Guns at Batasi.*

FIFTEEN

A script by Neil Simon, direction by Vittorio De Sica, a flamboyant and multi-personality role for himself, sunny Italian locations filmed in Technicolor, and even a featured part for Britt. Peter's next film project looked promising. After all of Brookfield's fits and starts, *After the Fox* (1966), a heist spoof, would be Brookfield's first actual production.

Given her glamour, Britt Ekland was continually offered film roles, but Peter, in a mix of professional expertise and jealousy, tended to talk her out of them. One nixed project, for example, was to star Dean Martin. "Do you really want Dean Martin breathing bourbon fumes all over you?" he asked his wife. Britt's role in the De Sica film had one distinct advantage: Peter was the star of the film and would therefore have to be there all the time.

Peter had met Neil Simon the previous August, and, soon thereafter, Simon showed him the first forty pages of his first screenplay. According to John Bryan, Peter "flipped over it," saying it was "the best screen material submitted to him in years." Peter's enthusiasm grew when Simon suggested a director: De Sica, whose groundbreaking *Bicycle Thieves* (1948) was one of the cornerstones of Italian neorealism. (The union of a preeminent Italian neorealist and a hot American comedy playwright was not quite as idiotic as it may seem. De Sica had long since moved away from lyrical, black-and-white urban dramas to slick, candy-colored, international money-makers like *Marriage Italian Style*, 1964.)

Sellers got along well enough with Simon and invited him at one point to Brookfield for a script conference. After the meeting concluded, Simon was surprised to find that Princess Margaret, Lord Snowdon, Harry Secombe, and Eric Sykes had been invited to join them for dinner and an improvised *Goon Show* routine. Simon's relationship with Sellers was friendly enough, but there were tinges of tension. Simon reports that on another occasion he, Peter, and Britt were sharing a limousine in London when they passed the West End theater at which Simon's latest hit stage comedy, *The Odd Couple*, was running. Britt mildly suggested to Peter that they see the show sometime, whereupon Peter turned hotly to Simon and demanded to know "what the hell's going on between you two?"

• • •

After the Fox is a farce about an Italian thief, a master of disguises named Aldo (Peter), who breaks out of prison to protect the morals of his loose sixteen-year-old sister, Gina (Britt). "It will be quite a challenge playing my husband's sister in the picture," Britt said at the time. "I hope I won't find it too strange." Simon's purposely farcical story requires Aldo to assume the guise of an Italian film director, Federico Fabrizi, who purports to film the actual smuggling of purloined gold bricks into Italy. Fabrizi then proceeds to cast a pompous, long-past-his-prime Hollywood star (Victor Mature) in the ersatz film along with Aldo's sister, whom he rechristens Gina Romantica.

Filming began in June on the island of Ischia, where Peter and Britt lodged at the Hotel Isobel Regina. For their residence in Rome, where the production moved at the end of July, they rented an elegant villa on the Appian Way, which Peter, true to form, had outfitted with multitudinous gadgets. They included his-and-hers walkie-talkies so that he could stay in touch with his wife when she was in a different part of the house.

With Peter assuming the role of de facto executive producer as well as star, his tendency to second guess his directors became even more detrimental than usual, since De Sica had to contend not only with a demanding star but a demanding financier as well, all wrapped up in the same moody man. De Sica's own attitude didn't help; he started telling friends and associates how much he detested Simon's screenplay. He didn't think too highly of Peter's performance, either.

The feeling was mutual; Peter grew equally disenchanted with De Sica. "He thinks in Italian, I think in English," Peter complained to Bert Mortimer. According to Hattie Stevenson, there was an even more intimate and painful problem: Peter "wasn't happy with Britt's performance at all, and so therefore that made home life very difficult."

At first, Peter took his frustrations out only on the film's unit publicist; in a typically roundabout way, Peter had him fired. But to spare Peter his characteristic spasm of remorse, he was told that the publicist had simply gone away on his own accord.

It was then that the color purple became not just a problem but one of the biggest and most long-lasting terrors of Peter's life. A script girl showed up one day in a purple outfit. Naturally she had no idea that this fashion decision would send Vittorio De Sica into an uncontrollable arm-waving frenzy. "It's the color of death!" De Sica revealed to Peter, who, suggestible and superstitious as ever, was haunted by purple for the rest of his life.

On at least one occasion Peter attributed the superstition to Sophia Loren, though he credited De Sica much more often. But no matter who planted the notion that purple could kill, Peter latched onto the belief fiercely. The mere hint of purple became a consistent trigger to Peter's easily erupting temper. In later years, publicists would scour Peter's proposed hotel rooms in search of the color of death; if they found it, the room would be changed. For Peter Sellers, the color ruined everything it touched. Purple was to life itself as Fred had been to Rembrandt.

• • •

Filming in Rome one day in early September, Britt was playing a scene with Victor Mature. Peter had stayed home that morning, but he just couldn't help himself but appear at Cinecittà later that day and, with the camera rolling and De Sica miming the expression he wanted from his leading actress, Peter came creeping up to his wife's side, so close that he was barely out of camera range, and whispered, "Play it as though you were *dreaming* of being beautiful!" De Sica took this usurpation in stride. To placate his star, who was also his boss, De Sica asked him to serve as Mature's stand-in for some close-ups of Britt that were taken later that day. But Sellers was growing even more irritated by De Sica—his English was too bad, his obvious distaste for the material too debilitating, and De Sica was simply the most obvious target for Peter's ire.

So he told John Bryan to get rid of him. Bryan resisted on financial as well as artistic grounds. Then, bizarrely, Peter demanded that British sausages be flown in for the cast and crew, De Sica objected, and Peter responded by telephoning his friend Joseph McGrath in England and asking him to take over the direction of the film. McGrath refused. De Sica appears to have completed the shooting—barely—though Peter himself took on the task of orchestrating postproduction work on the film.

Fed up, John Bryan terminated his relationship with Peter. *After the Fox* was Brookfield's first, last, and only production; the company dissolved.

At the beginning of filming *After the Fox*, Victor Mature was quoted as saying that "if Sellers plays his cards right, I may let him steal the picture." By July, Mature was disenchanted. "I just saw my rushes," the aging star told Sheilah Graham, "and I suggest you sell your United Artists stock."

When the film was released, the *New York Times* agreed with Mature: "Mr. Sellers acts on the level of Mr. [Jerry] Lewis, which is to say broadly, bluntly, and hoggishly." *Time* was also scathing: "a garlicky farce that could barely make the late late show on Sicilian TV."

Still, Peter's time in Italy was scarcely in vain. He bought a new Hasselblad camera, which he used to take a number of photos that ran in Italian newspapers as well as in London's *Daily Express* and *Daily Mirror*.

And he got his Ferrari Superfast at last.

Only five of the cars were made that year, but Peter managed to snag one—a sand-colored number with matching butter-leather seats. It was capable of revving up to 180 miles per hour, he was proud to say, though he was also forced to acknowledge that there was no place in England where he could actually drive that fast.

• • •

In public, Peter was buoyant, his marriage to Britt a visible success as long as it was outsiders who were watching. Once again, he had married an actress. Each member of the couple knew how to play a scene in front of an audience. They played things differently at home.

Neil Simon and his wife were staying virtually across the street from the Sellerses on the Appian Way during the production of *After the Fox*. They were awakened one night when Britt, after a particularly nasty fight with Peter—he threw a chair at her—climbed through a window in her nightgown and sought refuge at the neighbors'. The Simons were aghast, having had no idea Peter and Britt were anything less than fully content with each other.

"I tried so hard to understand Sellers," Ekland says in retrospect. "I related his dark moods to the pressures and ambiguities of his genius. Where was the warmth, humor, and humanity he generated on the screen? There were interludes when he was truly a loving, gentle, and generous human being, but these moments were like flashes of sunshine."

A few months earlier, Peter had penned a reflective piece for, believe it or not, *Seventeen* magazine. "Peter Sellers Talks to Teens" proved that on some skewed but fundamental level he knew himself better than anyone else did: "If I can't really find a way to live with myself, I can't expect anyone else to live with me," he wrote.

A more Goonish (but no less honest) bit of self-knowledge came out on *The Ed Sullivan Show* in the fall of 1966, when Peter appeared in the guise of his *After the Fox* character Federico Fabrizi. (For the purposes of historical placement, Sullivan's other guests that night were Judy Garland, Sophie Tucker, Tom Jones, Topo Gigio, and the Marquis Chimps.) Asked by Sullivan to explain the symbolic meaning of his film *No More Pasta*, in which a beautiful woman drowns in a vat of minestrone, Fabrizi waxed poetic: "We are all in a thick soup, swimming around in our own vegetables! With our arms outstretched, calling for human compassion! And—*come formaggi?*—a little cheese."

• • •

Habitually, many of the films Peter wanted to make were either made by other actors or not made at all. In April 1965, the Mirisch Brothers—who evidently bore no grudge over the *Kiss Me, Stupid* debacle—bought the rights to Kingsley Amis's new novel *The Egyptologists*; Bryan Forbes was to develop the film with Peter. Soon there was a deal for Peter as well: $600,000 for a ten-week shoot; living expenses of $1,000 per week; and 10 percent of the gross after the break-even point. Peter was no longer concerned about putting in long days; the contract specified studio days lasting nine hours and location days of ten hours. Peter would get top billing, script approval, and the right to make changes in the film after it was shot. Shooting was to start on or around October 1. But October passed, and by the end of the month Peter was still holding off on *The Egyptologists* pending another rewrite. It never got made.

In August, he mentioned to the Hollywood columnist Army Archerd another project in which he was most interested in participating. Charles Chaplin would direct the picture; Sophia Loren would costar. He hadn't seen a screenplay yet, he said, but he was confident that it would be there when the time came. One month later, Chaplin began filming *A Countess from Hong Kong* (1967) with Sophia and Marlon Brando.

Then came *Waterloo*. "Is there any truth in Mike Connelly's report that you want me to play Napoleon?" Peter cabled John Huston from the Hotel Maurice in Paris in late October. "If so, very interested."

The next day Peter returned to Brookfield, where he received Huston's unpunctuated reply a few days later: "Information is news to me but nevertheless a fine idea we have however already contacted Richard Burton regarding the role stop in case anything should go wrong may I please get in touch with you?"

Disappointed, Peter responded kindly but with a touch of self-protection: "Agree Burton would be marvelous casting and on second thoughts am not sure I would be right stop." He tagged on a marvelously absurd philosophical conclusion: "However what is to be will be even if it never happens."

• • •

To the handsome tune of $25,000 a day, Bryan Forbes convinced Peter to appear for three days' work on *The Wrong Box*, Forbes's adaptation of a novel by Robert Louis Stevenson and Lloyd Osbourne. Sellers's role was, as the *Financial Times* described it, that of the "befuddled, cat-ridden abortionist."

Dr. Pratt (coughing): "Yes, I'm . . . I'm . . . I'm all right. It's just a fur ball, it's nothing. Strange, I haven't had fur for a fortnight."

Forbes had asked Spike Milligan to appear in a small role as well for only a token fee, but Spike would have none of it. "Suddenly last year I woke up to the fact that everybody else was driving a Rolls Royce while I was driving a Mini Minor," Spike told Forbes, "so I decided to put an end to it and go into this business strictly for money like everybody else. When I have got a Rolls Royce and money in the bank I will start doing it for kicks again, but not till then."

Peter was in Rome when he got the script on June 10, but he didn't go before the cameras until mid-November, when, as planned, he worked for three full days, sharing the doctor's cramped attic office set with twenty-five hired cats. He plays his two all-too-brief scenes with Peter Cook, whose character, Morris Finsbury, turns to the decrepit and disreputable Dr. Pratt for a blank death certificate, which Finsbury intends to fill in later with the pertinent details. "All I want is the *death certificate*, Doctor," Finsbury stresses impatiently. "Don't we all," Pratt replies while pouring himself another drink. Under a bulbous makeup nose and hideously pallid complexion stare two weary, vacant eyes. "I was not always as you see me now," Pratt explains.

When Finsbury returns later that night, he has to rouse the doctor once again from his habitual slumbers. "I tell you the woman was already dead when I came in!" Pratt frantically cries, flustered at the brutal exposure of his own consciousness. Immediately after signing the death certificate to Finsbury's great relief, Dr. Pratt uses a squeaking kitten as his inkblotter. "Particularly delirious are two passages with Peter Sellers," Dilys Powell raved in the *Sunday Times*; "Peter Sellers is a positive gem, the finest thing in the film," wrote Michael Thornton in the *Sunday Express*.

• • •

Near the end of the year, Peter filmed a segment of a Granada television special, *The Music of Lennon and McCartney*, for the producer George Martin. After Lulu sang "I Saw Him Standing There," Marianne Faithfull sang "Yesterday," and Henry Mancini played "If I Fell" on the piano—not to mention the Beatles themselves performing (actually lip-synching) "Day Tripper" and "We Can Work It Out"—another familiar British face appeared.

PAUL: What's all this, John?
JOHN: It's Peter Sellers!

Cut to a stark Shakespearean set with incidental madrigal music on the sound track. Peter, dressed as Richard III, sits on an Elizabethan chair and, in the voice of Laurence Olivier, begins reciting the lyrics of "A Hard Day's Night." It is indescribably hilarious.

Peter had done the routine for release as a record earlier in the year, with Martin acting as producer, but it's the televised visuals that push the bit onto the level of Olympian comedy. The combination of Sellers's petulant, mad Olivier imitation with his near-instinctive talent for striking wildly funny facial expressions, made Peter's brief TV appearance in November not only the highlight of the program but also the best nugget of work he did that year.

During the taping, he had had some difficulty with his lines and called, rather saltily, for cue cards. No one seems to have minded, however, since Peter lightened the mood by abruptly launching into "A Hard Day's Night" as recited by Spike Milligan's goofy Eccles. Then he did it as Fred Kite.

The final, taped product, however, was pure, leering Olivier. With a declamatory and nasal delivery, Sellers barks certain words and bites others, glances out of the corners of his slitty eyes, and brings out in full force the song's underlying filth. The Beatles themselves couldn't get away with it; Peter could—and did:

A grumpy *dog* and *log*. A sly, insinuating *do*. A most self-satisfied *everything*. And, with a final smirk, *alright*.

Then Richard stands and delivers his outraged plea: "Can I do all this, yet cannot get a hit?"

The wish was granted within a month. Peter Sellers's recording of "A Hard Day's Night" reached number fourteen on the British pop charts in December.

• • •

"He could write his own ticket with me if he'd write and direct *Casino Royale*."

This was Charles K. Feldman talking to *Variety* in June 1965. Feldman had a dream—to produce a big, splashy James Bond spoof in Technicolor and Panavision, with lots of gaudy sets and costumes and mid-sixties psychedelic wackiness and gorgeous babes and multiple 007s and a roster of glamorous international movie stars. Peter would be perfect for it, he thought.

They had been talking since late April. First it was on, then it was off, then it was maybe—Peter kept changing his mind—and by June, Feldman had taken to wooing his star in the press as well as through cajoling telephone calls and flattering letters. Peter wasn't the only one to respond to Feldman's entreaties by hesitating. Bryan Forbes had been very close to agreeing to be the film's director, but he backed out before signing anything.

By late August, *Casino Royale* was on again. Columbia Pictures was putting up the money, and Peter, in Rome, was finally agreeing to terms: $750,000 plus $10,000 expenses. This time, Feldman got the insurance he needed to cover Peter—$5 million worth—and Peter seemed happy. He insisted that his friend Joe McGrath be the film's director, and Feldman approved. Peter had had an idea for a costar, too.

Sophia.

• • •

Everybody liked Joe McGrath, Feldman told Peter in the fall, but McGrath wasn't much help to Feldman in terms of convincing top-of-the-line performers like Sophia to sign onto the project since McGrath had never directed a feature film before. (McGrath had considerable television experience, but no movies.) If Feldman had been able to present McGrath to Sophia as an important director, then some of her reluctance might have been assuaged. But he couldn't, he was sad to say, so Miss Loren had declined the chance to appear with Peter in *Casino Royale*.

There were still script problems, too, Feldman told him. The first three drafts had been written by the veteran screenwriter Ben Hecht (*Scarface*, 1932; *Notorious*, 1946; and many others), who had died the year before. Feldman had acceded to Peter's wishes when he'd hired Terry Southern to write new dialogue and bits of comedy business. (According to Southern's son, Nile, Sellers specified in his contract that "he would have the exclusive services of Terry Southern to write his dialogue. And a white Bentley.") Peter had asked Terry to meet with him in Rome, and at the time both men thought they understood each other's minds about the direction of the script. But, it seemed to Feldman, they hadn't really heard each other as much as they believed they had. Still, Feldman said, he was certain that they would have a great screenplay before shooting began.

In early September, Feldman flew to Rome to meet with Peter and discuss casting. McGrath joined him. So did Peter's Hollywood agent, Harvey Orkin. So did *Casino Royale*'s latest screenwriter—Wolf Mankowitz.

One scarcely had to be as superstitious as Peter Sellers was to see that this was a distinctly bad omen, a human version of purple. Sellers and Mankowitz had tried and failed, furiously, to form a production company together in 1960, and Mankowitz distrusted Peter greatly. Still, their meetings appear to have gone smoothly enough—while they were actually happening, that is—and together the key members of the production team began to come up with a cast list. *Casino Royale*, they all agreed, should costar Shirley MacLaine and Trevor Howard.

A few days later, Feldman was back in Los Angeles meeting with MacLaine over dinner at Trader Vic's. They called Peter from their table and spoke for half an hour about the film's story and characters. The next day, Peter called Feldman. He didn't like the way Mankowitz was developing the script, he said; he suggested that they bring Terry Southern back. Peter was also complicating matters by talking to Columbia about doing another picture called *A Severed Head*, which was scheduled to shoot in mid-February. Charlie Feldman knew that *Casino Royale* would take more than a month's worth of Peter's time, and he was worried that his star was overcommitting himself.

In November, with a late-January start date having been scheduled at

Shepperton, Feldman arranged for Dr. Rex Kennamer to check up on Peter, just to make sure. Kennamer found Peter to be in good health, and *Casino Royale* was on its way. Sort of.

Casting was still in flux. MacLaine and Howard were out. Orson Welles, David Niven, and Ursula Andress were in. Eventually, of course, so were a few others, including William Holden, Charles Boyer, Woody Allen, Deborah Kerr, Joanna Pettet, Daliah Lavi, John Huston, Jacqueline Bissett, Jean-Paul Belmondo, and George Raft.

Casino Royale is categorically chaotic, but that was its nature all along. David Niven plays Agent 007, but so does Peter Sellers. In fact, so does Ursula Andress, and Joanna Pettet, and Terence Cooper. Niven's Bond reluctantly agrees to return to Her Majesty's service after the death of agent M (John Huston), whose fake widow (Deborah Kerr) fails to seduce him and becomes a nun. The evil SMERSH has gone bankrupt, and the baccarat mastermind Le Chiffre (Orson Welles) tries to win back funding in the casino but loses to a man named Evelyn Tremble (Sellers), who has been hired to play James Bond; Le Chiffre responds to the loss by torturing Tremble/Bond, who meanwhile has been seduced by the voluptuous Vesper (Ursula Andress), and on and on, until the purest evil on earth is found to exist in the form of Woody Allen.

● ● ●

Joe McGrath recalls his close friend Peter with a refreshing lack of malice: "There was a kindness there—a soft kindness, do you know what I mean? It was a side of him a lot of people never saw. So, I would forgive him most things. I mean, we had a bad time on *Casino Royale* because he went off and disappeared for three weeks. He was chasing Britt. They had trouble, and she went back to Sweden. But meanwhile Orson Welles and two thousand extras were waiting. Orson said, 'Where's your thin friend, Joe?' "

Wolf Mankowitz was not as forgiving of Peter. In fact, he was downright nasty: "He was a treacherous lunatic," the screenwriter later swore. "My advice to Charles Feldman was not in any circumstances to get involved with Sellers. But Sellers was at his peak at that time. I told Charlie that Sellers would fuck everything up—he wanted different directors, he wanted to piss around with the script. He knew nothing about anything except going on and doing funny faces and funny voices, and he wasn't really a great actor.

"He was *terrified* of playing with Orson and converted this into an aversion for Orson before he even met Orson," Mankowitz went on. There are a number of stories of bad behavior regarding Sellers and Welles: Peter overheard a young woman comment, about Welles, "Isn't he sexy?" and immediately became jealous. Peter, together in his suite with Orson, tried to get Welles to laugh, failed, and never got over his resentment. Peter met Orson in a Dorchester Hotel elevator. Sellers was coming down from his penthouse, and Orson and Mankowitz got on on a lower floor and Peter remarked that he hoped the elevator wouldn't collapse from the weight.

Princess Margaret was the last straw. Welles had developed a friendship with Margaret some years earlier when he was in London directing his stage production of *Othello*. Sellers, having no idea that she and Welles even knew each other, invited her to stop by the already greatly troubled set on February 18 for lunch. He made the mistake of crowing about it to Welles. "Then Princess Margaret *came*," Welles later gloated, "and passed him by and said, 'Hello, Orson, I haven't seen you for *days!*' *That* was the real end. 'Orson, I haven't seen you for days!' absolutely killed him. He went white as a sheet because *he* was going to get to present *me*."

"That's been blown up to ridiculous proportions," Joe McGrath retorts. "Peter never resented Orson at that lunch. I think the problem was really that Britt left and Sellers just got the scent and chased. When he came back, Orson was just sitting there sort of smiling. And Peter lost his courage. I talked to Milligan, and Milligan said, 'Well, yeah—he's obviously so ashamed that he just doesn't want to face up.'"

In fact, Peter had already decided the weekend before the fatal Margaret luncheon to issue a new demand to Feldman. He insisted that his scenes with Welles be shot in what Feldman's production log calls "single cuts—thereby avoiding having both of them working together."

Whatever the reason for his attitude and conduct, Peter proceeded to make the filming of *Casino Royale* substantially more difficult than such a heaving, overproduced extravaganza was already destined to be. At one point he departed the set and simply left a sign that said "Yankee Go Home."

Describing the Welles imbroglio, McGrath says that Peter informed him that " 'as long as I'm not in the same setup I'll go back.' I said, 'No! What are we doing, a home movie? This is *Orson Welles* you're talking about. And not only that, Peter, but you *wanted* Orson Welles. You said, "Wouldn't it be wonderful if we got Orson Welles?" And we get him and suddenly *this* happens.'" McGrath also pointed out to Peter that from a technical perspective alone it would be ridiculous to shoot a Panavision film with two stars in different setups; the point of *any* widescreen pro- cess, after all, is to shoot *wide*. Keeping Sellers and Welles in separate spaces and cutting back and forth between them would look, in a word, dumb.

Peter's sharp aversion to Orson was not the only problem for McGrath. "At one point he said to me, 'Sorry, I was a bit late coming back when you called me. I had something important to do. I was trying to get a new stylus for my record player.' I said, 'Oh, that's very funny. Don't treat me like you treat everybody else. Come on. What's going on?' 'No,' he said.

"I said, 'Who do you think you are? Peter Sellers?'"

"He said, 'Yes. I fucking *am* Peter Sellers!'"

"I said, 'This is getting out of control. We call you and you don't come. I'm not talking for Charlie Feldman, but Feldman did give you the chance with *What's New Pussycat?*, you know, and here you are, and Charlie is frightened to ask you, to tell you, to get here on time. *He is the producer.* And he is frightened to actually say, "Get here on time." *He is saying to me, "Would you tell him please to get there on time?"* So what game are you playing? Either get here on time or don't get here at all.'

"And then there was a break, and we went into the trailer to talk about another scene, and he said, 'I've had enough of this,' and he swung a punch at me.

"He hit me on the side of the jaw, and it sort of bounced off me, you know—it was halfhearted—but I thought, What the hell? If you want to hit me, come on. So I tried to hit him. Jerry Crampton, a stunt man, was outside, and he opened the door. Peter and I were, as Terry Southern later said, 'aiming blows at each other like school girls trying to hit wasps.' Crampton grabbed us and separated us and said, 'I love you both; I do not know which one of you to hit.' Sellers and I started laughing, and that was it.

"Then he disappeared again, and he was afraid to come back because of embarrassment. If he came back and I was still directing, and he walked onto the set and Orson was there, everybody was going to say, 'Oh what a shit you are.' So he said to me, 'I'll come back if I don't play any scenes with Orson,' and I said, 'Get lost,' and that was it." And with that, Joe McGrath left *Casino Royale*.

Actually, Feldman had been against McGrath from the beginning and later claimed only to have hired him because Peter had demanded it. Feldman claimed that he'd wanted multiple directors from the start. If that was really the case, then the producer got exactly what he wanted.

As early as February, Feldman tried to get Bryan Forbes to come on board again, but Forbes refused, particularly after he learned that Columbia executives, still stung by his refusal to accept the job originally, were reacting to his tough financial demands by calling him a blackmailing whore behind his back. Feldman turned to Blake Edwards, who said that all it took was a million dollars. Feldman didn't have a spare million dollars, so he turned to Clive Donner, whom Peter rejected. Feldman then hired Val Guest. And Ken Hughes. And Robert Parrish. And Richard Talmadge. And John Huston.

All in all, the filming of *Casino Royale* took place not only at Shepperton but at the Pinewood studios and at MGM's studios as well, with different directors directing different actors in different scenes with three directors of photography—Jack Hildyard, John Wilcox, and Nicolas Roeg. The whole thing took eight months to shoot.

None of this was easy on Charlie Feldman. There were midnight meetings with Peter and Britt, whom Peter was at one time pushing to be cast in the film. Phone calls and meetings with five new directors along with a growing list of writers. More meetings with Peter and his slew of agents and managers and lawyers—Harvey Orkin, Bill Wills, Freddie Fields, John Humphries. . . . Explanations by letter and wire to Columbia executives in Hollywood, who were becoming apoplectic at the rising costs. Then Orson decided he'd had enough and left for Barcelona.

Feldman brought Robert Parrish onto the project not only because Parrish was an experienced director (*Fire Down Below*, 1957, with Rita Hayworth and Robert Mitchum, among others), but because he was an experienced editor, too, having cut such films as John Ford's *The Battle of Midway* (1942) and Max Ophuls's *Caught* (1949). (Parrish had also been a child actor; he's one of the mean boys who pitch spitballs at the Tramp in Chaplin's *City Lights*, 1931.) Feldman's hope was that Parrish would know what to do with the countless reels of disjointed footage into which his multimillion-dollar baby, the still far from complete *Casino Royale*, had degenerated. (The final cost was at least $12 million, at that time a very high price tag.)

Parrish was also known for being a gentleman, someone who could handle a temperamental movie star—or two—so at Feldman's behest, Parrish flew to Barcelona to meet with Welles and convince him to return.

Delicately and with characteristic charm, he told the director of *Citizen Kane* (1941), *The Magnificent Ambersons* (1942), and *Touch of Evil* (1958) that he and Charlie Feldman would be very grateful to him if he would please come back to London so that they could finish filming *Casino Royale*. He'd be delighted to return, Orson replied. He'd just gotten bored waiting for Peter to show up on the set and thought he'd take a holiday in Spain.

There was just one thing, Parrish then mentioned. "Peter doesn't want to film any more scenes with you." And with that, Parrish later declared, "Orson got up from the table, came over, kissed me—square on the lips— and said, 'That's the best news I've ever heard!' "

The two men returned to London, but shooting still didn't proceed on schedule. According to Parrish's wife, Kathleen, Peter would drive around in his car and constantly call the studio on his car phone to see whether Welles was on the set. For his part, Welles would start drinking champagne at nine in the morning and continue all day long. The hours went by— Orson was quite the life of the party—and then Peter would stick his head in the door and Orson would immediately and loudly needle him and nothing would get done that day.

• • •

Charlie Feldman's contracts alone were creating a massive pile on his desk. John Huston, the director of such films as *The Maltese Falcon* (1941) and *The Treasure of the Sierra Madre* (1948) turned up in March as one of the *Casino Royale*'s directors as well as one of its actors. Huston had not only just finished directing *The Bible* (1966). He'd played Noah, the narrator, and the Voice of God, too. Maybe Feldman thought that only He could control Peter Sellers.

The screenwriter John Law began work in March, too. Peter insisted on it. Law was a television writer who worked, along with Graham Chapman, John Cleese, and Denis Norden, on David Frost's program, *The Frost Report*. Peter thought he'd be great for *Casino Royale*, and so Law was added to the lengthening list of rewriters.

John Law was just the latest in what was to be a very long line of scribes; at least eleven people wrote dialogue for, restructured the story of, tinkered with, and destroyed the work of others on the script of *Casino Royale*. Only Mankowitz, Law, and Michael Sayers got screen credit. Woody Allen, Val Guest, Terry Southern, and Peter himself contributed to it as well, uncredited. (On top of everything else, Peter and Feldman spent March and April going back and forth with each other over whether Sellers would get a writing credit. He didn't.) The novelist Joseph Heller (*Catch 22*), the television writer Lorenzo Semple, Jr. (*Batman*), and none other than Peter's Hollywood nemesis Billy Wilder were also brought on board by Feldman at one point or another to try and salvage this great, wobbling behemoth, but nobody has ever really sorted out exactly what any of them wrote or whether any of it managed to find its way into the finished film.

John Huston was ensconced in style at Claridge's when the screenwriter Nunnally Johnson, also in London, tried to get into the act as well. He sent over to Huston some new script pages for *Casino Royale* with a little note that might have just as easily applied to the whole fiasco: "If you can use the enclosed, help yourself. If not, tear it up."

By springtime, rumors of the conspicuous catastrophe were raging through Hollywood and London like two clouds of loud mosquitoes. They continued to bite until well after the film's release. Peter "got hung up on safety," a Hollywood reporter divulged, "and his constant calls from his Rolls squad car to Scotland Yard to report traffic violations frequently made Page One. He insisted on immediate police action and often got so carried away [that] he would make the arrest himself. Several afternoons of production were lost when Sellers appeared in court with his civilian arrests." This was an exaggeration, though it is true that on one occasion Peter did bring a reckless driving charge against another driver, and he only seems to have had to appear in court once (on April 1). After some protracted discussions with Feldman's assistant, Jerry Bressler, he agreed to give the production a free day of shooting to make up for the day lost to the court appearance.

Ursula Andress was growing so weary of the interminable production that she started complaining to the press hounds. "I started the film on January 11," she sighed to Sheilah Graham in April. "It was to be just a few weeks. It is already three months, and we can't finish before June. Why? There are so many things. If Peter feels tired, we must slow down. We are never allowed to rush because of him. . . . [And] he writes a lot."

Andress, for example, was originally supposed to have performed a scene with Peter atop an elephant, but Peter nixed it and decided that the scene should really feature bagpipers. The deleted elephant had, however, provided Peter with an opening, which he seized, in one of his early battles with Orson Welles. Welles and Sellers were shooting the key scene in which

LeChiffre and Tremble play the crucial rounds of baccarat. Welles decided it was time for *him* to do a little improvising, so instead of going along with the script, which required his character to lose the game, he performed some off-the-cuff card tricks and won. Sellers is said to have blown a gasket. "No!" Peter shouted in front of the assembled crowd of technicians and extras. "I've had enough from *one* elephant."

The stories keep coming. According to McGrath, there was to have been a scene with "a giant roulette wheel when Sellers had a dream. And he's the ball, spinning around on this giant roulette wheel, and the red and black divisions of the roulette wheel are girls' legs in dresses—they're in black and red. He's spinning around the rim, and then he rolls into someone's crotch." The sequence was shot but discarded; Peter didn't like it.

Then, in what Jacqueline Bisset recalls as a "sick joke," Peter shot her in the face with a blank. In the scene in question, Tremble creeps into a window with his gun drawn and is most surprised when the occupant, Miss Goodthighs (Bisset) recognizes him and calls out his name. Tremble was supposed to turn and fire the gun in her general direction, but Peter pointed it right at her and pulled the trigger. "First I thought I had actually been actually shot," Bisset later said. "Then, when I realized it had been a blank, I thought I had been blinded. My face looked like a shower spout of pin-pricks leaking blood. To get shot in your first scene with a big star—that's a nightmare."

And day after day, everybody was kept waiting for everybody else to show up on the set. In the annals of *Casino Royale*, Peter has taken the brunt of the blame for the delays. But the production logs tell a more nuanced story: "Waiting for Mr. Sellers." "Waiting for Mr. Welles." "Waiting for Miss Andress." "Waiting for Mr. Welles." "Waiting for Mr. Sellers." "Waiting for Crowd . . ." By mid-March, with *Casino Royale* already running weeks over schedule, Peter was calling in sick. "Only able to shoot fifteen seconds." "Only able to shoot twenty seconds." "Only thirty seconds possible." By the beginning of April, Feldman had calculated the total of Peter's delays at fourteen-and-a-half days at a cost of $705,000. Peter simply left the production sometime in May or June, which is the reason Terence Cooper suddenly takes over as yet another 007. At that point, somebody had to replace Peter, and it didn't much matter who.

• • •

Casino Royale was the biggest, most overproduced mess of Peter's career, but even *it* has a few good moments, one of which features Peter in a ridiculous striped outfit of no discernable category—a one-piece affair with shorts and a revealing V-neck (in the back), a sort of Matelot pajama—spinning with Ursula Andress on a round and revolving fuschia-covered bed surrounded by mirrors. Andress's character, Vesper, is filming home movies at the time, after which, meaninglessly, she shoots still photos of Evelyn Tremble as Hitler, Napoleon, an anonymous flaming queen ("Hello, sailor!"), and Toulouse-Lautrec.

Peter's card game with Orson is pretty much the disaster it promised to be, given that the two actors appear together in only one setup, with the rest of the sequence being filmed in individual shots. The characters look like they're worlds apart; even with the flagrantly artificial mise-en-scène of *Casino Royale* the camera doesn't lie. And despite some marvelous special effects, the subsequent scene in which Le Chiffre tortures Tremble is obviously filmed not only in separate shots but in separate *sets*. "The most exquisite torture is all in the mind," Le Chiffre tells Tremble before pulling the switches. He may be right, but by the time the spaceship lands in Trafalgar Square, one just doesn't care anymore.

Casino Royale opened in April 1967, with a royal command performance in London. Kathy Parrish remembers the queen sitting in one row laughing and enjoying herself and Feldman sitting in the row behind her, knowing the gargantuan thing just wasn't any good. Notices were mixed, but the film did find its audience and made at least some of its money back. It has but a few critical defenders today. One is the film scholar Robert Von Dassanowsky, who sees in its fragmented pastiche a grander philosophy: "The failure of modernity and a celebration of what Umberto Eco would call the postmodern 'crisis of reason' permeates nearly every scene of *Casino Royale*." If Von Dassanowsky is right, then Peter Sellers himself really may turn out to be the quintessential postmodern man.

SIXTEEN

Fragmentation reigned, as it must for every postmodernist. Peter's constant dieting continued, as did his marital discord and bad-tempered parenting, all broken up with pleasant evenings spent around a piano with friends, singing, laughing, and being the man he could have been if he hadn't been so many other less agreeable people in the meantime.

Joe McGrath and Peter Sellers made up after Peter himself walked away from *Casino Royale*. McGrath reports: "I got a letter from Peter later, apologizing, saying, 'I'm terribly sorry about what happened, I was wrong. We will work together again, I promise you.'" They were having drinks at the Dorchester bar soon thereafter when a Columbia executive came by the table. "Joe!" he cried. "God! I'm so sorry that you left the film! It was that bastard Sellers that fucked everything up. And it's a pleasure to meet you, Mr. Allen."

To keep the weight off, Peter ate nothing but spaghetti for a time. There was also a Chinese vegetable diet, a macrobiotic diet, and a yoga diet. There was a wine-and-steak diet, too. For a while he consumed only bananas.

The children continued to find life with their father to be difficult. Spike once commented that "he used the children as pawns. He loved them, but on his own terms. They had to love him when he demanded it."

"He threw me out of home for the first time when I was eight or nine," Michael Sellers says. "He asked us who we loved more, our mother or him. Sarah, to keep the peace, said, 'I love you both equally.' I said, 'No, I love my mum.' He threw the two of us out and said he never wanted to see us again." But of course he did, and of course their encounters were just as troubled, if not quite so memorable. Michael was shuttled around a lot, and not only between his parents. "By the time I was twelve I'd been to about eight or nine different schools." He and Sarah liked their stepmother, though. "Britt was interested in us," says Sarah. "None of his other women was."

As for Peg, her hostility to Britt seemed to wane a bit over time, perhaps in response to Britt's obvious affection for Michael and Sarah. Baby Victoria didn't get much affection from Grandma, though. "Peg did not like the role of Grannie," says Ekland. "And she would always refer to Victoria as 'it.' "

• • •

Peg Sellers, the former vaudeville showgirl, cut an increasingly bizarre figure around mod, swinging London in the mid-1960s. "She liked to wear little-girl dresses and even flaunted mini-skirts although she was well past sixty," Britt reports. "She also painted thick lashings of rouge on her face and bright, glossy lipstick."

Peg's heavy consumption of liquor and cigarettes had done nothing but increase throughout her widowhood. Britt couldn't help but notice that she hid her smokes under the cushions of the couch and decanted her booze into empty medicine bottles, which she then stashed in the bathroom cabinet, all to keep Peter from confronting his mother's vices directly. Still, says Ekland, "I got along with Peg well and I knew that as long as I didn't betray the secret of her gin reservoirs, I always would."

• • •

Through it all, Peter's closest and most trusted friends provided him with the greatest comfort. "The thing about psychiatry, I found, is just talking to someone," he mentioned to a British newspaper in 1966, "and in England if you have some good friends, as I have, then you don't need to go to a psychiatrist." Maybe, maybe not.

But the fact is, Peter did find compassion and solace among his mates. Spike, Joe McGrath, Graham Stark, Kenneth Griffith, David Lodge—these men showed him the kind of mercy that most frail people deserve but rarely receive. Their companionship was genuine, particularly when, from Peter's perspective, the rest of the world appeared inexplicably to become more and more hostile to him. His friends saw Peter's oddities—how could they help but notice them, since he wore his eccentricities on his sleeve?—but they saw the tender core beneath. Also, he was hilarious.

"He could be very, very funny," says McGrath. "There used to be an Italian restaurant called the Tratou in London. Milligan, Peter, Eric Sykes, and myself—we would get our wives or girlfriends, whoever we were with at the time, and we'd go around at ten at night and have dinner. Then they would close the restaurant, but we were allowed to stay. There was a pianist called Alan Claire, who they used to use a lot in television shows—Frank Sinatra always used him when he came over—and he'd be there, and we would finish dinner and sit around till three or four o'clock in the morning, and Peter would sing. He'd sing standards, and Spike would play the trumpet. That's a side that other people never saw."

For other people, the so-called normal, it takes great trust to expose their ugliest aspects to those closest to them. Typically, though, Peter Sellers got it backward. He trusted only his closest friends enough to reveal to them his essentially good heart.

• • •

In June of 1966, shortly after walking out on *Casino Royale*, Peter was named Commander of the British Empire by Elizabeth II in the Queen's Birthday Honors List. The queen named Harold Pinter as well.

Then destiny called: Peter spent four days shooting *Alice in Wonderland* (1967). He was the befuddled King of Hearts.

"I didn't want a lot of famous featured performances with lots of animal heads," the director Jonathan Miller declares of his adaptation of Lewis Carroll's philosophically absurd children's book. The physician-turned-satirist and *Goon Show* fan had something darker and more cerebral in mind: "It's rather melancholy. The film was designed to be a re-creation of Victorian life and the melancholy of growing up—the Victorian thing about childhood being an innocent time and everything else being sad and decaying." Miller made *Alice in Wonderland* on a relatively low budget for BBC television, a fact that did not discourage some of Britain's best performers from appearing in it. "I asked John Geilgud, Michael Redgrave, Leo McKern, and Peter Cook, and then I went to Sellers [and] said, 'Would you do it for as little as £500, which is all you'll get paid by the BBC?' "

Miller had worked with Peter in 1961. "I once appeared on what was then called a gramophone record with him—'The Bridge on the River Wye.' Peter Cook and I figured as minor characters in that, with Sellers rather brilliantly playing Alec Guinness, and it was quite funny. We spent a day doing it, and he was very jolly. There was lots of laughter then." (The record, a spoof of the 1957 film *The Bridge on the River Kwai*, costarred Spike and used an old *Goon Show* episode, "The Africa Incident," as the core; George Martin produced it. After the record was cut, but before it was released, the producers of the film threatened to sue, so Martin was forced painstakingly to remove the sound *k* from every utterance of "Kwai." Hence "Wye.")

Miller couldn't help but notice the change in Sellers, who was markedly troubled during the production of *Alice in Wonderland*. "He was a moody bugger, you know? He was very superstitious. If things had gone badly on the way to the location, if his stars hadn't read right, he'd be sunk in a gloom and would be unwilling to film." Still, Miller knew, "you could amuse him, and a sort of strange, mischievous smile would spread across his face." The rest of the time, though, Peter "kept to himself and often sat apart in a deck chair in a starry gloom."

Peter Eyre, who played the Knave of Hearts, retains no fond memories of working with Sellers in *Alice in Wonderland*. "I thought Peter Sellers was going to be like an actor. But he wasn't, really. He absolutely didn't relate to any of the other actors. He had to be slightly polite to the old actress who played the Queen of Hearts, Alison Leggatt, but otherwise he was completely closed off as a person. He only ever loosened up when Snowdon came to photograph. There were a lot of well-known actors in the production; I don't remember him actually speaking to anybody. And those other famous actors, like Michael Redgrave and John Gielgud—they weren't like that at all. Then again, they didn't have cars with chauffeurs. Sellers was a movie star."

As he had with Spike Milligan, Eyre attributes Peter's distance to the fact that he was, at his core, a comedian: "They can't bear the idea that somebody else is going to get a laugh. It's like an illness."

Without contradicting those who found Peter to be generous to them in front of a camera, Eyre is probably right about what might be called the comedian's curse. Apart from his closest friends, Peter's richest relationships were with his audiences, particularly the ones he never saw. It was with the disconnected listeners and spectators of radio, television, and film that he most securely bonded, and he did so instinctively and spontaneously in flashes of raw creation.

"He improvised very beautifully in the same tone as Carroll wrote," Jonathan Miller explains. "I didn't let anyone improvise unless they actually had the logic Carroll did." Miller suggested that Peter play the King of Hearts as a familiar *Goon Show* routine: "I borrowed a character of his—that feeble old man, Henry Crun—very vague and unfocused. He improvised wonderfully at one moment—when the letter gets picked up, and the White Rabbit brandishes it and says, 'This letter's just been picked up,' and the foreman of the jury says, 'Who's it written to?' and he opens it up and says, 'It seems to be a letter written by the prisoner to somebody.' Sellers then said [in Henry Crun's voice-of-the-shakes], 'It must be *that*. I mean, it can't just be written to nobody. You can't just write to nobody. I mean, if you did that all the time, well, the post office would come to a standstill! I mean, you've got to have *somebody*, I mean, well—we-ee-ll—it's not allowed!' That was just the sort of thing that Carroll would have written."

When the camera wasn't rolling, Sellers's strangeness could be less appealing. Miller goes on: "He was fascinated by wealth and his Rolls Royce and his various attendants who looked after him and the peculiar sort of Barbie-doll wife he had. He gave a party for my wife and me and a number of other people at his house, and I remember there was an enormous champagne bucket filled with caviar. It did seem rather immoderate.

"He was a difficult man—sort of show biz, sort of genius, but completely empty when he wasn't playing anyone. He was a receptacle rather than a person. And whatever parts he played completely filled the receptacle, and then they were drained out. And the receptacle was left empty and featureless. Like a lot of people who can pretend to be other people very convincingly and change their characters, he could do so because he hadn't had any character himself—not unlike Olivier in that way." But, Miller quickly adds, "He was much more subversive and interesting and modern than Olivier."

• • •

As early as June 1966, with *Casino Royale* still stumbling forward in production, *Variety* reported that two Hollywood producers, Jerry Gershwin and Elliott Kastner, had grown so skeptical of Peter's Hollywood agent Harvey Orkin's dismissive treatment of them—Orkin told the producers that Peter was booked solid for the measurable future—that they had taken it upon themselves to get on a plane, fly to London, and deliver a new screenplay to him personally, and that Peter had agreed to do the picture. One week later, everybody having been sufficiently embarrassed by the story, *Variety* noted that Gershwin and Kastner vehemently denied the whole thing. No, the producers categorically stated in Hollywood's trade paper of record; they had made Peter's deal for *The Bobo* (1967) directly with Harvey Orkin.

Bobo means *fool* in Barcelona. The script had much to recommend it, including a European location, an accent, a bizarre sight gag, and a role for Britt. The ridiculous yet somehow suave Juan Bautista arrives in Barcelona from a remote village and bills himself as the greatest singing matador in all of Spain. ("I sing before, after, and during, but not so much during, as it is difficult to sing when I am running.") A corpulent impresario agrees to book him in his theater on one condition: that he conquer and humiliate the greatest blond in all of Spain—Olimpia (Britt), a spoiled, capricious, voluptuous ball-breaker who has, of course, spurned the impresario. An elaborate masquerade ensues before Olimpia discovers Juan Bautista's true identity and exacts her strange revenge by dyeing him blue from head to toe. He ends up in a Barcelona bull ring as "the singing blue matador" and performs before a cheering crowd. She drives off with a genuinely rich suitor, a man more her speed.

Originally, Peter hoped to direct as well as star in *The Bobo*, which was scheduled for production at Cinecittà in the fall. But by the middle of the summer he'd decided to limit himself to performing, and Robert Parrish took over as the film's director. "The trouble is," Peter explained, "my role starts early in the movie and goes right through to the end. So does Britt's. In order to make the most of my role and the scenes with Britt, I've had to concentrate on acting, not directing, this time."

• • •

The Bobo became, as Parrish's widow, Kathleen, describes it, "a disaster that we considered a death in the family and never mentioned." Parrish himself told one comparatively benign tale in his memoirs: "After three weeks' shooting in Rome, Peter called me aside and whispered, 'I'm not coming back after lunch if that bitch is on the set.' 'Tell me which one and I'll take care of it,' I cringed. He had already had the script girl fired. I figured it was the makeup girl's turn. 'The one over my left shoulder, in the white dress. Don't look now,' he said, and slinked away to charm the cast and crew. The girl in the white dress was his wife and costar, Britt."

To Parrish's surprise, he ran into the couple an hour or two later. They were lunching together at the Cinecittà commissary. "As I passed their table they raised their glasses to me."

One piece of information unavailable to Parrish is supplied by Michael Sellers, who reports that a few days before shooting began on *The Bobo*,

Peter "got his solicitors to write to Britt and tell her that he intended to file for divorce."

• • •

Peter took a few days away from *The Bobo* and flew to Paris to film a scene with Shirley MacLaine in MacLaine's multicharacter comedy *Woman Times Seven* (1967). Directed by Vittorio De Sica, *Woman Times Seven* features MacLaine as the eponymous number of characters opposite an array of costars including Alan Arkin and Michael Caine. Peter's scene was simple; there was little room for arguments with De Sica, and besides, his wife wasn't his costar.

As a funeral cortege makes its incongruous way through the park beneath the Eiffel Tower, a physician (Peter, looking very much like Auguste Topaze) comforts the widow, Paulette (MacLaine). The doctor's comfort slides into a passionate declaration of love, prompting Paulette to cry all the harder—briefly. Soon they're discussing where they're going to live together, and before the casket has even reached the cemetery they diverge from the funeral route and walk off in each other's arms.

• • •

On Monday, October 17, Peter arrived on *The Bobo*'s Cinecittà set at 4:10 P.M., having just watched all the rushes to date. "I've just seen the most wonderful film!" he exclaimed enthusiastically. "It's marvelous!" He shot a scene or two with Parrish and finished at 7 P.M. At 8:30 P.M. Parrish picked up his ringing telephone. "I'm low on the film," Peter told him. It was Britt's fault. "Her reading of lines is amateurish," her husband opined.

It got worse.

"Peter called Britt 'a cunt' in front of the entire cast and crew," Kathleen Parrish states. Everyone froze, but the Italian crew members were especially mortified at Peter's vulgar treatment of a woman—his own wife, a Scandinavian bombshell to top it all off, a lady whose toes they would gladly have kissed.

A gregarious group, *The Bobo*'s crew enjoyed fixing a fairly elaborate lunch for themselves and a few select guests. They liked Robert Parrish—everyone did—and they invited him to join them once or twice. But they never wanted to have much to do with Peter at all, let alone share a meal they cooked themselves. And Peter, as always, wanted very much to be invited. According to Kathy Parrish, the "cunt" incident only served to cement the crew's enmity, and afterward they became even more open in giving Peter the cold shoulder.

So, in a grossly misguided effort to get the crew to like him and invite him to lunch, Peter bought a dozen knockoff Rolex watches and began doling them out as gifts.

He approached the camera operator and handed him one of the cheap watches. The camera operator literally spat on it and threw it on the ground at Peter's feet.

At one point, Kathy Parrish invited Peter to lunch, and he was completely at ease and low-key. "Peter could be charming," she notes. They did a jaunty strutting dance together, the Lambeth Walk, and had a fine time in each other's company. But as far as the production of *The Bobo* was concerned, she says, "it was ugly from beginning to end. Everything around Peter was awkward."

Peter and Britt had returned to the Appian Way—to a somewhat smaller villa than the one they'd rented during the production of *After the Fox*—but by this point the marriage was in even more drastic trouble. More (and bigger) furniture was hurled. During one rage Peter actually flipped the bed over. One of the castors hit Britt in the mouth and chipped a tooth. She proceeded to leave the production for several days—the mirror opposite of her behavior during *Guns at Batasi*, for this time she was fleeing *from* her husband.

In the middle of it all, Peter got a phone call from London. Peg had suffered a heart attack.

Robert Parrish asked Peter if he wanted to fly back to be with her. Peter replied that it wasn't necessary, he spoke to her all the time. She died a few days later, without him.

• • •

"He used to be quite terrible to her at times," Dennis Selinger once said of Peter and his mother, "and yet, probably she was the only woman in his life who really meant anything to him."

Peter and Britt flew to London for the funeral, after which Peter sent his mother's ashes to North London to be interred with Bill's at the Golders Green cemetery and columbarium. There is a plaque there, placed by Peter, who nonetheless did not visit the cemetery until 1980. As for Peg's clothes, Peter gathered them from her apartment, took them to Brookfield, and burned them in the garden.

Peg had moved on, but the mother-and-son heart-to-hearts are said by some to have continued from beyond the grave. "After she'd gone," Selinger claimed, "he used to have conversations with her. He'd get into a room and talk to her for quite some time." Evidently she succored him.

Later, Peter periodically told people he carried some of Peg's ashes around with him on his travels. Joe McGrath finds it hard to believe. "He would make up a lot of it, you know. I mean, if he thought that somebody would believe he was carrying his mother's ashes around, it would be very funny. I know he told people stories about his death experiences—when he had his heart attacks and stuff like that—but he never told *me* any of that, and I know he never told Spike Milligan. Spike said, 'No—he'd never tell us any of that because we're gonna say, "You're putting me on—don't give *me* any of that shit." ' "

• • •

Peter Sellers was in such terrible emotional shape during the production of *The Bobo* that even his close friend Kenneth Griffith felt the sting. At Peter's insistence, Griffith played the role of Pepe, one of Olimpia's discarded lovers. "I came on the set one day and Robert Parrish was sitting like Little Jack Horner in the corner of the studio. *Peter* was directing.

"The scene I had was with Britt Ekland. I thought, 'Geez, somebody could have warned me. Well, perhaps they forgot.' So I did the scene, which was quite difficult, with Miss Ekland. She always showed goodwill and tried very hard, but she was having problems. I think we were into forty-odd takes—which was quite difficult for me because if *she* got it right it would be printed and that's it. But we went on. At the end of the day I got my makeup off and got changed and sought Robert Parrish—nice man, lovely man. He was sitting alone. I said, 'Robert, you didn't tell me what was going to happen this afternoon.' He said, 'I'm sorry, Kenneth.' I said, 'Is it all with your agreement?' I thought maybe Peter had said, 'Look, I can handle it.' But Robert very quietly said, 'No. He just announced that he was taking over, and I felt that I had a duty to sit quietly and be a servant to the film. You know, the number-one job is to get this film finished.'

"When the film was finished, the big man in film publicity here [in London] asked if he could come and see me. He said, 'You know Peter wants everyone on the film in a significant capacity to write a piece about what they think of him as a director' [for use as publicity]. I said, 'I can't do that, because it would imply that I supported what happened. And I don't.' And he got up—because he'd had orders from Peter—and said, 'Well, Kenneth, you know everybody on the film has done it. You are the only one who has said no.' I said, 'Look, I love Peter dearly, but I can't be a party to this.' After that Peter cut me dead for six months."

Actually, Robert Parrish never left the picture entirely in Peter's hands. In late November, with the production still grinding on—Peter was by that point insisting on reshooting scenes without even seeing the rushes—Parrish told his London-based agent that he was getting along "as good as ever" with Peter and with Elliott Kastner as well. "Peter leans on me when he needs to and flails out on his own when he doesn't. Elliott holds his stomach and says, 'Bob, what am I going to do?' "

Then Harvey Orkin showed up in Rome and helpfully told Peter that he, Orkin, didn't like Peter's interpretation of his role.

Orkin's asinine remark—had he never *met* his client?—sent Peter into a tailspin so predictable that one wonders if there was malicious intent on Orkin's part. Like most artists, Peter needed a constant, smooth flow of reassurances, not a sudden stab of criticism, which human beings generally take badly and actors and writers take even worse. Unfortunately, Peter's response to Orkin's insensitivity was not to question his relationship with Orkin but rather to insist on reshooting even more scenes in a desperate attempt to develop an entirely new character.

They were all still at it in late January when Peter demanded a codirecting credit. First he fought with Kastner about it—Kastner told Peter he was "full of shit"—and then he approached Parrish, who patiently reminded him that he had told Parrish earlier that he'd only wanted credit as the film's star. According to Parrish at the time, "Peter accepted this and said he would never bring it up again."

"Dear Bob," Peter cabled on January 31. "Since I have directed *The Bobo* I also want to cut it, but alone with [the editor] Johnny Jympson. Just Johnny Jympson and I, in other words. I hope you will agree to this as I must tell you I intend to go all the way."

"Dear Bob," Peter wrote on February 14. "Thank you for your letter in which you state that you do not agree that I directed *The Bobo*. I wonder if you would now be good enough to let me know upon what facts you base this statement." There were other less-than-pleasant exchanges with Parrish and others over the musical score, which Peter insisted on reworking as well. In the end, though, Robert Parrish received sole credit for directing *The Bobo*.

When *The Bobo* was released, it was not widely slammed. On the contrary. The critic Richard Schickel wrote only one of a number of glowing reviews. Schickel captures the spirit not of that performance, particularly, but of Sellers's best work nonetheless: "There is in his character a wonderful scramble of guile and innocence, humility and dignity, not to mention a certain wise, romantic rue. . . . What is so good about Sellers' performance is that he never insists upon these emotional generalizations at the expense of specific characterization, is never excessively sweet or sour and never, never tries obviously to turn the Bobo into an Everyman, as so many lesser actors have when they have tried to work a vein that is so trickily laced with fool's gold. . . . Peter Sellers may be the finest comic actor of his time, and it is a boon to be able to study him at length and at leisure instead of merely glimpsing his face in the crowd of those all-star productions where he has lately been lurking so much of the time."

• • •

"A certain wise, romantic rue" was indeed what Peter Sellers radiated onscreen. But offscreen, there was little wisdom, and his romances inevitably turned sour—all that was left was rue. An "atrocious sham" is the way Britt Ekland describes her marriage to Peter at this point. Like Anne, she was the object of his increasingly incendiary rages and follow-up periods of deep remorse. One day, for instance, she returned home at the end of her day to find Peter in a white-hot jealous fury. Convinced that she was with another man, Peter grabbed her gold Cartier watch, stomped on it, threw the pieces in the toilet, and flushed. Soon awash in guilt, he bestowed more gifts.

One of his favorite domestic games was the treasure hunt—"Treasure Trove," he called it—in which he would hide valuables around the house or apartment and watch delightedly as Britt searched for them. On one of these hunts, which took place in their suite at the Dorchester, Britt found a scarf, a cigarette lighter and case, perfume, luxury soaps, and another gold watch. Yet they spent less and less time together.

Despite the fact that the Sellerses' time in England now had to be strictly limited for tax reasons—the jet set was largely a group of celebrity tax refugees—Peter bought another new apartment, a four-bedroom affair on Clarges Street in Mayfair. When the couple was together and not at Brookfield, or Mayfair, or Los Angeles, or sailing in the Mediterranean, they paused at Saint Moritz, where, in April, Britt and Peter threw a birthday party for Michael. Spike Milligan came with his wife and children, and everyone had a great time, except for Peter, who went to bed.

His behavior was finally becoming too much for Britt, so one day she swallowed a fistful of sleeping pills. "It wasn't a deliberate attempt to commit suicide, but I wanted to find oblivion."

• • •

As with any big star, there were many blanks for every bullet. One of the projects Peter was involved in that year was *The Russian Interpreter*, to be directed by Michael Powell. They met at the Dorchester on March 4, 1967, at which time Peter told Powell, the director of such classics as *The Red Shoes* (1948) and *Peeping Tom* (1960), that he wasn't the right director for his own project. Powell asked him who he would suggest. Peter replied, "I don't know, but not you." When Powell recorded the incident in his diary, the entry was a single word: "Peterloo."

The screenwriters Paul Mazursky and Larry Tucker also proposed *The Russian Interpreter* as a Peter Sellers project later in 1967. In fact, the three men considered forming a production company called Peter, Paul, and Larry. But neither the film nor the company ever came into being.

Peter wanted Graham Chapman and John Cleese to write a script called *The Future Began Yesterday*: a man uses a copying machine to duplicate his wife. Peter wanted one particular actress to play the wife.

Sophia.

Peter also wanted to do Eugene Ionesco's absurdist *Rhinoceros* set in modern Hamburg; it was to be directed by *The Ladykillers'* Alexander Mackendrick, but his agent, David Begelman, talked him out of it.

There was *Pardon Me, Sir, But Is My Eye Hurting Your Elbow?*, a collection of skits that boasted an impressive lineup of talent: scripts by Allen Ginsberg, Peter Cook, Gregory Corso, Terry Southern, Philip Roth, and others; a score by Leonard Bernstein; direction by Arthur Hiller. At one point Peter was said to be ready to play nine different roles in the omnibus film, but the picture never came together. Several of the skits, later published in book form, would have been excellent vehicles for Peter. Southern's entry, "Plums and Prunes," is about a Westchester ad executive named Brad, his wife Donna, and their nubile sixteen-year-old daughter, Debbie, whose sexual attractiveness dawns all too disturbingly on Brad, who proceeds to punch, choke, and beat Debbie's boyfriend to death. Ginsberg's "Don't Go Away Mad" is a surreal farce about a bearded middle-aged man who gets picked up by the cops in Central Park for not having an identity. To cure him, he's given electroshock therapy, drugs, a lobotomy, and an exploding hydrogen bomb.

Peter got as far as offering Kenneth Griffith a role in yet another picture. "Typical of Sellers," Griffith declares, referring to their estrangement, "six months later the phone rang. 'How are you, Kenny? Look I'm doing this film, and I'm playing two parts—brothers! Any other part in the film you want, you can play. My dad!' (I wasn't all that old.) 'Anything! Whatever you want to play. *Please be in it.*' So I went round and we read the whole script and then I chose my role—because it went right through the film and I would get more money. Suddenly I was told that Peter Sellers wouldn't do it." (Griffith no longer recalls the name of the film, but it could well be *The Bed Sitting Room*, 1969, directed by Richard Lester from a script by Spike Milligan and John Antrobus and starring Ralph Richardson, Rita Tushingham, Peter Cook, and Dudley Moore.)

In addition, there was an adaptation of Graham Greene's story "When Greek Meets Greek," which Kenneth Geist optioned with an eye toward producing the film. Geist wanted to cast Peter, Alec Guinness, John Lennon, and Lynn Redgrave. "I want to do it," Peter told Geist, who asked John Mortimer to write the script. "I'll do it," Mortimer told Geist. Then Peter referred Geist to his accountant, Bill Wills. "It was a *Waiting for Godot* situation," says Geist, who calls Wills "a great dullard." The film never got made.

Mel Brooks approached Peter about starring in Brooks's first film, a comedy about a failed theatrical producer and a nebbish accountant who put on a Broadway show, but Peter was too distracted to listen. Brooks describes his experience of trying to interest him in *The Producers* (1967): "I sent the script to Peter Sellers, and I told him about the project, and he had to go to Bloomingdale's. So we walked around Bloomingdale's—he was shopping, I was talking. I'd be in the middle of a very important moment—where Bialystock says to Bloom, 'Do you want to live in a gray little world, do you want to be confined, don't you want to fly?'—and he'd say 'You like this buckle? What do you think of this buckle?' "

As Brooks experienced the odd interaction, Peter didn't mean to be rude, or dismissive, or regal: "It was just a series of different focuses. Foci. He'd focus on something and get lost in it." It was Dennis Selinger who ultimately responded to Brooks on his client's behalf, saying that he really didn't know whether Peter had read *The Producers* or not, but the fact was (as Brooks tells it, quoting Selinger), "He's so meshuggeneh—so crazy— he's locked into so many things now. . . . This is not the right time to approach him with new material."

And there was *God Bless You, Mr. Rosewater: or, Pearls Before Swine*, an adaptation of Kurt Vonnegut's 1965 novel. The movie was to have been directed by Blake Edwards, but Edwards and Sellers made a different film in the meantime and had a few difficulties with each other. *God Bless You, Mr. Rosewater*, too, went by the boards.

• • •

In the spring of 1967, the Hollywood trade papers excitedly scattered details of Peter Sellers's imminent return to Tinseltown. "I've wanted to come back here and make a film on happy circumstances," Peter told Army Archerd. The circumstance was Blake Edwards's *The Party* (1968).

Sheilah Graham reported that Peter and Britt were scheduled to sail to New York on the *Queen Elizabeth*, then fly to Los Angeles. And once they arrived in Hollywood, Graham remarked, the couple wouldn't "be living in separate houses as they have done recently in England." (In addition to Brookfield and what appears to have been a standing reservation at the Dorchester, they'd taken yet another apartment—this one on Curzon Street in Mayfair. Who knows who stayed where?) Britt was supposedly packing twenty trunks of clothes along with one of the couple's Yorkshire terriers.

In late April, Peter arrived in L.A. He alone had taken the *Queen Elizabeth* after all. Britt had gone to Sweden to be with her mother, who had just been diagnosed with cancer. He was accompanied by two-year-old Victoria, with whom he made the traditional trip to Disneyland in her mother's absence.

• • •

An interviewer showed up one day at the Goldwyn Studios, where *The Party* was being filmed. "Why do you have all that dark stuff on your face?" he inquired of Peter. This was quite the wrong thing to say. "If you don't know why I have this stuff on my face you have no right to interview me!' Peter roared before ordering the unprepared hack off the set. "Go ahead— print all the dirty things you want to!" he shouted after him.

Originally titled *R.S.V.P.*, *The Party* is about a polite, inept Indian actor, Hrundi V. Bakshi, whose name is mistakenly added to the guest list of an exclusive Hollywood bash, which he inadvertently destroys. Peter plays the role in blackface, and it's very funny as long as one isn't terribly concerned about issues of race and representation. Clad in a pale lavender suit, bright red socks, and white shoes, Hrundi Bakshi is essentially a one-man subcontinental minstrel show, though a sympathetic one. It's the smug white Hollywood types who are contemptible in *The Party*. Producers and bimbos, studio executives and their shallow wives—they bear the brunt of Edwards's scorn, with Hrundi V. Bakshi being the object of both the director's and the audience's sympathetic identification. It's more the pity that *The Party*'s Deluxe color registers Peter's dark-brown makeup so poorly.

Peter's Indian accent features prominently, as it should, but *The Party* is largely about physical, cinematic sight-gag humor. Hrundi's shoe floats away on a preposterous stream that runs through the ultramodern house. A drunken waiter (Steve Franken) wreaks havoc with the salad. Hrundi's Rock Cornish hen flies off his plate in one shot and impales itself on a woman's pronged tiara in the next, all in less than two seconds. The drunken waiter proceeds to retrieve it, along with the woman's blond beehive wig, which he places on the dismayed Hrundi's plate. The wracking tensions of dinner party etiquette are the scene's main focus, and even under the blackface Peter expresses them charmingly, naturally. One would never guess that he and Blake Edwards were once again said to have stopped speaking to each other at some point during the production. Assistants relayed messages: "Ask Mr. Sellers if he's comfortable crossing to the phone while he's doing the dialogue." "Tell Mr. Edwards I'm very comfortable . . ."

In *The Party*, Edwards gives Leo McCarey's comedic "pain barrier" theory a literal twist in a meticulously constructed ten-minute sequence in which Hrundi cannot find a proper place to urinate. The most accessible bathroom is occupied by several women. His hands clasped in front of him, he finds another; it's taken up by a group of men smoking pot. Still another is used by a waiter in red bikini briefs enthusiastically flexing in front of the mirror. All the while, Sellers is tensing his body, his gait becoming more and more warped and constricted. Hrundi wanders out to the lawn and sets off the sprinklers. Then a waif-like aspiring starlet (Claudine Longet) decides to sing a Henry Mancini song just as Hrundi rushes, dripping, through the living room.

Politely, he waits for her to finish. With a wretched grin plastered on his face, he leans against the wall, crosses his legs, clenches his fists, torques from the waist, and looks to heaven for salvation. As the song concludes, he creeps away in baby steps.

The sequence goes on for two more excruciating minutes. Hrundi tears frantically from room to room to no avail before he finally gets to pee, and, at the moment of relief, the look on Peter's sweaty face is inimitable. In close-up, his head lolls around in coarse ecstasy while his facial expression suggests the more beatific joy of a martyred saint at the moment of ascension, and it's still not the end of the sequence. An entire roll of toilet paper unspools by itself, Hrundi stuffs it all in the toilet, breaks the toilet's lid, flushes, stops up the plumbing, and floods the bathroom before Sellers and Edwards's tour-de-force of bladder agony concludes.

• • •

As fundamentally visual as this film is, it's nevertheless in *The Party* that Peter Sellers, in his exquisite front-of-the-mouth Indian accent, utters one of the choicest lines of his career, the immortal "Birdie num-num." The birdie is a parrot in a vast bamboo cage. The num-num is its seed.

"Birdie num-num," Hrundi V. Bakshi announces, gazing at the feathered thing. "Birdie num-num. Birdie num-num!"

Seed by seed, he feeds the parrot for a few moments and then pitches in a fistful. "I give you a lot," he explains before wandering away. He spies an elaborate electronic contraption built into the wall and flips a switch. "Num-num. Num-*num*! Birdie num-num!" Hrundi V. Bakshi proclaims to all the guests through the whole-house intercom. Then he makes an impromptu series of chicken noises.

This is quintessential Peter Sellers—silly, insane, brilliant. "Birdie num-num" is funny for reasons that remain entirely obscure: a phrase verging on meaninglessness, an accent both accurate and farcical, a bland and indefinable comportment that manages somehow to register as purely hilarious. For no apparent reason, the bit coalesces into something precise and emblematic. It is impossible to imagine anyone other than Peter Sellers achieving glory with "birdie num-num." He remains to this day the master of playing men who have no idea how ridiculous they are.

• • •

When *The Party* opened in April 1968, *Time* was snide: "This party, in short, is strictly for those who don't get around much." The *New York Times* was offended: "When, eventually, Sellers is reduced to mugging the poor Indian's pain at not being able to empty his bladder, the picture hits a low point from which it never recovers." When the British royal family watched *The Party* together at Balmoral Castle, however, Elizabeth II laughed so hard that tears rolled down her face. The queen got it right.

SEVENTEEN

Let me see—how is it to be managed?
I suppose I ought to eat or drink something or other;
but the great question is, what?

It was 1967. The Beatles had their maharishi, Peter had his yoga, and the counterculture, regardless of its income level, turned to the jangling rhythms of southern Asia for druggy inspiration.

Peter became friendly with Ravi Shankar, the world's most famous sitar master. When Peter was in Los Angeles that year, he invited Shankar to his rented house to perform a private concert. Paul Mazursky, one of the guests, reports that Peter imitated Ravi's accented voice directly to Ravi's face— much to Ravi's amusement. And in fact it was Shankar who demonstrated the elements of sitar technique for Peter on the set of *The Party*, when Hrundi, early in the film, sits alone and plays.

Sellers's friendship with Shankar led to an even closer friendship with George Harrison. "I got to re-know him through Ravi Shankar," Harrison says. "He liked Ravi a lot and became close friends with him, and at that time, you know, I was with Ravi all the time learning the sitar. We hung out together, the three of us, which was quite an unusual combination."

Harrison also reports that Peter was quite immersed in his spiritual quest: "He was doing a lot of yoga and trying to hone in on 'Who am I?' 'What is it all about?' " He hadn't discovered any lasting answers.

• • •

Peter could be social and outgoing if the mood suited him. He, Britt, Edwards, Edwards's new and as-yet unannounced girlfriend, Julie Andrews, and other key *Party* people did, in fact, party in a grandiose, Hollywood sort of way—when Edwards and Peter were speaking, at least. As filming neared completion, Peter threw a fifty-guest cocktail do, after which everyone climbed onto the busses he had chartered and headed to the Greek Theater in Los Feliz, where Henry Mancini was opening that night. There was also a three-hundred-person wrap party thrown by the producers on the *Party* set, with music provided by the onscreen band (The Party Four). On a more sober note, Peter returned to Cedars of Lebanon Hospital to address a group of cardiologists about his experiences as a heart-attack survivor.

Peter made new friends, too. The closest by far was Roman Polanski. They met in an Italian restaurant near the Paramount lot, where Polanski was filming *Rosemary's Baby* (1968) with Mia Farrow. "My first impression of him was of a sad, shy man who hid his essential melancholy behind a fixed smile that revealed his rather prominent teeth," Polanski writes in his autobiography. "His manner conveyed profound depression."

Asked to elaborate on this observation in person, however, Polanski is quick to clarify: "He was at that time in such a mood, but it doesn't mean that it prevailed throughout the years that we knew each other. He had a lot of reasons to be depressed, like everybody else. I don't think that he was particularly stricken by depression throughout his life." Obviously bored by all the one-dimensional "Mad Peter" lore, Roman Polanski defends him. Still, Polanski acknowledges, "Peter's idiosyncrasies could be a drag." For example, Sellers tended to walk out of restaurants mid-meal. "This often happened at The Luau," Polanski writes. "I grew to dread the moment when, after ordering, Peter would whisper, 'Ro, I can't stand it—bad vibes in here—let's go somewhere else.'"

• • •

Going somewhere else was Peter's way of life. At the end of July, Peter and Britt flew to Paris, then to Marseilles, where they began a two-week cruise of the Mediterranean. "When the Sellerses discovered that they couldn't get all their belongings they'd picked up during their Hollywood stay on their plane," the columnist Dorothy Manners gasped, "they ordered a second freight plane just to transport the haul. The only thing they were forced to leave was Peter's new car."

It was a Corvette Stingray. There hadn't been one available in Los Angeles, so Peter—who once described himself as being "auto erotic"—got his press agent to call Detroit and have General Motors ship one to him immediately so he could drive it around Beverly Hills during the filming of *The Party*. He had to have it.

"You tell them you want a car as soon as possible," Peter said at the time, "and you'll bloody well get it two weeks from now. You tell them you want it *today* and they know you mean business." He got away with this sort of thing precisely because he could.

• • •

If it weren't for the tremendous talent, the domestic horrors, and the periodic fits of public charm, Peter Sellers's life could be described in the form of a warehouse inventory and an accompanying list of the stamps on his passport. He had commissioned a new yacht while on a side trip to Genoa during the production of *The Bobo*—a fifty-foot number, which he christened *The Bobo*—and in August 1967, he and Britt sailed to Sardinia to spend a little time with the Aga Khan. The couple, divorce postponed, were accompanied by Margaret and Tony Snowdon; the Aga was tossing the princess a birthday bash. Kirk and Anne Douglas were there, too; Peter had met them in Monte Carlo on the way. Margaret's cousin, Princess Alexandra, and her husband, Angus Ogilvy, came along as well. So did Michael, Sarah, and Victoria Sellers, the youngest being cared for by her Swedish nanny, Inger.

"It was the real jet set period," Roman Polanski declares. "It was, like, one day in Rome, one day in L.A., then we'd suddenly be in London. Our jobs would take us to various places, and we would meet like that, you know." Paris, Rome, London, Los Angeles, Monte Carlo; Peter, Margaret, Roman, Kirk, the Aga; films, income, houses, taxes, luggage. . . . It was rather like a progressive dinner, where guests go from house to house for each new course, only in 1967 they were jetting, not driving, and the food was better, and there was unlimited champagne and lots of drugs, and everybody was famous. Through Roman, Peter met Warren (Beatty). Warren introduced him to Julie (Christie). "You have to look back at what London was like in the '60s," says Peter's friend Gene Gutowski, who had been Polanski's producer on *Repulsion* (1965), *Cul de Sac* (1966), and *The Fearless Vampire Killers, or: Pardon Me But Your Teeth Are In My Neck* (1967). "We were young, we were successful, and everybody's star was on the rise. It was limited to much more of a select group than today. Let's put it this way: there were not as many celebrities around in those days."

With Roman, Peter enjoyed playing an odd game of their own invention: Sellers, assuming the personality of a cretin, would climb into the driver's seat of his latest Rolls Corniche, and Roman would give a driving lesson as though to the mentally handicapped. "Press the right-hand pedal, gently—no, too hard! . . ." And so on, through the busy streets of London. According to Polanski, it was especially amusing to play the game stoned on hashish.

In the late fall of 1967, the Polanski circle got together to plan a communal Christmas holiday in Cortina. Roman and his magnificent girlfriend, Sharon Tate, took Peter out to dinner at a Chinese restaurant to talk about the trip and introduce him to some of the other guests. A physician named Tony Greenburgh—described by Gene Gutowski as "a society doctor"—was seated across the table from Peter. The talk turned to the question of whether doctors bore any moral responsibility to patients who seemed driven to self-destruction. Not knowing Peter at all, Greenburgh all-too-calmly stated his opinion: that doctors were unable to stop hell-bent patients from killing themselves, whether it was through drinking, drugging, smoking, or overwork, and therefore he bore absolutely no responsibility for his patients outside of the particulars of his practice.

Peter became wildly enraged, his reaction so abrupt and extreme that the other guests naturally assumed it was one of his impromptu comedy routines. Their amused disbelief continued even after Peter got up from the table, marched around to Greenburgh's side, shrieked "You're wrong, Doctor—you're wrong, you're *fucking wrong!*" and grabbed the physician by the throat and began to choke him. Someone at the table giggled and casually told Peter to stop acting silly. Greenburgh, for his part, was turning blue.

Polanski sprang to the doctor's defense and pried Peter's fingers loose from his throat. He then asked Peter to sit down, whereupon Peter, according to Polanski, "buried his face in his hands and began to sob."

• • •

These were trying times for certain people with whom Peter Sellers came into contact; some had it easier than others. Many years after inspiring mutual unpleasantness during the production of *I Love You, Alice B. Toklas!* (1968) Peter and one of the film's writers, Paul Mazursky, ran into each other at the Beverly Hills Hotel. They greeted each other warmly after their long estrangement. "I was wrong, Paul," Sellers is said to have confessed. "Will you ever forgive me?" "There's nothing to forgive," Mazursky benevolently replied, only to chronicle the whole ugly thing later, lavishly and at Peter's expense, in his autobiography.

They met while Peter was filming *The Party*. Freddie Fields, Peter's Hollywood agent, had read the script, which Mazursky wrote with his collaborator, Larry Tucker, and forwarded a copy to Peter, who agreed overnight to do the film. They were all taken aback by Peter's first suggestion for director. "Hello, Freddie," Peter said into the phone during one of his early meetings with Mazursky and Tucker. "I'm here with the boys, and we all agree that our first choice is Fellini." If Fellini was too busy, Peter added, then they'd "move on to Bergman." Fields is said to have told Tucker and Mazursky privately that he had no intention of approaching either the director of *Juliet of the Spirits* (1965) or the director of *Persona* (1966) with a film that centered on pot brownies.

Somebody suggested George Roy Hill. Peter responded by saying that he refused to work with Hill again after *The World of Henry Orient*. Mike Nichols's name came up and was shot down. Jonathan Miller was proposed. Miller actually flew to Los Angeles for a meeting, but when he brought up the subject of the film's musical score, Peter went pale and terminated the conversation. In Mazursky's account, Peter is said to have then suggested Mazursky.

But Peter rejected him, too, supposedly after the writer gave Britt a kiss on the cheek and Peter accused him of having sex with her. Mazursky to Freddie Fields: "The only thing I did was tell Peter *The Bobo* stank!" Fields to Mazursky: "That's almost as bad as telling Sellers you fucked his wife."

Peter eventually chose Hy Averback to direct *I Love You, Alice B. Toklas!* and barred Mazursky from the set until the day he asked him back.

At one point during the production, which occurred in December 1967 and January 1968, Mazursky was summoned to Peter's rented house in Beverly Hills, where he was greeted warmly by a smiling Peter, who then burst into tears. "The ship is sinking, Paul. Sinking, I tell you." And on and on.

Peter's strange sociability—ebullient one moment, despondent the next—led him to launch an informal cinema club to keep him focused on the art he loved, with other pleasures on the side. The first film he chose to screen was Satyajit Ray's *Pather Panchali* (1955), to be screened with an accompanying dinner of lamb curry. And hash brownies. With Britt having left for New York to shoot William Friedkin's *The Night They Raided Minsky's* (1968)—in which she plays an Amish burlesque dancer—Peter eagerly invited his pretty young costar, Leigh Taylor-Young, on whom he had developed the predictable crush.

During the screening, "Peter sat in the back of the small screening room holding hands with the exquisite Leigh-Taylor," Mazursky writes, referring to Taylor-Young.

The club's next film was to be Fellini's *I Vitelloni* (1953), to be accompanied by Betsy Mazursky's spaghetti Bolognese and more brownies, but when the guests showed up, there was no film. According to Mazursky, nobody remembered to order it. As Mazursky tells it, Peter's response was something on the order of "I don't want spaghetti, and I don't want *Vitelloni!* I don't *ever* want *Vitelloni!* Never, ever, never!" "Fuck you, Peter," Mazursky said. "Fuck *you*," said Peter. The projectionist saved the day by screening *The Producers*.

As an afterthought, Mazursky mentions that Peter's "work on the film was impeccable. He was prompt, fully prepared, and very generous to his fellow actors."

Peter's own account is much less acrimonious than Mazursky's:

"One night we all wanted to see a Fellini film, see? We were all just nicely high, and all the girls had baked hash cookies. But the owner comes in and says, 'I'm sorry to tell you guys, but they didn't wanna give us the Fellini film.' I said, 'Oh shit, fuck it.' But this guy says, 'No, listen, I got a film by Mel Brooks. It's called *Springtime for Hitler* (the original title). So we gave out a few more cookies, things were very heavily hashed up, and we got ripped out of our minds. We started watching this film and were hysterical. I actually had to crawl out of the room on my hands and knees and go to the lavatory because I was almost sick with laughing. When I went back in, I just saw white on the screen. We were all just looking at the white until someone knew enough to say, 'Change the reel!' "

Studio executives didn't quite know what to make of Brooks's stomach-hurting laughmaker, and *The Producers* was still looking for distribution support. Sellers thought he could help: "The following day I got hold of as many producers as I could, urging them to come and see this film. I got a good turnout. I took out full-page ads in the *Hollywood Reporter* and *Variety*. The movie is one of the greatest comedies that's been made recently." He had been unable to listen to Brooks's lines because of the distractions of Bloomingdale's, but once it was finished, he could *see* and *hear* it; even through his spiked-brownie haze, Peter saw what Hollywood executives were dismissing. His championing of *The Producers* gave it the industry attention that turned it into a smash hit.

• • •

I Love You, Alice B. Toklas! is a flower-power comedy, a classic of its genre thanks almost entirely to Peter's performance. Harold Fine (Peter), a middle-aged, asthmatic, Lincoln-driving lawyer, undergoes a profound life transition after his hippie brother's breathy girlfriend, Nancy (Leigh Taylor-Young), bakes him some "groovy" Pillsbury brownies—"groovy" owing to the pot she adds with a liberal hand. Harold himself becomes groovy. He leaves his fiancée, Joyce (Joyce Van Patten) at the altar, outfits himself in glorious hippie duds, grows his hair into a shaggy, John Lennon-ish cut (a moderately less ludicrous version of Dr. Fassbender's Prince Valiant in *What's New, Pussycat?*), and takes to reading *The Psychedelic Experience* naked with the free-spirited Nancy.

While his histrionic mother (Jo Van Fleet)—her voice full of whining, her hair full of bluing—consoles Joyce with such splendidly grating comments as "women are built for hurt," Harold seeks the advice of a white-robed guru. It doesn't quite work. They walk together on the beach. "But how can you know what a flower is, Harold, if you don't know who *you* are?" the guru asks. "I'm trying, guru, I'm really trying!"

"When you stop trying, then you'll know who you are."

Harold, meanwhile, is gingerly stepping over seaweed and bits of shell. "Well, I'm trying to stop trying." This is not coming easily to Harold.

Harold cringes at the touch of cold ocean water on his Jewish feet as the guru goes on about flowers, energy, and life. Harold shivers and is pained. The words are amusing; Peter's gestures and expressions are extraordinary.

Harold's transformation ends when a gang of freeloading hippies overrun his hippified apartment. He reunites with Joyce but walks out on their marriage ceremony a second time. His life as a hippie has taught him nothing if not how to be even more selfish than he was at the beginning, but in 1968 this appears to have been considered a happy ending, because as he escapes down the sidewalk, a hippie calls out, "Hey! Where ya goin', man?" "I dunno," Harold Fine replies, breaking into a run. "I don't know. And I don't care! *I don't care!* There's got to be something beautiful out there! There's got to be! I know it!" Peter was still organizing his life through his films' dialogue. He still believed he could find solace somewhere.

• • •

Paranoia about his wife, paranoia about his performance. . . . At one point in late December 1967, Peter demanded that the *Alice B. Toklas* set be closed. Apparently it was for a love scene with Leigh Taylor-Young; Peter may have worried about becoming overenthusiastic. But whatever the cause, two police officers stood guard at the outer door of the sound stage as nonrequired technicians were ushered away and screens were arranged tightly around the set.

Photoplay got the scoop: "Peter Sellers has his cast, crew, and friends so confused with his demands. Sellers, I'm told, 'is behaving like a brat.' Most popular joke on the Warners lot is when someone asks, 'Was that a sonic boom?' Answer: 'No, that's Sellers blowing his top.' "

While Peter was filming *I Love You, Alice B. Toklas!* in Hollywood, Britt was in New York filming *The Night They Raided Minsky's*, which left Peter more than enough room to come on to Leigh Taylor-Young. And yet Peter sent Britt at least twenty benevolent telegrams while they were separated. One was signed "Elizabeth and Philip," another "Margaret and Tony." "Richard and Elizabeth," "John, Paul, George, and Ringo," "Carlo and Sophia," "Alec Guinness and Peter O'Toole," and "Maharishi Yogi" were also among the well-wishers.

Despite the violence and the grilling, Britt was still making an effort, however doomed, to be the wife Peter wanted, or claimed to want, so she shuttled back and forth between the *Minsky's* shoot in New York and Peter in Los Angeles. Some weekends, one of her costars, Elliot Gould, would fly with her to Hollywood to spend two days with his wife, Barbra Streisand, who was filming *Funny Girl* (1968). The two couples sometimes had dinner together at Barbra's beach house in Malibu.

• • •

On the set, Peter Sellers continued to live up to the gossip, but his brilliance when the camera was running kept striking his colleagues as well. He was "a magnificent artist," declares the actor Salem Ludwig. "It was a pleasure to be on the set with him. Once the camera was on, you wouldn't want more from an actor. He was really *with* you. He was so supportive on camera—he did everything to make you comfortable."

Then comes the inevitable caveat. Ludwig also had the opportunity to view Peter at his temperamental worst when he caused an incident with Jo

Van Fleet on the day the pot brownies scene was scheduled to be shot. Though no one realized it at the time, the contretemps had actually begun brewing the day before. Knowing that one of the film's key scenes would occupy them the following morning and afternoon, the actors, director, and crew wrapped up quickly, and everybody left the set except for the four brownie principals (Peter, Van Patten, Van Fleet, and Ludwig), the director Averback, and the two writers, Mazursky and Tucker. Ludwig recalls that a vague conversation began to arise—few words but lots of implications— but nobody said anything explicit until finally it had to be spelled out for Ludwig and Van Fleet: Everybody was supposed to head over to Peter's place and get stoned. The plan was to use their experiences when the cameras rolled in the morning.

Van Fleet and Ludwig each expressed concern about the illegality of smoking marijuana. Van Fleet was especially nervous about it and begged off, claiming to be allergic to the stuff. Besides, the two older actors said, they were *actors*. They could *pretend*. As Ludwig made a point of observing at the time, "You don't have to actually explode an atomic bomb to get the effect of a mushroom cloud." And so neither Ludwig nor Van Fleet went to Peter's house to get high.

There was a 7:30 A.M. call the next morning, but Peter didn't show up. Everybody sat around waiting until finally, at about 11:30, Peter surfaced, smiling very broadly and greeting almost everyone with unusual effusion. (Ludwig figures the delay cost at least $40,000, but Sellers was characteristically unperturbed by that kind of expense.) The crew then launched into what Ludwig describes as the standard routine of filming with Peter, which is to say that Peter disappeared, the crew arranged everything precisely for him, and only then did they call him onto the set. Jo Van Fleet was sitting on the couch when he arrived. Sellers appeared and realized that she was the only person he hadn't greeted yet.

What he didn't understand was that she was in character already. And unfortunately for Peter, her character was that of his mother. Clearly, she had her own idiosyncracies.

In the manner of a six-year-old, Peter tiptoed up to the side of the couch and whispered, in a little-boyish way, "Jo." She didn't respond. He repeated it: "Jo." And again she didn't respond. He tiptoed around to the other side of the couch and tried again. "Jo." Then he blew up. "I hope you're feeling better this morning!" he shouted.

"Oh, good morning, Peter," Van Fleet said matter-of-factly.

As Ludwig puts it, "Peter vituperated." It was all directed at an astonished Jo. She was awful in the picture, Peter declared to the room, over and over, and with increasing amplitude. She was ruining the whole film, he roared. And by the way, she was ruining everyone else's morale, too.

"I realized he was talking about himself," Ludwig observes.

Joyce Van Patten slipped quickly away in a successful effort to distance herself from the acrimony. But Hy Averback simply froze in place, as did Mazursky and everyone else. Peter kept on yelling for a full twenty minutes. No one made any attempt to calm Peter down, nor did anyone come to Jo Van Fleet's defense.

"Peter?" Ludwig finally broke in. "Is there some grievance? Let's go into your dressing room and talk about it." "*Yes*," Peter snapped. "It's something very specific. It's her general attitude!" And with that he marched off the set.

Ludwig began to follow him but was restrained from doing so on the grounds that Peter needed no further encouragement. "If you do this," someone said, "he'll get on his yacht and we'll never see him again."

Jo Van Fleet "went to pieces." Distraught, she called her psychoanalyst and discussed it with him over the phone, after which she invited Ludwig to dinner that night and talked it through with him as well, at which point Mazursky telephoned and invited himself over for more conversation about Peter and his perceptions and what it all meant and what they were going to do about it. Mazursky expressed regret. "You did something I should have done," he told Ludwig.

The problem was easily but awkwardly solved the following day. The scene was shot in two parts. Peter and Joyce Van Patten performed on one side of the soundstage, while Jo Van Fleet and Salem Ludwig performed on the other. The editor Robert C. Jones pieced it all together later. (In fact, there is a single shot of the four characters all in the same space; the rest is done in close-ups and two-shots.)

Sad to say, grudges were held. When *I Love You, Alice B. Toklas!* was about to open, Salem Ludwig was left conspicuously uninvited to the cast and crew screening. He called the production office and was told just to show up. He did so—and was promptly snubbed by Paul Mazursky.

Sellers went on to bad-mouth the film in the press. "You should have seen it before they got at it. . . . They set up this marvelous Jewish wedding ceremony and at the last moment they lost their nerve and dubbed the rabbi into English! Now if the audience hadn't gathered by then that he was a rabbi speaking Hebrew, I don't see that there's much hope for the human race." (In fact, the brief shot of the rabbi's lips moving proves that indeed Warner Bros. did embrace the lowest common denominator by overdubbing Hebrew into English.)

A more outlandish complaint came much later, in 1980, when Peter expressed what appeared to be his long-standing outrage in a *Rolling Stone* profile:

"I wish you'd seen the original one with the interviews with Allen Ginsberg and Tim Leary. Paul Mazursky and Larry Tucker and myself, we got into the lab at night and *we* cut the film. Can you believe it? We bribed the guard, we spent all night with an editor, and when the schmucks came in the following day, we were there bright and early as though we'd just arrived, and we said, 'Listen—we don't like the finished film. We think you should see our attempts.' So they see it and they say [impersonating a crass Hollywood executive] 'Too weird. Who the *fuck* is Ginsberg? Who the *fuck* is Leary? People are going to know about Ginsberg and Leary in Orange County? I mean, dat's ridiculous!' I said, 'They're not for Orange County! They're for the world!' "

One must wonder one of two things: At what points were the narrative of *I Love You, Alice B. Toklas!* disrupted by interviews with two reigning gurus of the counterculture, or at what point did Peter fabricate the tale?

• • •

With Britt in New York, London, or Sweden, and with Peter never being one for monogamy and Roman having introduced Peter to Mia Farrow, the two couples—Peter and Mia, Roman and Sharon—went into the desert.

Their destination: Joshua Tree, California, a lunar terrain with parched, desolate earth punctuated by bizarre cacti, all conveniently located within a few minutes' drive of Palm Springs. "Because of its reputation for UFO sightings," Polanski recounts, "it was very much in vogue." Necessarily, they all smoked some pot, after which Peter and Mia wandered into the dry wasteland holding hands. Unknown to them, Roman followed. He eavesdropped as they engaged in a deeply spiritual, mystical, ludicrous, and entirely appropriate dialogue about eternity, stars, and alien life forms. The puckish Polanski then tossed a stick at them from the darkness. "Did you hear that?!" Peter whispered. "What *was* it?" Mia asked.

"I don't know," Peter replied, "but it was fantastic. *Fantastic!*"

Peter and Mia were of their time and place, and it is only because their extraordinary talent and celebrated friends enabled them to remain famous for the next thirty or thirty-five years that their behavior during the sixties remains mock-worthy while the rest of us maintain our comfortable anonymity as though we never did anything similar at the time.

Like anyone who could afford it, Peter and Mia enjoyed, as Polanski describes it, "dressing up as rich hippies, complete with beads, chunky costume jewelry, and Indian cotton caftans." The Mamas and the Papas' John Phillips recalls that Peter once walked in on a very stoned Mia and John and declared, colorfully, that he would get Mia "down from that drug if I have to pull you down by the pubic hairs."

At Christmastime 1967, Roman and Sharon invited Peter for a skiing holiday in Cortina. On Christmas Day, Sellers insisted on dressing as Santa Claus and handing out the gifts. Sharon helped him fashion the outfit— her fox fur coat, a red ski cap as a hat, and a white ski cap as a beard. But by the next day he had become so depressed and miserable that he left.

On January 20, 1968, Peter was one of Roman and Sharon's wedding guests at London's Playboy Club; the club was run by Victor Loundes, who, as Gene Gutowski describes him, "had a very open house." Naturally Warren Beatty, Rudolf Nureyev, Keith Richards, Brian Jones, Sean Connery, Vidal Sassoon, Kenneth Tynan, and Laurence Harvey came to the party, too.

Also that year Sonny and Cher hosted a party for Twiggy in their house in the Hollywood Hills; among the guests were Peter, Steve McQueen, Marlon Brando, Robert Mitchum, Tony Curtis, and Kirk Douglas.

In 1968, Peter Sellers was surveying the world from a very lofty perch. The air at the top may have been growing thinner by the month, but it was still exceedingly fresh—if you didn't notice the smoke.

• • •

The Mirisch brothers put another *Pink Panther* film on the drawing boards. But Blake Edwards wasn't directing; the job went to Bud Yorkin.

Inspector Clouseau (1968) "was first offered to Peter, and he refused it," Edwards later said. Instead, the role went to Alan Arkin. "In all the years I knew Peter, in spite of all the times when he swore he was never going to do another *Panther*, he never stopped complaining about the fact that the Mirisch Company had chosen Arkin. Peter was a collector of grievances, but he seemed to bear more of a grudge concerning the Arkin thing than just about anything else. For the sake of my own sanity, I have long since stopped trying to figure it out." Edwards goes on to say that *Inspector Clouseau* was the only unsuccessful *Panther*, but Peter took no consolation in its failure.

Still, Peter did return, however briefly, to the familiar in the summer of 1968 when a televised *Goon Show* aired in Britain in early August. Written by Spike, directed by Joe McGrath, and produced by Peter Eton, the program was not an attempt to present Crun, Bluebottle, Minnie, Eccles, and Seagoon in action, as one might expect from a visual medium, but rather simply to film the three veteran Goons standing at microphones doing their voices, just as they had done on BBC radio. (Strangely, this TV *Goon Show* was not produced by the BBC but by Thames for ITV.)

The show was not terribly successful. Milligan, who had originally been hired to write a new script, failed to be inspired to do so, and the Goons were forced to revert to the already late in the game "Tale of Men's Shirts" from 1959. As a result, what might have been a promising television series was cut short by a weak pilot.

• • •

Richard Lester once observed that the trouble with Peter Sellers having reached and sustained international superstardom was that he stopped coming into contact with ordinary people. Lester's point is not simply that he was emotionally isolated. More at issue for his work was that Peter's luxurious detachment, punctuated by parties with the glitter bunch, left him without everyday models on whom to draw for character development. "If you're in limousines all the time you don't meet many people," Lester said.

According to Siân Phillips, Kenneth Griffith "used to try and get him to travel on the underground. He used to say to Sellers, 'I honestly think it would give you a lot of interest in life—and peace of mind—if you mingled more and went on the subway with people.' But you know how Sellers was. He was completely insane and had absolutely no intention."

At the same time, the benefits of interactions with the ordinary are thoroughly overrated as far as celebrities themselves are concerned. Movie stars' lives can quickly turn grotesque whenever fans barge in. Peter told of his experience on a plane from Barcelona to Rome during the production of *The Bobo*. He was in first class when a group of tourists, in coach, learned there was a star on board: "For an hour they came in shifts of three to look at me. One man told me his brother-in-law had done the titles on one of my films and seemed offended when I didn't know him. He asked me to write a note to his brother-in-law on a menu card saying I bumped into Ethel and George on the plane. Then Ethel and George argued about what I should say." And at a Hollywood get-together, Peter once told, "a long, thin thing glided up to me at a party and said, 'I do find all of your films terrifyingly boring.' "

Robert Parrish was an independent witness to another such deformed encounter between Peter and his so-called fans. The two men were on a plane together—heading to Barcelona this time—when a group of Americans got on. They were each wearing a lapel button that read, "We smile more!" One of the smilers marched right up to Peter and said, "Mr. Sellers! I just saw one of your pictures recently, and it wasn't very good, and I didn't think your performance was very good either."

Sellers froze. "Thank you for pointing that out to me," he muttered.

As Spike Milligan once put it, "He sees himself as a clean person in a colony of lepers—can't afford to mix with them too much if he's to come out alive."

• • •

For reasons with which only bitterly divorced people can perhaps fully sympathize, Peter and Britt flew to Venice for another reconciliation. Accompanied by Britt's three terriers—Scruff, Pucci, and Fred—they sailed *The Bobo* through the Gulf of Trieste and down the Adriatic, ending the cruise at Brindisi. They flew over to Rome, checked into the Excelsior, and proceeded to have such a vicious fight that the night porter showed up and humbly made known to them their neighbors' complaints. Britt took a few Valium and went to bed. She was awakened by Peter placing a telephone call to his Italian agent. "Franco," Peter announced, "I want you to come to the hotel immediately and collect my wife. She is leaving Rome this instant. Our marriage is finished." To his groggy wife he said, "Just get out of here and don't ever come back. I never want to see you again, you bitch." So she left.

By midmorning of the following day, Peter had ordered the crew of *The Bobo* to throw all of Britt's belongings onto the dock. Among the detritus were Scuff, Pucci, and Fred.

Britt served Peter with divorce papers. Peter convinced Britt to have lunch with him. "I know I can't live without you," he told her, but she pursued the divorce anyway. "For the first time in my life I was alone,"

Britt writes, though her solitude didn't last very long, for she soon took up with Count Ascanio "Bino" Cicogna, an Italian playboy who went out and bought a bigger yacht than *The Bobo*.

The divorce was finalized on December 18, 1968. Spike sent Britt a congratulatory telegram.

Two days later, Peter arrived at London's fashionable Mirabelle restaurant for a dinner party with Roman, Sharon, Warren, Julie, and the producer Sam Spiegel. Not surprisingly, Peter's date was a beautiful and fashionable blond film star. Oddly, she was Britt Ekland. The date ended at Peter's place when Peter pulled down his £1,200 shotgun and threatened to shoot his ex-wife to death. "Don't be silly, Peter," was Britt's adept reply. Knowing who she was dealing with, she kept talking to him in a soothing voice until she could slip the gun out of his hands. Then he burst into tears.

EIGHTEEN

On his own—at least away from Britt—Peter kept running with the fast-living Polanski crowd, which, in addition to Roman and Sharon and Warren and Julie, included Yul Brynner, Peter Lawford, Gene Gutowski, the playboy Jay Sebring, and the screenwriter James Poe.

As Polanski himself describes it, "There was quite a bunch of friends during this period; we were all usually in a very happy mood. Having had a few drinks or having just smoked a joint, we would start joking and kidding around, and it would develop into a kind of routine. We would start playing Italians, you know—just pretending we spoke Italian. There were always two arguing, and one other would sort of stand and observe, and then he would get involved in the argument of the other two. One of the two would start arguing with *him*, leaving the other one out. And it would go around like this—we could do it for hours. Sometimes we would do operas, make up singing. Often we would do Spaniards—whatever came to our minds. It was dependent on the kind of drink we had had and the extent of our drunkenness. It was really great fun."

"There was a fabulous happening," Gene Gutowski fondly recalls, "the premiere of *Rosemary's Baby* in Paris. Peter was very much in attendance. We took over a whole hotel—the little place where Oscar Wilde had lived and died. It had become a showpiece, boutique-type hotel. We had a magnificent three-day party, the whole place reeking of, uh, substances, controlled or uncontrolled, mostly un-. Peter liked to indulge."

Asked whether Peter's drug use made his mood swings more drastic, Gutowski answers, "It's difficult for me to judge. He definitely had mood changes, but I couldn't tell you if it was under the influence of whatever he was taking or smoking or was just simply his nature. He would be quite happy and suddenly become very depressed and dark. That was typical of him."

Peter took a casual attitude toward carrying drugs across international borders. "He was very friendly with a great friend of Roman's," Gutowski explains, "a Moroccan Jewish film director by the name of Simon Hessera. Simon was forever trying to make a picture, and he became very friendly with Peter. Peter spent some time in Rome, and before he left, he left me a note: Would I please collect a jar of honey from an English lady at an address in Rome and have Simon bring it to him in London? It was as simple as that.

"When I sent Simon to pick up the honey, it was an extraordinary amount of money—something like $200. Simon was quite amazed and upset about it: 'What is this stupid thing? What kind of honey is he eating?' I said, 'Simon, I really don't know. He's a health freak. Maybe it's royal jelly. Just shut up and take it to London.'

"Poor Simon, shaking his head, carried it to London. Soon after, he realized that this honey was heavily laced with hashish. Peter was giving it out in tiny spoonfuls to his friends. When Simon found out what he'd carried past customs he was very upset."

• • •

Michael Sellers started smoking marijuana at age thirteen. Peter didn't realize it at the time, but he was his own son's drug connection, for the boy simply snitched it from his father's stash, which Peter kept stored in empty film canisters around the house. "There was so much of the stuff that I knew he wouldn't miss a little. . . . It was like his pills. He had thousands of them, and I would help myself to amphetamines or Mandrax sleeping pills."

Sarah kept a defensive low profile. A cute, quiet child, she let her mother raise her. When Peter demanded her presence, she went along.

Victoria Sellers's first memories are of Brookfield, its ducks and geese, the chicken coop, the trampoline Peter put up in the yard, and the pastel-pink bedroom in which she slept, always with the lights on, for she knew the house was haunted.

Peter sold Brookfield to Ringo Starr in 1969 for £60,000.

• • •

His offscreen concerns seem mostly to have been money and women. Peter could be as cheap as he was extravagant. It depended on his mood. He'd treat his friends to dinners, trips on his yacht, baubles; then, without warning, he'd make them foot the bills. A friend of his, the skiing instructor Hans Moellinger, got a taste of this after a trip with Peter to Vienna. "He was always telling me about buying property in the Seychelles, and this and that—he was obviously very rich—but in a way he was very stingy. Once we were staying at the Hotel Sacher with two beautiful girls, and. . . ." Asked who Peter's companion was, Moellinger is vague. "I was with Miss Sweden at the time, and she always had five or six friends around. . . . And we went to the opera and did the usual sightseeing, and finally we left. The bill was the equivalent of about two or three thousand dollars nowadays. I thought he paid it. One or two weeks later I got an invoice. It said, 'Mr. Sellers thought you should pay the bill.' Can you imagine? At that time my monetary situation was not so good," the ski coach notes.

As for the ideal woman, Peter had a dream—one of many. "These photographs you see of Gorky or Goethe," Peter remarked to Joe McGrath one day.

"What are you talking about?" the confused McGrath replied. "He said, 'Well, I don't have any photographs of Goethe. But those Russian writers, and those early American writers—they're all sitting there, and there's a cottage in the background, and there's always a woman, slightly out of focus, drying her hands on a towel. That's what I want—that sort of woman. I really want somebody that's going to be a cushion for me.' "

Peter did not go wanting for women after his second marriage ended, but most appear to have been cushions of a very different sort. He revealed to one girlfriend the secret of his success: as a pickup line he'd tell them he was descended from Lord Nelson, a throwback to his chubby childhood. But faking lineage can't have been his only skill. Peter Sellers was a desirable man: funny, glamorous, rich, handsome (yes, he was handsome), and world-famous. His good looks were precise and curious, distinctly unconventional. He radiated on a physical level—the flashing smile, the slim frame he worked daily to carve from a naturally larger mass, sad eyes that pierced nonetheless. And he was sexy; and women knew it. Britt Ekland once revealed that Peter displayed what she called "extraordinary talents as a lover." She knew his flaws better than almost anyone, but, as she acknowledged, "If some things disappointed me in our marriage, that was never one of them." Among the beautiful women he dated around this time were Zsa Zsa Gabor's daughter Francesca Hilton and Alice Joyce, a Pan American Airlines flight attendant, to whom Peter actually proposed.

Emotionally, he was perpetually disappointed; sexually, he got what he

wanted. The paradox tore at him. "His intimate life, with the women . . . ,"
Polanski says, trailing off and beginning again. "It was not always what you
would call the happiest relationships."

In the drawing rooms of London, Peter's skills at seduction led to
increasing speculation about the precise nature of his friendship with Princess Margaret, particularly when her own marriage to Lord Snowdon became more publicly rocky. With Tony causing talk about his relationship
with Lady Jacqueline Rufus Isaacs, Margaret was rumored to be spending
time alone with Peter at his Mayfair apartment. According to Margaret's
biographers, the source of the rumor was—guess—Peter himself.

Siân Phillips saw him in action one evening "at dinner when I was in
a show in the West End. I got there after my performance, and I thought,
well, I know everybody—except for one little woman I didn't know at all.
'She's obviously not in the business, I'll catch up with her later.' " And so
Siân Phillips sat down. "O'Toole was laughing, of course, because he didn't
give a damn, but Sellers was looking absolutely ashen because I reserved
her for later. Of course, it was Princess Margaret. She was the only one I
hadn't recognized. Sellers really wanted to impress her. He wanted everything to go really well; he didn't want any hiccups." Phillips notes, "You
had to be careful around her. I don't know if those stories about him and
her are true or not, but certainly she was terrifying to be out with. She'd
be a nice little person singing songs and playing the piano, and then suddenly she was HRH and you had to grovel. You couldn't overstep the
mark."

"Well, I obviously don't know how intimate they were," Joe McGrath
states. "But they were very, very close. Oh yeah, very. They were *all* close.
I mean, so was Tony."

As for Margaret's feelings about Peter, she once remarked that he was
"the most difficult man I know." He proved the point when he called her
on the telephone one day and did an excruciating imitation of her husband
describing in obscene detail one of his dates with Jackie Rufus Isaacs.

• • •

One day about twenty years earlier—he and Anne were still married—
Peter Sellers looked across a London park and spied a pretty little three-
year-old girl. He began dating her in 1968, when she was twenty-one.

Miranda Quarry was delicate but curvy, with long, straight hair and an
aristocratic bearing. Her stepfather was noble in the technical sense of the

word; he was Lord Mancroft, a former junior minister in Parliament. Miranda was a patrician hippie without any of the distracting dirt or politics. She moved in the circles expected of her; her peers were literally so.

She and Peter crossed paths since their earliest encounter in the park. A modern debutante, Miranda had once taken a come-and-go job creating floral arrangements in the Dorchester's flower shop, where Peter used to buy bouquets for Britt. They met again on the set of his new picture, *The Magic Christian*—she was a publicity assistant at that point—and soon began dating. It was an affair of convenience. She liked to hang around with Peter and his movie people, Peter enjoyed romancing a delicious aristocrat, and they got together when it was convenient.

Peter's first wife and two daughters comment on his relationships with women during this period:

Victoria: "As any man would be who is no longer married, he went out with a lot of different women, and traveled here and there, and decided to rent a house in this country for a few months, and then, no, no, we're going to rent a house *here*, and then we're going to stay in *that* hotel. . . . It was all mixed up and jumbled but, I would say, interesting."

Sarah: "That's how he operated. Once he got bored with one toy, he wanted the next. It was a constant quest, really, and I think the women were just a part of that. . . . I think he found it very difficult to have a decent relationship. It probably boils down to his mother."

Anne: "He used to bring me all his new acquisitions in the way of girl-friends, so that 'Mum' could see them and tell him what I thought of them."

If some men seem unable to deal with women apart from the categories of the virgin and the whore, Peter Sellers, as usual, provided a novel twist. *His* classifications were the virginal sexpot and his own mother. Anne, never either, now found herself hideously transformed into a woman she despised and thus had no desire to emulate for her ex-husband. Peter wasn't able to help himself, and she was unable to stop him.

• • •

"It started off with Terry Southern," says Joe McGrath. "We were going to do *Flash and Filigree*, his other novel, but Peter said, 'No, let's do *The Magic Christian* [1969]'."

Given Peter's recent history with directors, McGrath found himself the object of warnings from friends and associates. "Some people said, 'You accepted the poison chalice.' I said, 'I don't really see it like that, you know.'

"He could be very depressive. If you got him on a bad day he could fuck up the day's filming for you. But I got to know him well enough that I could say to him, 'You're obviously exhausted' and just send him home. He had this great thing that comedy *is*—energy. And if you are not feeling fit or good, you can't be funny.

"He always avoided confrontations, so I think an awful lot of people thought him devious. He would never face up to confrontation. He would say, 'Excuse me' or something and go somewhere else, then have a minion tell the person, 'This is what we're doing.' I got past that with him. He would *have* a confrontation with me. Not on the floor. He would say, 'Can we go to the dressing room?' or something, and then we would figure it out and argue it and discuss it and then he would come back and do it. By that time I knew Peter well; I could tell him what I thought. As Spike Milligan always said, 'Once you go past that barrier with Peter, you're a friend. But if you don't, he'll always look on you as some servant he's telling what to do.' "

Peter was in Hollywood on January, 22, 1969, when he held a combination cocktail party and press conference for *The Magic Christian* at the Beverly Hills Hotel. But it was his costar who fielded many of the questions, and they mostly didn't have to do with *The Magic Christian*. Ringo Starr was about to join the other Beatles for their final public performance on the roof of the Apple building in London the following week.

John Lennon had been the first choice for the role, but Lennon wasn't able to do it. Hence Ringo. The good-natured drummer's last picture, *Candy* (1968), called on him to play a Latino gardener in hot pursuit of the title character, a nubile female Candide. (*Candy*, scripted by Buck Henry, is based on Terry Southern's novel of the same name.) In *The Magic Christian*, he plays Peter's character's adopted son. It was less of a stretch.

Ringo found the experience of acting with Sellers to be particularly strange, owing to the two men having known each other for years without cameras rolling in the background. "I knew [him] quite well, but suddenly there he was going into character, and I got confused," said Ringo.

"The amazing thing with Peter was that, though we would work all day and go out and have dinner that night—and we would usually leave him laughing hysterically, because he was hilarious—the next morning we'd say, 'Hi, Pete!,' and we'd have to start again. There was no continuation.

You had to make the friendship start again from 9 o'clock every morning. We'd all be laughing at 6 o'clock at night, but the next morning it would be, 'Hi, Pete!,' then 'Oh, God!' We'd have to knock the wall down again to say 'hello.' Sometimes we'd be asked to leave the set, because Peter Sellers was being Peter Sellers."

For his part, Sellers had only positive comments about Starr's performance. "Ringo is a natural mime," said Peter. "He can speak with his eyes." Ringo said of Peter, "He would always say, 'It's your eyes, Ring. It's your eyes. They'll be two hundred feet big up there, you know.' "

• • •

The story goes: Sir Guy Grand, KG, KC, CBE (Peter), a lonely but immensely wealthy aristocrat, meets a homeless youth (Ringo) and immediately adopts him. (KG stands for Knight, Most Noble Order of the Garter, and CBE for Commander, the Most Excellent Order of the British Empire. There is no KC in the British system of honors, so let's call it an informal abbreviation of KCB, which stands for Knight Commander, the Most Honourable Order of the Bath.) "Well, then, Youngman Grand," Guy states after the brief ceremony. "Father!" Youngman cries. Together they spend a lot of money in a series of colorful, seemingly pharmaceutically oriented, more or less disconnected adventures.

Guy and Youngman attend a performance of *Hamlet*; the lead, Laurence Harvey, performs the soliloquy as a strip show routine, getting down to—and past—the Danish prince's bodkin, in this case a black leather jockstrap. ("You've got to hand it to that Laurence Harvey," Youngman Grand remarks to Guy. "He really knows his job.") A train trip turns into a psychedelic burlesque show with a strobe light sequence. A shooting expedition becomes a World War II battlefield complete with machine guns, artillery, and tanks. (They barbecue a bird with a flame-thrower.) At a fine art auction, Guy notices a dark portrait and engages a Sotheby's representative (John Cleese) in conversation. The rep tells him that while the painting has not been specifically attributed to the master himself, it is decidedly of the school of Rembrandt:

> GUY: (in Peter's parody-Eton-ish lockjaw voice) I like "School of Rembrandt." Yes, I enjoy all the French painters.
>
> SOTHEBY'S REPRESENTATIVE: (without the parody) Uh, well, Rembrandt was, in a sense, Dutch.

Guy purchases the painting out of auction for £30,000, cuts out the nose, which he keeps, and orders Sotheby's to burn the useless rest. With its purposeful incoherence and stabs at druggy social satire, *The Magic Christian* is, like Peter and Mia's cosmic walk in the desert, distinctly of its time and place.

• • •

According to Terry Southern's son, Nile, "Peter would get agitated when he wasn't working. He would just get really eager and impatient and just start working on the material, and he'd bring in his other friends to start working on it, and it ended up that, like, nine people ended up working on that script." Terry used to joke that Peter would just run into someone at a cocktail party and the next thing anyone knew, that person was re-writing the script of *The Magic Christian*.

Graham Chapman and John Cleese were among them. Chapman once declared that the future *Monty Python* stars—*Monty Python's Flying Circus* premiered on the BBC a few months later in October 1969—had originally been hired "to write in a part for Ringo Starr. The reason given was so that the financiers could find the money to make the movie." Joe McGrath remembers the situation rather differently: "Cleese and Chapman were pretty unknown at the time, but Peter wanted them. Terry resented them quite a lot, [but] Peter insisted on bringing them in because he was going to play Guy Grand as an Englishman. We got the money in this country, so it was set in England." McGrath adds, "At one point, before he could find his voice, he was actually playing it like Groucho Marx."

In any case, Chapman described his experience on *The Magic Christian* as "an ordeal-by-fire." According to him, he and Cleese wrote a scene in which a very nervous man was to sit on a hostess's Pekinese and kill it. Sellers "laughed hysterically at it, but the next day when we came back to see Peter, he'd gone off it totally. He'd actually read this piece of script to the man who delivered his milk, and he hadn't laughed. So it was out."

Cleese, says McGrath, is "very funny in the Sotheby's scene, but I had to bring him back. The first day he was a nervous wreck. He couldn't play opposite Peter. He said, 'My God, I never realized the heat that comes off him.'

"At the end of the first day [of shooting Cleese's sequence], Peter said to me, 'We've really got to get rid of him and cast somebody else. Surely we can cast somebody else and bring him in tomorrow.' He'd just blown the first day, [so] I said, 'Let me talk to him.' Sellers said, 'I'm going home—you obviously want to see yesterday's dailies—so give me a call later.'

"I went up to see John in the dressing room. He was really in tears. He said, 'I know I have blown this, I understand if you don't want me back tomorrow, I understand what's going on. . . .' I said, 'Now look. Peter has gone home, so what we'll do is we'll have an early call tomorrow, and we'll shoot some reverses on the scene we did today.' We got him in early, and we shot the reverses, and I sent that reel off immediately to be developed. Peter came in about 10:00 A.M. and I showed it to Peter, who looked at it and said, 'Oh, yeah, we can use it. I think he's just very nervous.' Peter and I went up to John's dressing room, and everything was okay."

Gail Gerber, Southern's companion, recalls chaos of a more literary nature:

"Terry became nonplussed the *first* time when he realized that the producers had decided it was 'episodic' and needed something to tie it together. They thought, or maybe Terry thought, that Guy Grand could adopt a son or something. Terry always took suggestions in good faith.

"He was prepared to write in the son, which he did, and fortunately Ringo got to do the part. He was great in it—weird and great. Of course the book had nothing to do with any of that, but this was a pretty off-the-wall production anyhow.

"There were lots of phone calls. 'You've got to get to London! You've got to get to London!' We were going to leave Burroughs in our apartment on 36th Street [the poet William S. Burroughs, the author of *Naked Lunch* and *Junkie: Confessions of an Unredeemed Drug Addict*] and go to London, but Terry kept dragging his feet for some reason until finally we got on a plane and went. Meanwhile they'd already started shooting.

"Because Terry wasn't there, Peter got all these other writers. They went for a whole different sort of slapstick thing. By the time we got there, several scenes were, in Terry's estimation, ruined. There was the hunting scene, where they were blowing away birds until they were charcoal, and what mostly offended Terry was the scene at the auction house. Guy Grand was a very kind person and a great connoisseur of art, and he would never, *ever* plunge a knife into a fine painting. But they got carried away in their own funny way."

One day, says Gerber, "Terry came back from the set and said, 'You'll never believe what they said today. "We've got Raquel Welch!" ' "

"Terry said, 'I don't have a *part* for Raquel Welch.'

"They said, 'Well, write one.' "

• • •

Cameos abound in *The Magic Christian*.

Spike Milligan turns up as a traffic warden. He gives Guy Grand's black Mercedes limousine a parking ticket, only to be told by Grand that if he eats the ticket he'll get £500. So he eats it.

Michael Sellers appears as a teenage hippie.

Wilfrid Hyde-White plays the ship's captain. (*The Magic Christian* is the name of the oceanliner.)

Christopher Lee is the ship's vampire.

Roman Polanski sits alone at the ship's bar. A large, diamond-brooched blond approaches him and asks, "Would you like to buy a girl a dwink?" Through the haze of Polanski's cigarettes, she begins to sing "Mad About the Boy," parades theatrically around the room, and pulls her wig off to reveal the head of Yul Brynner.

Everyone adjourns to the engine room, where they find seventy bare-breasted women rowing the ship forward. Their slavemistress: Raquel Welch. She's "the Priestess of the Whip." "In, out! In, out! *In, out!*" Raquel cries. King Kong then kills Wilfrid Hyde-White.

Terry Southern wanted Stanley Kubrick to appear in a cameo, too, but as McGrath notes, "Stanley was just never available."

Peter himself performs an eerie sort of cameo in *The Magic Christian*. McGrath explains: "He plays the part of a nun. You just see this nun occasionally in the back of the train." With a demented smile on her face, the good sister shoots photos during the strobe-light sequence. "That's Peter. He had the nun outfit on, and he called up and said 'Joe, quick, *quick!* Come up to the dressing room!' Of course I rushed up there. I thought there was something wrong with him.

"He had the wimple on and said, 'Who am I?'

"I said, 'You're Peg.' "

" 'Yes,' he said. 'I'm Peg.' He looked exactly like her."

• • •

"The last scene in the movie is a shit vat, where everybody goes into the shit for money," observes McGrath. "Terry and I insisted that we do this in the States under the Statue of Liberty."

So the cast and crew finished up in London and prepared to go to New York to film rich people wallowing for dollars in a tank full of feces.

"We were having this wrap party in London," Gail Gerber looks back. "There were about thirty of us at a giant round table. Peter was dating Miranda Quarry at the time, and we're onto coffee and, well, you know how a hushed silence can fall? Well, it fell. And my voice rang out saying that I had never had an ocean voyage. Peter picked up on it immediately and said, 'Yes! We must take the QE2 to New York! Don't you think, Miranda?' "

It was not an idle question. At the time, Lord Mancroft, Miranda's stepfather, was a director of the Cunard Line, of which the *Queen Elizabeth II* was the flagship. Luxury transatlantic passage was swiftly arranged. "We all got a free trip," says McGrath.

Gail Gerber recites the passenger list on the *QE2*: "There was Peter, and Miranda, and a BBC crew following them, and the producer, and his wife, and Derek Taylor (because of Ringo), and his wife, and five children, and nanny, and Ringo, and Maureen, and was it one or two kids?, and a nanny, and Terry and me. Allen Klein was on the ship as well. What the hell was he doing there?" McGrath adds, "John Lennon was supposed to come with us, but he got turned back at Southampton because of the visa thing. He'd come down from London with us. In fact, we'd all gone down in the big Mercedes limo we used in the film." (Derek Taylor was the Beatles' friend and press agent; Maureen was Ringo's wife; Allen Klein was in the process of becoming the Beatles' manager, a relationship that soon soured and ended in protracted litigation. John Lennon was denied a visa by the United States Embassy in London because of his arrest and conviction for marijuana possession in October 1968.)

"Hash oil, tobacco, cannabis, dynamite-like opium. . . ." Terry Southern is reciting the drug list on the *QE2*. "Peter became absolutely enthralled—he couldn't get enough. For five days we were kind of in a dream state."

"They were all out of their heads," McGrath notes. "There were blankets being rolled up and stuffed under doors."

On the first night, there came a rap on McGrath's door. He opened it to find Peter dressed as the leader of a gang of nineteenth-century London street urchin pickpockets. "Good evening," said Peter. "I am the ship's Fagin. Tomorrow I shall be the ship's purser, but tonight I am the ship's

Fagin!" All night long he knocked on people's doors and greeted them singing "You've Got to Pick a Pocket or Two."

The stabilizers weren't working properly—those of the *QE2*—and not only Gail Gerber but some members of the crew became violently seasick. Luckily, Sellers had brought along a remedy. "Peter had a great big jar of honey," Gerber relates, "and a big, long-handled spoon. It was laced with hash oil. And with everybody he would meet, he'd dip the spoon in and pass it around. He thought it was absolutely wonderful. He saw me all green, and he dipped the spoon in and gave me some. I felt a lot better."

An advance team had flown across the Atlantic and, as McGrath continues, "set up to do the shit vat on the island under the statue. At the last minute Commonwealth United, which put the money up, said no. 'We're not going along with this—it's making it too hot for us.' 'You mean hot for the money men,' Terry said. Sellers then paid out of his own pocket, and we shot it down on the banks of the Thames with St. Paul's and all that in the background. Sellers paid for that himself, and later on Commonwealth United gave him back the money. But they wouldn't do it under the Statue of Liberty. They wanted the movie, they wanted Peter Sellers, 'We'll give you anything, do it, do it, do it. . . .' But, when it came to that, as Terry said, it was too hot for them."

The Magic Christian, shit scene and all, was given a Royal Charity world premiere at the Kensington Odeon Theater in London on December 11, 1969, to benefit Britain's National Society for the Prevention of Cruelty to Children, Princess Margaret, president.

Spike Milligan provided the last word some years later: "It's a very funny film. I loved every inch of it. You've really got to hate people to love this film."

• • •

Throughout 1969, as the Beatles' personal behavior toward one another deteriorated—Paul was getting bossier, John wanted the group to break up, George resented Paul telling him how to play the guitar, Ringo was very nice—they recorded an anthem not of mere tolerance but of a more genuine *acceptance*, touched as it was with resignation. "Let It Be," they sang. Some of their recording sessions—not only for "Let It Be" but other songs as well, along with their rooftop concert—were filmed for inclusion in the film *Let It Be* (1970).

Peter turns up in a scene that wasn't used in *Let It Be*'s final cut, for obvious reasons. The band is sitting on couches taking a break when their good friend Pete shows up and pleasantly offers them some knockout grass. It's a facetious conversation punctuated by a lot of merry laughter, but it still doesn't seem terribly far off the mark in terms of Peter's habits at the time, not to mention the Beatles' own drug use.

Alas, the deal doesn't go down. Paul claims that he's stopped smoking pot; to be precise, Paul claims that a fictitious biographer has claimed that he has stopped smoking pot. Peter expresses great disappointment at this news, especially, he says, because he so fondly recalls the fantastic weed they'd once shared. As the dejected Peter makes his exit, Paul pushes things a little too far by advising Peter not to leave any syringes on the floor of the studio on his way out. Paul explains that he's worried about the band's notoriety since John Lennon's 1968 drug bust. Cut to a close-up of Lennon sitting apart from the others. John is noticeably displeased at Paul's little joke.

• • •

Peter helped three other friends make another film in 1969—the disastrous *A Day at the Beach* (1970). Simon Hessera directed and Gene Gutowski produced, from a script by Roman Polanski.

"We wanted Hessera to make his debut as a director," Polanski relates. "That's what *he* wanted to do, and he was really fantastic at acting and imitations, and we were convinced that he could do a good picture. Simon sat down with Gérard Brach, a writer with whom I wrote several scripts, and wrote a script called *The Driver*. [Brach cowrote the screenplays for Polanski's *Repulsion* (1965), *Cul-de-sac* (1966), and *The Fearless Vampire Killers* (1967).] Peter wanted to play a lead in the film—whatever he could do—[but] when I read that script I didn't believe there could be a movie made out of it. I thought we'd better find something else. I read a book by a guy called Heere Heeresma, a Dutch writer, did an adaptation of it, and suggested that Hessera do the film. Peter volunteered to do a cameo, and that was it.

"We were having a little party or dinner or something like that at the home of my partner at that time, Gene Gutowski, and [the producer] Robert Evans was there with Charlie Bludhorn, the head of Paramount; we were pushing for Paramount to finance the picture. Simon was there, and Peter was there, too, and of course we started doing one of our routines. They were tremendously amused—particularly Charlie—at what Simon and Peter were doing, and somehow started the notion that they were going to give some money for this film to be made." *A Day at the Beach* was reportedly financed at a cost of $600,000. "In those times that was a lot of money," Polanski comments. "I mean, it was sufficient to make a low budget movie."

As Gutowski describes it, "*A Day at the Beach* is the story of the relationship between an alcoholic and his little daughter. He tries to have an outing at the beach and promises his ex-wife that he will not drink. Of course he falls apart and gets blind drunk. We shot it in Denmark—on the beach and in Copenhagen. Peter spent about a week or two with us. We had a very good time. He was always in pursuit of amorous adventures, always in pursuit of being introduced to the woman of his life and, you know, always in love or falling in love. That was Peter."

In an apparent attempt to make the film even more raw than its subject matter destined it to be, Hessera cast an unknown and inexperienced actor, Mark Burns, in the lead. Burns plays "Uncle Bernie," so nicknamed because his estranged wife refuses to tell her daughter, Winnie (Beatrice Edney), that the abysmal drunkard is really her father. It's a one-dimensional performance, the dimension being surliness.

Midway through the film, after a snack of three bottles of beer at a seaside cafe, Uncle Bernie leaves Winnie to fend for herself on the beach, in the rain, and staggers into a beachside trinket shop. He asks the proprietor for a shell. Peter Sellers's face appears in sudden close-up. He's wearing a white sweater and smart print ascot. His right shoulder is thrust forward. "Why don't you come in and choose one," he asks, toying with his earlobe.

Enter a grinning Graham Stark in a bright red shirt and print ascot; Peter's unnamed character addresses Stark as "Pipi." (The film's credits cite "The Partners: A. Queen and Graham Stark.") Peter tells Pipi to get some beer "while I keep this young man happy." Biting his finger, he declares that Pipi "goes and ruins *everything, always.*"

Peter takes his sunglasses off and sucks on the earpiece. Pipi returns. "She wants three bottles and an opener," he says, referring to Uncle Bernie. (By this point, Hessera has cut away to the little girl, who is now tangled up in fishing netting and screaming in terror, but Uncle Bernie is shopping for shells and cannot hear her.) Uncle Bernie tells off Pipi for ruining Peter's life and leaves.

Bernie retrieves Winnie, who has somehow managed to extract herself from the netting, and they spend the rest of the day together, he drinking beer, she wandering around. The final scene occurs at night in an empty, cobblestoned town square. The bottomed-out Uncle Bernie staggers in, led by little Winnie, abruptly pitches forward, slams his head against the cobblestones, and croaks. The film's last words belong to the wailing little Winnie: "Uncle Bernie!"

"It's not good," Polanski acknowledges. "The problem is, I'm afraid, the director, and also insufficient funds. But the main problem is the actor. You can't watch a man playing a drunk for one-and-a-half hours unless he's a really great actor and has some charisma. That guy had none.

"Other than that, I mean, the film. . . . If there had been a great performance. . . . The film is done well enough to work. What *didn't* work was the casting. Simon was not a director, and, let's face it, we were a little bit cavalier."

• • •

What Polanski doesn't mention is that his work on *A Day at the Beach* was interrupted. He and Gutowski were in London when, in the early hours of Friday, August 8, 1969, some intruders creepy-crawled their way onto Polanski's rented estate in the hills above Bel Air, shot a young man to death in the driveway, and then murdered everyone inside the house. The victims were Sharon Tate, who was only a few weeks away from giving birth to a son; Jay Sebring, Abigail Folger, Wojiciech Frykowski, and Steve Parent, the youth in the driveway. No motive, no mercy, no sense, no solace.

Gene Gutowski remembers: "Shortly after Sharon's murder I flew with Polanski from London to California. His friends gathered around him. There was Peter, Warren Beatty, Yul Brynner. . . . We kept a vigil, cheering him up as best we could and giving him support and friendship. Peter was instrumental. It was a tough time for everybody, absolutely." Peter attended Sharon's funeral on Wednesday, August 13, at Holy Cross Cemetery.

One month later, Roman and some friends offered a $25,000 reward for information leading to the arrests of the killers. Polanski himself doesn't remember the details anymore: "Peter Sellers . . . ? I don't recall—not enough. I remember putting up the reward, and I know that the reward led to the capture of the people because it was paid out. Somehow no one mentioned it afterwards. If it was reported there must be some truth in it—I just don't remember. I mean, that period, I never go back to it, you know, voluntarily, and if you don't refresh your memory by going back to it, it fades out much faster."

Gutowski, however, is very clear about Peter's help. He did put up part of the reward money, Gutowski says, and "he was motivated by pure friendship and his desire to help find the guilty." Polanski, Beatty, Brynner, and others provided the rest.

At the time, Peter spoke out in public: "Someone must have knowledge or suspicions they are withholding or may be afraid to reveal. Someone must have seen the blood-soaked clothing, the knife, the gun, the getaway car. Someone must be able to help."

By December 1969, Charles Manson, Susan Atkins, Patricia Krenwinkle, Tex Watson, Leslie Van Houton, and Linda Kasabian had all been charged with the murders. Charges against Kasabian were dropped when she agreed to be the star witness for the prosecution. The rest were convicted and are spending their lives in jail. A biker named Danny DeCarlo, who was familiar with the defendants and who felt the need to extract himself from a host of legal problems by sharing what he knew, evidently got some of the reward money; so, it seems, did Ronni Howard, a.k.a. Shelley Nadell, a.k.a. Connie Schampeau, to whom Susan Atkins had spilled some gory details in prison.

Peter Sellers was capable of enormous compassion, tenderness, and love—so much so that you thought you were going to be friends for life. And then hours, days, weeks later, the scale would tip the other way, and a very unlikable, aggressive person would emerge."

The director Alvin Rakoff is describing his experience of making the small scale, too-little-known *Hoffman* (1970). "I look back at Peter with great affection, and love, and puzzlement. He was an extraordinary firecracker, and yet you were in danger of being burnt."

Filmed in the fall of 1969 in seven weeks at Elstree Studios, with one additional week on location (Wimbledon Common, the Thames Embankment), *Hoffman* is the story of a middle-aged man who blackmails a pretty young woman into letting him dominate her, potentially sexually, for a one-week period after he discovers that her boyfriend, his employee, has been cheating him at work. The comedy-drama—of which there is substantially more unnerving drama than comedy of any sort—introduced the twenty-one-year-old Irish actress Sinead Cusack, the daughter of the actor Cyril Cusack, to the screen.

Rakoff had directed an earlier, shorter version of *Hoffman* for television, but as the project headed for the big screen, he found himself in some trouble. Donald Pleasance had played the role on TV, but he wasn't considered big enough for the silver screen. So Peter was hired, thanks to Bryan Forbes, who had become head of production at Elstree Studios, then controlled by EMI. But after a meeting at Peter's apartment on Clarges Street, Mayfair, Peter decided, as Rakoff describes it, that "he and I would never get on with each other, and I should leave the picture. I left the meeting.

"But Bryan Forbes said to Peter, 'I'm not paying him off. If you want him to go, *you* pay him off.' And the next thing I know, there's a call from

Peter, saying 'I'm sure we can get on with each other—shall we try?' So there I was—fired from the picture by the leading man and reluctantly taken back. But then we got on like a house on fire—a very warm friendship."

"I auditioned Sinead with Peter, and Peter liked her," Rakoff reports. "It was essential that there be some sort of chemistry between the two of them." That there was. As Rakoff describes it, they got along "too well."

"Peter said, 'Let's have dinner tonight,' and she said yes, so he said, 'I'll pick you up.' About 8:00 o'clock I heard the helicopter Peter had ordered. He took her to Paris for dinner. 'Let's have dinner' became not 'dinner' but a love dinner at a very good Parisian restaurant. I would defy any beautiful girl not to fall in love with such a man. He was a very lovable guy when he wanted to be."

The affair was intense, rather brief, and sequentially joyous and harsh. "Oh, they had terrible riles, those two, but again, who wasn't riled with Peter Sellers?" says Rakoff.

Miranda Quarry didn't go entirely missing while Peter was romancing Sinead. According to Rakoff, Miranda "was around all the time. She was around the night Peter said, 'I don't think you and I are going to get on.' She was around then, and I knew it was fairly disastrous then. I told him— 'There's nothing to this love, Peter.' He hadn't had his eye opened. He had certain questions about other women, so it didn't appear that he was overwhelmingly, passionately single-minded about Miranda Quarry."

• • •

"Please make yourself look as if you want to be *fertilized*."

That's Benjamin Hoffman (Sellers), leaning up against the bathroom door with a lascivious grin. Miss Smith (Cusack) has locked herself inside in terror. The film is full of such unpleasant lines, but that is its nature; it's about a mean, lonely, middle-aged man and a mousy, trod-upon young woman. "What you're doing to me is atrocious," she spits. "It's the filthiest thing I've ever heard of." "Yes, I am filthy, yes," he replies with a smirk, "but there's no escaping one's fate."

"Miss Smith, you are here to be two arms, two legs, a face, and what fits in the middle."

"There are two people in all of us—the child in the snapshot and the monster the child grows into."

"Women are always hungry for something—fallopian tubes with teeth."

He shows her the new flat he's building for himself:

MISS SMITH: What's wrong with the old place?
HOFFMAN: Oh, well, you know—treacheries, miseries, failure, despair.

At times, Peter inhabits Benjamin Hoffman so wholly that he appears to be speaking from his own heart:

"You were afraid to go out with me because of my maniac face," he mentions. "Yes, girls all over the world are afraid of men with my expression—plain, sad-faced men. You look at us, all of you, and you're right." (In fact, of course, Peter Sellers rarely experienced this phenomenon in his life. Even before he glamorized himself for Sophia Loren, the *actual* sad-faced man generally got the beautiful women he sought, and their fear, if any, came later.) As he concludes his speech, he walks past the picture of Daniel Mendoza that happens to be hanging on Hoffman's wall, glances up at it, and declares, speaking of the millions of melancholy men in the world, "Their day is coming. . . . Hope never dies in a man with a good, dirty mind."

According to Alvin Rakoff, this was all scripted: "He was certainly capable of any sort of improvising he wanted. All you had to do was tell him to improvise. But the text of the script was there, and that's the script we did."

It is an astute, actorly performance on Sellers's part. He plays Hoffman differently when Hoffman is not in Miss Smith's presence; when she's not around he becomes mutedly fidgety and insecure. When he knows she can see or hear him, he acts the cool lothario, spinning each line with insinuating inflection (or infection as the case may be). But even from her perspective it's a failed performance. She sees through it and falls in love with him.

• • •

Hoffman may be a miniature, but it does contain one striking technical feat. There is a single shot that lasts for about eight minutes. Rakoff explains: "Peter said, 'Can't we . . . ?' He was always asking, 'Can't we . . . ?' "

The shot—which begins when Hoffman escorts Miss Smith back into the bedroom after she attempts to flee—was complicated to design and treacherous to execute. According to Rakoff, there were 118 camera positions for the cameraman and tracking crew. But they only had to do several takes, and Rakoff believes they used the first or second; Peter's fears of brain damage from the heart attack were certainly given the lie by his ability to remember all the lines, gestures, and movement cues. Rakoff remains impressed by the social aspect of it as well. "Peter wanted to do a long take, so he put his teeth into it. It helped pull the unit together because they thought it was a remarkable achievement that, as a film crew, they could do this. Everyone kept saying it was impossible. But Peter liked the idea; he liked going for broke. I kept saying, 'Okay, we'll stop *there*,' and he'd say, 'No, let's keep going.' Sinead was in awe of him, of course, so she, too, was motivated."

He wasn't always in such control in front of the camera, the worst problem being a certain unreliability. "He was an actor who giggled a lot—that's an endearing quality," says Rakoff. "Once, right after lunch, he got a fit of the giggles, as actors can do. *Anything* we tried doing, he couldn't stop giggling, and he had to leave the set—and the studio. That's another thing—I'd never know if he'd ever come back. I said, 'Okay, Peter, we'd better call it a day,' and he was just giggling, and said, 'I'll try to come back tomorrow. I can't be sure.' "

Rakoff recalls that Peter "arrived on the last day of shooting with gifts for everybody. He gave the camera operator a color television set—that was pretty rare in 1969. He gave Leica cameras, tape recorders, small portable radios. . . . His factotum, Bert, distributed them. When he came to Ben [Arbeid, the film's producer] and me, he put his arm around both of us and said, 'You two guys—I didn't know what to get you, so what I want you to do is to take your wives, go on a trip to anywhere that you've wanted to go—anywhere in the world! And send me the bill.' I looked at Ben, and Ben said, 'Oh, that's lovely—that's a terrific gift!' And I said, 'Please, Peter, can I have a color television set?'

"He just laughed and went away. Ben said, 'Why did you say that?' I said, 'Because it will never happen.' He was like a bouncing ball. You know things are going to go wrong. Sure enough, Ben did go on a trip and sent Peter the bill. Peter ignored it.

"He *meant* it," Rakoff is convinced. "At the time he absolutely *meant* it. He wanted us to go—that day."

• • •

Rakoff always thought *Hoffman*'s pace was too slow: "It does have faults. I am to blame for some of them because I couldn't cajole, applaud, *whip* Peter to play it faster. I couldn't get it out of him, and that, I think, is the principle felony. But character-wise, it works. *Sellers*-wise it works."

Actually, the film's chief fault lies not with its pace but with its sound track, where an easy-listening 1970-vintage score belies both the cruelty and the poignancy of the drama. Hoffman treats Miss Smith abominably, and yet the musical score is that of a light romantic comedy. Even when their emotional tenors begin to shift, the slight and forgettable music sets the wrong tone.

Commercially, the film was a failure that never had the chance to be a critical flop. According to Bryan Forbes, Peter "entered into one of his manic depressive periods" during the production and demanded, upon completion, "to buy back the negative and remake it. . . . I had to take the blame." According to Rakoff, Forbes's own disputes within Elstree led to the film's exceedingly poor distribution—so poor, in fact, that *Hoffman* waited until 1982 to be screened in a New York repertory house.

• • •

His faulty heart was necessarily on his mind, and together with his declining cinematic fortunes, Peter's thoughts turned morbid. At the time, according to Rakoff, Peter talked about dying quite a bit. He told the director that he was planning to be cryogenically preserved. "He told me more than once. We're talking about a man who had been pronounced dead and was brought back to life. He said he'd arranged to be frozen. You could either have just your head frozen or your whole body frozen. I think he said he had arranged for the whole body; maybe it was just the head; I don't really know. I said, 'Aren't you worried? We know that everything deteriorates when frozen, so when you come to, you won't be the same. If, a thousand years from now, they know how to revive a dead man, you won't be the *same* dead man. You'll be a freak!' And he said, 'I don't care. At least I'll be alive.'"

• • •

In October, with *Hoffman* still in production, Peter mentioned to the *Evening Standard* that he was set to return to the stage. It wasn't going to be a splashy exercise like *Brouhaha*; Jane Arden's *The Illusionist* would play at the Open-Space theater, which was located in a Tottenham Court basement. "The main character is a music-hall illusionist who does tricks," he said. "It's a very evil part. The play is a strange piece. It has an edge of great horror." *The Illusionist* would have a ten-week run beginning in January.

Then it changed; *The Illusionist* would play at the Round House theater, and Peter's costar would be Charlotte Rampling.

It changed once more—Peter never appeared in *The Illusionist*. It all ended in a little lawsuit and was forgotten.

• • •

"Very een-ter-est-ing," Artie Johnson murmurs in a 1969 episode of *Laugh-In*. Peter pops up out of the bushes in matching German military gear. He stares intently at Johnson. "I sink zat *you* are very een-ter-esting, too!" says Peter, cracking up at the end of the line and descending back into the bushes together with a giggling Johnson.

Dan Rowan and Dick Martin's *Laugh-In* was the hippest American comedy show of the period—Burbank's answer to *Monty Python*. (*Laugh-In* actually predated *Monty Python's Flying Circus* by a year.) Guest stars turned up regularly to add a certain celebrity kick to the series' regulars—Johnson, Judy Carne, Ruth Buzzi, Henry Gibson, Goldie Hawn, Alan Sues, and Joanne Worley. Richard Nixon once appeared, famously saying "Sock it to *me?*" On the program on which Peter turned up, the other special guests were Johnny Carson and Debbie Reynolds.

Some of Peter's jokes were defiantly lame. "Thanks for the tea, Dan," says Peter, "but it is awfully weak, I'm afraid." "I'm sorry, Peter," Rowan responds. "Say, how long *should* the tea be left in the water?" "Well, let me put it this way: the tea in the Boston Harbor is just about ready." A better bit occurs with Artie Johnson, when Peter turns up as Artie's friend in Johnson's classic, black-coated Dirty Old Man routine. They molest Ruth Buzzi together on a park bench. She beats Peter back with her pocketbook. Peter (in Henry Crun voice): "You've just made an old man very happy!" whereupon he and Artie fall off the bench together and die.

"Hel-lo!" Peter sings out as he pulls open a window in the magnificent Joke Wall. "You really have done a remarkable job in your experiment with the democratic system here in America. Just think! It was only a hundred years ago when President Lincoln freed the black people. And already some of them are even going to school!"

• • •

Always generous to his friends, Peter lent his support to Graham Stark by agreeing to appear as himself in Stark's thirty-minute silent comedy short, *Simon Simon* (1970), along with Michael Caine and David Hemmings. A pair of blokes of limited intelligence (Stark and John Junkin) involve themselves in a series of misadventures involving a truck and short underpass, a mock firing squad, a stranded cat and a cherry picker, an aerial dogfight between two cherry pickers, and so on. Peter's scene lasts all of forty seconds. In the midst of a car chase—the car is chased by two cherry pickers—there occurs a minor crash. The driver of the chased car hits a sleek blue sports car. Peter is inside. It's a hit and run accident, but Peter isn't concerned about legal issues. With a troubled expression on his face, he gets out, inspects the dent, and gestures impatiently to someone offscreen. An assistant rushes into the image, gets into the car, and drives away. Peter gestures again to another offscreen factotum, his new *red* sports car pulls up, he gets in, and speeds away.

• • •

"I really don't know if he fell in love with me," says Goldie Hawn, Peter's costar in his next picture, *There's a Girl in My Soup* (1970). "I only know that I gave him a surprise party in my home some time after the film. He spent all evening looking at my things and said, 'This is the kind of house I've always dreamed of having, with all the warmth and stability that I feel here.' Afterwards he sent me this absolutely gorgeous armoire, which I still have."

The project carried with it certain ominous specters. *There's a Girl in My Soup* was made by the Boulting brothers, John and Roy, who had had increasingly rough times with Peter on the four films they made together—*Carlton-Browne of the F.O.*; *I'm All Right, Jack*; *Only Two Can Play*; and *Heaven's Above!*, the last having been made seven years earlier, even before the debacle of *Casino Royale*. *There's a Girl in My Soup* was financed by Columbia Pictures, which made *Casino Royale*. And finally, *There's a Girl in My Soup* was coproduced by Mike Frankovich, who declared after *Casino Royale* that Peter would never be permitted to make another picture for Columbia Pictures.

Despite its catchy title, the film is a pretty dreary exercise. In London, the amorous, patrician, middle-aged Robert Danvers (Sellers), the host of a televised gourmet show, picks up a promiscuous nineteen-year-old American girl (Hawn) who is in the process of breaking up with her handsome, oafish, more or less worthless boyfriend (Nicky Henson). A free spirit with a smart mouth and a hard, cruel edge, Marion is scarcely the kooky dumb blond Goldie Hawn played so triumphantly on *Laugh-In*. Marion is mean. And Danvers, for his part, is selfish and singular, consumed by his career, resistant to intrusions, obsessed with sex—in short, and despite his wealth, an ordinary middle-aged male.

The sexual revolution of the late 1960s, along with its concomitant dismissal of censorship regulations, gave free rein to the Boultings' love of smut. At one point, Danvers makes love to a beautiful girl while watching himself on television talking about impaling a piece of meat, the video Danvers completing the joke with a matching finger gesture. Later, when a Frenchman employs the word "happiness," he accents the second syllable. And so on.

Still, Sellers is quite accomplished at conveying the depressing trials of masculinity in middle age. He knew what he was doing. With his own hair thinning, he covered it with a toupee to go with his capped teeth, exercises, and constant dieting. Onscreen, when he flexes, shirtless, in front of a triple mirror, he manages to look both virile and pathetic. It's a shame that the character as written is so colorless; Terence Frisby's script, based on his own stage play, lacks wit and verbal flair. What saves *There's a Girl in My Soup* is Goldie Hawn, who lends her unpleasant character an air of relaxed prepossession. Aside from his short bit with Shirley MacLaine in *Woman Times Seven*, Peter Sellers had never before played opposite such a deft and naturalistic actress.

Roy Boulting later wrote of Peter that "during the making of *There's a Girl in My Soup*, the relationship had been a very abrasive one. I emerged from it, worn, shaken, and swearing that I would never endure such an experience again." According to Boulting, Peter was "nervy, irritable, and deeply unhappy," during the production, characteristics that Boulting attributed to his relationship with Miranda.

Nineteen seventy does appear to have been a particularly strange, strained year for Peter. In the late spring, the time during which *There's a Girl in My Soup* was shooting, Peter announced that he was in the market for a new house in a very particular location. A friend had told him, as Sellers put it, that "when the great nuclear blow-up occurs, and the Earth is shifted on its axis, there will be only two safe places in which to live." It was between Stonehenge and the Ozarks. He chose Stonehenge.

He did not end up moving to Stonehenge, but he did marry Miranda.

• • •

London's *Evening Standard*, August 24, 1970:

> Peter Sellers and Lord Mancroft's stepdaughter, Miranda Quarry, were
> married at Caxton Hall today. About 300 people waiting outside the
> register office cheered as the couple emerged. Miranda, 23, and Sellers,
> 44, have been close friends for about two years but had previously
> denied marriage plans. About three dozen guests were at the wedding.
> They included actor Spike Milligan, who wore a cream safari-style
> shirt and black corduroy peaked cap.
>
> Miranda arrived with Lord and Lady Mancroft at 12 noon exactly.
> She was wearing a gypsy-style dress with a full length skirt in puce
> printed silk and a black velvet bodice. She had a black sombrero hat
> and carried a posy of white roses. With her were her two three-year-
> old Pekinese dogs, Tabatha and Thomasina. "They are my brides-
> maids," she said with a smile. . . .
>
> Witnesses at the ten minute ceremony were Sellers' closest friend,
> Bert Mortimer, who was also best man, and solicitor John Humphries.

With two rings did he wed. He slipped both on Miranda's finger—a
traditional platinum band and a more elaborate Russian ring that signified
love, fidelity, and happiness.

• • •

"Every man's dream is still, I'm sure, finding a virgin," Peter told an *Esquire*
interviewer shortly before the wedding. He and Miranda were married by
the time the profile was published, so his remarks became an unfortunate
historical record. "That's why marriage has gone on the rocks," he persisted.
"The original idea was that the girl had never been with anyone else, and
it was so pure. That's not quite the word. So I came to the conclusion that
to be in love with the girl of one's dreams—who if possible was a virgin—
was the ultimate happiness."

His notions about the desirability of virgins went quickly by the boards.
Peter clearly harbored grave misgivings about his long-term prospects with
Miranda. And, as was his custom, he took his complaints to an ex-wife, in
this case Britt. In one of their disconcertingly frequent telephone conversations during this period, he was markedly perplexed. "I don't know if I'm

doing the right thing," he whined, "but Miranda says it's now or never."
Anne was consulted as well.

Despite his insistence to *Esquire* that he wasn't at all the sad, neurotic
clown that his first biographer, Peter Evans, had just gotten through por-
traying in *The Mask Behind the Mask* (a good book that Peter hated), Peter
was often quite morose. Siân Phillips recounts the melancholy nature of a
man adrift in a sea of material splendor: "He turned up in Rome in
O'Toole's suite at the Excelsior and said, 'Could I sleep on your couch?'
He wanted to come to England, but he wasn't allowed—he'd be arrested
for tax or something, I don't know—so he pitched his tent, as it were, in
O'Toole's sitting room. O'Toole thought this was great fun for a bit and
then got very tired of it and said, 'Go and stay with my wife in Hampstead.
I know she won't tell anybody. You can just sneak in and hole up there,
and just don't go out, and nobody will know you're there.'

"Now, I had two children and a house full of people, and the only bed
was in the study on the ground floor, where all the phones were as well. So
I thought, 'Right, okay, I'll do this, he probably won't be here for very
long.' So he arrived with Bert, his trusty, chauffeur, companion, friend,
whatever, and they moved in with a mountain of luggage. I've never seen
more Louis Vuitton in my life—there were *trunks!* I couldn't believe it. I
thought, 'This is not very good.'

"I told my mother, who looked after the house for us. I said, 'Peter
Sellers is coming to stay.' 'When's he coming?' 'I don't know. He's sneaking
in under cover of darkness.' 'Never mind—I'll make a big *boef bourguignon.*' So she spent most of the day making a very authentic, exquisite *boef
bourguignon*, and Peter arrived, and she said, 'Settle down, Mr. Sellers'—
she was Welsh—'and I will get you your supper. I've got a very good *boef
bourguignon.*'

" 'Oh, I'm a vegetarian.'

"*Consternation.*

"People were sent out to comb Hampstead for vegetables at that hour
of night, and from that moment on, the kitchen was piled high with
chopped vegetables. There were pyramids of vegetables all the way up and
down the work tops. Nobody could get anything done because my mother
was always making homemade soup for Peter Sellers. He said, 'This is the
best soup I have ever tasted in my life.' I said, 'Well done, Mummy, you
know, but what is it?' She said, 'Well, I put bones in it, of course. And
marrow.'

"He was there for over a month, using both phones constantly, night and day. Nobody could make a phone call. He had all these charts of Eastern—I don't know what they were, pictures of Buddhists. . . .

"He would just stay in his study communing with himself or with Bert on the phone. He was just terribly, terribly sad. I have to say that as a house guest he was the most depressing person I've ever had in the house. I used to creep in at night and try to sneak past the study door so I could get to bed without Peter intercepting me, because he would sit down and cry. He would talk about his life, and, oh, it was so. . . . I was sorry for him, but it was so depressing having him around. Not one joke from beginning to end. Not a laugh."

And so he married Miranda.

• • •

"I was the best man at that wedding, and the bridesmaids were the dogs," Bert later said. "Then they went off to their honeymoon. I accompanied them. We were in the south of France on the yacht, and it's honeymoon time, and then one morning we couldn't find him. The ship-to-shore phone rang, and it was him. He'd booked himself into a hotel, and he'd left his bride of weeks on the yacht with me, and we couldn't work out why."

Neither could he. As any actor knows, most entrances require an exit. Even *with* Miranda he kept moving. For tax reasons, the newlyweds moved to Ireland; they bought the coach house of a 1,000-acre manor near the village of Maynooth in County Kildare, about an hour's drive from Dublin. Periodic privileges at the immense manor came with the deal.

He and Peg remained in touch. As he told the British entertainment reporter Roderick Mann, "When I was living in Ireland with Miranda, we kept chickens. And one day the hen got lost. I thought the fox had got it, but as Miranda was distressed we held a séance. When Peg came through I asked her, 'Do you know where the hen has gone?' 'Of course I do,' she said. 'It's up in the rafters of the stable.' 'Hang on,' I said. 'I'll take a look.'

"Well, I couldn't find the damn thing and I told her so. 'It's not there,' I said. 'Of course it's there,' she said. 'Go and have another look. But don't be long. I'm not sodding about all night looking for a perishing hen.' " They found the hen the next day. It was trapped in the rafters, just as Mother promised.

But the tale is suspect because, on other occasions, Peter claimed that, no, he did not actually speak to Peg directly but rather to an intermediary; another departed soul relayed her messages. According to Peter, the medium was the spirit of an American Indian named Red Cloud.

• • •

"I've been in pictures since Jesus was a lance corporal," declares Rod Amateau, the director of Peter's next picture, *Where Does It Hurt?* (1972). "I never treated him with any reverence. Only respect."

Where Does It Hurt? is a gleefully sour comedy about a guy named Hammond (Rick Lenz) who comes into Valley Vue Hospital for a chest X-ray but has no health insurance. It looks bad for him until he mentions that he owns his own house. "You have a house!" the receptionist cries, her eyes lighting up as she pushes the secret toe buzzer that alerts Albert Hopfnagel (Peter), the fast-talking hospital administrator, to the presence of an easy mark. Hammond is whisked away and given a variety of procedures, a good deal of which pertain to his anus—blood work, a high colonic, an electrocardiogram, a rectal probe, urinalysis, and a barium enema, all leading up to a pointless appendectomy.

The comedy is raw, bitter, and misanthropic. "Let me add this up," Hopfnagel snaps at one of the doctors in Peter's most pinched American accent to date. "A) Your sister-in-law, Mrs. Manzini, needs a hysterectomy; b) she wants you to operate; and c) she wants to pay for the hysterectomy with S&H Green Stamps. Does she have any idea of how many S&H Green Stamps this operation would take?" "She has," the doctor replies. "She was president of the Blessed Sacrament Ladies' Auxiliary. They collected Green Stamps. They broke up over birth control, and she kept the stamps." Hopfnagel works with this information: "As you know, our customary charge for a hysterectomy is $500. We shall have to charge her $2,000 because we are taking Green Stamps. *Yes or no?!*"

Where Does It Hurt? is an equal opportunity offender. "So much for faggot power," Hopfnagel mutters discontentedly after a gay informant fails to provide precise information on the potential visit of the city's hospital commissioner. He then calls the hospital's Japanese-American lab technician (Pat Morita) a "greedy little Buddha-head." "If it hadn't been for my creative white cell count," Mr. Nishimoto retorts, "that sore-ass Hebe wouldn't even *be* a patient." (Patient Hammond has been confused with patient Epstein and has been treated accordingly.) "So much for the Yellow Peril," says Hopfnagel after throwing Mr. Nishimoto out of his office. It's a nasty comedy, but that's its aesthetic. In its bitterness, if not its political incorrectness, *Where Does It Hurt?* was ahead of its time.

• • •

According to Rod Amateau, money was the key to understanding Peter Sellers. In the director's words, Peter was "economically determined." ("The word is *penurious*," Amateau adds by way of clarification.) In a meeting in Ireland at what Amateau calls Peter's "drafty manor—it was terribly cold," they agreed to finance the film fifty-fifty and take equal shares of the profits. (*Where Does It Hurt?* was coproduced by Josef Shaftel.) "This was an independent production done on the cheap," Amateau bluntly states. "About $600,000. I mean, *really low*." "We can make this picture for short money," Amateau remembers telling Peter, which provoked the following reply. Peter (in Hopfnagel's reedy American twang): "Rod, yer my kinda guy."

There was a brief rehearsal period before shooting began in Los Angeles on July 7, at which point Peter called and asked for his limousine. Rod replied that he could certainly provide a limo for Peter if that was what Peter wished, but since their deal was to split the costs evenly as well as the profits, the car would cost Peter $50 a day. The following morning, Peter left his rented Benedict Canyon house and arrived at the studio in the passenger seat of the key grip's pickup truck. "He lives near me," was the way Peter explained his transportation to Amateau, who adds that "from then on there wasn't one moment of delay on the whole picture. He couldn't have been nicer. He was watching the clock the whole time."

Peter was very well liked by the cast and crew. He was efficient, helpful, and methodical in getting the film completed on schedule. Asked if he was doing any drugs at the time, Amateau replies, "Who *didn't* do drugs?"

"It wasn't a very good picture," Amateau acknowledges, but it did end up in the black. "It made money not because it was a great picture but because it was cheap. Peter was very happy to go home with a full wallet."

For a birthday present, Peter gave Amateau a copy of the *Encyclopedia Britannica* in two condensed, microprinted volumes, along with an accompanying magnifying glass. "You want to know everything," Peter told his director, "here's your chance to know everything else." Soon thereafter, Peter and Amateau happened to be in Rome at the same time, and the three of them—Rod, Peter, and Bert—went out to dinner in Trastevere, where Peter and Rod launched into an argument about Fellini. "He's great," said Rod. "You're crazy," said Peter. "You like everybody." No, Rod pro-

tested, Fellini is a very nice man. . . . No, said Peter. Amateau doesn't remember precisely what they argued about—there was wine involved—but
he does recall that Fellini's tendency (as Amateau describes it) "to direct by
the numbers" made no sense to Peter, who found it offensive to actors.
(Fellini, with whom Amateau had worked, often directed his actors to move
around the set in a series of numbered positions, and he rarely gave them
dialogue when they shot but instead filmed them without sound and
dubbed in the dialogue later. Sellers, who never worked with Fellini, found
the director's habits to be obnoxious.)

"Fuck him," said Peter.

As the Fellini argument escalated, Bert began to make silent no-no
gestures on the sly. Rod changed the subject. The men parted when dinner
was over. Peter was a little chilly. Rod returned to his hotel, took a shower,
and the doorbell rang. "It's not me," said Bert. "You've got to understand
Peter. You won't like it, but he wants the encyclopedia back. He's mad at
you. Don't say he's childish! I've told him that. And don't say no or you'll
get me in trouble." Amateau gave Bert the encyclopedia. Bert left.

A little while later, the phone rang. "In other words," said Peter's voice
through the receiver, "you thought so little of my gift that you gave it back
without protest. If you'd have really liked it you'd have fought for it."

Rod: "I don't fight for anything except women and money."

Peter: "You're off my list." Then he hung up.

For the next few months, Peter kept calling from wherever he happened
to be—Switzerland, England, Italy, Ireland—and begging Amateau to
please let him send it back. "Don't send it, Peter," said the amiable Amateau. "Bring it with you the next time we get together."

Eventually they found themselves in London at the same time,
whereupon Bert arrived at Rod's door bearing the encyclopedia. "He's
downstairs," said Bert. Amateau went to the window and saw Peter sitting
in his car, waving up to him in the queenly manner.

"I had the best of him because I appealed to his worst nature," Amateau
fondly concludes. "And lemme tell you, it takes one to know one. He was
a lot more talented, but what the hell?"

• • •

Where Does It Hurt? was lucky. Many projects didn't pan out at all. "Spike
Milligan and I are working on an idea now," Peter had declared in 1970.
"I can't tell you what it is, but it's similar to spiritualism and that sort of

thing. Not spiritualism, but in a similar area." Spike was less circumspect. It was to be, in Spike's words, "a comic version of the Bible." Lo, it did not come to pass.

The Last Goon Show of All was sufficiently antediluvian to make up for any missing biblical tale. Recorded on April 30, 1972, at the Camden Theatre (to be broadcast on radio May 10 on Radio 4 and televised on BBC1 at Christmastime), it marked a reunion between Peter, Spike (who wrote the script), Harry, Ray Ellington, Max Geldray, and the announcer Andrew Timothy, who had been onboard for the first *Crazy People* in 1951. "When I announced the first *Goon Show* I was thirty," Timothy declares in the opening moments. "I am now ninety-three."

"I will now whistle the soliloquy from *Hamlet*," Peter announces in stentorian tones to the assembled studio audience, which included Prince Philip and Princess Anne. (Prince Charles was in the navy at the time and telegrammed that he was "enraged" that he couldn't attend.) And the soliloquy Peter did whistle, trailing off after the first few recognizable bars and moving slightly away from his microphone, at which point Andrew Timothy dryly breaks in:

"That was Mr. Sellers practicing his comeback."

TWENTY

Down, down, down. Would the fall never *come to an end?*

He hoped to solve his career problems by making a movie about a cretin. Shortly after Jerzy Kosinski's newest book hit the stands in 1971, the émigré novelist received a brief and cryptic telegram: "Available my garden or outside it. C. Gardiner," followed by a telephone number. Curious, Kosinski dialed it. Peter picked up. Kosinski had created *Being There*'s Chauncey Gardiner to express the life and soul of Peter Sellers, Peter Sellers said. As Kosinski later described it, "He sees his life as dictated by chance." They met at an Italian restaurant in London. "He was responsible for the worst diarrhea of my life," Kosinski later declared.

Gene Gutowski took an option for the film rights. "I had a deal with MGM—a very quick one I made when the book was a bestseller. Kosinski gave me the rights because he thought I had done such a good job with the Polanski pictures, and he trusted me. Through a social friendship with Kirk Kerkorian, I was able to get it right through the management of MGM, and very quickly I had an okay to go ahead with the picture. It was then on the basis of Gore Vidal writing the screenplay. Gore was happy to do so. It all happened in forty-eight hours. Then Kosinski changed his mind under the influence of a friend of his, a Polish cameraman who wanted to direct the picture and said to Kosinski, 'Look, with Gore Vidal writing the screenplay, you'll never have full control.' It was very self-serving, because he wanted to direct the picture. The project disintegrated, and of course MGM stepped out."

• • •

What Peter made instead was another filmed production of *Alice's Adventures in Wonderland* (1972), which consisted entirely of famous featured performances with lots of animal heads. Peter plays the March Hare. He filmed his rather short sequence at Shepperton in June 1972.

Despite its all-star cast—including Michael Crawford, Spike Milligan, Dudley Moore, and Ralph Richardson—*Alice's Adventures in Wonderland* turned out to be, in Peter's words, "a lousy film." He was publicly enthusiastic about the movie's prospects while it was still being shot, but as he announced to the press after seeing the thing, "We all feel—I'm speaking on behalf of all the actors because we all spoke about it—that it's a poorly constructed piece of movie." Fortunately for Peter, or at least for Peter's art, he left London soon after completing his work on *Alice* and went off to the Channel Islands to film one of the best but least-known movies of his career.

• • •

The Blockhouse (1973) is about a group of Allied prisoners of war who happen to be building fortifications on the northern coast of France when D-day hits. With bombs falling all around them, their Nazi guards flee, leaving the prisoners unsupervised. They dive into a well-stocked bunker, where a perfectly targeted Allied bomb seals them in, and they die, one by one, over time.

"It's based upon a true story," the director Clive Rees explains. "Actually, they were German soldiers who were looting a warehouse when the Red Army was coming. The entrance was blown up by the Germans, who trapped their own people inside. Years later the place was opened up. Two people were found alive, four or five dead and bathed in flour, and of the two people who came out alive, one died ten minutes after rescue, the other thirty-six hours later, blind and insane."

Sellers plays the Frenchman, Rouquet, a quiet former teacher. There was little difficulty in piquing his interest in the role. "Oddly enough, we just rang him up," says Rees. "Anthony Rufus Isaacs, who was the producer, knew him greatly. He was in Ireland and married to Miranda, who was a bit ill—she was recovering from meningitis—and we went over to see him. *She* liked it a lot and told him to read it, and he should do it, and we talked briefly, and he said yes.

"Dennis Selinger then got on to us, and said that Peter had changed his mind and wouldn't do it at all, because obviously the kind of money we had would only be enough for a bit part. So we rang Peter up and said, 'You don't want to do it?' He said, 'That's rubbish. I *do* want to do it. I *will* do it.' So he did it." Always a Goon at heart, Peter evidently appreciated the ultimate absurdity of being buried alive by the greatest liberation army in human history.

"William Morris told us that Charles Aznavour (who plays Visconti) didn't want to do it either," Rees adds, "and yet he *did* want to do it. We flew over to Paris, where his agent met us early in the morning and took us out to lunch. When she asked what was the budget of the film, we said, 'About £75,000.' She presumed that that was Charles's fee." Then Rees and Rufus Isaacs met with Aznavour himself. "The agent made it quite apparent that she thought that Anthony and I were from Warner Brothers—serious film-type people, which we weren't. Then she said, 'What is the budget for this film?' We said '£75,000,' and she said, 'I think you should leave.' " They were at the front door of Aznavour's house, Rees says, when Aznavour assured them, " 'Don't worry. I'll do your film.' In fact, he did it for seven grand. When we ran out of money during the film he never asked for it. He never pushed us at all. Peter, on the other hand, did.

"I got a call from Peter saying, 'I'm not coming to your fucking rehearsal until I get my fucking money.' Well, we didn't have very much, so Anthony got on to my bank manager and said, 'We've got Peter Sellers, we owe him ten grand, he wants it now, or he's not going to continue.' So he lent us *twenty* grand. When we got it, we asked Peter who we should pay it to, and he said, 'Pay it to Hare Krishna in Geneva, Switzerland.' That's what happened, and I haven't the faintest idea."

• • •

The Blockhouse is about being buried alive and yet remaining alive. Stocked plentifully by the Gestapo, the bunker is a cavernous warehouse full of water, canned food, sacks of flour, wine, and candles, so the men can survive for quite some time, knowing all the while that they must die there. It's a social drama, cerebral but raw—part Samuel Beckett, part Samuel Fuller. "I've been studying these candles," Rouquet gently announces early in the film. "They last about five hours each. Since we have been in this room we have burned exactly twelve. My pulse rate is normally seventy-two beats per minute. If you multiply that by sixty it will give you four thousand three hundred twenty beats per hour. We had been down here about twenty-four hours before we came to this room. That makes three days in all, exactly. It seems a pretty reliable way of keeping time—provided we have candles and my heart doesn't stop."

Clive Rees describes another moment: "There's a kind of ridiculous party scene. Rouquet thinks he'd like a drink, so he asks Visconti at the bar to give him some brandy, and being a typical kind of Nepalese rat, Visconti says, 'Get it yourself.' So Lund (Per Oscarsson) offers to get him something. Rouquet is so childishly grateful that he looks over, food falling out of his mouth, and tears are running down his face. That's genuine—Peter just cried. He was an extraordinary man to work with.

"To me there's a humanity in it. I don't expect anybody else to see it, but I think there's a kind of poetry. As I say, I'm very pretentious, but it starts off very conventionally, and gradually it gets more and more interior; there's more and more silence, and people's thoughts and feelings are expressed not by what they say but by what is registered in their faces. To me it was like a series of icons, and therefore there was a sort of beauty. Harry Crafton, the makeup person, contributed a great deal to that film because although they're getting more and more wrecked, they're actually getting rather beautiful. At least that was the idea.

"The whole film was shot underground. We were seventy feet down, and it was so incredibly quiet and depressive. And what with the nature of the story, it kind of got to people. Sellers could really feed on that. It enabled him, I think.

"It was filmed in Guernsey, a small island just off the French coast," says Rees. "Peter would be standing on his head in the morning, eating his special macrobiotic food and all that," and causing no difficulties. "The fact was," Rees notes, "we were virtually trapped on an island. No one had anywhere to go, so we sort of *lived* it, in a way. There weren't any night clubs to go off to; there weren't any distractions."

Still, there was the obligatory Sellers-as-bad-boy incident. One morning, Rees relates, "He told the makeup and hair people what they should put him in. He turned up in this incredible wig. Peter had designed a punk show, and he looked ridiculous. He was also stoned out of his head. He'd been smoking dope like nobody's business, and he was writing stuff like 'Bruce Sucks' all over the walls. I really didn't know what to do.

"It was a scene in which each of the actors had, by that time, established his own little section of the room. So I decided, Sellers was *here*, so I'd start *there* and work my way around the room and get to him last. When I finally got around to him, he'd fallen asleep. I woke him up and said I wasn't feeling too well and we'd continue it tomorrow.

"At 3:00 o'clock that morning, I got a phone call from Peter saying, 'You didn't like my wig, did you?'

"I said that, no, I thought it was wrong in the circumstance, and I explained the thing about the aging and the changing and the icons and that kind of stuff, and he agreed, and that was the end of it. He was amazingly helpful and sympathetic, once we got his money off to Hare Krishna."

• • •

In the film, Rouquet eventually commits suicide. Rees describes the long take in which he filmed the scene: "He does it in such a careful, methodical, considerate, kind sort of way. He's a schoolteacher—a compassionate and careful man. The candles are running. He looks at his photograph. (That's his old school, you see. I mean, you don't know that, but *he* knows it.) He's very tidy. He puts everything back in the little box, thinks a bit, carefully rolls his sleeve back, opens his box, and gets from it a knife. He puts his hand into a sack of flour; he's neat—he doesn't want to bleed anywhere. He puts the knife in, pauses, and winces as he's cutting himself. His hand comes out, and you can just see a little blood and flour, and he just puts his hand on the candle, and it fizzles out."

Bert Mortimer, who witnessed the filming, later said that "he was so wrapped up in the part I believed he actually might do it. And Peter was so nervous himself that it might actually have come about."

Clive Rees sums up his association with Peter: "I knew him very well as the man who played Rouquet—as an actor who was fantastic to work with, who was very sympathetic, polite, and physically quite touchy. I mean, he would hold you. I don't mean *hug* you, like we do today. But he would touch you. We had a close relationship, but it was about what we were doing, and that's where it began and ended. I was aware that I was working with a genius—not just a great actor. A genius. He was *different*. Aznavour is, I think, a really good actor. He's an entertainer, a really wonderful bloke. But I wouldn't use the word *genius*. Peter had that."

• • •

By the time *The Blockhouse* was being filmed in the summer of 1972, Peter's marriage to Miranda was essentially over, though it took a long time for the legal formalities to be arranged. Hans Moellinger recalls Peter's emotional state, the ambivalence of a paranoiac: "We were in Munich. He was still with Miranda then and was always speaking in cheerless terms that he was afraid that she was cheating on him. All of a sudden, in the middle of the night, he said, 'Hans, I must go back to Dublin!' I said it was impossible—night flights are forbidden in Munich. But he said, 'You *must* get me a plane, I have to go back immediately, Miranda is cheating on me!' I said, 'Wait until morning, you'll fly back and you'll see that. . . .' 'No no no no!' he said. 'Get the plane!'

"We tried to get a plane in Munich, in Berlin—it was impossible. Finally we got one in Geneva. The plane came to Munich at 2:00 A.M.—for about 37,000 Swiss francs. I called the director of the airport and told him that Peter Sellers, who had had a heart attack—everybody knew he had a weak heart—had to get to his doctor in Dublin. He said, 'I'll try to organize something.' At about 4:00 or 4:30 in the morning, I went with my girlfriend and Peter to the airport. We were sort of dragging him into the hall, left and right, holding him, schlepping him through to the plane. But now the problem came: 'Hans, I can't fly alone.' "

Moellinger's girlfriend at the time was nineteen years old and still in school, and she didn't happen to have her passport with her at the airport. Moellinger hadn't thought to bring his along either. "Peter said, 'It doesn't matter. We'll fly to Dublin and the plane will fly you back.'

" 'I can't, Peter.'

" 'You *must*.'

"So finally I arranged it so that the girlfriend stayed there and I flew with him to Dublin, and I arrived back at about 9:30 in the morning, and the whole trip cost about 170,000 [Swiss] francs. When I get back the telephone rings, and Peter says, 'Hans, I knew it. She was cheating on me. She was in the arms of another man, I promise you.' I said, 'How did you know?' He said, 'I *felt* it.' "

• • •

While living in Ireland, Peter and Miranda had renovated a house in the county of Wiltshire, about sixty miles west of London. Stonehenge is in Wiltshire, for example. But Miranda was now living there by herself.

With Miranda, or even without her, there seems never to have been the ardor of his obsessive love for both Anne and Britt. Miranda was pretty and amusing in a kicky, cusp-of-the-sixties sort of way, but her breeding got in the way. It's insensitive, not to mention inaccurate, to label Peter's interest in Lord Mancroft's stepdaughter as nothing more than crass social-climbing, as others have done; after all, a queen, a princess, and a prince each trump the stepdaughter of a lord. But he does appear to have been delighted, at first at least, to expand his social circle to include the established gentry. Still, as with all things Peter, it didn't last long. (As Lady Mancroft noted at the time, "I'm not surprised at anything to do with Peter.") He hated the Miranda-engineered parties at which half of *Burke's Peerage* would demand instantaneous comedy routines. Also, he later said of his third wife, "She was my intellectual superior."

• • •

On December 9, 1972, at the Rainbow Theater in London, The Who—Roger Daltrey, Keith Moon, Peter Townsend, and John Entwistle—backed by the London Symphony Orchestra and Chamber Choir and joined by an almost all-star cast, performed their rock opera *Tommy* onstage—twice—before live audiences as a charity event. An orchestra-backed studio album, released two months earlier, had been a smash hit, but The Who wanted to take it live.

Onstage at the Rainbow, Daltrey was Tommy, Moon the depraved Uncle Ernie, Entwistle was Cousin Kevin, and Townsend served as the narrator. Steve Winwood (of the groups Blind Faith and Traffic) played Tommy's father, Maggie Bell (of the Scottish group Stone the Crows) appeared as his mother, and Merry Clayton was the Acid Queen; Clayton is the belting singer best known for her feverish backup vocals on the Rolling Stones' "Gimme Shelter." Peter Sellers played the doctor who attempts to cure the legendary deaf, dumb, and blind boy in the song "Go to the Mirror." (Richard Harris performs the role on the album.) The show was taped and broadcast in the United Kingdom later that month and raised £10,000, for a group supposedly called the Stars' Organisation for Spastics.

It was from the Who's drummer, Keith Moon, that Peter felt the strongest and most reciprocal pull of friendship. Moon was also, as the critic Ira Robbins describes him, "an irrepressible adolescent, reckless, fearless and merciless in his need to entertain and be amused. His destructive exploits—hotel rooms, cars, stages, drums—made The Who more dangerous than other groups," though somehow, as Robbins points out, it all seemed to be in harmless fun. In person, "Moon the Loon" lived big. He was relentlessly inventive, openly friendly, and completely off his rocker. In private, Keith Moon was, in Robbins's words, "a sad, needy guy incapable of basic human experience."

As a drummer, says Robbins, "Keith was less a timekeeper than an explosive charge that detonated on time, every time." Peter was much the same as an actor, and the two became friends. Moon's improvisations weren't those of a jazz drummer; he was too undisciplined for that. Who concerts were more like open adventures than structured series of impromptu riffs. Robbins points out that as performers neither Moon nor Sellers tended to do the same thing twice or follow a previously agreed upon plan. "And that may be the key to Moon's similarity to Sellers," says Robbins. "In a sense, those anarchic characters improvised because that was the only way they could function. They lacked the ability *not* to."

• • •

Peter was full of plans in the spring of 1973. For the Boulting brothers, there was to be a six-role comedy set in France during the Occupation. He mentioned to the press that he hoped to adapt Richard Condon's latest thriller, *Arigato*. (Condon wrote *The Manchurian Candidate*.) He was still hoping to make *Being There*, too, as well as a film called *Absolute Zero*, to be scripted by Ernest Tidyman (who had cowritten *Shaft*, 1971). Stanley Kubrick also had something in mind for him, he said, but Peter had to be secretive: "Stanley doesn't want to mention what it's going to be about."

At the time, he was shooting yet another small and depressing film— *The Optimists* (1973)—in which he plays a decrepit busker. His character, Sam, at one time a successful and popular music hall star, now lives in a ratty flat with Bella, an elderly dog. Two children (Donna Mullane and John Chaffey), regularly vacating their unhappy home, enter his life, and Bella dies.

Directed by Anthony Simmons, *The Optimists'* title is ironic, though a new dog shows up at the end. Peter, of course, fully immersed himself in his North Country character's voice and mannerisms—so much so that when he filmed his scenes as a street performer in the West End, he seemed so authentic that passersby were oblivious to his identity and reportedly donated money into his hat. (The camera was hidden across the street.) There is even the tale of a real-life busker who became incensed that another performing vagrant was horning in on his turf and angrily shooed the movie star away. When filming was completed for the day, Peter simply rounded the corner in costume, got into his red Mercedes, and drove away.

Peter modeled Sam on several old North Country comics he recalled from his youth as well as the nineteenth-century variety clown Dan Leno, whom Peter had met during a séance. "We went back to his writings for some of the dialogue," Peter said at the time. "Phrases like 'this morning I was in such a state that I washed my breakfast and swallowed myself' are lines Leno used in his act." Peter had already revealed in the *Esquire* profile that he'd been receiving career guidance through the years from the dead Leno. To complete his characterization, Peter's longtime makeup artist, Stuart Freeborn, applied a prosthetic nose and strange, subtly disfiguring teeth.

"Peter and I became friendly on that film," recalls the cinematographer Larry Pizer. "He was a guy who played games with people for inexplicable reasons. He was a brilliant comedian, but not a happy one. Some people enjoy being funny. He didn't."

At what point does peculiar behavior become so consistent that it ceases to be erratic? For example, the cast and crew of *The Optimists* arrived on location one day to find Peter standing on his head in the snow. Pizer found it showy—private yogic devotion turned into a piece of public performance art. Another day the prosthetic teeth went missing, but as Pizer says, "It could have been a game." Peter's spur-of-the-moment inventions usually achieved their artistic aim—dialogue changes, new bits of actorly dexterity—but they did tend to disrupt the shooting schedule. For instance, there is a scene in which Sam returns to his flea-bitten home very drunk—so much so that he can barely make it up the stairs. According to Pizer, it was Peter who decided to add some small but important business: The staggering Sam methodically empties his coat pockets of drained liquor bottles every few steps. "It took forever to shoot," Pizer reports. "Hours were ticking by." Then again, this was Peter's craft, and it worked on film, where it mattered.

• • •

After completing *The Optimists*, Sellers found himself in a nostalgic mood and contacted his girlfriend from the 1940s, Hilda Parkin. "Peter phoned me out of the blue," Hilda reports, "and he told me about his film about the busker. He said, 'I think you would love it—I'd love you to see it.' We had a long chat. I said, 'Hey, how about *you*? Haven't you done well!' "

Hilda Parkin and her husband, Ted, were in show business, too, and Ted was active in the benevolent British theatrical club the Water Rats; Hilda was in the women's auxiliary, the Lady Ratlings. "I told Peter I was a Lady Ratling and that Ted was a Water Rat, and he said, 'You know, Peg always wanted me to be a Water Rat.' Within no time at all he approached the Water Rats to become one."

He was accepted. "Ted went to his 'making.' When they introduced him, he just looked up at the sky and cried. It's what his mother wanted him to do. Ted said it was a bit embarrassing, really, because he couldn't speak—he was just looking up and crying."

• • •

Nine years earlier, in late 1964, Peter and Britt had spent some time in the company of Judy Garland, her companion Mark Herron, and her eighteen-year-old daughter, Liza Minnelli. In May of 1973, Liza, twenty-seven, was back in London and starring at the Palladium. Peter was in the audience, entranced, at Liza's Friday evening performance, and three days later they were engaged to be married.

Billie Whitelaw reintroduced them after Friday's show. She remembers that Peter was in one of his peculiar moods that night: "Liza kept looking at me, as if to ask, 'Hey, is this guy putting me on?' I told her I wasn't sure, but if I were her, I'd watch it. Anyway, they went home together." On Saturday night the giddy couple dined at Tratou and adjourned to the piano after dinner, where Liza soloed on "Can't Help Lovin' That Man." It was true; she couldn't help it. On Sunday, Liza held a press conference at the Savoy to announce their love. "I'm going to marry Liza," Peter said on Monday.

This news came as a surprise to Liza's other fiancé, the one in Holly-wood. "My engagement to Desi Arnaz [Jr.]—well, the relationship has been deteriorating for some time. There is no engagement," Liza told the press. Desi's mother, Lucille Ball, responded by exclaiming, "*Peter Sellers?* Who's kidding who? Liza must be *crazy!*"

Liza showed up one day at Shepperton, where Peter was shooting his new comedy, *Soft Beds, Hard Battles* (1973). During a break, they talked again to the press. "I'm in love with a genius," Liza stated. Peter mentioned that his and Miranda's divorce "would go through the courts in its own time." Liza was asked if she was worried about becoming Peter's fourth wife. She replied in the voice of Sally Bowles: "Oh, no! Four is my lucky number, my dear."

Peter and Liza—and Charles Chaplin, Laurence Olivier, Lord Snowdon, David Niven, Ralph Richardson, and David Frost—were among the mourners at Noel Coward's funeral May 24, 1973, at St. Martin in the

Fields. Niven recalled Peter's mood at the end of the service—an inexplicable one, given the extraordinary interest his new romance was generating at the time. "As we walked out into the sunshine, Peter said, 'I do hope no one will ever arrange that sort of thing for me.' Niven asked why. 'Because I don't think anyone will show up.' "

Liza had to return to the States briefly at the end of May for a scheduled concert, but in less than a week she was back in London and moving into Peter's Eaton Muse house, where she competed for space with Peter's multimedia equipment and toys as well as pictures of his children and Sri Swami Venkatesananda. Liza's godmother, the irrepressible actress and author Kay Thompson, moved in, too. (Kay Thompson appeared with Audrey Hepburn and Fred Astaire in Stanley Donen's *Funny Face*, 1957, and wrote the children's book *Eloise* and its several sequels.)

Eccentricity reigned. One night, at three o'clock, Liza declared that she simply had to see the gravesite of the fictional dog Bella from *The Optimists*, so Peter picked up a bottle of chilled champagne and off they went to a cemetery. Peter led Liza to the tiny burial ground in Hyde Park, where they climbed over the fence and prowled. "Where is it?" Liza kept crying out in the darkness.

Like a vast Venus flytrap snapping shut on two desirable and helpless flies, the British media fed. Peter grew annoyed by the frenzy and called his friend Joan Collins (whose husband, Ron Kass, had been *The Optimists'* executive producer) to arrange an escape to her house. He traveled incognito. Collins describes the disguise: "an SS officer's uniform, complete with leather jacket liberally festooned with swastikas and an SS armband, [and] a steel helmet covering his whole head." At the end of the visit, Collins says, he sped away in his Mercedes holding his arm stiffly out the window and shouting " 'Heil Hitler! Heil Hitler! Sieg Heil' in his most guttural German."

One day, BBC radio featured one of Maurice Woodruff's competitors, the psychic Frederick Davies, who divined that Peter Sellers and Liza Minnelli would in fact never marry. Liza's response to this intrusion on her intimate life was to call and make a personal appointment with Davies. "I read the Tarot cards for her [and] told her that the romance was ill-fated," Davies reveals. "She became slightly emotional."

Magical cards were not the only issue in the relationship. According to Theadora Van Runkle, a friend to both Peter and Liza, "Peter was mad about Liza. He told me she was really sexy. But he got really angry with her one night at dinner because she crept up behind him and pulled off his toupee. He was livid with her, and that was the end of the relationship."

Michael Caine thought the couple was very much in love at the luncheon party he threw at his house. Peter brought along his Polaroid camera and took many pictures; at one point, he handed the camera to Caine, who took a snapshot of Peter and Liza.

There was another party the following Tuesday; Peter and Liza had split the day before. Either Kay Thompson or Marlene Dietrich—Caine says Dietrich, logic says Thompson—advised Caine that he should tell his good friend Peter that she thought "he is a rotten bastard for the way he has treated my beautiful Liza." Liza herself showed Caine the Polaroid, which Peter had given her as a memento. "Thanks for the memory, Pete," he wrote on the back. She flew back to New York on June 20.

Peter told the *Daily Mail*, "I don't think marriage is my bag." A few days later he jetted to Paris to photograph Marisa Berenson.

• • •

"I'm going back to the Boultings after this film," Peter told the press during the production of *The Blockhouse*. "We always brought each other good luck." The film in question was *Soft Beds, Hard Battles*.

Roy Boulting seems not to have seen his association in quite in the same way. For one thing, Boulting had found their most recent collaboration, *There's a Girl in My Soup*, to be especially trying because of Peter's moody whims. For another, that movie flopped.

Based on a verbal commitment from Peter, *Soft Beds, Hard Battles* was scheduled to go before the cameras in the late summer of 1972, but whatever luck the Boultings may have had with Sellers ran out when he suffered one of his inexplicable changes of mind and the production had to be called off. A few weeks later, Peter was considering doing the movie after all. This time, his agent Denis O'Brien put it in writing. Filming began in mid-April, 1973, at Shepperton.

The first scene: 1940, a Parisian bordello. As a narrator (Peter doing his broadly American "Balham—Gateway to the South" voice) provides background, an old man dresses after an encounter with a pretty prostitute. General Latour (Peter with the voice of a hoarse French geezer) looks like Marshal Pétain and General de Gaulle's superannuated love child. Cut to another room in the whorehouse, where a British officer (Peter doing David Niven) puts on his clothes after a similar romp. Peter proceeds through the course of the film to play four more roles—another French officer, the head of the Paris Gestapo, the Crown Prince of Japan, and Hitler.

A military sex farce set in an ornate bordello, *Soft Beds, Hard Battles* is an awful movie—"an almost creepily witless endeavor," as Vincent Canby wrote in the *New York Times*—that may have looked even worse on paper. It makes *There's a Girl in My Soup* seem like Molière. Men insistently jerk their batons, poke their swords, and tilt champagne bottles up at the crotch. Hitler appears at the bordello to pay his respects to the madam, Madame Grenier (Lila Kedrova), but when an African prostitute comes into view, the Fuehrer is disgusted. "Eine schwartze!" he cries. When the first of Peter's Frenchmen, General Latour, goes before a firing squad, he slumps forward and his toupee falls off. "The truth cannot be camouflaged," the narrator intones. Comedy bits include beds that spring up suddenly and hurl hapless Nazis down an air shaft as well as flatulence-inducing elephant pills slipped into glasses of champagne. The Nazis fart themselves to death.

Toward the end, the whores flee to a convent where they masquerade as nuns. That's where Prince Kyoto comes in—Peter in waxen yellowface, foldless eyes, and an overbite. "Fetch watah an' towah!" Prince Kyoto barks after a bumbling "novice" spills a tray of food on his pants. It ought to go without saying that she rubs the stains off his groin. It is very sad.

• • •

The pirate comedy *Ghost in the Noonday Sun* (1973) is even worse. Spike Milligan cowrote the script, based on Sid Fleischman's successful children's novel. Spike costarred in the film as well. Peter Medak, who made the successful satire *The Ruling Class* two years earlier, directed. It was shot in sunny Cyprus, and it's *still* ghastly. Peter fought with Tony Franciosa (who plays the Fairbanks-like Pierre) and walked off the set twice. The production team built a tall ship to specifications, but the specs were off; it was *too* tall and rocked violently and couldn't be steered.

Peter personally asked Larry Pizer to shoot the film. One day well into the production, Peter invited Pizer to a small, intimate party. Victoria Sellers sat on Larry's knee. They all sang songs and had a good time. The following day Peter had Larry fired.

Says Pizer, "I had to leave the island that day, like I had the fucking plague or something." A few weeks later, Pizer got a letter. "Chaos is supreme here," Peter wrote. "Don't be unhappy. It has nothing to do with you."

Even at the time of the firing Pizer knew it wasn't personal. "He wanted to get at Peter Medak," is Pizer's simple explanation; like Peter's harassing the *After the Fox* publicist as a way of venting his rage toward Vittorio De Sica, Peter still needed to communicate his desire to get rid of his director by proxy. A year or so later, Pizer ran into Peter at a party. Peter wanted to talk about it and explain, but Pizer turned away and they never spoke again. And yet, Pizer concludes, as so many did, "He was a pleasure to work with in many ways."

Peter plays a pirate named Dick Scratcher. Spike plays his rival, Billy Bombay. The unpleasant film itself ends in bickering: The last shot is of Dick Scratcher buried up to his chin in the dry ground, with Billy Bombay tied to a tree with rope so thick and plentiful that it verges on mummification, and they're bickering interminably. On the day it was shot, the production crew of *Ghost in the Noonday Sun* saw the chance to exact their revenge. They recorded a parody calypso number detailing every rotten thing that occurred during the shoot and forced the helpless Peter and Spike, physically restrained, to listen to it.

• • •

The Blockhouse was brilliant, but it wasn't released. Neither was *Ghost in the Noonday Sun*. Nor *Hoffman*. (*The Blockhouse* was finally shown in New York in 1981; *Hoffman* in 1982; *Ghost in the Noonday Sun* was released later on video.) *Where Does It Hurt?* made money because it was intensely cheap. *The Optimists* was dreary, *Alice's Adventures in Wonderland* and *Soft Beds, Hard Battles* were dreadful disasters. With six duds in a row, Peter's most personal project, *Being There*, hadn't a chance of getting made.

Gene Gutowski kept trying: "Kosinski wrote his own screenplay, and I was able to resuscitate it with Peter. Sidney Lumet would direct it. I had discussions with Hemdale in London, but they backed out at the last minute. At that time Sellers was not really bankable."

The director Hal Ashby was also interested in directing *Being There*. Peter approached him while Ashby was doing postproduction work on *The Last Detail* (1973). Ashby met with Sellers in London in the summer of 1973, but the meetings were more or less futile because, as Ashby later admitted, "Neither one of us had the power then to raise the money for it."

• • •

So he made one more dud, just to top it off. Like most of the others, *The Great McGonagall* (1974) was artistically well-intentioned, but it just didn't work. Joe McGrath directed the picture for Spike Milligan; the two old friends were great admirers of the eponymous and dreadful Scottish poet. "Peter insisted on coming and guesting in it," says McGrath. His role was that of Queen Victoria. "He played it all on his knees in a Victorian dress wearing roller-skates."

A series of absurdist vignettes strung together as a kind of bitter vaude-ville routine—as the end credits note, the film was shot "entirely on location at Wilton's Music Hall, 1-5 Grace's Alley, Cable Street, London E1"—the picture was meant to be a showcase for Spike, who plays the talentless bard. One fine exchange occurs when Spike, as McGonagall, takes the witness stand, where he is asked his trade by a prosecutor. McGonagall answers: "For twenty years now, I have worked patiently as an unemployed weaver, and I am currently training to be a poet." "*Who employs you, and what are your wages?*" the prosecutor booms. "I am self-employed," McGonagall calmly responds, "so there's no wages. . . . It's not what you'd call regular employment." "What would you call it?" the prosecutor demands. "Un-employment!" McGonagall cries.

Victoria appears at the beginning of the film and returns later on wear-ing a black dress and white lace veil; she's seated at a piano playing jaunty jazz. The visual gag is mildly funny, and Sellers's comportment defies de-scription, but then he turns around: Queen Victoria is wearing precisely the self-satisfied smirk of a cocktail lounge pianist acknowledging his nightly applause. It's worth the whole movie.

The Great McGonagall flopped, like everything else had of late. Peter later said, "I had six or seven years of one flop after another—so much so that I just didn't work. I was getting to the stage where people were crossing the road so they wouldn't have to embarrass themselves by saying hello."

His money was running out. After several quick moves around London, he ended up in a stark, almost Brutalist high-rise in Victoria; the building looked like the residential equivalent of the Bulgarian Ministry of Defense.

The money wasn't *gone*, just dwindling. Unlike Daniel Mendoza, Peter Sellers wasn't heading for debtors' prison. But, like his great-great-grandfather, he did tend to spend.

He was on the run, as always. He went to the lush Seychelles in late December, but it turned out to be a little *too* lush—it rained for ten days straight—so he flew to Gstaad for New Year's to do some skiing. He told the press that he didn't like the sport and gave it up after a week of trying, but his ski instructor and friend, Hans Moellinger, disagrees. Moellinger had known Peter for years:

"I had met Peter with Roman in Gstaad. He was not a very good skier, so I gave him some lessons. (I'm sort of the ski instructor for famous people—Jack Nicholson, Yul Brynner, Prince Charles. . . . The oldest was Helena Rubinstein.) Roman was renting a beautiful chalet, where Jack, Peter, and a few others were staying for about two weeks. It was always a great time in Gstaad. The boys always expected me because I always brought along three or four girls. There was always a big hello when I arrived.

"He was not a good skier, but he kept listening. Skiing is a very easy thing to learn if you listen and are not nearsighted. It wasn't difficult to teach him. After one or two weeks he could do a snowplow, so we could do mountains, no problem." Peter's own claims to the contrary notwith-standing, he didn't give up skiing after his initial attempt, which certainly predated this particular New Year's excursion. On at least one occasion Moellinger even took him helicopter skiing on the riskier high-altitude slopes near Zermatt. Peter enjoyed it, but there was a problem: "He nearly had an accident. We went up to the glacier, about 3,500 meters high, and started with a traverse. All of a sudden he couldn't hold it anymore and went into a fall line situation and nearly went over a ridge. At just the last minute I threw him over so that he fell about ten meters before the rock."

(A snowplow is generally the first thing one learns in downhill skiing—a way to slow down and maintain control by pointing the skis in a v-shape in front while bending the knees. A traverse—skis together with all the weight on the downhill ski—is just a way to glide across the mountain. The "fall line situation" to which Moellinger refers means simply that Peter started to go straight down the slope. Nobody but the most expert skiers ever attempts to head purposely down the fall line, so Moellinger caused Peter to fall to keep him from heading over a cliff.)

Skiing itself was not the only thrill of the Zermatt excursion: "We were staying at the Zermatthof. They're very conservative people, the Swiss. We celebrated one evening with champagne and two girls. We had an enemy in one of the hotel waiters. I don't know why, but he didn't like us—maybe because of the girl situation." So Moellinger and Sellers decided to pull a weird prank on the surly servant. In the middle of the night, they got one of the women to strip and sit naked on the bed, and then they called room service. The waiter's knock at the door was Peter's cue to begin loudly intoning, "Ohmmmmmmm." Moellinger remains amused by the result: "The waiter put the bottle down and walked backward toward the door— like in the old days with kings. He thought there was some sort of sex party going on."

As for the skiing, Moellinger says that Peter "did enjoy it very much, because he said so. I once taught Robert MacNamara [the Secretary of Defense during the Kennedy and Johnson Administration and later president of the World Bank], and he said that skiing was the only time he could really relax because he had to concentrate so much. Peter felt the same way. He liked the whiteness of the snow, the absolute quietness— especially in the high altitudes like Zermatt. It was very special to him— the only place he could relax. But with his heart problems we couldn't stay very long at a high altitude, so for him it was better at Gstaad."

Lots of things were better in Gstaad. Michael Sellers recalls the high-octane party he attended with his father at Polanski's rented chalet; Michael was around twenty at the time, which places the event in the neighborhood of 1974. "Someone produced some grass," Michael writes, "and Dad got me busy rolling joints—until someone arrived with cocaine. I was then equipped with a razor blade and asked to cut the cocaine on Roman's marble table."

• • •

Drugs aside, work went on.

"Clouseau never died," Blake Edwards said, in late 1974, of the idiot detective's sudden reemergence in the public eye after ten years of moribundity. "Over the years Peter and I kept him alive. He would call me up with Clouseau's voice on the phone at all times of the day and night, and we'd spend hours thinking up ideas, talking and laughing like idiots."

The film's executive producer, the British impresario Sir Lew Grade, reported a rather different regeneration. It was he, Sir Lew wrote in his memoirs, who instigated *The Return of the Pink Panther* (1975) by approaching Blake with the idea of reviving Clouseau. Edwards was then living in London with his wife, Julie Andrews, having fled the States after their oddly melancholy and violently overpriced musical, *Darling Lili* (1970), tanked at the box office and effectively, albeit temporarily, wrecked their Hollywood careers. According to Grade, Edwards's response was simple: He told Grade that he was under the impression that Peter Sellers would never make another *Pink Panther* comedy or work with him in any capacity on any project ever again.

But Grade placed a call to Peter anyway, met with him for several hours, and got him to agree. On one point at least, it seems, Edwards and Sellers were absolutely in tune with each other, particularly in the downer period of 1974. Clouseau, Edwards once said, "is a man who eventually survives in spite of himself, which is, I guess, a human condition devoutly to be wished."

• • •

It's another jewel heist. The "Pink Panther" diamond goes missing. Sir Charles Litton, the gentleman thief from the original *Pink Panther*, is the prime suspect.

Edwards asked David Niven to reprise his role as Litton, but he had already committed himself to film *Paper Tiger* (1975) in Malaysia. Then Douglas Fairbanks Jr. was announced and dropped before the role was taken by Christopher Plummer. Catherine Schell costarred.

Peter was by all accounts astoundingly cooperative during the production of *The Return of the Pink Panther*, a fact Edwards later attributed to a certain penitence mixed with revived ambition: "If you caught Peter when he was on a downgrade, he'd be okay. He was manageable and rational. He wanted it to be successful so he could get back up on top again. I was able to negotiate almost *for* him. There was a certain amount of risk taking, but if it worked, the rewards would be enormous. Peter was extremely happy. He got quite wealthy from that project. We had a fun time—really enjoyable."

The Return of the Pink Panther begins with a magnificent credits sequence (by the British animator Richard Williams) in which the luridly coated panther's ass swings back and forth in a gesture of jaunty pride. But Sellers's Clouseau is even more cartoonish than the cartoon. For one thing, the accent has become extreme—a parody of Peter's own parody.

At the beginning, while Clouseau concerns himself with a street accordionist and his accompanying pet, thieves rob the bank next door. In the following scene, Chief Inspector Dreyfus (Herbert Lom) is outraged. Clouseau explains:

> CLOUSEAU: I did not kneau ze benk was being reubbed because I was *en*-gezhed in my sworn duty as a police officer. . . . Z'ere was some question as to whez'er ze beggar or his minkey was breuking the lew!
> DREYFUS: Minkey?
> CLOUSEAU: What?
> DREYFUS: You said "minkey"!
> CLOUSEAU: Yes, shimpanzee minkey! So I left them beuth off with a warning-*ge*.
> DREYFUS: The beggar was the lookout man for the gang.
> CLOUSEAU: Zat is impossible! He was blind! How can a blind man be a lookout?
> DREYFUS: How can an idiot be a policeman?! Answer me that!
> CLOUSEAU: It's very simple, all he has to do is enlist.

Dreyfus soon seeks the healing wisdom of a psychoanalyst.

• • •

Even more than *A Shot in the Dark*, the comedy is grisly. Clouseau's loyal servant, Cato (Burt Kwouk), reappears—Clouseau calls him his "little yellow friend" with "little yellow skin"—only to get blown up by the insanely commonsensical Clouseau. The doorbell rings and Clouseau opens it, graciously accepts the burning bomb that a masked visitor hands him, calmly closes the door, comprehends, and tosses it away from himself—toward Cato, thereby blowing Cato into the next apartment, whereupon a little old lady bashes him on the head with her handbag.

A cigarette lighter in the shape of a gun finds its way to Dreyfus. He then picks up the wrong "lighter" and shoots his nose off.

On a more benign note, in one sequence Clouseau was shown to a terrible and tiny hotel room by an obnoxious concierge and manic bellhop. The three men could barely move, at which point the chambermaid walked in. Peter loved what he called "that strange, 'wild peasant' look" on Julie Andrews's face when she made her entrance as the rustic servant, complete with chunks of apple stuck into her cheeks to create an air of Alpine plenitude. At the end of the scene, when the maid began softly humming "Edelweiss," Peter was overcome by a fit of the giggles—the camera was still rolling—and had to run out of the room. Unfortunately, the scene was cut and the footage destroyed.

With its larger, seventies-era budget came a certain lack of old-fashioned narrative coherence; set pieces took the place of a coherent narrative. A critical commonplace has it that the Clouseau films got worse as the money increased, but that's not the case, though *The Return of the Pink Panther* does work best not as a tightly wrought comedy but rather as a series of exemplary, often morbid moments.

Sellers and Edwards got along well enough that they were also planning to make *Zwamm*, to be written and directed by Blake. According to *Variety*, *Zwamm* was going to be about a "comic space odyssey excursion . . . in which Sellers would play a space creature who comes to Earth." And as *Variety* frighteningly added, "Pair would like Mickey Rooney to join 'em." *Zwamm* never got made.

Prince Charles was in Montreal when he saw *The Return of the Pink Panther*. It was his favorite Sellers film to date, he wrote to his friend. In fact, Charles claimed, he'd laughed so hard that he wet the dress of the woman in the next seat.

• • •

Peter spent his birthday, September 8, in the Seychelles, where he was buying land for possible real-estate development. Miranda Quarry's present to him, delivered the following day, was the initiation of divorce proceedings. Peter later joked that his epitaph should read: "Star of stage, screen, and alimony."

By the beginning of November, he was back in London, lodging in a suite at the Inn on the Park in Mayfair. The high rise in Victoria was history; he'd leased a house in Chelsea near King's Road. (Miranda got the Wiltshire house as part of the divorce settlement.) He and some old friends—Spike, Michael Bentine, Prince Charles—got together the following week for a private dinner at the Dorchester to celebrate the publication of *The Book of the Goons*, a collection of Spike's scripts and drawings, photographs of the Goons in various guises, and a series of private letters and telegrams among the Goons themselves. The book reveals, for example, that in 1952 Peter had had letterhead printed for the law firm of Whacklow, Futtle, and Crun just to write an absurd letter to Spike. Spike, meanwhile, was representing himself as the solicitors Wiggle and Fruit to supervise the public auction of Harry Secombe, who was to be sold in lots at the Sutcliffe Arms at Beaulieu. Also from Spike, the Messers Chew, Threats, and Lid ("Chemists and Abortionists by Appointment") prescribed a remedy for Peter's constipation. Harry, meanwhile, sent a single-word telegram to Milligan:

"Fire."

• • •

With *The Return of the Pink Panther* approaching its release, but not yet certain of the fortune it would earn him, Peter signed a deal with Trans-World Airlines to make a series of commercials. At first he was to play three characters—an aristocratic Brit named "Piggy" Peake-Tyme; an open-shirted Italian playboy, Vito D'Motione; and a parsimonious Scotsman named Thrifty McTravel. Stan Dragoti directed the series, to which was eventually added a fourth character—a genial American businessman. His deal included provisions for him to appear in a taped TWA trade show short as well.

At the time, Peter himself was flying with Titi Wachtmeister. The daughter of Count Wilhelm Wachtmeister, who was the Swedish ambassador to the United States for a time, the perky blond countess was introduced to Peter two years earlier by Bengt Ekland, Britt's brother, at which point he and Titi began their on-and-off affair.

Titi was already well known in London. A top model in the late 1960s—"a blonde Jean Shrimpton" is how the London *Times* described her—Titi sparked some notoriety in 1970 when George Harrison tried to rename his nightclub, Sybilla's, in her honor. For some reason, the Crown Estates office found a nightclub named Titi's to be objectionable—their word was "vulgar"—and they insisted that Harrison drop the plan. He settled on renaming his nightclub in a much more wholesome but still-Swedish way—Flicka.

In April 18, Peter was in New York attending—and performing at—

a tributary dinner in honor of Sir Lew Grade at the Hilton. He was on television that night, too, on Julie Andrews's prerecorded special, *Julie— My Favorite Things*, directed by Blake in London. "I must be the squarest person in the world," the white–bell-bottomed Julie realizes, so she seeks the advice of a psychiatrist—Peter as Dr. Fritz Fassbender from *What's New Pussycat?*, only now, in combination with his dark 1970s glasses, Peter's wig makes him resemble less Prince Valiant than Yoko Ono.

> JULIE: Aren't you the famous Fritz Fassbender?
> PETER: Yes, of course I am! Heidelberg, Class of '39! Ph.D., LLD, SS . . .
> JULIE: SS?!
> PETER: No, no, it's a lie! Liar liar, pents on fire! I vas only following orders!

Dr. Fassbender demands that she prove that she's really Julie Andrews. "Supercalifragilisticexpialidocious," Julie gamely responds, so Peter offers her a joint and says, "Have a dreg on zis and try saying zat again! Zupak-elafragalidzniks. . . . Lizzen, Julie, you are getting hipper and hipper all ze time by ze minute! One more drag on this and you'll be practically Cheech and Chong!"

If Cheech and Chong served as the ideals of hipness in 1975, Peter himself was *there*. Here is an entry from Kenneth Tynan's diaries that year:

> "The phrase to remember is: 'The necessary tinge of wham.' This is how Peter Sellers (I think it was) summed up, tonight, the salient quality of Terry Southern. . . . Peter taught us how to get the best out of pot by spreading tinfoil across the top of a wine glass, prodding holes in it (and a gash) with a needle, then crumbling the pot over the holes, igniting it, and sucking the fumes in through the gash."

> Another entry dated a few days later: "More reminiscences of the pot-smoking night with P. Sellers. As one sucks the smoke through the gash in the tinfoil, the hash embers glow, and the close-up view is exactly like that of a burning city seen from the air. This led me into an improvisation, accompanied by Peter, of a Bomber Command navigator talking to the rest of the crew as they go in through the flak to prang Dresden."

• • •

On May 5 Peter and Titi, accompanied by Michael Sellers, arrived at the La Costa resort in San Diego for three days of *Return of the Pink Panther* previews for select press and guests (including Fred MacMurray and Dick Martin). Sellers, Plummer, and Catherine Schell were each trotted before the horde of gorging reporters; what with the hotel rooms, cocktail parties, dinners, entertainment, limousines, and gift bags, the three-day junket cost United Artists over $125,000. On May 11, Peter was driven back to Los Angeles for several more days' worth of publicity work, after which he flew to New York to appear on *The Merv Griffin Show*. Mervin devoted his entire ninety-minute program to *The Return of the Pink Panther*.

While in New York, Peter, dressed and accented as Clouseau, was named an honorary detective by the New York Police Department. He and Titi hightailed it out of the city on May 22, bound for Heathrow.

"All I'm trying to do is get through the day—that's all," he told a British journalist before flying back to Los Angeles in July to appear on *The Tonight Show*.

• • •

In August, there was a special premiere in Gstaad. Peter requested of United Artists that they provide a few round-trip tickets: one for Michael Sellers, one for Sarah Sellers, one for Victoria Sellers, one for Bert Mortimer, one for Peter Sellers, two for George Harrison, and one for Peter's as-yet-unknown date—unknown because, by that point, Titi was history. During their acrimonious breakup in July, Peter demanded that Titi return the £2,000 Cartier watch he gave her while Titi frantically attempted to retrieve a stuffed dog.

The Gstaad junket's locus was the Palace Hotel. Peter flew in along with his family and George Harrison, Lew Grade, Catherine Schell, Christopher Plummer, Henry Mancini and his orchestra, and, for some reason, John Boorman. Liz and Dick turned up as surprise guests at the gala dinner for 250 journalists.

Peter was seeing multiple women in August alone. One was the eighteen-year-old Tessa Dahl, the daughter of the novelist Roald Dahl and his wife, the actress Patricia Neal. Another was the model Lorraine Cootamundra, née MacKenzie. "In the past ten days," a British tabloid gasped that month, "he has taken out Susan George three times and is also seeing Scandinavian beauty Liza Farringer, who is in her late 20s." By the end of the month he was high in the Rockies—Vail, Colorado, to be exact—for

a lunch with the First Lady of the United States, Betty Ford, and her eighteen-year-old daughter, Susan, whom he was photographing for *Vogue*.

In September Peter hosted a party at his rented pad in Beverly Hills. Cary Grant showed up. So did Bill Wyman and Ron Wood of the Rolling Stones, Keith Moon, and David Bowie. The party turned into an impromptu jam session, with Peter doing his bit on drums. Bowie played the saxophone. Earlier that year, Moon had invited Peter and Graham Chapman to his Beverly Glen home, where the three Brits amused themselves with reenactments of old *Goon Show* sketches.

September also had him in London, where he was a presenter at the glittering Society of Film and Television Awards. Princess Anne was the honored hostess. Peter handed Joanne Woodward her award; Hayley Mills gave one to John Gielgud; Jack Nicholson's trophy was proffered by Twiggy. By early October Peter was back in Los Angeles, where he attended Groucho Marx's birthday party along with Elliott Gould, Sally Kellerman, Milton Berle, Red Buttons, Carroll O'Connor, Sally Struthers, Jack Lemmon, Lynn Redgrave, Roddy McDowall, and Bob Hope. Peter was subdued. "Just to sit there and realize you are in the same room with Groucho Marx is a delightful experience," he remarked.

In October, Keith Moon took a short break from the beginning of his yearlong tour with The Who and booked a room at the Londonderry Hotel on Park Lane, in which he threw a rambunctious party for a group of select friends, including Peter, Ringo, and Harry Nilsson. The party got out of hand when a sizable chunk of plaster suddenly blasted into the adjacent room. According to Moon, he was just "trying to show Peter Sellers how to open a bottle of champagne without touching the cork. It involves banging it against the wall."

• • •

With Peter back in the movie game, and with so much time having elapsed since the unpleasant closing of *Brouhaha*—and with few people having remembered the unproduced *The Illusionist*—the producer Bernard Miles tried to convince him, again, to return to the theater. *Richard III*. Peter turned it down in favor of more films.

Clouseau was a cash cow, but not a perfect one. "God forbid that I should do a whole series," Peter said in May, while Blake Edwards was industriously preparing the script of *The Pink Panther Strikes Again* (1976). But money mattered to Peter, as it should have, given his previously dete-

riorated fortune; by the time *The Return of the Pink Panther* opened in Europe in September, it had already taken in $36 million in the United States alone, second only to *Jaws* (1975). And so he soon agreed to another round of Clouseau. One early idea for the fourth *Pink Panther* was that Peter would take four roles: in addition to Clouseau, he'd play (or replay) James Bond as well as playing Dr. Phibes and the fiendish Fu Manchu.

But before the *Panther* comedy had a chance to go before the cameras in early 1976, he made Neil Simon's detective spoof, *Murder by Death* (1976). His role: Sidney Wang, a hideous parody of the already-appalling Charlie Chan. His costars were Maggie Smith and David Niven as the *Thin Man*-esque sleuths Dick and Dora Charleston; Elsa Lanchester, with a nod to Agatha Christie, as Jessica Marbles; Peter Falk as Humphrey Bogart as Sam Spade; James Coco as Milo Perrier (another, more strained, Agatha Christie joke); Eileen Brennan as the flamboyant Tess Skeffington; the unnaturally hilarious Truman Capote as their host, Lionel Twain; Nancy Walker as the deaf maid; and Alec Guinness as the blind butler. ("It's nice to hear guests again," says the butler. "Thank you," says Dora Charleston; "You are . . . ?" "Bensonmum." "Thank you, Benson." "No, no, Bensonmum. My name is *Bensonmum*.")

Peter prepared for his role by flying to Los Angeles—on TWA, of course—to see as many Charlie Chan pictures as Raystar, Ray Stark's production company, could find for him. *Murder By Death* went into production in the fall of 1975 and concluded just before Christmas.

"He behaved very peculiarly," Alec Guinness said shortly before his death in 2000. "I think he was a little bit round the bend then. He had a ring with some sort of crystal in it that changed color with his mood," said Guinness, who found such things baffling. "One day he didn't turn up at all. Everyone sat around, sat around. . . . Then we all went home. David Niven went back to his hotel and saw Peter having lunch with someone. He was fine."

Guinness related another whimsy: "We all had identical caravans [dressing room trailers], set up in alphabetical order. Peter insisted on having a bigger caravan than everyone else. Eventually they did find him one—a hideous thing—that was six inches longer. David Niven and I saw him out with a tape measure measuring it."

Peter also got into a pissing match with Peter Falk—as Guinness described him, "that one-eyed actor." "Neither would come on to the set before the other one. The whole thing had to be timed with stopwatches so they would arrive at the same time." The dueling Peters simply couldn't deal with having to wait for the other to show up. "It was just a stupid game they were playing," Maggie Smith declares.

Dame Maggie also found Peter to be difficult, unpredictable, and strange. One evening, she relates, he corralled everyone in the cast and the key members of the creative team to watch one of his films; Smith cannot recall which one—only that it was very long and very dull. After it was over, Neil Simon turned and said, "I hate to sleep and run. . . ."

Smith also remembers the day Eileen Brennan showed up in one of the snazzy outfits the film's costume designer, Ann Roth, had fashioned for her—a brilliant purple gown with matching boa. Peter flipped out on the spot and insisted that the deadly gown be stricken from the wardrobe and remade in another color. "Poor Ann Roth had to stay up all night making a new costume," Smith sighs. It ended up being apricot.

"David Niven finally cracked," Dame Maggie comments. "He became very irritated and upset and said to Sellers, 'How dare you behave this way?' It was so unlike David." Niven had always been so even-tempered, quiet, and polite that, according to Smith, "Peter did listen to him," however briefly.

His friends found him easier to bear than his costars. The actor Malcolm McDowell, with whom Peter shared the agenting services of Dennis Selinger, describes it well: "Peter's thing was, you never knew whether he'd be talkative or not because he was a manic-depressive. But I knew not to worry if he didn't say anything—just to ignore it, and eventually he'd come round, which he invariably did. I remember a private dinner in a restaurant called Julie's [in London], for Dennis Selinger's sister—she was 70—and all the clients were there. Roger Moore, Michael Caine, all those people. . . . I sat next to Peter, and he was completely silent through the whole dinner. And at the end of it, one of the ladies got up and said, 'Oh! I've lost my diamond earring!' Everyone started to look for it, whereupon Peter stood up and did a whole Inspector Clouseau thing. Everybody was in tears laughing. It was incredible, a mark of genius. It was the first time he'd spoken all night."

• • •

In February, Peter and his newest costars—Colin Blakely, Leonard Rossiter, and Lesley-Anne Down—began the production of Blake Edwards's *The Pink Panther Strikes Again*, in which Clouseau inadvertently prevents the now-mad (and now-former) Chief Inspector Dreyfus from destroying the world. The critic Jim Yoakum observes that the fifth *Panther*'s storyline bears more than a passing resemblance to that of *The Mouse That Roared*: a kidnapped, bearded scientist and daughter; a doomsday device; Peter's character succeeding despite himself.

His accent worsens further; now even his own name verges on unintelligibility. ("Yes, this is Chief Inspector Clyieuzaeauh.") The disguises go just as far: Clouseau purchases a new "Quasimodo Hunchback Disguise Kit" with an inflatable helium hump and ends up floating over the rooftops of Paris and past Notre Dame until he shoots off the helium release valve in his crotch and plops into the Seine. ("Feurtunately zere was sufficient air still left in my heump to keep me afleut until the rescyeau.")

There's an anachronistically eerie moment when the evil Dreyfus causes the United Nations Building in New York City to disappear. It's violent insanity as a response to gross stupidity:

DREYFUS: What do you suppose they will call the crater? "The Dreyfus Ditch"! (He laughs maniacally.)
KIDNAPPED PHYSICIST: There shall be no crater.
DREYFUS: No crater? But I *want* a crater! I want wreckage! Twisted metal! Something the world will not forget!

But the laser beam Dreyfus sets off only makes the building disappear from the Manhattan skyline without a trace.

"What kind of a man are you?" the physicist asks Dreyfus. "A madman," Dreyfus replies.

• • •

The Pink Panther Strikes Back contains the most purely ghastly comedy sequence in Peter Sellers's career. The comic tone is beyond baroque:

Dreyfus has a toothache. Clouseau, dressed with a frizz of white hair, a sort of Alpine Einstein, administers laughing gas to himself and to Dreyfus and extracts the tooth—the *wrong* tooth—with a pair of pliers while, because of the excessive heat in Dreyfus's lair, Clouseau's latex-laden geezer makeup begins to melt off his face. To the sound of the two men's incessant spastic laughter, Clouseau's face dangles in great, pendulous globs from his nose. The laughter becomes shriller and more mirthless as Clouseau, physically disintegrating, frantically grabs handfuls of his face and packs them back onto himself. Following through perfectly on Clouseau's philosophical trajectory all through the *Panther* series, his disguise decays at the same pace as rationality. It's ugly to watch, as it was clearly meant to be.

"How's this?" Clouseau asks Dreyfus of his own badly reconstructed head. "Grotesque!" Dreyfus shouts, both of them laughing in agony.

Peter Sellers's innate ability to sustain such a complex and peculiar tone has rarely if ever been matched. Attempts by others to play Clouseau—Alan Arkin in *Inspector Clouseau* (1968), Roger Moore as Jacques Clouseau in *Curse of the Pink Panther* (1983), Roberto Benigni as Jacques Clouseau, Jr., in *Son of the Pink Panther* (1993)—necessarily ended in dull failure. One of the world's foremost Peter Sellers fans, Maxine Ventham, makes a crucial point when she observes that "Clouseau would be unbearable—and *is* unbearable when played by other actors—if he didn't have those sad, vulnerable, dark eyes peering out at the world." Look at Peter's melancholy eyes as Clouseau's face falls off in globs and you will see precisely what she means.

• • •

It wasn't a happy shoot. Lesley-Anne Down was not a happy trouper. Each day, she says, "There would be at least an hour of doing absolutely nothing. It would just be Peter being very silly. Little by little we would start working on an idea. And it would be just one shot. Very often, that's all we would get in a day—one shot. A film that had a schedule of eleven or twelve weeks ended up taking twenty weeks to do."

"He had terrible feuds with other people," Herbert Lom recalls with a certain distaste, "for instance, Blake Edwards. They were not on speaking terms. He used to send messages to Blake about the scene, and Blake used to send messages through his assistant to Peter, and we all stood around looking at the ceiling till they stopped playing their game." Moreover, Lom adds, "Blake showed me telegrams he had received: 'You are a rotten human being.' 'You are a shit and I can afford to work without you.' 'I don't need you to get work. Love, Peter.'

"Peter wouldn't tolerate Blake, who needed to *direct* everybody. But Peter wasn't going to be directed by Blake. He didn't like him as a person. Peter thought at the time that Blake was a shit, and he wasn't going to be bossed around by a worthless human being, and all that kind of crap." Their relationship was like a screwball marriage—comedy and combat in equal measure—and it was based on mutual need.

Still, Lom insists on one point: "*I* never found him to be difficult. *Never.*"

For his part, Blake Edwards offers a stark account of Peter's troubles: "He talked to God, what can I tell you? He called me up in the middle of the night and said, 'Don't worry about how we're going to do that scene tomorrow. I just talked to God, and He told me how to do it.' "

• • •

"I'm very protective of Peter," Burt Kwouk insists. According to Kwouk, the reason is simple: "Respect. Respect for what he was. There's too little respect in our business. There are very few actors who are not troubled people." Asked if Peter Sellers was more troubled than most, Kwouk answers, "I happen to think that he wasn't. He wasn't any more fucked up than I am." For Kwouk, the difference was this: "When you're somebody like Peter Sellers, the media latch onto it and make it much bigger than it seems. That's what the media do. What the hell, they've got to make a living.

"He was a complicated man. Some of us loved him, some of us hated him. *Of course.* That's true of *everybody*. There were people who didn't like Jesus Christ. They nailed him to a cross, for chrissake. The business of being a human being is what it's all about. It's not about being a movie star, not about being an actor, not about being world famous. It's about being a human being. We all go to the toilet every morning, whoever we are."

• • •

In the south of France in July, in London in August, in Los Angeles in September, and with a side trip to the Seychelles sometime in between, Peter, fifty, was beginning to keep company in the form and figure of Lynne Frederick, a wild little thing of twenty-one. An actress (she appeared as Catherine Howard in *Masterpiece Theatre*'s *Henry VIII and His Six Wives*) and girl about town (by the time she hooked up with Peter, the precocious Lynne had already enjoyed affairs with both the thirty-seven-year-old David Frost and the fifty-year-old West End gaming club operator Julian Posner), Lynne was a striking beauty, confident beyond her years. And ambitious.

Sellers himself described her as having what he called an "extrasensory instinct" that told her precisely what he needed at any given moment. She, in turn, provided it. She was four months younger than his son.

On December 15, 1976, *The Pink Panther Strikes Again* received its Royal World Charity Premiere at London's Odeon in Leicester Square. A single invitation was sent to Mr. Peter Sellers, who was insulted at being unable to invite his chosen date, specifically Lynne, since royal invitations cannot be altered, even for close friends of the royals. "If Lynne is not allowed to be there I'm bloody well not going myself," he said. And so he boycotted the British premiere of his own film, to much stir in the British press.

Now it was Prince Charles's turn to be offended. Charles was aghast at his old friend's behavior and the scandal it caused. It was still bloody: "I was bloody annoyed that he didn't turn up," the Prince declared at the time. "I wish I could take *my* girlfriend to functions, but I can't. I'm going to tell him how I feel when I see him."

Peter, Lynne, and Victoria left for Gstaad two days later.

After eleven months passed, a reporter was curious. "Are you still in the doghouse with Prince Charles?" Peter was asked. "Don't know," Peter replied. "Haven't seen him since."

• • •

Malcolm McDowell was already acquainted with Lynne Frederick. "I'd just worked with her on a film called *Voyage of the Damned* (1976) so I was rather. . . . I would have warned him off, had I known. But you can't, can you?"

At a party, McDowell recalls, "Peter actually said to me, 'I will walk into a room of forty women, and there is one woman in that room that is poisonous for me, and I will walk straight up to her and ask her to marry me.' "

The wedding took place in Paris on February 18, 1977. They soon flew to their new summer house at Port Grimaud near Saint-Tropez.

Lynne's mother, Iris Frederick, a Thames television casting agent, was pointedly *not* invited to the ceremony. "I wouldn't have gone in any case," Iris declared to reporters. "I will never, *ever* talk to him. There is the age difference, but more important, there is Mr. Sellers's track record. He has three failed marriages behind him. Three women can't be that wrong." She and Lynne had stopped speaking three months earlier and remained estranged for quite some time.

As for the precise cause of the marriage itself—Peter and Lynne had been living together for months before tying the knot—it seems to have been a form of coercion on Peter's part. It was he who demanded that she marry him; she'd been offered a five-month television job in Moscow, and he didn't want her to go and leave him alone.

• • •

As Spike Milligan once told Michael Sellers, Peter "was always searching for a bloody heart attack as if it were a letter he knew had been posted and hadn't arrived." The mail was delivered on March 20, 1977, on board an Air France Boeing 727 from Nice to Heathrow. The plane was about twenty-five minutes away from London when Peter's chest seized; a flight attendant described him as looking "dreadful." There was a doctor on board, and he made Peter comfortable and reassured him while air traffic controllers gave the plane top priority for landing. After a brief examination by a physician at Heathrow's medical unit, he was rushed to Charing Cross Hospital.

"It is not a heart attack and there is nothing to worry about," Lynne told the press. It was all the result of bad oysters in Saint-Tropez, she said. The senior cardiologist at Charing Cross took a different opinion.

Strangely, Peter had been quite friendly with the world's best-known heart surgeon, the jet-setting Dr. Christiaan Barnard, since the early seventies. And yet Peter never allowed Dr. Barnard to operate on him, nor anyone else for that matter. He's said to have considered open-heart surgery at Charing Cross, but he decided simply to go with a new electronic pacemaker instead. It was installed, after which he and Lynne flew back to Saint-Tropez.

• • •

In May, they flew to Gstaad.

In June, Peter fired Bert Mortimer.

Sue Evans, Peter's secretary, remembers the moment well: "I got a call really late one night. It was Peter, and he said, 'I'm going to dictate a letter, and I don't want you to say anything. Just take it down, and *don't say anything*.' He started dictating the letter, and it was dismissing Bert. His loyal chauffeur, personal assistant, and friend was gone."

"I just could not understand why he would want to break that relationship," says Bert. "Even today I can't tell you."

Kenneth Griffith recalls Lynne Frederick terribly well. He paid the couple a visit. "She was very friendly, pleasant, and nice, but I wasn't convinced that he wasn't in trouble. *Serious* trouble. Which proved to be correct. Because of my sense about her, I said, 'Pete, you remember when you were living in the Dorchester?' "

Peter recalled precisely the occasion to which Griffith referred: Griffith was appearing in a West End play at the time and not making very much money at it. Griffith continues: "I'm sitting there eating wonderful food and feeling a lot better when he suddenly says, 'Here, Kenny—something worrying you?' 'No, no, Pete,' I said, 'I'm feeling great. Lovely to see you and be here.' Four minutes later: 'Kenny, something *is* worrying you and I want to know what it is.' I said, 'I've had a bad time you know, I shouldn't be doing this fucking play, it's hard work, I do two performances six nights a week. . . . And I bought a house, it was a struggle to get the money to buy it on top of everything else, and I've been doing such rubbish as an actor in films. And,' I said, 'it nearly beat me.' He said, 'How do you mean "nearly beat you"?' I said, 'Well, I think there's about two thousand quid left. It's done.'

"He gave me a check for $2,500. I said, 'No, Peter—out of the question.' 'Aw Kenny,' he said, 'Don't, don't, *don't* tear it up, don't, because it would give me great pleasure, and I'll speak to Bill [Wills] in the morning. All I'll do is tell Bill to lose it—who will know? *No one* will know, but it will give me great pleasure.' I did tear it up.

"Now—with his new wife there, I said, 'You know how memory can play tricks with you, Pete?' 'Yeah, yeah,' he said. But I wasn't really speaking to him; I was speaking to *her*. And I said, 'Was that true? You put a check for $2,500 in my pocket?' 'Yes,' he said. 'You probably tore it up, didn't you?' That's all. But it was information that I felt she ought to know about her husband. I don't think she cared at all." In short, Griffith saw Sellers's generosity; according to him, Lynne saw his bank accounts.

• • •

Sarah Sellers recalls Lynne very well, too: "We were told that she would like to take me and Michael out for a meal and get to know us. She seemed quite nice to begin with. She came across as very bubbly and friendly and warm. Once they got married things definitely changed."

"Lynne was like the nurse," Victoria Sellers maintains. "He needed help doing things—he had pill-taking times, and we couldn't do this, or that, because we couldn't get Dad all excited." Sue Evans agrees: "She took over the running of his life. He had alienated so many people by this point that he saw Lynne as the one person who was there."

Except for Bert, whom Peter fired. That he did so within months of marrying Lynne explains it.

• • •

Army Archerd mentioned Peter's newest film project, *Curse of the Pink Panther*, in August. Lynne Frederick would appear with him in it, Peter told another Hollywood columnist a few weeks later, fresh from a trip with Lynne to Disneyland. "In fact," he said, "I think her role should be enlarged." Then they left for London.

Curse of the Pink Panther, soon retitled *Revenge of the Pink Panther* (1978), began shooting in Paris in November. Lynne played no role onscreen.

Clouseau goes in pursuit of the drug lord Douvier (Robert Webber), whose turf (the world) is threatened by rivals; Douvier's secretary-lover, Simone (Dyan Cannon) helps him until she turns on him and aids Clouseau. They all end up in Hong Kong.

Clouseau shows up at the costume shop of Professor Balls (Graham Stark) to try on his new disguise—a leg-shortened Toulouse-Lautrec number complete with blue smock, beard, and straw hat. At first, he stumbles and totters, unused to the absence of tibia, but then he gets it. It's the end of *Dr. Strangelove*:

BALLS: That's it, Chief Inspector! You can *walk!*
CLOUSEAU: I ken . . . ! *I ken'a weuk!*

At which point he tips his hat and launches into "Zank 'eaven for Leettle Girls."

A henchman at the front door hands him the requisite bomb. Clouseau accepts it, reaches into his pocket for a tip, and announces his dismay: "I'm sorry. I'm a little short."

Then: "A beum? Wear yeu expicting weune? *A beum!*" He tosses it, as is his habit, away from himself and toward the nearest person—Balls.

December found the cast and crew in a Shepperton soundstage, where, just before Christmas there was a friendly reunion when Princes Charles, Andrew, and Edward paid a visit. (They watched Peter film the scene in which Clouseau and Cato attempt to gain entrance to a drug speakeasy-disco, Le Club Foot.) By the first week of February, the production had moved to Hong Kong for extended location shooting, and the film wrapped in April on the French Riviera.

Peter and Lynne seem to have been getting along well at the time. "It's a whole new second-stage rocket," Peter said of his marriage around that time. "Mind-boggling and marvelous . . . ! I knew that we had met before in a previous incarnation, and I know we shall meet again after this."

• • •

With each passing *Panther*, Burt Kwouk couldn't help but notice the escalation in comic extremism, not to mention the soaring costs and metastasizing scope: "Peter's accent got worse and worse, we all started to look older, and the pictures, for some reason, became larger in scale as they went on. *A Shot in the Dark* was pretty small scale; the last one was a huge epic." But, Kwouk quickly adds, "I'll tell you the honest truth—I can no longer tell one movie from the other. It just seems like one enormous twelve-hour movie that took twenty years to shoot."

Given the huge financial successes of *The Return of the Pink Panther* and *The Pink Panther Strikes Again*, the whiff of another enormous blast of cash was in the air in the offices of United Artists, so the company arranged another lavish press junket, just to make sure. At a cost of $300,000—nearly triple the price of the *Return* affair—UA invited three hundred guests including seventy-five reporters, their spouses, Steve Martin, Bernadette Peters, and Don Ho, to Kahuku, Oahu, to celebrate the Fourth of July. Only a week before the extravaganza, with studio executives giddily preparing to buy favorable worldwide press, Blake Edwards was seized with misgivings about a portion of the fireworks scene, so he summoned Peter and Dyan Cannon to an MGM studio set on June 24 and 25 and hastily reshot the sequence.

Despite the strain of orchestrating what one disgruntled publicist called "this goddam junket"—"Blake and Tony [Adams] are scum and I really don't give a shit anymore how it turns out," the publicist privately opined—it was a big success. Media coverage of the film was most extensive.

At the press conference with Edwards, Dyan Cannon, Burt Kwouk, and Herbert Lom, Peter was asked about his heart attacks. "I'm trying to give them up," he replied. "I'm down to two a day now. It's about time for one *now*! It all began when I met Sue Mengers." (Sue Mengers was the powerful, notoriously abrasive Hollywood agent later parodied by Blake Edwards in the form of Shelley Winters's character in *S.O.B.*, 1981.) Blake quickly diverted the conversation in another direction: "The only thing *I* worry about is mouth-to-mouth resuscitation. It might excite him too much." Peter and Lynne flew to London for the British premiere the following week.

Revenge of the Pink Panther was highly successful at the box office. Like *The Pink Panther Strikes Again*, it took in an estimated $100 million in revenues.

Since both Sellers and Edwards had repeatedly said that each would never work with the other again, the occasion of the fifth *Pink Panther* (and, with *The Party*, their sixth collaboration) necessitated some sort of explanation for the radical change of heart. Edwards took his pragmatic, workhorse stance: "I guess it's the old Hollywood thing—'I'll never work with the guy again—until I need him.' " Edwards also provided an astute evaluation of Peter's physical comedy style: "Peter is not really a physical comedian in the sense that Chaplin or Keaton were. He is not that kind of an acrobat, and he is not trained that way. But he has a mind that *thinks* that way."

With his combined share of all the *Pink Panther* revenues reported to have been $4 million, Peter was rich again. And he'd reached his limit: "I've honestly had enough of Clouseau myself. I've got nothing more to give."

• • •

On the small screen, Peter stands in a straggly brown wig topped by a horned Wagnerian helmet and performs a brief imitation of Queen Victoria to a fascinated Kermit the Frog. *The Muppet Show*, with Peter as the week's guest star, aired during the last week of February 1978.

Kermit tells Peter that while he really loves all of Peter's funny characters, it's perfectly okay for him to just relax and be himself:

> PETER: (in the stentorian voice of a very old, very grand British thespian) But that, you see, my dear Kermit, would be altogether impossible. I could never be myself.
>
> KERMIT: Uh, never yourself?
>
> PETER: No. You see, there is no me. I do not exist.
>
> KERMIT: (uncomfortable) Er, I beg your pardon?
>
> PETER: (leaning in close and looking nervously around for eavesdroppers) There used to be a me, but I had it surgically removed.
>
> KERMIT: (looking nauseated) Uh, er, can . . . can we change the subject?

In a minute, Kermit. Peter Sellers was terribly self-conscious about his lack of a self, and it must have been taxing to sustain such a robust contradiction. What does it mean to have no self if you yourself think you have none? Sellers had *selves*, just as everyone does; his were just more extravagant, and most of them were played out under high-key lights in movies, television, and publicity photos. They were provisional, performative selves, and they popped up whenever the need for a particular one arose. His favorites were fictional, snapped on spontaneously and crafted over time. These selves made him a fortune and a lot of clever and successful friends who enjoyed his company. His least pleasant selves, the remorse-producing ones, were, in a word, selfish—hungry, impulse-driven selves bent on gratification at any cost. Expensive car, beautiful wife, willing girlfriend, latest camera, compliant child—*he had to have it*, and he had to have it *right away*, and, completing the performance, he had to *let everyone know*. Once he got it, of course, the selfish self faded away, satisfied but empty. Surgically removing that set of selves must have seemed less painful than living with them.

• • •

Peter and Lynne returned from Hong Kong to a domestic disruption in London. They were living in an elegant apartment in Roebuck House. The apartment, done in Indian-techno-Goon, featured saffron-colored walls, a lot of burning candles, a small carved Buddha, a prominent picture of Spike, acres of electronics and photographic equipment, and a huge blow-up photo of Lynne that had been taken by Peter.

Peter had been living there from the time before Titi; Tessa had briefly moved in. Now they found themselves faced with a 300 percent rent increase. Peter's upstairs neighbors were outraged, too—Lord Olivier and his wife, Joan Plowright, who according to Peter had a habit of dropping marbles on the hardwood floor. "We tried living in France last year," Lynne told the press, "but it wasn't a success. I don't know where we would go now. I hope it won't be America." They abandoned Roebuck House with no London residence to take its place.

Lynne described Peter as "incredibly volatile. He'll say, 'We're going to Egypt tomorrow night.' He needs someone to gently pull him down to earth a bit. . . . You need incredible patience. But I think I have it. I think I'm perhaps the first calm woman he's found. He thinks he's difficult to get along with. Past wives and girlfriends have put forward this moody, broody image. But I don't see him like that."

"What went wrong with my marriages?" Peter asked rhetorically some time later. He never condemned Anne, toward whom he remained friendly and needy. Miranda was too sophisticated and aristocratic for him, but he never ripped into her in public. He was now saving it all for Britt, to whom he generally referred tersely as "Ekland." "She's a professional girlfriend, so there's no more to be said," he declared on one occasion. On another he added this: "Every move she makes, she ruins a life. It's her hard, driving, ruthless ambition." Peter also made a point of letting Victoria know the depth of his feelings about her mother.

• • •

Physically, Peter's heart was kept going by a pacemaker, but emotionally it was fracturing to the point that in the early summer of 1978 he flew with Lynne to the Philippines for several sessions of shamanistic surgery. As Michael Sellers describes it, the shamans "conducted their 'surgery' by invisibly passing their hands into a patient's body and plucking out the diseased tissues." Michael tried to talk him out of it. Lynne thought there was no harm in trying, so off they went.

Peter endured twenty grueling "surgeries," which apparently involved the psychic doctors yanking pig spleens out from their concealment under the operating table.

He pronounced himself cured. Lynne herself went under the psychic knife to heal a persistent back problem and made a show of being equally impressed with the doctors. "They really are incredible," she declared. "Aren't they, darling?"

• • •

In late April 1979, when Peter viewed his next film, *The Prisoner of Zenda* (1979), in a screening room at Universal Studios in Burbank, he had a strong, sour reaction. The lights came up, he told Walter Mirisch, "You'll be hearing from me," and then he departed.

The next morning, he sent Mirisch a thirteen-point memo that described in excruciating detail how much he detested *The Prisoner of Zenda*. Halfway through the screening he began sweating and swearing; by the end he was in a blind rage. "I don't know how I held myself in check that evening," he told the durable British journalist Roderick Mann. "The version I saw was so bad! Mirisch has tried to turn it into a sort of poor man's *Pink Panther* and shot extra scenes using doubles which I knew absolutely nothing about. I'm so upset and disappointed. I even thought of renting a billboard to voice my protests, or hiring the Goodyear blimp and putting a message on it. Don't see it. It's a disaster.

"I'm just not going to sit back and be clobbered. After all, I do know something about comedy."

Stan Dragoti had originally been slated to direct *The Prisoner of Zenda*, but he was replaced by Richard Quine, the director of such slick and commercially successful pictures as *My Sister Eileen* (1955), *The Solid Gold Cadillac* (1956), and *The World of Suzie Wong* (1960). The film features Peter in three roles; his costars are Lionel Jeffries (with whom Peter had appeared in *Two-Way Stretch, Up the Creek*, and *The Wrong Arm of the Law*), Elke Sommer, and Lynne Frederick.

The story: King Rudolph IV of Ruritania (Peter as a sort of Bavarian Methuselah), floating high above his domain in a balloon filled with hot air, opens one too many bottles of champagne, pops a hole in the balloon, and stands in befuddled terror at his sudden descent. He lands in a tree in a faraway village and promptly falls into a well.

Meanwhile, in Ruritania, plots are afoot as General Saft (Jeffries) moves to subvert the monarchical process; meanwhile, in London, the king's debauched son (Peter doing a particularly jaded Terry-Thomas) is amusing himself in a gambling hall when he's told of his father's demise. "The king is dead. Long live me," Rudolph V pronounces.

Ruritanian ministers then hire a look-alike carriage driver named Syd (Peter doing a fairly standard Cockney) to impersonate the new king; he eventually falls in love with Princess Flavia (Lynne) and, in the end, assumes the throne himself. *The Prisoner of Zenda* is an expensive, flabby dud.

Peter's Terry-Thomas voice is a bit florid, especially since he combines it with a speech impediment—*w*s serve as *r*s—which renders many of Rudolph's lines unintelligible. Some are quite funny—"The cwown is mine!"—but all in all it's still not one of Peter's better efforts.

With Peter flush with cash and fame again—*Revenge of the Pink Panther* was the tenth-top-grossing film of 1978—he was firmly back in the groove as far as on-set antics were concerned. In some cases, he was probably right; the script was terrible, Quine's direction indecisive, Walter Mirisch's meddling unproductive. The film may legitimately have seemed to him to be headed for failure. But in other cases, Peter was just being Peter at his worst. Lionel Jeffries told (the real) Terry-Thomas privately that Peter's behavior had been truly dreadful on the set one day, and that Peter had telephoned Jeffries about it later that night. "Was I really awful today?" Peter asked. "Well, yes," Jeffries said, at which Peter laughed and hung up.

• • •

The cut of *The Prisoner of Zenda* Peter had seen with Walter Mirisch was not the final one; the picture still required some dubbing on Peter's part. He refused to do it.

A few days later, under threat of legal action, he did it.

Then he flew to Barbados for a month. Lynne stayed in Los Angeles. He rented the theater designer Oliver Messel's old place by himself. From Barbados he flew to Switzerland to oversee the move into his new house in Gstaad.

He changed his mind about *The Prisoner of Zenda*, at least in public, by the time the film was released. "I think it's a wonderfully entertaining movie," he penned in a letter to Roderick Mann. The print he'd seen, he explained, didn't have a musical score and was even missing several scenes. Lynne, separately, put her two cents in, too: "Part of the trouble was we saw the film by ourselves, not with an audience. So there was no laughter. And Peter got upset."

By that point, Lynne had moved into her own house. As Roderick Mann put it, the move occurred "with Sellers's blessing."

He hadn't found lasting, unconditional love, and he hadn't found spiritual contentment either. Michael Sellers takes a harsh tone when describing his father's religious life: "If someone offered a cut-price, special-offer, gift-wrapped religion that guaranteed miracles and a personal audience with the Maker, then Dad would apply for instant enrollment." Peter was scarcely alone in trying to fashion a spiritual quilt out of appealing and available scraps without worrying too much about how the seams would fit. But few people other than the half-Jewish, Catholic-educated, Buddhist-Hindu-yogic-Castanedaesque Peter Sellers would go so far as to fly a wondrous Catholic priest from Mexico to Gstaad, install him briefly in a hotel, and get him to offer him Holy Communion. Michael dutifully knelt alongside.

Peter had also paid a visit to a Beverly Hills numerologist, he told a friend. "She said that in one incarnation I had been a priest in Roman days. You know—it's the old déjà vu thing, but every time I've been to Rome I've felt it—especially one night in the Circus Maximus. It's now a car park. About three in the morning I was sitting right in the center thinking about all the Christians who had been sacrificed to the lions and feeling that I must have been there."

• • •

For most of the 1970s, Peter Sellers was obsessed with playing a nobody who became a somebody nobody could really know. As his secretary Sue Evans once said, "You have to understand that *Being There* was a daily conversation" from the time Peter hired her in 1973 until 1979, when the film was shot and released. Jerzy Kosinski concurred: "For seven and a half years, Peter Sellers became Chauncey Gardiner. He printed calling cards as Chauncey Gardiner. He signed letters Chauncey Gardiner." Peter often made a point of acting like Chauncey Gardiner, too. At a mid-seventies meeting with Kosinski in a Beverly Hills hotel room, Peter ordered champagne to be sent up. When the waiter arrived, Peter was staring at the television set. Only it wasn't on. "Would you mind not stepping in the way?" he kindly asked the mystified waiter, who stepped gingerly all around the room in a strained effort not to block Peter's view of an empty screen.

At one point a year or two later, Peter was in Malibu renting Larry Hagman's beach house. "Jerzy Kosinski came over all the time," Victoria Sellers remembers. "He and my dad hit it off really well." Conveniently for Peter, the thin, white-haired, white-bearded director Hal Ashby lived in Malibu, too. Ashby was still interested in making the picture, and by that point,

Ashby himself was becoming most bankable; his 1978 film *Coming Home* ended up winning three Oscars—for Jon Voight, Jane Fonda, and the screenwriters Waldo Salt and Robert C. Jones—and was nominated for six more.

In late 1978, Peter was renting an expansive blue and white house on Summitridge Place in Beverly Hills, where he flew the Union Jack above the driveway, just to make a point: He wasn't one of *them*. After years of frustration and disappointment, and after a preparatory face-lift, he reached a joint agreement with Ashby, the producer Andrew Braunsberg, and the film and television production company Lorimar to make his most cherished project as a big-scale feature film. In 1973, the entire proposed budget for *Being There* had been $1,946,300. By the time production began on January 15, 1979, Peter alone was getting $750,000 for sixteen weeks' work, plus a percentage of the gross, plus living expenses of $2,500 per week during the shoot, plus first star billing above the title, with nobody else getting credit in larger type. Through his agent Marty Baum at Creative Artists, Peter also tried to make it impossible for any other star to share billing space above the title.

"I did it just to see a genius at work," said Shirley MacLaine, explaining why she agreed to take what she called a supporting role at that stage of her spectacular career (*The Trouble With Harry*, 1955; *The Apartment*, 1960; *Irma La Douce*, 1963; *Sweet Charity*, 1969; *The Turning Point*, 1977). Still, MacLaine's agent successfully played the bad cop in negotiations with Braunsberg, Ashby, and Lorimar and made sure that his client got her name above the title immediately below Peter's. Jack Warden and Melvyn Douglas's agents followed suit, so by the time everything was said, signed, printed, and screened, a total of four movie stars' names preceded the words *Being There* in the opening credits.

Finally, in mid-January 1979, Peter Sellers began to make the film of his life. Literally, he thought.

• • •

Being There is the story of a man named Chance, a mindless, nearly emotionless middle-aged fool forced by the death of his ancient benefactor to leave the mansion and small garden in which he has spent his life and, alone, to take to the streets, where, quickly, and luckily, he is hit by a limousine owned by the wife of one the richest men in the world, who doctors him, houses him, feeds him, and sets him up for superstardom.

MacLaine plays the wife, Eve Rand. Hal Ashby originally considered

Laurence Olivier for the role of Eve's dying husband, Benjamin Rand, but Lord Olivier turned it down. As Shirley MacLaine explained during the production, "I called Larry about it the other day. He didn't like the idea of being in a film with me masturbating." After briefly considering Burt Lancaster, Ashby ended up with Melvyn Douglas.

As for the role of Chance, Peter once explained facetiously that "Jerzy Kosinski wanted the part himself. That's why he wrote it for a young man of Olympian, god-like beauty." (In fact, Kosinski was a slight and rather rat-faced man—not ugly, but not Olympian either.) "I saw Chauncey Gardiner as a plump figure, pallid, unexercised from sitting around watching television. [Am I] too old? A lot of people said that. I just told them, 'You're wrong, I'm right.' "

Given the fact that Peter had spent most of the last decade trying to embody Chauncey Gardiner, it hurt to be told that he was now too old to play him. The face-lift helped. It eliminated the haggard quality that had begun to creep in with *The Pink Panther Strikes Again*. Owing to his heart condition and the lack of a sustainable treatment, Peter was fundamentally unhealthy, though he didn't look it onscreen.

To create Chance's voice, Peter said that he had, as usual, "messed around a long time with sounds. I have a whole sound set-up, and I spoke into a tape recorder and then listened. I compared one sound with another until I found the one I was happy with." The result was a voice with "very clear enunciation, slightly American, with perhaps a little Stan Laurel mixed in." David Lodge maintains that in Chance's voice there's a touch of Peter's old, taciturn gardener from Chipperfield as well.

• • •

Peter had been a problematic figure in the world of big-budget motion pictures for quite some time by the time *Being There* was filmed, and he required no small degree of personal handling, let alone public explanation. Andrew Braunsberg felt the need to make excuses for some of Peter's recent (and not-so-recent) work, but Braunsberg handled the awkward issue deftly and accurately by saying simply that "he knows he's done some junk, but everyone who makes a lot of films has." (As if there was any doubt about Braunsberg's theory, it is proven by Laurence Olivier's *Inchon*, 1981, and Katharine Hepburn's *Olly Olly Oxen Free*, 1978, to name only two of the hundreds of crummy films made by fine performers.) And his weirdness was by that point an old cliché that tinkered on the edge of grand myth.

Inevitably, for example, Peter announced to the cast and crew of *Being There* that he refused to work with anyone who wore purple, leaving the explanation to Hal Ashby, who dutifully obliged.

Peter kept to himself most of the time during the production. At Peter's insistence, reporters were turned away left and right, although two—Mitchell Glazer of *Rolling Stone* and Todd McCarthy of *Film Comment*—were allowed to visit the set with the promise of interviews at a later time. Shirley MacLaine later wrote that she repeatedly invited Peter to lunch or dinner, but that he kept refusing, despite their shared interest in what Shirley herself itemized as "metaphysics, numerology, past lives, and astrology." Peter himself said that "Shirley used to have a go at me for always going off into a corner. But I had to. I didn't want to break my gardener for the day."

On the other hand, Melvyn Douglas told of a more genial and social Peter. "Jack Warden and Peter Sellers are theatre raconteurs as well as wonderful actors," Douglas later wrote in his autobiography. "The two of them hardly ever left the set. Shooting on their scenes would end and they would retire to another part of the room and go on telling stories, gesturing and laughing until tears ran down their faces."

In early February, Peter was filming on location in Washington, D.C.—Chance wandering the streets of the ghetto; Chance walking down the median strip of a crowded artery, seemingly headed for the brilliantly lit Capitol. By mid-February, the cast and crew had moved to another location—Biltmore, a 10,000-acre estate owned by George W. Vanderbilt in Asheville, North Carolina. The producers made a point of setting aside one of the mansion's vast rooms to serve as Peter's dressing room, but Peter took one look at it and hurried back to his own trailer.

On Valentine's Day, Peter sent Shirley five dozen red roses—anonymously, but she knew. Shirley thanked Peter for them, but he refused to acknowledge the gift.

• • •

"You're always going to be a little boy, ain't you?" says Louise, the black maid, as her parting words after the old man dies and leaves the helpless Chance to fend for himself. And so, to the tune of Eumir Deodato's souped-up, synthesizer-ridden "Also Sprach Zarathustra," the overgrown infant opens the front door for the first time in his life, closes it behind him, negotiates the few steps down to the sidewalk, and enters the world. Later that morning, when a young black gang leader pulls a knife on him, Chance responds by yanking his television remote control device out of his pocket, pointing it at the street tough, and trying to change channels to someone more pleasant.

In front of an electronics store, Chance stands dumbfounded before a big-screen TV that plays images of the sidewalk in front of it. He backs up in horrified confusion at finding himself to be a video image and is immediately hit by Eve Rand's immense Cadillac. In the limousine's backseat, Eve gives him a drink. Assuming that the liquid is water or some form of juice, Chance drinks alcohol for the first time and promptly chokes just as Eve asks him his name:

"Chance—achhkk—achkg—actgk'he gardner."

"Chauncey Gardiner?"

Chance has a new name. "Are you related to Basil and Perdita Gardiner?" the luxurious Eve asks in a hopeful tone. "No," Chance replies in the flat near-monotone that expresses the full extent of his emotional life. "I am not related to Basil and Perdita."

It's not that Chance has *no* affect. Sellers periodically knits the muscles of his forehead to create an expression of mild and regular bewilderment. Chance appears at those moments to think, but it is thinking without thoughts, a kind of vestigial reasoning that leads nowhere. He is a mental earlobe trying to be a fin. It's not surprising that American audiences accepted the plot of *Being There*, in which an idiot becomes a national hero, for after all, they elected Ronald Reagan to the presidency the following year.

• • •

Ben Rand suffers from aplastic anemia; steroids, transfusions, a fully equipped personal intensive care unit, and a live-in physician (Richard Dysart) struggle to keep him alive in his American palace on the outskirts of Washington. While Ben gets his daily dose of fresh blood, an orderly wheels Chance into the mansion's clinic so that Ben's doctor can examine the leg that Eve's car came close to crushing. Chance spies an African-American medical attendant, whose skin calls the gang leader to what passes for Chance's mind. Chance asks the man if he knows Rafael, the shadowy figure to whom the gangster had urged Chance, at knifepoint, to relay a message. Chance proceeds to repeat the message in his vacant, colorless tone, the antithesis of the vivid communiqué itself:

" 'Now get this, honky. You go tell Rafael that I ain't taking no jive from no Western Union messenger. You tell that asshole that if he got something to tell me, to get his ass down here himself.' Then he said that I was to get my white ass out of there quick or he'd cut it."

The problem was, Peter couldn't get the speech out without breaking into uncontrollable laughter; as *Hoffman*'s Alvin Rakoff and others have noted, Peter could be a giggler. Ashby ordered take after take as Peter attempted vainly to compose himself. The cast and crew couldn't help laughing, too, and so the scene never worked as written, and the entire speech had to be cut. In the finished film, Chance simply lies back down on the hospital gurney and keeps his mouth shut.

This painful episode brought into stark relief the challenge Peter faced in reciting *any* of his lines, of which "now get this, honky," and so on, was only the most overtly ludicrous. Throughout *Being There*, Peter achieves the pinpoint-sharp exactitude of nothingness. It is a performance of extraordinary dexterity. As the critic Frank Rich wrote in *Time* when *Being There* was released, "The audience must believe that Chance is so completely blank that he could indeed seem to be all things to all the people he meets. Peter Sellers' meticulously controlled performance brings off this seemingly impossible task; as he proved in *Lolita*, he is a master at adapting the surreal characters of modern fiction to the naturalistic demands of movies. His Chance is sexless, affectless, and guileless to a fault. His face shows no emotion except the beatific, innocent smile of a moron. . . . Sellers' gestures are so specific and consistent that Chance never becomes clownish or arch. He is convincing enough to make the film's fantastic premise credible; yet he manages to get every laugh."

As Rich astutely observes, Chance is a modern, absurdist human vacuum, but a genial and naturalistic one—a schismatic personality that Peter had to convey with strenuous vocal and gestural technique. To break Chance's strict, meditation-like state would be to destroy Chance's being. A lesser actor would have made the character's mental dysfunction flamboyant and drastic. A Hollywood ham, all but winking directly at the camera, would find a way to reiterate soundlessly what a magnificent performance the audience was lucky enough to witness—how fantastically smart the actor had to be to play a dullard. Think of Dustin Hoffman in *Rain Man* (1988). Peter Sellers's intelligence was always deeper, his onscreen confidence greater, his technique much more finely honed.

• • •

The President of the United States (Warden) shows up at the mansion to marshal Ben Rand's political and financial support. There he meets Chance. As the three titans discuss national affairs, the conversation turns to the best way to stimulate economic growth. Chance pauses for a moment, moves his eyes slightly, pauses again—all meaningless gestures that register as cogitation—and says, "As long as the roots are not severed, all is well—and all *will* be well—in the garden."

The president is taken aback, forced to regard Chance's remark as a metaphor in order for the statement to make any sense at all. Chance follows through: "In a garden, growth has its seasons. First comes spring and summer. But then we have fall and winter. And then we get spring and summer again."

THE PRESIDENT: (*confused*) Spring and summer?
CHANCE: (*flatly*) Yes.
THE PRESIDENT: (*as if speaking to a cretin*) And fall and winter?
CHANCE: (*delighted to be understood*) Yes!

Rand, the cadaverous multibillionaire, is truly overjoyed with Chance's pointless words. "I think what our young friend is saying is that we welcome the inevitable seasons of nature, but we're upset by the seasons of our economy!" "Yes!" Chance cries. "There will be growth in the spring!" The president is duly convinced. "Well, Mr. Gardiner, I must admit that is one of the most refreshing and optimistic statements I've heard in a very very long time." Rand applauds. "I admire your good, solid sense," the president continues, obviously pleased to be receiving a cretin's wisdom. "That's precisely what we like on Capitol Hill."

Later, a book publisher responds to Chance with a similar sense of spiritual kindredness by greeting him warmly and offering him a book contract with a six-figure advance. "I can't write," says Chance. "Well, of course not!" the publisher replies with a hearty laugh. "Who can nowadays?"

The president mentions the sage advice of Mr. Chauncey Gardiner at a televised speech at the Financial Institute, whereupon Chance is hurried onto a talk show. His dopey remarks, delivered with a sort of puckish grin, begin as standard, late-night, getting-to-know-you comedy banter. Chance clearly knows the drill, having spent his life watching television. Ashby cuts to Ben and Eve Rand watching proudly from Ben's bed and the president and first lady watching nervously from the White House. Things turn more sober on television when Chance opines that "it is possible for, uh, everything to grow stronger. And there is plenty of room for new trees and new flowers of all kinds." The audience applauds enthusiastically.

"It's for sure a white man's world in America," Louise snaps, watching him from the lobby of her apartment building.

As the president, the CIA, the FBI, and countless newspaper reporters attempt to find any information whatsoever on the nonexistent Chauncey Gardiner, Chance lies in his lavish bed eating breakfast from a tray and watching the happy, happy opening number of *Mister Rogers' Neighborhood*. With Fred Rogers singing a song about his special friend, Eve arrives and climbs into bed with Chance. He continues to watch Mister Rogers as Mister Rogers sings the spelling of the word *friend*, whereupon Eve misinterprets Chance's babylike indifference to sex by attributing it to gallantry. "A long time ago, people didn't have television," Mister Rogers tells his little viewers. "But they still liked to look at interesting pictures." Eve departs.

Fortunately for Eve, Chance happens to be viewing a steamy romantic scene on TV when she returns to his room late at night. He grabs her and begins kissing her passionately in direct imitation of the images he is watching at the time. When the onscreen kissing stops, so does Chance.

Eve: Chauncey! What's wrong? What's the matter, Chauncey? I don't know what you like!
Chance: I like to watch, Eve.

And so she performs for him on a bearskin rug. Switching channels to a yoga program, he does a handstand on the bed while Eve moans and comes to her own relaxed and delighted laughter.

Throughout *Being There*, but here in particular, Shirley MacLaine's performance is as exceptional as Peter's. A scene that could have turned farcical, grotesque, or pathetic—the vivacious wife of a decrepit old man masturbating before a brainless cipher—becomes instead distinguished, compassionate. MacLaine invests Eve with a mix of sophistication and innocence, delicacy and fresh sexual passion. Though it might seem to have been Peter's due to play opposite great actresses throughout his career, the fact was that he rarely did; Peter was lucky to have one more chance to act alongside a bona-fide star.

• • •

The film ends with Ben Rand's burial. The president delivers a platitudinous eulogy (the selected quotations of Ben) as Chance wanders into the seemingly unending forest of the Rand estate. As Ashby himself described *Being There*'s original ending, "Shirley MacLaine goes after Peter Sellers when he leaves the funeral and goes into the woods. She finds him and she says she was frightened and was looking for him. He says, 'I was looking for you, too, Eve.' And they just walk off together." Ashby had already filmed that scene when a friend of his, the screenwriter Rudy Wurlitzer, asked him how the *Being There* shoot was progressing. "It's wonderful," Ashby replied. "Peter Sellers and Melvyn Douglas are achieving such clarity, such simplicity, it looks like they're walking on water." It was a moment of inspiration.

Ashby shot a new ending.

Chance wanders through the snowy woods while the president continues with his platitudes and Ben's pallbearers whisperingly agree to nominate Chance for the presidency. On the edge of a lake, Chance straightens a sapling that has been weighed down by an old, broken branch. He moves toward the shoreline and walks into—rather, on top of—the lake. He pokes his umbrella gently in, plunges it down, looks up and around in characteristic incomprehension, and continues strolling on the surface of the cold winter water. What choice did Peter Sellers have, let alone Chauncey Gardiner?

TWENTY-THREE

Never imagine yourself not to be otherwise
than what it might appear to others that what you were
or might have been was not otherwise
than what you had been
would have appeared to them to be otherwise.

On April 18, 1979, the last day of shooting *Being There*, MacLaine and Sellers were filming the scene set in the backseat of Eve Rand's limousine. "Peter had been to a numerologist the night before," Shirley reports. "Looking into my eyes, he told me that the numerologist had warned him that his wife's numbers didn't match his own numbers. Peter was clearly most concerned about this information."

He was worried about his mind as well as his heart; the actual, blood-pumping muscle was giving him as much cause for concern as his love life. He found himself musing over the possible effects of his two minutes of clinical death in 1964. "I think I'm probably going a little soft in the head," he told *Time* magazine a little later, "which is why I have something in common with Chance."

Peter's renewed obsession with Sophia Loren did not help his deteriorating marriage with Lynne. Thoughts of Sophia had resurfaced because Sophia had just published her memoirs, and the name "Peter Sellers" had not appeared therein. Peter was shocked and hurt. "Our relationship was one of the things that helped break up my first marriage!" he complained to the columnist Roderick Mann. Referring to Sophia with icy formality, Peter continued: "Miss Loren was always telephoning me, and I'd go rushing all over Italy to be with her. It's odd that someone who apparently meant so much in her life—or so she said—should not figure in her life story. The only reason I can think is that she was married at the time. But it's not as if her husband didn't know. Carlo knew very well."

Peter's remarks became a scandal, one which did not please Sophia, who was swiftly pestered to respond to Peter's public despair. "I could not write about every partner I have had in the movies," she told one reporter. "It would have taken volumes. I only wrote about the most important events of my life. Peter lived in Los Angeles and it was too far to go to see him from Italy." At this point Sophia became angry: "I will not answer any more questions about Peter Sellers! I wrote the book to tell the truth about my life, not for gossip columnists!"

"I know the men I've slept with," Sophia told Shirley MacLaine privately. "And Peter, bless his phantasmagorical mind, was not one of them."

MacLaine was soon surprised to find herself in the same phantasmagorical boat. During the production of *Being There*, she later wrote, "He did tell me in detail of his love affairs with Sophia Loren and Liza Minnelli. I wondered about his lack of discretion but sometimes found his reenactments very funny." Then she discovered, after filming had concluded, that Peter was describing to others the details of his torrid affair with Shirley MacLaine. In fact, one Hollywood producer reported that he had been in the same room with Peter when Peter was "whispering sweet nothings" to MacLaine on the telephone. "Then he was whispering to a dial tone," is MacLaine's response.

• • •

His fourth marriage's denouement seemed inevitable to the point of redundancy. Just before *Being There* began shooting, Peter was asked about Lynne. "I'm so lucky," he answered. "She's a beautiful girl in every sense. I just wish I'd met her long ago. It's been a long, bumpy road to find her, but God at last has smiled on me. . . . Lynne is exactly the kind of girl whom Peg would have wanted for me. She [Peg] is always around, always giving me help and advice. . . . She loves Lynne and wants us to be happy together."

Lynne's own mother, Iris, still hadn't spoken to her daughter since the marriage, though she did continue speaking to the press. "What mother can be expected to approve of the marriage of her daughter to such a man?" Mrs. Frederick declared to the *Los Angeles Times* in late January. "Their marriage was doomed from the start."

Iris was right.

Lynne saw a shrink. The doctor's diagnosis was one to which Peter failed to cotton. "A psychiatrist she went to was crazy enough to suggest that because I loved my mother I was still looking for another mother figure!" he declared in exasperation. "When my mother was alive," he explained, "she did everything she could in her life to help me. She was content and always there, both for my father and me. I said to Lynne one day that because of her kindness, she reminded me of my mother. . . . Sometime later she went to a psychiatrist in Hollywood. Those shrinks are awful! What he told Lynne was that the trouble between us—the strain which I hadn't noticed—was caused by my looking for another mother figure. And it was that incestuous feeling that prevented us from having children. Now that is mad, isn't it? Quite mad!"

Peter wanted a divorce. Typically, he told a reporter about it first. "That was what hurt," Lynne said, "reading in a newspaper that our marriage was finished. It's true we had discussed divorce, but no decision had been reached when he left. We've both consulted lawyers, but nothing's happened yet."

It seems that in the third week of April, just after *Being There* wrapped, Peter left Los Angeles for Barbados, alone and in a rage, because Lynne had refused to accompany him on the vacation. He stayed in Barbados a single day and then flew to London. "From there he telephoned me to announce that his marriage was over," Roderick Mann wrote in the *Sunday Express* on April 28. "A few days later he made the same statement to London newspapermen."

The whole thing continued to be played out in newspapers and, in a secondary sense, in daily telephone calls between the two aggrieved parties, who clung to each other long distance. In early May, Peter was in his room at the Inn on the Park in London and sleeping in until 4 P.M. He was "haggard and bleary-eyed" when he answered the door, found a reporter, tried to slam the door in the reporter's face, and ended up slamming it on his own foot.

"I don't mind being alone," he told still another scribe. Yet in mid-May, he mentioned to a third journalist that he'd asked Lynne to fly to London for what he called a "love summit"; he himself having left London briefly to make an appearance at the Cannes Film Festival. "For tax reasons I cannot work in London," he said to a fourth reporter, "but I can certainly go there to save my marriage." To a fifth he added that "up till now all the discussions regarding our future life together have been on the telephone."

"Really," he said, "I am a romantic, so I can't rule out getting married again. But this time it will be to an older woman—someone who is thirty-one or thirty-two."

One of Lynne's friends told the *Daily Mail* that "she doesn't appear upset about anything."

• • •

In May, Peter announced that he was starting work on a new record album. *Sellers Market*, which was recorded in France in June. It was originally going to feature a conversation between Prime Minister Margaret Thatcher and *I'm All Right, Jack*'s Fred Kite; it would have been a classic, but the final selection includes no such cut. Instead, *Sellers Market* includes among its highlights an unusual rendition of Cole Porter's "Night and Day"—it's done in Morse code—and an equally warped version of Freed and Brown's "Singin' in the Rain" done as a military march.

The best track, though, is "The Cultural Scene: The Compleat Guide to Accents of the British Isles," in which an American professor, Don Schulman (Sellers) tours the United Kingdom and finds a wide variety of rhythms and inflections, all done by Sellers: London (Cockney), Surrey (Russian), Birmingham (Indian), Wales (lilting singsong), Edinburgh (kilty), and Glasgow (virtually incomprehensible and belligerently drunk).

He kept himself occupied in other ways, too. He had several new film projects in mind: *The Romance of the Pink Panther*, to be directed by Sidney Poitier; *Chandu the Magician* for Orion; *The Fiendish Plot of Dr. Fu Manchu*, also for Orion; and a remake of Preston Sturges's classic 1948 screwball comedy *Unfaithfully Yours* for Twentieth Century-Fox. He even talked about making a science-fiction film with Satyajit Ray.

The Romance of the Pink Panther would be different than the other *Panther*s, Peter told the Hollywood columnist Marilyn Beck. Clouseau will "expose a side of himself no one has seen. He's going to be involved with a woman who's deeply in love with him, and we'll see his reaction to that." There was still no word on who would play the woman, Anastasia Puissance. In fact, the script was not yet completed at the time. According to Peter, production wouldn't begin until August 1980, at the earliest. Reportedly, Peter would be getting $3 million up front for the film—half of which, he claimed, had already been paid. He would also get 10 percent of the gross.

Estimating from the financial success of the last *Panther*, *The Romance of the Pink Panther* alone might earn him $8 million.

That Sidney Poitier rather than Blake Edwards was set to direct *The Romance of the Pink Panther* seems not to have been the result of animosity between Peter and Blake. He'd filmed a cameo for Edwards's latest picture, *10* (1979), which starred Dudley Moore, Julie Andrews, and Bo Derek. Peter played drums in a jazz band, but the scene was cut before the film's release.

• • •

In the beginning of August, *Rolling Stone*'s Mitchell Glazer conducted his interview with Peter in Gstaad. He found the words "Om Shanti" inscribed over the front door of Peter's chalet and an autographed photo of Stan Laurel hanging on the wall. "It's nice to walk around here and get stoned," Peter told Glazer for publication. "This place is so beautiful even *I* can relax."

• • •

In December 1979, when the latest issue of Britain's *Club International* magazine hit the stands, readers and gossip columnists were delighted to find what the magazine billed as "exclusive" nude photos of Britt Ekland and Lynne Frederick. Britt's were full-frontal, Lynne's simply bare-breasted. "It's gossiped that Sellers himself snapped the pics, but not for publication," the *Hollywood Reporter* noted.

• • •

In January 1980, *Being There* was screened for President Jimmy Carter and the first lady, Rosalynn, at the White House. President Carter particularly enjoyed the exchange between Chance and the president—the one during which the president thinks he is getting political advice but in fact is receiving the basic facts of plant life. "That's better advice than I get," said President Carter.

• • •

Before embarking on *The Romance of the Pink Panther*, *Unfaithfully Yours*, *Chandu the Magician*, or the unlikely space alien picture for Satyajit Ray, Peter made *The Fiendish Plot of Dr. Fu Manchu* (1980) with Helen Mirren and Sid Caesar.

Roman Polanski had once been mentioned as a director for the film, but nothing came of it. John G. Avildson spent a week with Peter discussing the possibility of his directing it, after which Orion paid Avildson $100,000 to walk away. Richard Quine was approached; he too dropped out after arguing with Peter about the direction the film should take. Piers Haggard was finally hired. Haggard had directed such films as *The Blood on Satan's Claw* (1970).

Filming began at the Studios de Boulogne in Paris at the end of September.

Fu Manchu, the eponymous fiend, had long held a special appeal for Peter: "I listened fanatically to the Fu Manchu radio serials on the BBC. They were more terrifying than the BBC's light musical programs." Now, in performing the role himself, Peter strove to avoid what he called "the stilted stereotype of swapping *r*s for *l*s. It's demeaning, it's been done to death, and it's not funny." (In other words, it *had* been funny in *Murder By Death*, but now he was bored with it.) Instead, Peter provided Fu Manchu with the backstory of an English prep-school education—in Peter's words, "where he learned the meaning of torture, like any proper British schoolboy"—and then claimed to have based Fu Manchu's British accent on Lord Snowdon. Peter swore that he'd asked Snowdon for his permission, which Snowdon is said to have swiftly granted, but in point of fact the fiend's voice sounds a good bit too Chinese for the tale to be true.

Peter also claimed that he was focusing on Fu Manchu's astounding sex appeal. "After all," Peter explained, "if you've devoted 150 years to depravity, you're bound to get good at it."

His makeup: a spray-applied rubber that hardened into crow's feet and wrinkles; twelve molded sponge devices to create Asiatic features; tinted contact lenses; a beard; and long black plastic fingernails. It was all painful. "The bloody lenses made my eyes run, my skin itched from the spirit gum on the beard, and the fingernails were a bore. I kept poking myself in odd places. I don't know how women manage with them," Peter remarked.

In early November, the production moved to St. Gervais, the Alpine resort, for some location work, after which *The Fiendish Plot of Dr. Fu Manchu* moved back to the Studios de Boulogne. Just before Christmas, Peter flew to Gstaad for some rest, promising to return after the holidays. He did return, whereupon he promptly fired Piers Haggard, whom, like several other directors over the years, he had grown to hate for reasons of his own. Peter took over the filming himself.

In January, Peter summoned David Lodge to Paris, where Lodge found Lynne to have become "very hard—not the same person" he had met earlier. In some sense they were back together, but since their relationship had always included long separations followed by intense reunions, their current togetherness was simply par for the course.

According to Lodge, Peter retained the contractual right to reshoot anything he wanted, and he could reshoot any given scene *as often* as he wanted. So to Lodge's amazement, Peter reshot Lodge's scene entirely in close-ups. (A scene shot entirely in close-ups would produce a rather avant-garde effect.) Lodge tried to just sit there and let Peter film him, but, from Peter's perspective, Lodge just couldn't seem to get it right. "Your eyebrows are popping up and down like a fiddler's elbow!" Peter told him before insisting that they retake the scene yet again.

"Do what Gene Hackman does," Peter advised his oldest continuous friend. "Fuck all." (By this Peter meant something on the order of "don't do anything—just sit there.")

Lodge concludes his tale by noting that despite Peter's right to reshoot anything he pleased, Orion was under no obligation to *use* any of it, so Lodge's scene ended up on the cutting room floor.

• • •

The Fiendish Plot of Dr. Fu Manchu has two remarkable performances, both by Peter, some beautiful set designs by Alexandre Trauner (who designed *The Apartment*, 1960, for Billy Wilder, among other films), no script, and few laughs. The film opens with Fu's minions singing "Happy Birthday to Fu" on the occasion of his 168th birthday. He prepares ritualistically to drink the *elixir vitae* that keeps him alive, but a servant drops the bottle. ("You look familiar," Fu remarks to the servant, played by Burt Kwouk.) Fu spends the rest of the film assembling the exotic ingredients, all the while pursued by a retired Scotland Yard inspector, Nayland Smith (Peter), and alternatively thwarted and aided by Inspector Alice Rage (Helen Mirren).

Michael Caine had once been mentioned as a possible Nayland Smith, but Peter took the role himself, and his Nayland Smith couldn't be more opposed to anything Caine could have produced. Peter's Nayland is a peculiarly flat-voiced old man—Henry Crun with no affect, having had it tortured out of him by previous encounters with Fu Manchu. In fact, there is something oddly cerebral about both of Sellers's performances in this

lackluster film. Because of the film's basic storyline, it isn't a stretch to say that both Fu Manchu and Nayland Smith spend much of the time meditating on their own mortality. The result is weirdly affecting—a badly written, practically undirected comedy played as warped eulogy.

"Peter was fucked up," his costar Helen Mirren acknowledges. "He could be very cruel, but he was also incredibly vulnerable, like a child." But like most other of the sensitive people with whom Peter Sellers worked, Mirren adds a crucial filip: "He was very, very nice to me. He did the sweetest thing—he laughed at my jokes. That's such a kind thing to do to anyone. Especially [for] a great comedian."

• • •

March 1980 saw the usual swelling tide of pre-Oscars jockeying, handicapping, and hype. Peter flew from Gstaad to London, and from London to New York, where, on March 12, he appeared on the *Today* show to promote *Being There*, for which he was nominated for a Best Actor award. "I'm looking for a girl with a sick mind and a beautiful body," he told Gene Shalit, though he was, of course, still married.

He told Marilyn Beck that he had no plans to appear at the Oscars ceremony at the Dorothy Chandler Pavilion in Los Angeles on April 14. "I'll be busy in London editing *The Fiendish Plot of Dr. Fu Manchu*. But even if I weren't, I wouldn't attend the Oscars. I never go to those do's, never go to anything. I'm very anti-social."

He was also by that point engaged in a public feud with Jerzy Kosinski, who for his part was running around informing everyone about Peter's face-lift. Peter, meanwhile, was claiming that Kosinski had not actually written the shooting script of *Being There*; instead, Peter said, *Being There* had really been significantly rewritten by Robert C. Jones, who had won an Oscar for *Coming Home*. This may seem to be an outlandish claim, given Kosinski's international stature, but in point of fact Hal Ashby, too, supported Jones when Jones took the matter to Writers Guild arbitration after Kosinski refused to share the credit. Unfortunately for Jones, Ashby, and Sellers, the Guild supported Kosinski and awarded him sole credit for the cowritten script.

Peter made the cover of *Time* on March 3. All six of him.

Backed by images of Chance, Quilty, Strangelove, Clouseau, and the Grand Duchess Gloriana XII, the face of a well-known, little-known actor looked inscrutably toward the camera. The headline was, "Who Is This

Man?" Peter was actually pleased by the article, which was written by the critic Richard Schickel—so much so that he wrote an appreciative letter to the editor: "I would like to thank you very much for taking the trouble to probe accurately the deeper recesses of whatever the hell I am."

At the Dorothy Chandler Pavilion on the fourteenth, Jane Fonda strode across the stage, opened the envelope, and announced that Dustin Hoffman won the Best Actor award for *Kramer vs. Kramer* (1979). By that point Peter had also lost the New York Film Critics Circle award to Hoffman, too. (That one wasn't even close. Hoffman got thirteen votes, Peter only three.) He had to settle for a Golden Globe and a Best Actor award from the National Board of Review, and he was bitterly disappointed.

He didn't fare better in Europe. Nominated by BAFTA as Best Actor in 1981, Peter lost to John Hurt for *The Elephant Man* (1980).

Peter was devastated not only by his failure to win an Oscar; he had been just as upset when he saw the release print of *Being There*. Without Peter's approval, Ashby and Braunsberg decided to end the film not with Chance walking on the surface of the lake, but with the outtakes of Peter laughing hysterically, trying and failing to deliver the "now get this, honky" line. The outtakes do pull some easy laughs—it's hard not to break up when listening to *anybody* suffering a laughing jag—but to Peter, the essence of his most austere and technically controlled performance was utterly ruined. He sent an angry telex to Ashby:

"It breaks the spell, do you understand? Do you understand, it breaks the spell! Do you hear me, it breaks the spell! I'm telling you how it breaks the spell. . . ."

• • •

"I've got an illegitimate daughter running around somewhere," he claimed in April 1980. He was speaking of the baby he believed he and the unnamed mystery woman had conceived while he was serving in the Royal Air Force—the one Peg had invited to dinner while Anne was recovering from her miscarriage. He had three children, whom he treated more or less poorly, if at all, but thoughts of his maybe, maybe-not lost daughter only intensified as his health deteriorated.

Of his three children, Michael Sellers enjoyed the least troubled relationship with his father. There had been periods of tension, but the two males seemed to get along well enough. Michael had his mother for emotional support; his father was there for infrequent fun.

Michael and Sarah were each the beneficiaries of a one-time gift of £20,000 when they turned twenty-one. It wasn't much, considering Peter's wealth, but, as usual, it was all he had to give them.

Peter had never quite gotten around to setting up a trust for his third child. Victoria Sellers had spent most of her life forced into playing the role of pawn in a nasty chess game; Peter was the black king, Britt the blond queen. With an unerring sense, the early-teenage Victoria once showed up for a visit clad entirely in purple. Peter threw a typical fit, but soon whisked her away on a shopping spree, both to make up for his rage and to ensure that she wouldn't wear the offending color in his presence. On another occasion, Peter canceled Victoria's planned visit to Port Grimaud at the last minute, thereby enraging Britt, thus provoking Peter to tell Sue Evans to write a letter to Victoria on his behalf and tell her, as Michael Sellers puts it, "that she should no longer regard him as her father."

That one blew over, slightly, but at the end of March 1980, the fifteen-year-old Victoria made the mistake of telling her father what she thought of his work: "He asked me if I'd seen his latest film, *Being There*. I said yes, I thought it was great. But then I said, 'You looked like a little fat, old man.'

"I didn't mean to hurt him. I meant his character in the film looked like a little old man. But he went mad. He threw his drink over me and told me to get the next plane home."

Sarah Sellers usually knew enough to keep her distance. She tried to please her father, but for reasons she never understood, she kept on failing. "When I was a student and rather poor," she says, "I didn't know what to give him and Lynne for Christmas, so I got her some lace doilies and him an old print. I got a letter back from him saying, 'I know it's the thought that counts, but what a thought. Yours, Dad.' I was devastated. But then he turned up a few months later as if nothing had happened."

But when Sarah put her two cents in over Victoria and the drink-throwing episode, she received the following telegram: "Dear Sarah, After what happened this morning with Victoria, I shall be happy if I never hear from you again. I won't tell you what I think of you. It must be obvious. Goodbye, Your Father."

• • •

Entertainment writers' conventional wisdom, if one can call it that, holds that movie stars demean themselves by appearing in television commercials.

It's considered far more honorable for stars to demean themselves on celluloid. But when Barclay's Bank offered Peter £1 million for a series of four
commercials, he accepted, and rightly so. It was a great deal of money. He
may not have needed it to survive, but he needed it nonetheless. After all,
he certainly wasn't acting for his health.

The commercials were shot in Dublin, with Joe McGrath directing.
Peter's character is a con man called Monty Casino, who bilks the unsuspecting out of their quid, the suggestion being that Barclay's Bank offered
protection against such shady scams. (The name plays not only on Monte
Carlo's casinos but also Monte Cassino, where Spike Milligan nearly got
blown up during World War II.) In the first, Monty swindles a young
musician out of his money; in the second, he cons a stately manor's aristocratic owner. The third featured Monty gulling a student out of his rent
money. The fourth was never filmed.

"He had a heart attack, and we couldn't finish," McGrath relates. "He
started to get palpitations and said, 'My God.' I said, 'Is it your heart?'
'No,' he said, 'it's the Pacemaker—it's gone into top gear. Quick—give me
that bag!' He took out this tiny leather case which had green and red things
on it. I said what is it? He said, 'It's Gucci jump leads, you can start me
up. What are friends for?'

"He said, 'We've got to get a specialist.' So, I phoned downstairs and
said we needed a specialist for Mr. Sellers. They said, 'You can't get a
specialist unless an MD comes and examines him.' So I said to Peter that
an MD would come up and then we'd get him into a hospital. He was
lying in bed. I had come in from my room and was still in a dressing gown,
and I had dark glasses on, and there was a knock on the door. This guy
was standing there, and he said, 'You look terrible, Mr. Sellers! You should
get to bed!' Peter said, 'That's what I need—an Irish doctor.'

"I took him into intensive care. The last thing he said was, 'I'll see you
in London.' He was in there for a couple of days, and then he was out.
And, like the fool he was, he went to Cannes."

• • •

McGrath is getting ahead of the story.

Nurse Lynne flew into Dublin from Los Angeles and announced to the
press that it was just a false alarm and not a heart attack at all. This time
it wasn't oysters but a bicycle. Peter had had to ride a bike in one of the
Barclay's commercials, she explained, and he'd simply overdone it. Her

motive seems clearly to have been commercial in nature; she was trying to protect his insurability.

Nevertheless, shortly after leaving the hospital and flying down to Cannes for the film festival, Peter endorsed an advertisement for the British Heart Association. The ad, printed in London newspapers, featured a photo of Peter; it was captioned "Heart Attack Survivor." Accompanying the pictures was a quote:

"I'm lucky—I survived!"

• • •

Lynne accompanied Peter to Cannes, where *Being There* was in competition for the Golden Palm. He kept a fairly low profile, except for the little garden party arranged by Lorimar for about 450 guests. "I'm fine, thank you, I'm feeling very fit; I'm fine, thank you, I'm feeling very fit," Peter kept repeating as he made his way through the horde. But the journalists kept asking.

"Please, I am not an invalid," he insisted to the crowd of reporters, who were legitimately confused by his remarks because they were being told simultaneously by Lorimar staffers that Peter was "not a well man."

Paparazzi, kept out of the affair by a wrought-iron fence, simply poked their lenses through the iron bars while a string quartet played in the background. The Los Angeles *Herald-Examiner's* Wanda McDaniel described the turmoil: "When Sellers arrived, the roots of garden party etiquette got severed to smithereens. At one point, the crush took on shades of panic until bodyguards convinced the curious that there are better ways to go than getting trampled to death at a garden fete."

The garden party certainly helped the film's publicity, but it scarcely mattered as far as the awards were concerned. The Golden Palm went to two films that year: Bob Fosse's *All That Jazz* (1979) and Akira Kurosawa's *Kagemusha* (1980).

And the Best Actor? Michel Piccoli for *Salto nel vuoto* (1979).

• • •

"The only rocks in this marriage are the rocks other people are throwing," Lynne declared at the end of May. And furthermore, she made a point of noting, "My mother and I are enjoying a very good relationship once again because she now approves of Peter. She assumed our marriage would last only a couple of months. Instead we have been together almost five years

and we celebrated our third wedding anniversary in February. We are prov-
ing my mother wrong, so she has finally had to accept Peter."

"My mother still hasn't met him," Lynne went on to say. "One of the
reasons is that she lives in Spain and we have no plans to go there."

Instead, Peter and Lynne went in precisely the opposite direction. They
embarked on a yachting trip to the Aegean Sea.

• • •

It was probably wise of both Peter and Lynne to stay away from Iris Frederick, but even a luxurious sail could only do so much. The effects of the
face-lift were wiped away by Peter's worsening heart condition. His face
was taking on a gaunt quality; the precise shape of his skull emerging more
clearly with every pound of weight he lost, not to mention every added line
of worry and stress. And yet, typically, and despite his increasing frailty, he
continued to develop new film ideas. It was the only therapy he trusted.

The writer Stephen Bach, then an executive with United Artists, flew
to Gstaad in June. "Peter Sellers was wraithlike," Bach later wrote. "The
smile he wore seemed paralyzed in place, and I thought I had never seen
so delicate a man. His skull, his fingers, the tightly drawn, almost trans-
parent skin—all seemed frail, infinitely fragile. . . . [He was] a spectral presence, a man made of eggshells."

Peter had been working on the script of *The Romance of the Pink Panther* with a writer named Jim Moloney; the film's producer, Danny Rissner,
had sent Peter some script notes, and Peter, after reading them on the yacht
in the Aegean, had threatened to jump overboard. He insisted that Lynne
be named as executive producer. If UA balked, he would walk.

It must be said that Lynne Frederick had her hands full with Peter,
as did each of his other wives. The difference was that none of his friends
could stand this one. They knew *him* too well, for one thing. And they
trusted neither her motives nor her personal performances—the ones she
gave privately for them. It was relatively distant business associates who
got the full treatment. Bach, for instance, believed Lynne's benevolent
routine on his trip to Gstaad to salvage the project. "The atmosphere was
uneasy only until Lynne Frederick came into the room, exuding an aura
of calm that somehow enveloped us all like an Alpine fragrance. She was
only in her mid-twenties but instantly observable as the mature center
around which the household revolved, an emotional anchor that looked
like a daffodil."

At the same time, Lynne Frederick deserves a bit of compassion herself in retrospect. It was the helpless Peter she nursed, the dependent and infantile creature of impulse and consequent contrition. Patiently, she ministered to him. And eventually, as Bach observes, Peter was moved to cooperate. At the end of the meeting, Bach observes, "I noticed, as he rose, that not once in the long, talkative afternoon had he let go of Lynne's hand, nor had she moved away. She transfused him simultaneously with calm and energy and the hand he clung to was less a hand than a lifeline."

• • •

The Romance of the Pink Panther was not the only project on Peter's mind. Marshall Brickman's *Valium*, now called *Lovesick*, was still in development. Brickman still possesses a tape recording of Peter practicing his scenes as a Viennese psychiatrist. *Unfaithfully Yours*, too, was moving forward, as was a sort of reunion project with Terry Southern. The proposed title: *Grossing Out*.

It was to be a satire based on someone Peter claimed to have met. Peter had, the story goes, once been invited to the wedding of a Saudi princess and found himself sitting on an Arabia-bound airplane next to a man who appeared to be a fabulously dressed rock star but who turned out to be an international arms dealer. "He had an accent that Peter couldn't pin— Mediterranean, but you couldn't tell where," Southern's companion, Gail Gerber, relates.

" 'This jacket is bulletproof,' " the weapons trader explained. "Peter was fascinated. 'And these buttons are the shell casings of bullets that were shot into it.' That knocked Peter out."

From that point, spinning out script ideas with the gloriously warped Terry Southern must have been great fun—the scenes taking place in the international arms marketplace, for example. "As Peter explained it to Terry, it was just like going to a shopping mall," says Gerber. On much the same wavelength as Peter and Terry, Hal Ashby expressed interest in directing *Grossing Out*, and the Hollywood trade papers reported that Peter would be getting $3 million for his appearance.

To the list was added *The Ferret*; written and directed by Blake Edwards, the comedy-on-the-drawing-boards was to be a spin-off of the *Pink Panther* series, still involving the character of Clouseau, but redefining the story that surrounded him.

"Without my work, life would be intolerable," Peter said. "It is the only panacea I know."

• • •

From Gstaad in early summer, Peter called his British lawyer, Elwood Rickless, and told him that he had finally agreed to the angiogram—an X-ray of one or more blood vessels of the cardiovascular system—that his cardiologist had recommended, the point being to determine whether his heart was strong enough to withstand surgery. He arranged to fly to London and then to Los Angeles, where he would check into Cedars-Sinai Medical Center for the exam. He chose Cedars-Sinai because of his positive experience there in 1964. If the cardiology team recommended it, Peter agreed that he would undergo immediate open-heart surgery.

"I was speaking to Peter on the phone," Spike Milligan said. "The subject of children came up, and he said, 'You know, I'm a bloody fool. I keep leaving them in and out of the will. Some weeks I put them in, others I take them out. It depends on how I feel.' " Spike offered his opinion—that he thought *all* children were entitled to inherit at least some of their father's estate. "Yes," Peter responded, "I really must change my will."

Meanwhile, in Los Angeles, Malcolm McDowell ran into Lynne: "I was sitting in Ma Maison restaurant on Melrose Avenue in West Hollywood, and I looked over and there was Lynne Frederick Sellers. Because I had worked with her, of course, I went over to say hello, and she introduced me to her lawyer. We chatted for a minute, and I started to walk off, and then she came over and said, 'Malcolm, I'm meeting with my lawyer because I've had it with Peter. It's over.' I said, 'I'm very sorry to hear that, Lynne.' She said, 'I'm really sick of him. I'm sick of him! I mean, this has gone too far. I should have done this ages ago, *and that's it!* ' "

Peter had the same idea. "She annoys me," he told his son in July, expressing in ever more distinct terms the ambivalence of his feelings all along. "I just wish the divorce was over and done with."

• • •

The novelist Auberon Waugh interviewed Peter in Gstaad. Peter's personal assistant, Michael Jeffery, was caring for him in Lynne's customary absence. Stephen Bach's trip to Gstaad had been business related, so Lynne had an interest in being present. Now she was in Philadelphia.

Waugh describes Michael Jeffery: "a young costume designer in tight corduroy trousers who wore a gold stud in one ear and walked with the unmistakable skip of a former ballet dancer. It is Mike who cooked him his meals, made sure he kept his appointments, and scolded him if he forgot to put his boots on when going out of doors. Without disrespect to either, one could say that he had found his mother-figure, although there seemed a certain amount of aggravation in the air between them."

Peter was dressed for the interview in a "navy blue track suit with various bits of string attached." As for the house, Waugh writes, "The main floor was like an open-plan bungalow, with sitting room, kitchen, and dining areas, and another area where Mike Jeffery slept, his bed surrounded by impressive photographic equipment." Peter slept on the floor below. In the basement was a bomb shelter, which came with the house.

At Waugh's prompting, Peter named the four films of which he was proudest: *I'm All Right, Jack*; *Dr. Strangelove*; *The Party*; and *Being There*. Waugh noted that, for Peter, Spike "remained—usually by telephone, and often at very long distance—the chief guru in his life." The other, of course, was Swami Venkesananda, who kept an ashram in Mauritius. But Waugh was skeptical of Peter's devotion to the swami: "I could not avoid the suspicion that part of his fascination is that Mr. Sellers could study his accents, his intonations and gestures, and practice them quietly to himself in the bathroom afterwards."

• • •

On Monday, July 21, Peter and Michael Jeffery flew to London from Geneva in Peter's private plane. They landed at Stansted Airport in Essex (Peter preferred to avoid Heathrow), drove down to London, and checked into the Dorchester. He wanted to stay in the Harlequin Suite, but it was already booked, so he made do with the Oliver Messel suite, named for—and designed by—the noted theater designer. In addition to his clothes, he made sure to bring along the script-in-progress for *The Romance of the Pink Panther*.

Peter had spoken to Spike before arriving in London, and Spike, rather morbidly, had told him, " 'We're all getting old. How about one more dinner?' 'Yes, of course!' he said. 'One more dinner.' " Harry Secombe got "a message from Spike saying 'Let's go and have dinner with Peter before one of us is walking behind the coffin.' " The three old friends set up their reunion for the following night.

Before turning in, Peter, accompanied by Jeffery, climbed into a limousine, drove to North London, and paid his first visit to the Golders Green crematorium and memorial garden where Peg and Bill's ashes lay.

He woke up early the next morning, showered and shaved, put on his loose blue workout suit, ordered some coffee and melba toast, called Michael Jeffery's room, ordered a massage, and then called Sue Evans, who arrived around 9 A.M. Peter took a nap while Evans and Jeffery went over the day's affairs. His lawyer, Elwood Rickless, showed up and got Peter to sign a document setting up the long-delayed trust for the fifteen-year-old Victoria, and then it was time for lunch. Peter asked for a double order of grilled plaice, a salad, and a little cheese; he requested the double order of plaice because he was convinced that the Dorchester was stingy with its fish. After finishing his meal, Jeffery helped Peter select his outfit for the evening—black, black, and black (pants, shirt, lizardskin shoes)—topped with a black and white check jacket. Sue Evans got ready to leave. "Sue, don't go yet," he asked. "Sit on for a bit and talk to me."

Then, "I do feel frail. Really, I feel faint," he said, and before he got a chance to get back into bed, his face turned deep purple and then very pale, he closed his eyes, and he died.

• • •

"It's hard to say this, but he died at the right time," said Spike.

"Anything to avoid paying for the dinner," said Harry.

• • •

To be pedantic about it, Peter's clinical death was actually a more protracted process. He was rushed to Middlesex Hospital and hooked up to machines that kept him going for another thirty-six hours. Sue Evans called Michael, who was in London. Sarah was in Portugal. Victoria was in Sweden with her mother. They all had time to assemble at the hospital before the Widow Sellers arrived in dark glasses, fresh from the Western Hemisphere.

Peter's body didn't give up easily, but this time it had no choice. A little after midnight on July 24, it was over.

• • •

"Peter was a well-loved actor in Britain," Burt Kwouk observes. "The day he died, it seemed that the whole country came to a stop. Everywhere you went, the fact that Peter had died seemed like an umbrella over everything."

The headlines screamed, the newscasters intoned. And in a bit of irony both gruesome and cruel, thieves stole Lynne's crocodile handbag and matching wallet—they were gifts from Peter, she said—while she was shopping for a black dress the next day.

• • •

Peter's funeral was held at Golders Green on Saturday, July 26.

Anne was in Portugal with Ted Levy when Peter died. She didn't return to London, she says, "because I knew it would be a circus."

She was correct. The surge of fans, reporters, photographers, and morbid sightseers was magnificent in the pouring rain.

Britt made a discreet entrance in a blue Rolls Royce. Miranda, after placing a sympathy telephone call to Lynne (a call answered by Sue Evans) stayed away.

Peter's aunties, Ve and Do, were there, along with Spike, Harry, Michael Bentine, his cousins Ray Marks and Peter Ray, Canon John Hester, Lord Snowdon, Brother Cornelius, Dennis Selinger, Graham Stark, David Lodge, and Baron Evelyn de Rothschild.

• • •

As one of the Ray cousins said of the funeral, the wives were crying and the Goons were laughing. This was especially the case after Canon Hester, at Michael's suggestion, made an announcement at the end. Just before Peter's body was wheeled away to the furnace room to be turned into ash, Canon Hester solemnly told the assembled mourners that Peter wanted them to listen to one last song.

And so it was that Peter Sellers exited the world, riding in swingtime into the flames, to the tune of Glenn Miller's "In the Mood."

Ever drifting down the stream—
Lingering in the golden gleam—
Life, what is it but a dream?

A memorial service for Peter Sellers took place at St. Martin in the Fields on September 8, 1980. It would have been Peter's fifty-fifth birthday.

In addition to Lynne, Michael, Sarah, Victoria, Spike, Harry, David Lodge, Graham Stark, and Michael Bentine, guests included Lord Snowdon, David Niven, Michael Caine, Sam Spiegel, Herbert Lom, and about 490 less famous people.

Snowdon recited the twenty-third Psalm. Harry sang "Bread of Heaven." Niven offered the eulogy. "It was a joy and a privilege to have known him for so long," Niven said. "Yet how many of us really did know Peter? After twenty-five years of friendship, I had to ask myself." Niven noted with candor that some of Peter's many obituaries described him as having been "difficult, ungracious, despotic, bitter, depressed, lonely, in a constant state of turmoil, vexatious, quarrelsome, and neurotic." Niven acknowledged that, well, yes, Peter had been some of those things at least some of the time. But, he went on to say, "luckily he was not all these things all of the time, because if he had been, St. Martin's and the surrounding fields would be empty this morning instead of full."

According to the terms of Peter Sellers's last will and testament, 50,000 Swiss francs was to go to the city of Gstaad, £5,000 to his lawyer Anthony Humphries, £5,000 to his accountant Douglas Quick, and $2,000 each to Michael, Sarah, and Victoria Sellers. The rest of Peter's estate would proceed to Lynne Frederick.

Thanks to his tax lawyers and accountants, Peter's British estate was virtually worthless. His foreign estate hovered in the neighborhood of $9.6 million.

On behalf of Michael, Sarah, and Victoria, Spike Milligan appealed personally to Lynne's sense of decency, but since she had none, she had none of Spike's appeal, so Peter's children were forced to contest his will in court, where they eventually lost. Lynne's point was simple: "Why can't they leave his memory alone?"

Six months after Peter's death, Lynne Frederick married David Frost. Then she divorced Frost and married a cardiologist. She got all the money.

"It all went up her nose," Anne Levy once said with uncharacteristic spite, not to mention exaggeration. Anne was referring to the fact that Lynne developed severe addictions to drugs and alcohol and died in 1994 at the age of thirty-nine. Yes, there was a lot of cocaine in the later years of Lynne Frederick. But there was even more money.

Lynne's mother, Iris, found the body. It was taken to the Los Angeles County Morgue, where it became Case Number 94-3840 and was tagged with a note reading, "history of alcohol and seizures."

Then Iris got the money.

Iris Frederick lives in a lovely home in Cheviot Hills, California. She controls all access to Peter Sellers's papers and personal effects, she has trademarked his name, and she is currently developing his property in the Seychelles as a high-end resort.

When Iris dies, Peter Sellers's fortune will all go to a girl named Cassie, the daughter Lynne had with the cardiologist.

• • •

Michael Sellers went on to write a book about his father, *P.S. I Love You*. He also coedited *Sellers on Sellers*, a collection of reminiscences, and *Hard Act to Follow*, in which he and some other sons and daughters of celebrities chronicle their wholly justified difficulties in being famous people's offspring.

Victoria Sellers turned up in the news in the spring of 1986 when she appeared nude in *Playboy*. The glossy magazine spread reveals her recreating famous moments from classic films: a bare-breasted "Ingrid Bergman" in white silk panties and high heels at the end of *Casablanca* (1942); "Elizabeth Taylor" in *Cleopatra* (1960), clad in a snake; and "Sophia Loren" in *Yesterday, Today, and Tomorrow* (1963) with her bush exposed.

Victoria was also indicted that spring for her role in a cocaine-trafficking gang. The ringleader was her agent. Facing twenty years in jail, she agreed to testify for the government and was placed on three years' probation. In the early 1990s, she and her friend and housemate, Heidi Fleiss, found employment as high-priced prostitutes; the so-called "Hollywood madam" scandal broke in 1993.

The following year, Victoria was questioned about a series of armed robberies committed by her boyfriend.

Sex Tips with Heidi Fleiss and Victoria Sellers was released on DVD in time for Christmas 2001.

Sarah Sellers lives quietly in North London.

Anne Levy lives near her daughter.

After "Bino" Cicogna committed suicide, Britt Ekland continued to live a life of glamour and glory with such short- and long-term mates as Warren Beatty, Rod Stewart, George Hamilton, and the record producer Lou Adler, with whom she had a son.

Liza Minnelli went on to achieve some great performances (*New York, New York,* 1977, and *Arthur,* 1981) and equally well-publicized addictions.

Titi Wachtmeister moved on from Peter Sellers to King Carl Gustaf of Sweden. She returned to the public eye in the late 1980s when she launched a line of expensive T-shirts called "T-T's T's." She died of a brain hemorrhage in 1993.

Sinead Cusack married Jeremy Irons in 1978; the couple has two sons.

In 2000, Sophia Loren wrote a loving tribute to Peter Sellers for a British awards ceremony. She was, she wrote, "amused and permanently entertained by his wit and his vivid intelligence. After him nobody else has reached his level and his originality. I will always remember him with love and endless regrets."

Miranda Quarry is now Lady Nuttall.

• • •

Blake Edwards attempted to assume control of *The Romance of the Pink Panther* after Peter's death and offered the role of Inspector Clouseau to Dudley Moore, who turned it down.

Edwards then compiled a selection of outtakes from previous *Pink Panther* films, released it as *The Trail of the Pink Panther* (1982), and was promptly sued by Lynne Frederick, who claimed that the film insulted the memory of her dear husband. A British court ordered the various producers of *The Trail of the Pink Panther*—Edwards, United Artists, and Lakeline

Productions, which was owned by Julie Andrews—to pay $1 million in damages, 3.15 percent of the film's profits, and 1.36 percent of its gross receipts.

Edwards's more successful films after Peter's death include *S.O.B.* (1981) and *Victor/Victoria* (1982), which he and Julie Andrews later turned into a smash Broadway musical. Edwards has recently rewritten *A Shot in the Dark* as a Broadway play and *The Pink Panther* as a Broadway musical.

• • •

In Hollywood, a cinematic remake—or postmillennial rethinking—of *The Pink Panther* is in development for Mike Myers, who claims that his father used to provide him with comedy lessons that took the form of Mr. Myers waking up young Mike in the middle of the night and making him watch Peter Sellers's films on TV.

Peter Sellers's roles in *Lovesick* (1983) and *Unfaithfully Yours* (1984) were taken by Dudley Moore. The rest of Peter's projects died with him.

David Lodge, Kenneth Griffith, and Graham Stark live in or around London. Roman Polanski lives in exile in Paris. Terry Southern died in 1995, Stanley Kubrick in 1999. Hal Ashby died in 1988. Michael Bentine died in 1996. Sir Harry Secombe and George Harrison died in 2001.

Spike Milligan died in February 2002.

New York
March 2002

Penny Points to Paradise (1951). Harry Secombe (Harry Flakers), Alfred Marks (Edward Haynes), Peter Sellers (The Major, Arnold Fringe), Spike Milligan (Spike Donnelly), Paddy O'Neil (Christine Russell). Director: Tony Young; screenwriter: John Ormonde. Advance and Adelphi Films, 77 minutes.

Let's Go Crazy (1951). Peter Sellers (Groucho, Giuseppe, Crystal Jollibottom, Cedric, and Izzy Gozunk), with Manley and Austin, Keith Warwick, Jean Cavall, Pat Kaye and Betty Ankers, Maxim & Johnson, and Freddie Mirfield and his Garbage Men. Director: Alan Cullimore. Adelphi Films, 33 minutes.

Down Among the Z Men (1952). Harry Secombe (Harry Jones), Carole Carr (Carole Gayley), Peter Sellers (Colonel Bloodnok), Michael Bentine (Prof. Osric Pureheart), Spike Milligan (Private Eccles). Director: Maclean Rogers; screenwriters: Jimmy Grafton and Francis Charles; producer: E. J. Fancey; director of photography: Geoffrey Faithfull. E. J. Fancey Productions, 82 minutes.

The Super Secret Service (1953). Peter Sellers, Graham Stark, Dick Emery, Bryan Johnson, Raymond Francis, Anne Hayes, Dickie Martyn, Frank Hawkins, and the Ray Ellington Quartet. Director: Charles W. Green; screenwriters: Spike Milligan and Larry Stephens; producer: John H. Robertson. New Realm, 24 minutes.

Beat the Devil (1953). Humphrey Bogart (Billy Dannreuther), Jennifer Jones (Gwendolen Chelm), Gina Lollobrigida (Maria Dannreuther), Robert Morley (Petersen), Peter Lorre (O'Hara), Peter Sellers (uncredited voices, including that of Humphrey Bogart). Director: John Huston; screenwriters: Truman Capote and John Huston; director of photography: Oswald Morris; producer: John Huston. Romulus/United Artists, 100 minutes.

Orders Are Orders (1954). Margot Grahame (Wanda Sinclair), Maureen Swanson (Joanne Delamere), Brian Reece (Captain Harper), Raymond Huntley (Colonel Bellamy), Sid James (Ed Waggermeyer), Tony Hancock (Lt. Wilfred Cartroad), Peter Sellers (Private Goffin), Eric Sykes (Private Waterhouse), Donald Pleasence (Corporal Martin). Director: David Paltenghi; screenwriters: Geoffrey Orme and Eric Sykes, based on the play by Ian Hay and Anthony Armstrong;

producer: Donald Taylor; director of photography: Arthur Grant. Group 3/ British Lion, 78 minutes.

Our Girl Friday (1954). Joan Collins (Sadie Patch), George Cole (Jimmy Carroll), Kenneth More (Pat Plunkett), Robertson Hare (Professor Gibble), Hermione Gingold (spinster), Peter Sellers (voice of cockatoo, uncredited). Director: Noel Langley; screenwriter: Noel Langley; producers: George Minter and Noel Langley. Renown Pictures, 87 minutes. Released in Britain as *The Adventures of Sadie*.

Malaga (1954). Maureen O'Hara (Joanna Dane), Macdonald Carey (Van Logan), Binnie Barnes (Frisco), Guy Middleton (Soames Howard), and Peter Sellers (multiple voices, uncredited). Director: Richard Sale; screenwriter: Robert Westerby; director of photography: Christopher Challis; producers: Colin Lesslie and Mike Frankovich. Columbia Pictures, 84 minutes. Released in the U.S. as *Fire Over Africa*.

John and Julie (1955). Colin Gibson (John), Lesley Dudley (Julie), Noelle Middleton (Miss Stokes), Moira Lister (Dora), Wilfrid Hyde-White (Sir James), Sidney James (Mr. Pritchett), Megs Jenkins (Mrs. Pritchett), Constance Cummings (Mrs. Davidson), Peter Sellers (Police Constable Diamond). Director: William Fairchild; screenwriter: William Fairchild; director of photography: Arthur Grant; producer, Herbert Mason. British Lion, 82 minutes.

The Ladykillers (1955). Katie Johnson (Mrs. Wilberforce), Alec Guinness (Professor Marcus), Cecil Parker (Major Courtney), Herbert Lom (Louis), Peter Sellers (Harry), Danny Green (One-Round), Jack Warner (police superintendent). Director: Alexander Mackendrick; screenwriter: William Rose; cinematography: Otto Heller; producer: Michael Balcon; associate producer, Seth Holt. Ealing Studios, 97 minutes.

The Case of the Mukkinese Battle Horn (1956). Peter Sellers (Quilt, Sir Jervis Fruit, Henry Crun), Spike Milligan (Brown, White, Minnie, Catchpole Burkington), and Dick Emery (Watchman, Nodule, Such, Ponk), with Pamela Thomas, Wally Thomas, Bill Hepper, and Gordon Phillott. Director: Joseph Sterling; screenwriters: Harry Booth, Jon Penington, and Larry Stephens, from a story by Larry Stephens, with additional material by Spike Milligan and Peter Sellers; director of photography: Gerald Gibbs; producers: Jon Pennington, Harry Booth, and Michael Deeley. Marlborough Pictures, 27 minutes.

The Man Who Never Was (1956). Clifton Webb (Lt. Comm. Ewen Montagu), Gloria Grahame (Lucy Sherwood), Peter Sellers (voice of Winston Churchill, uncredited). Director: Ronald Neame; screenwriter: Nigel Balchin, based on the book by Ewen Montagu; director of photography: Oswald Morris; producer: André Hakim. Twentieth Century-Fox/Sumar Film, 103 minutes.

Dearth of a Salesman (1957). Peter Sellers (Hector Dimwittie). Director: Leslie Arliss. A.B.-Pathé, 28 minutes.

Insomnia Is Good for You (1957). Peter Sellers (Hector Dimwittie). Director: Leslie Arliss; screenwriters: Lewis Greifer, Mordecai Richler; director of photography: J. Burgoyne-Johnson. A.B.-Pathé, 26 minutes.

The Smallest Show on Earth (1957). Virginia McKenna (Jean), Bill Travers (Matt), Margaret Rutherford (Mrs. Fazackalee), Peter Sellers (Percy Quill), Bernard Miles (Old Tom), Francis De Wolff (Hardcastle). Director: Basil Dearden; screenwriter: John Eldridge and William Rose; director of photography: Douglas Slocombe; producers: Sidney Gilliat, Frank Launder, and Michael Relph. British Lion/Continental, 81 minutes. Originally released in the U.S. as *Big Time Operators*.

The Naked Truth (1957). Terry-Thomas (Lord Henry Mayley), Peter Sellers (Sonny MacGregor), Peggy Mount (Flora Ransom), Shirley Eaton (Melissa Right), Dennis Price (Nigel Dennis), Georgina Cookson (Lady Lucy Mayley), Kenneth Griffith (Porter), David Lodge (Constable Johnson). Director: Mario Zampi; screenwriter: Michael Pertwee; director of photography: Stanley Pavey; producer: Mario Zampi. British Film/Rank Organisation, 91 minutes. Originally released in the U.S. as *Your Past Is Showing*.

Up the Creek (1958). David Tomlinson (Lieutenant Fairweather), Peter Sellers (Chief Petty Officer Doherty), Wilfrid Hyde-White (Admiral Foley), Lionel Jeffries (Steady Barker), Lionel Murton (Perkins), Sam Kydd (Bates), John Warren (Cooky), Liliane Sottane (Susanne), and David Lodge (Scouse). Director: Val Guest; screenwiters: Val Guest, John Warren, and Len Heath; director of photography: Arthur Grant; producer: Henry Halsted. Byron/Exclusive, 83 minutes.

tom thumb (1958). Russ Tamblyn (Tom Thumb), Alan Young (Woody), June Thorburn (Forest Queen), Terry-Thomas (Ivan), Peter Sellers (Tony), Bernard Miles (Father), Jessie Matthews (Mother), Peter Bull (the town crier), and the Puppetoons. Director: George Pal; screenwriter: Ladislas Fodor, based on the story by the Brothers Grimm; director of photography: Georges Périnal; producer: George Pal. Galaxy Pictures/MGM, 98 minutes.

Carlton-Browne of the F.O. (1959). Terry-Thomas (Cadogan deVere Carlton-Browne), Peter Sellers (Amphibulos), Luciana Paluzzi (Princess Ilyena), Ian Bannen (young king), Thorley Walters (Colonel Bellingham), Miles Malleson (resident advisor), Raymond Huntley (foreign secretary), John Le Mesurier (Grand Duke Alexis), and Irene Handl (Mrs. Carter). Directors: Jeffrey Dell and Roy Boulting; screenwriters: Jeffrey Dell and Roy Boulting; director of photography: Max Greene; producer: John Boulting. British Lion/Charter Films, 88 minutes. Released in the U.S. as *Man in a Cocked Hat*.

The Running Jumping & Standing Still Film (1959). Peter Sellers (photographer), Dick Lester (painter), Spike Milligan (record player, etc.), and Graham

Stark (kite master), with Audrey Stark, Mario Fabrizi, Leo McKern, and David Lodge. Director: Dick Lester; "Thoughts by Spike Milligan, Peter Sellers, Mario Fabrizi, and Dick Lester; devised by Peter Sellers." 11 minutes.

The Mouse That Roared (1959). Peter Sellers (Tully Bascombe, Grand Duchess Gloriana XII, and the Prime Minister, Count Mountjoy), Jean Seberg (Helen Kokintz), William Hartnell (Will), David Kossoff (Professor Kokintz), Austin Willis (U.S. Secretary of Defense), Leo McKern (Benter), and Jacques Cey (ticket collector). Director: Jack Arnold; screenwriters: Roger MacDougall and Stanley Mann, based on the novel by Leonard Wibberley; director of photography: John Wilcox; producer: Walter Shenson. Highroad/Columbia Pictures, 83 minutes.

I'm All Right, Jack (1959). Ian Carmichael (Stanley Windrush), Terry-Thomas (Major Hitchcock), Peter Sellers (Fred Kite, Sir John Kennaway), Richard Attenborough (Sidney De Vere Cox), Margaret Rutherford (Aunt Dolly), Dennis Price (Bertram Tracepurcel), Irene Handl (Mrs. Kite), Miles Malleson (Windrush, Sr.), Liz Fraser (Cynthia Kite), Marne Maitland (Mr. Mohammed), John Le Mesurier (Waters), Raymond Huntley (Magistrate), Victor Maddern (Knowles), Kenneth Griffith (Dai), David Lodge (card player), and Malcolm Muggeridge (himself). Director: John Boulting; screenwriters: John Boulting, Frank Harvey, and Alan Hackney, based on a novel by Alan Hackney; director of photography: Mutz Greenbaum; producer: Roy Boulting. British Lion, 101 minutes.

The Battle of the Sexes (1959). Peter Sellers (Mr. Martin), Robert Morley (Robert MacPherson), Constance Cummings (Angela Barrows), Jameson Clark (Andrew Darling), Ernest Thesiger (Old MacPherson), Donald Pleasence (Irwin Hoffman), and Moultrie Kelsall (Graham). Director: Charles Chrichton; screenwriter: Monja Danischewsky, based on "The Catbird Seat" by James Thurber; director of photography: Freddie Francis; producer: Monja Danischewsky. Bryanston/Continental/British Lion, 84 minutes.

Never Let Go (1960). Richard Todd (John Cummings), Peter Sellers (Lionel Meadows), Elizabeth Sellars (Ann Cummings), Adam Faith (Tommy Towers), Carol White (Jackie), Noel Willman (Inspector Thomas), and David Lodge (Cliff). Director: John Guillermin; screenwriter: Alun Falconer, from a story by John Guillermin and Peter de Sarigny; director of photography: Christopher Challis; producer: Peter de Sarigny. Independent Artists/Rank, 90 minutes.

Two-Way Stretch (1960). Peter Sellers (Dodger Lane), David Lodge (Jelly Knight), Bernard Cribbins (Lennie Price), Wilfrid Hyde-White (Soapy Stevens), Maurice Denham (the governor), Lionel Jeffries (Crout), Irene Handl (Mrs. Price), Liz Fraser (Ethel), Beryl Reid (Miss Pringle), Mario Fabrizi (Jones). Director: Robert Day; screenwriters: John Warren and Len Heath, with additional dialogue by Alan Hackney; director of photography: Geoffrey Faith-full; producer: M. Smedley Aston. British Lion, 84 minutes.

The Millionairess (1960). Sophia Loren (Epifania), Peter Sellers (Dr. Kabir), Alas-tair Sim (Sagamore), Vittorio De Sica (Joe), Dennis Price (Adrian), Gary Ray-mond (Alastair), Alfie Bass (fish curer), Miriam Karlin (Mrs. Joe), and Graham Stark (butler). Director: Anthony Asquith; screenwriter: Wolf Mankowitz, based on Riccardo Aragno's adaptation of George Bernard Shaw's play; director of photography: Jack Hildyard; producers: Dimitri de Grunwald and Pierre Rouve. Twentieth Century-Fox, 90 minutes.

Mr. Topaze (1961). Peter Sellers (Auguste Topaze), Herbert Lom (Castel Benac), Nadia Gray (Suzy), Leo McKern (Muche), Marita Hunt (baroness), John Ne-ville (Roger), Billie Whitelaw (Ernestine), and Michael Sellers (Gaston). Direc-tor: Peter Sellers; screenwriter: Pierre Rouve, based on the play *Topaze* by Marcel Pagnol; director of photography: John Wilcox; producers: Dimitri de Grunwald and Pierre Rouve. Twentieth Century-Fox, 97 minutes. Released in the U.S. as *I Like Money.*

Only Two Can Play (1962). Peter Sellers (John Lewis), Mai Zetterling (Eliza-beth Gruffydd Williams), Virginia Maskell (Jean), Kenneth Griffith (Jen-kins), Richard Attenborough (Probert), Raymond Huntley (Vernon Gruffydd Williams), Maudie Edwards (Mrs. Davies), John Le Mesurier (Salter), and Graham Stark (Hyman). Director: Sidney Gilliat; screenwriter: Bryan Forbes, based on Kingsley Amis's novel *That Uncertain Feeling*; director of photogra-phy: John Wilcox; producer: Leslie Gilliat. British Lion/Vale/Kingsley/Co-lumbia, 106 minutes.

The Road to Hong Kong (1962). Bing Crosby (Harry Turner), Bob Hope (Ches-ter Babcock), Joan Collins (Diane), Robert Morley (spy leader), Dorothy La-mour (herself), and Peter Sellers (Indian neurologist, uncredited). Director: Norman Panama; screenwriters: Norman Panama and Melvin Frank; director of photography: Jack Hildyard; producer: Melvin Frank. Melnor Films/United Artists, 92 minutes.

Lolita (1962). James Mason (Humbert Humbert), Shelley Winters (Charlotte Haze), Peter Sellers (Claire Quilty), Sue Lyon (Lolita), Gary Cockrell (Richard Schiller), Jerry Stovin (John Farlow), Diana Decker (Jean Farlow), and Mar-ianne Stone (Vivian Darkbloom). Director: Stanley Kubrick; screenwriters: Vla-dimir Nabokov, based on his novel, and James B. Harris (uncredited); director of photography: Oswald Morris; producer: James B. Harris. Seven Arts/MGM, 152 minutes.

Waltz of the Toreadors (1962). Peter Sellers (Gen. Leo Fitzjohn), Dany Robin (Ghislaine), Margaret Leighton (Emily Fitzjohn), John Fraser (Lt. Robert Finch), Cyril Cusack (Dr. Grogan), Prunella Scales (Estella Fitzjohn), Denise Coffey (Sidonia), Raymond Huntley (Ackroyd), John Le Mesurier (Rev. Grimsley). Director: John Guillermin; screenwriter: Wolf Mankowitz, based on the play by Jean Anouilh; director of photography: John Wilcox; producer: Peter de Sarigny. Rank Organization, 104 minutes. Released in the U.K. as *The Amorous General.*

The Wrong Arm of the Law (1962). Peter Sellers (Pearly Gates), Lionel Jeffries (Inspector Parker), Bernard Cribbins (Nervous O'Toole), Davy Kaye (Trainer King), Nanette Newman (Valerie), Bill Kerr (Jack Coombes), Ed Devereaux (Bluey May), Reg Lye (Reg Denton), John Le Mesurier (assistant commissioner), Graham Stark (Sid Cooper), Michael Caine (uncredited), and Mario Fabrizi (uncredited). Director: Cliff Owen; screenwriters: Len Heath and John Warren, with additional dialogue by John Antrobus, Ray Galton, and Alan Simpson, from a story by Ivor Jay and William Whistance Smith; director of photography: Ernest Steward; producers: Aubrey Baring, Cecil F. Ford, E. M. Smedley-Aston, and Robert Velaise. Romulus/British Lion/Continental, 94 minutes.

The Dock Brief (1962). Peter Sellers (Wilfred Morgenhall), Richard Attenborough (Herbert Fowle), Beryl Reid (Doris Fowle), David Lodge (Frank Bateson), Frank Pettingell (Tuppy Morgan), Audrey Nicholson (young Morgenhall's girlfriend), Tristram Jellinek (Mr. Perkins), Eric Woodburn (Judge Banter). Director: James Hill; screenwriter: Pierre Rouve, based on the play by John Mortimer; cinematography: Edward Scaife; producer: Dimitri De Grunwald. MGM, 78 minutes. Released in the U.S. as *Trial and Error.*

Heavens Above! (1963). Peter Sellers (The Rev. John Smallwood), Cecil Parker (Archdeacon Aspinall), Isabel Jeans (Lady Despard), Ian Carmichael (the other Smallwood), Bernard Miles (Simpson), Brock Peters (Matthew Robinson), Eric Sykes (Harry Smith), Irene Handl (Rene Smith), Kenneth Griffith (Rev. Owen Smith), and Geoffrey Hibbert (council official). Directors: John Boulting and Roy Boulting; screenwriters: John Boulting and Frank Harvey; cinematography: Mutz Greenbaum; producers: John Boulting and Roy Boulting. Charter Films, 105 minutes.

The Pink Panther (1964). David Niven (Sir Charles Litton), Peter Sellers (Inspector Jacques Clouseau), Robert Wagner (George Litton), Capucine (Simone Clouseau), Brenda De Banzie (Angela Dunning), Colin Gordon (Tucker), John Le Mesurier (defense attorney), James Lanphier (Saloud), Guy Thomajan (Artoff), Michael Trubshawe (novelist), Riccardo Billi (Greek shipowner), Meri Wells (Hollywood starlet), Martin Miller (photographer), Fran Jeffries (Greek "cousin"), and Claudia Cardinale (Princess Darla). Director: Blake Edwards; screenwriters: Maurice Richlin and Blake Edwards; director of photography: Philip Lathrop; producer: Martin Jurow. Mirisch Company/United Artists, 113 minutes.

Dr. Strangelove or: How I Learned to Stop Worrying and Love the Bomb (1964). Peter Sellers (Group Capt. Lionel Mandrake, President Merkin Muffley, Dr. Strangelove), George C. Scott (Gen. "Buck" Turgidson), Sterling Hayden (Gen. Jack D. Ripper), Keenan Wynn (Col. "Bat" Guano), Slim Pickens (Maj. T. J. "King" Kong), Peter Bull (Ambassador Alexi de Sadesky), Tracy Reed (Miss Scott), James Earl Jones (Lt. Lothar Zogg), Jack Creley (Mr. Staines), Frank Berry (Lt. H. R. Dietrich). Director: Stanley Kubrick; screenwriters: Stanley Kubrick, Terry Southern, and Peter George, based on the novel *Red Alert* by Peter George; director of photography: Gilbert Taylor; producer: Stanley Kubrick. Hawk Films/Columbia, 90 minutes.

A Shot in the Dark (1964). Peter Sellers (Inspector Jacques Clouseau), Elke Sommer (Maria Gambrelli), George Sanders (Benjamin Ballon), Herbert Lom (Charles Dreyfus), Tracy Reed (Dominique Ballon), Graham Stark (Hercule Lajoy), Moira Redmond (Simone), Vanda Godsell (Madame LaFarge), Maurice Kaufmann (Pierre), Ann Lynn (Dudu), David Lodge (Georges), André Maranne (Franois), Martin Benson (Maurice), Burt Kwouk (Kato), Reginald Beckwith (camp receptionist), Douglas Wilmer (Henri LaFarge), and Bryan Forbes (Turk). Director: Blake Edwards; screenwriters: Blake Edwards and William Peter Blatty, based on the stage play by Harry Kurnitz from the play by Marcel Achard; director of photography: Christopher Challis; producer: Blake Edwards. Mirisch Company/United Artists, 102 minutes.

The World of Henry Orient (1964). Peter Sellers (Henry Orient), Paula Prentiss (Stella), Angela Lansbury (Isabel Boyd), Tom Bosley (Frank Boyd), Phyllis Thaxter (Mrs. Avis Gilbert), Bibi Osterwald (Boothy Booth), Merrie Spaeth (Gil Gilbert), Tippy Walker (Val Boyd), John Fiedler (Sidney), Al Lewis (store owner), Peter Duchin (Joe Byrd). Director: George Roy Hill; screenwriter: Nora Johnson and Nunnally Johnson, based on the novel by Nora Johnson; directors of photography: Boris Kaufman and Arthur J. Ornitz; producer: Jerome Hellman. Pan Arts/United Artists, 106 minutes.

Carol for Another Christmas (1964). Sterling Hayden (Grudge), Peter Fonda (Morley), Ben Gazzara (Fred), Richard Harris (ghost of Christmas present), Steve Lawrence (ghost of Christmas past), Eva Marie Saint (Wave), and Peter Sellers (King of the Individualists), with Britt Ekland and Robert Shaw. Director: Joseph L. Mankiewicz; screenplay, Rod Serling, based on the novel *A Christmas Carol* by Charles Dickens; director of photography: Arthur Ornitz; producer: Joseph L. Mankiewicz. Xerox Corporation/Telsun Foundation, Inc., for the United Nations/American Broadcasting Co. Aired on December 28, 1964.

What's New, Pussycat? (1965) Peter Sellers (Dr. Fritz Fassbender), Peter O'Toole (Michael James), Romy Schneider (Carole), Capucine (Renée), Paula Prentiss

(Liz), Woody Allen (Victor), Ursula Andress (Rita), and Edra Gale (Anna Fass-bender). Director: Clive Donner; screenwriter: Woody Allen; director of photography: Jean Badal; producer: Charles K. Feldman. Famous Artists/United Artists, 108 minutes.

After the Fox (1966). Peter Sellers (Aldo Vanucci), Britt Ekland (Gina), Lidia Brazzi (Teresa Vanucci), Paolo Stoppa (Pollo), Tino Buazzelli (Siepe), Mac Ronay (Carlo), Victor Mature (Tony Powell), Martin Balsam (Harry), and Akim Tamiroff (Okra). Director: Vittorio De Sica; screenwriter: Neil Simon; director of photography: Leonida Barboni; producer: John Bryan. Delegate Productions/Nancy Enterprises/Compagnia Cinematografica Montoro/United Artists, 102 minutes.

The Wrong Box (1966). John Mills (Masterman Finsbury), Ralph Richardson (Joseph Finsbury), Michael Caine (Michael Finsbury), Peter Cook (Morris Finsbury), Dudley Moore (John Finsbury), Nanette Newman (Julia Finsbury), and Peter Sellers (Dr. Pratt). Director: Bryan Forbes; screenwriters: Larry Gelbart and Burt Shevelove, based on the novel by Robert Louis Stevenson and Lloyd Osbourne; director of photography: Gerry Turpin; producer: Bryan Forbes. Columbia Pictures, 105 minutes.

Casino Royale (1967). Peter Sellers (Evelyn Tremble), Ursula Andress (Vesper), David Niven (James Bond), Orson Welles (Le Chiffre), Joanna Pettet (Mata Bond), Daliah Lavi (the Detainer), Woody Allen (Jimmy Bond), Deborah Kerr (Mimi), William Holden (Ransome), Charles Boyer (Legrand), John Huston (McTarry), Jean-Paul Belmondo (Legionnaire), Jacqueline Bisset (Miss Good-thighs), and George Raft (himself). Directors: John Huston, Kenneth Hughes, Val Guest, Robert Parrish, and Joseph McGrath; screenwriters: Wolf Mankow-itz, John Law, and Michael Sayers; directors of photography: Jack Hildyard, John Wilcox, and Nicholas Roeg; producers: Charles K. Feldman and Jerry Bresler. Famous Artists/Columbia Pictures, 131 minutes.

Alice in Wonderland (1967). Anne-Marie Mallik (Alice), Wilfrid Brambell (White Rabbit), Alan Bennett (Mouse), Michael Redgrave (Caterpillar), Leo McKern (Duchess), Peter Cook (Mad Hatter), Peter Sellers (King of Hearts), Alison Leggett (Queen of Hearts), Peter Eyre (Knave of Hearts), John Giel-gud (Mock Turtle), and Malcolm Muggeridge (Gryphon). Director: Jonathan Miller; screenwriter: Jonathan Miller, based on the novel by Lewis Carroll; director of photography: Dick Bush; producer: Jonathan Miller. BBC-TV, 80 minutes.

Woman Times Seven (1967). Shirley MacLaine (Paulette, Maria Teresa, Linda, Edith, Eve Minou, Marie, Jeanne), Peter Sellers (Jean), Alan Arkin (Fred), Lex Barker (Rik), Rossano Brazzi (Giorgio), Michael Caine (handsome stranger), Vittorio Gassman (Cenci), and Robert Morley (Dr. Xavier). Director: Vittorio

De Sica; screenwriters: Peter Baldwin and Cesare Zavattini; director of photography: Christian Matras; producer: Arthur Cohn. Embassy Pictures, 100 minutes.

The Bobo (1967). Peter Sellers (Juan Bautista), Britt Ekland (Olimpia), Rossano Brazzi (Carlos Matabosch), Adolfo Celi (Carbonell), Hattie Jacques (Trinity), Ferdy Mayne (Flores), and Kenneth Griffith (Pepe). Director: Robert Parrish; screenwriter: David R. Schwartz, based on his play *The Bobo* and the novel *Olimpia* by Burt Cole; director of photography: Gerry Turpin; producers: Elliott Kastner and Jerry Gershwin. Warner Bros., 103 minutes.

The Party (1968). Peter Sellers (Hrundi V. Bakshi), Claudine Longet (Michele Monet), Marge Champion (Rosalind Dunphy), Stephen Liss (Geoffrey Clutterbuck), Gavin McLeod (C. S. Divot), Fay McKenzie (Alice Clutterbuck), Denny Miller ("Wyoming Bill" Kelso), and Steve Franken (Levinson the waiter). Director: Blake Edwards; screenwriters: Blake Edwards, Tom Waldman, and Frank Waldman; director of photography: Lucien Ballard; producer: Blake Edwards. Mirisch Corporation/United Artists, 99 minutes.

I Love You, Alice B. Toklas! (1968). Peter Sellers (Harold Fine), Jo Van Fleet (Mrs. Fine), Leigh Taylor-Young (Nancy), Joyce Van Patten (Joyce), Salem Ludwig (Mr. Fine), David Arkin (Herbie Fine), Herb Edelman (Murray), Grady Sutton (funeral director), and Louis Gottlieb (guru). Director: Hy Averback; screenwriters: Paul Mazursky and Larry Tucker; director of photography: Philip Lathrop; producer: Charles Maguire. Warner Bros., 92 minutes.

The Magic Christian (1969). Peter Sellers (Sir Guy Grand), Ringo Starr (Youngman Grand), Isabel Jeans (Dame Agnes Grand), Caroline Blakiston (the Hon. Esther Grand), Wilfrid Hyde-White (ship's captain), Richard Attenborough (Oxford coach), Leonard Frey (Laurence Faggot), Laurence Harvey (Hamlet), Christopher Lee (ship's vampire), Spike Milligan (traffic warden), Roman Polanski (solitary drinker), Raquel Welch (Priestess of the Whip), and John Cleese (Sotheby's director), with David Lodge and Graham Stark. Director: Joseph McGrath; screenwriters: Terry Southern and Joseph McGrath, from the novel by Terry Southern, with additional material by Graham Chapman, John Cleese, and Peter Sellers; director of photography: Geoffrey Unsworth; producer: Denis O'Dell. Grand Films, Ltd./Commonwealth United, 101 minutes.

Hoffman (1970). Peter Sellers (Benjamin Hoffman), Sinéad Cusack (Janet Smith), Jeremy Bulloch (Tom Mitchell), Ruth Dunning (Mrs. Mitchell), and David Lodge (foreman). Director: Alvin Rakoff; screenwriter: Ernest Gébler, based on his novel; director of photography: Gerry Turpin; producer: Ben Arbeid. Longstone/Associated British Films, 113 minutes.

Simon, Simon (1970). Graham Stark, John Junkin, Peter Sellers, Julia Foster,

Norman Rossington, Paul Whitsun-Jones, Audrey Nicholson, Kenneth Earle, Tommy Godfrey, Tony Blackburn, Michael Caine, David Hemmings, Bob Monkhouse, Eric Morecambe, Peter Murray, Bernie Winters, and Ernie Wise. Director: Graham Stark; screenwriter: Graham Stark; directors of photography: Harvey Harrison and Derek Vanlint; producer: Graham Stark. Hemdale, 30 minutes.

A Day at the Beach (1970). Mark Burns (Bernie), Beatrice Edney (Winnie), Peter Sellers (trinket shop owner), Graham Stark (Pipi), Fiona Lewis (Melissa), Maurice Roeves (poet), Jack Macgowran (beach attendant), Joanna Dunham (poet's wife), Eva Dahlbeck (café owner), Tom Heathcote (man from Ghana), Bertil Lauring (Louis), and Jorgen Kiil (Carl). Director: Simon Hessera; screenwriter: Roman Polanski, based on a novel by Heere Heeresma, translated by James Brockway; director of photography: Gil Taylor; producer: Gene Gutowski. Paramount Pictures, 90 minutes.

There's a Girl in My Soup (1970). Peter Sellers (Robert Danvers), Goldie Hawn (Marion), Tony Britton (Andrew), Francoise Pascal (Paola), Nicky Henson (Jimmy), John Comer (John), Diana Dors (John's wife), and Nicola Pagett (bride). Director: Roy Boulting; screenwriter: Terence Frisby, based on his stage play, with additional dialogue by Peter Kortner; director of photography: Harry Waxman; producers: M. J. Frankovich and John Boulting. Columbia Pictures, 96 minutes.

Alice's Adventures in Wonderland (1972). Fiona Fullerton (Alice), Peter Sellers (the March Hare), Michael Crawford (the White Rabbit), Ralph Richardson (the Caterpillar), Flora Robson (the Queen of Hearts), Robert Helpmann (the Mad Hatter), Dudley Moore (Dormouse), Spike Milligan (Gryphon), Peter Bull (the Duchess), and Michael Jayston (Lewis Carroll). Director: William Sterling; screenwriter: William Sterling, based on the novel by Lewis Carroll; director of photography: Geoffrey Unsworth; producer: Derek Horne. Wham! USA/JEF Films, 97 minutes.

Where Does It Hurt? (1972). Peter Sellers (Albert T. Hopfnagel), Jo Ann Pflug (Alice Gilligan), Rick Lenz (Lester Hammond), Harold Gould (Dr. Zerny), Eve Bruce (Lamarr), Pat Morita (Mr. Nishimoto), and Kathleen Freeman (Mrs. Manzini). Director: Rod Amateau; screenwriters: Rod Amateau and Budd Robinson, based on their novel *The Operator*; director of photography: Brick Marquard; producers: Bill Schwartz and Rod Amateau. Hemdale, 84 minutes.

The Blockhouse (1973). Peter Sellers (Rouquet), Charles Aznavour (Visconti), Nicholas Jones (Kromer), Jeremy Kemp (Grabinski), Leon Lissek (Kozhek), Alfred Lynch (Larshen), Pier Oscarsson (Lund), Peter Vaughan (Aufret). Director: Clive Rees; screenwriters: John Gould and Clive Rees, based on the novel by Jean Paul Clebert; producers: Edgar Bronfman Jr. and Antony Rufus Isaacs; director of photography: Keith Goddard. Audley Films, Galactacus, and Hemdale Film Corporation, 88 minutes.

Soft Beds, Hard Battles (1973). Peter Sellers (General Latour, Major Robinson, Herr Schroeder, Hitler, H.R.H. General the Prince Kyoto, M. le Président des Forces Spéciales, narrator), Lila Kedrova (Madame Grenier), Curt Jurgens (General von Grotjahn), Beatrice Romand (Marie-Claude), Rex Stallings (Alan Cassidy), Patricia Burke (Mother Superior), and Rula Lenska (Louise). Director: Roy Boulting; screenwriters: Roy Boulting and Leo Marks; director of photography: Gilbert Taylor; producer: John Boulting. Charter Film Productions/United Artists, 94 minutes.

The Optimists (1973). Peter Sellers (Sam), Donna Mulane (Liz), John Chaffey (Mark), Marjorie Yates (Chrissie Ellis), David Daker (Bob Ellis), and Pat Ashton (Mrs. Bonini). Director: Anthony Simmons; screenwriter: Tudor Gates and Anthony Simmons, based on the novel *The Optimists of Nine Elms* by Anthony Simmons; director of photography: Larry Pizer; producers: Adrian Gaye and Victor Lyndon. Cheetah/Sagittarius/Paramount Pictures, 110 minutes.

Ghost in the Noonday Sun (1973). Peter Sellers (Dick Scratcher), Anthony Franciosa (Pierre), Spike Milligan (Billy Bombay), Peter Boyle (Ras Mohammed), Clive Revill (Bay of Algiers), Richard Willis (Jeremiah), James Villiers (Parsley-Frack), Thomas Baptiste (Abdullah), Griffith Davies (Omar), and David Lodge (Zante). Director: Peter Medak; screenwriter: Evan Jones, with additional dialogue by Spike Milligan, based on the novel by Sid Fleischman; directors of photography: Michael Reed and Larry Pizer (uncredited); producer: Gareth Wigan. World Film Servers/Cavalcade Films, Heron Service Company Production, 90 minutes.

The Great McGonagall (1974). Spike Milligan (William McGonagall), Peter Sellers (Queen Victoria), Julia Foster (Mrs. McGonagall), John Bluthal (Mr. Giles, MacDuff, Herclues Paint, McLain, British soldier, policeman, sheriff, judge), Victor Spinetti (Mr. Stewart, Second-Lieutenant Rotlo, gentleman, revolutionary, cardinal, policeman), and Valentine Dyall (Lord Tennyson, sergeant, doctor, native messenger, policeman, fop). Director: Joseph McGrath; screenwriters: Spike Milligan and Joseph McGrath; director of photography: John Mackey; producer: David Grant. Darlton, 95 minutes.

The Return of the Pink Panther (1974). Peter Sellers (Inspector Jacques Clouseau), Christopher Plummer (Sir Charles Litton), Catherine Schell (Claudine), Herbert Lom (Chief Inspector Dreyfus), Peter Arne (Colonel Sharki), Peter Jeffrey (General Wadafy), Gregoire Aslan (chief of Lugash Police), Burt Kwouk (Cato), David Lodge (Mac), and Graham Stark (Pepi). Director: Blake Edwards;

screenwriters: Frank Waldman and Blake Edwards; director of photography: Geoffrey Unsworth; producer: Blake Edwards. Mirisch Corp./United Artists, 113 minutes.

Murder by Death (1976). Peter Sellers (Sidney Wang), Alec Guinness (Jamesir Bensonmum), Maggie Smith (Dora Charleston), David Niven (Dick Charleston), Eileen Brennan (Tess Skeffington), Truman Capote (Lionel Twain), James Coco (Milo Perrier), Peter Falk (Sam Diamond), Elsa Lanchester (Jessica Marbles), Nancy Walker (Yetta the maid), Estelle Winwood (Miss Withers), James Cromwell (Marcel), and Richard Narita (Willie Wang). Director: Robert Moore; screenwriter: Neil Simon; director of photography: David M. Walsh; producer: Ray Stark. Rastar/Columbia Pictures, 94 minutes.

The Pink Panther Strikes Again (1976). Peter Sellers (Chief Inspector Jacques Clouseau), Herbert Lom (former Chief Inspector Dreyfus), Burt Kwouk (Cato), Leonard Rossiter (Quinlan), Colin Blakely (Drummond), Lesley-Anne Down (Olga), Howard K. Smith (himself), Graham Stark (two hotel clerks), Dick Crockett (the president), Byron Kane (secretary of state), Richard Vernon (Professor Fassbender), and Briony McRoberts (Margo Fassbender). Director: Blake Edwards; screenwriters: Frank Waldman and Blake Edwards; director of photography: Harry Waxman; producer: Blake Edwards. Amjo/United Artists, 103 minutes.

Revenge of the Pink Panther (1978). Peter Sellers (Chief Inspector Jacques Clouseau), Herbert Lom (former Chief Inspector Dreyfus), Burt Kwouk (Cato), Dyan Cannon (Simone Legree), Robert Webber (Philippe Douvier), Robert Loggia (Marchione), Tony Beckley (Algo), and Graham Stark (Dr. Augus Balls). Director: Blake Edwards; screenwriters: Blake Edwards, Frank Waldman, and Ron Clark; director of photography: Ernest Day; producer: Blake Edwards. Jewel/United Artists, 104 minutes.

The Prisoner of Zenda (1979). Peter Sellers (Rudolph IV, Rudolph V, Syd Frewin), Lynne Frederick (Princess Flavia), Lionel Jeffries (General Sapt), Elke Sommer (the countess), Gregory Sierra (the count), Jeremy Kemp (Duke Michael), Catherine Schell (Antoinette), and Graham Stark (Eric). Director: Richard Quine; screenwriters: Dick Clement and Ian La Frenais, based on the novel by Anthony Hope; director of photography: Arthur Ibbetson; producer: Walter Mirisch. Universal Pictures, 108 minutes.

Being There (1979). Peter Sellers (Chance), Shirley MacLaine (Eve Rand), Melvyn Douglas (Benjamin Rand), Richard Dysart (Dr. Allenby), Jack Warden (the president), Richard Basehart (Vladimir Skrapinov), Ruth Attaway (Louise), Dave Clennon (Thomas Franklin), and Fran Brill (Sally). Director: Hal Ashby; screenwriters Jerzy Kosinski and Robert C. Jones (uncredited), based on the novel by Jerzy Kosinski; director of photography: Caleb Deschanel; producer: Andrew Braunsberg. Lorimar/United Artists, 130 minutes.

The Fiendish Plot of Dr. Fu Manchu (1980). Peter Sellers (Fu Manchu, Nayland Smith), Helen Mirren (Alice Rage), David Tomlinson (Sir Roger Avery), Sid Caesar (Joe Capone), Simon Williams (Robert Townsend), Steve Franken (Pete Williams), Stratford Johns (Ismail), John Le Mesurier (Perkins), and Burt Kwouk (servant). Directors: Piers Haggard and Peter Sellers (uncredited); screenwriters: Jim Moloney and Rudy Dochtermann, based on the Sax Rohmer novels; director of photography: Jean Tournier; producers: Zev Braun and Leland Nolan. Playboy Productions/Orion, 100 minutes.

B I B L I O G R A P H Y

Abele, Robert. "Idol Chatter: Helen Mirren." *Premiere* (July 1999): 52.

Adams, Tony, et al. "Three Production Points of View." *American Cinematographer* (July 1978): 662–663, 675, 692–693, 711.

Alexander, Shana. "Sellers' Last Role—Almost." *Life* 57, 5 (July 31, 1964): 27–30.

Allan, Hunter. *Walter Matthau.* New York: St. Martin's Press, 1984.

Allen, Steve. *Funny People.* New York: Stein and Day, 1981.

Amis, Kingsley. *Memoirs.* New York: Summit Books, 1991.

Anon. "Photographing 'Revenge of the Pink Panther.' " *American Cinematographer* (July 1978): 656–659, 706–707.

Anon. "Southern Compatibility." *Mean* 1, 5 (September–November 1999): 42–44.

Anon. " 'Come On Out, Pete.' " *Newsweek* (November 2, 1964): 99, 101–102.

Anon. "Best Sellers." *Playboy* (April 1986): 130–142.

Anon. "*Gallery* Interview: Peter Sellers." *Gallery* (November 1978): 31–35.

Anon. "Out of the Air: Being There." *The Listener* (July 31, 1980): 142.

Anon. "Peter Sellers: Funny Peculiar." *Economist* (May 28, 1994): 90.

Anon. "Peter Sellers: Goon-in-tune." *Films and Filming* (May 1959): 5.

Anon. "Playboy Interview: Peter Sellers." *Playboy* (October 1962): 69–72.

Anon. "Rickless and others. V. United Artists Corporation and others." *Journal of Media Law and Practice* (July 1987): 71.

Anon. "Sellers Season." *New York Times Magazine* (April 1, 1962): 80–81.

Anon. "Talk With a Star." *Newsweek* (May 9, 1960): 113.

Anon. "The Shy Man." *Time* (April 27, 1962): 74.

Anon. "The World of Sellers." *Newsweek* (September 9, 1963): 90–91.

Ansen, David. "The Great Impersonator." *Newsweek* (August 4, 1980): 43–44.

Arce, Hector. *Groucho.* New York: G. P. Putnam's Sons, 1979.

Ardmore, Jane. "Mrs. Sellers' Deathwatch." *Photoplay* (July 1964): 76–77.

Armes, Roy. *A Critical History of British Cinema.* New York: Oxford University Press, 1978.

Aronson, Theo. *Princess Margaret: A Biography*. Washington, D.C.: Regnery Publishing, Inc., 1997.

Bach, Stephen. *Final Cut*. New York: William Morris and Co., 1985.

Balcon, Michael. *Michael Balcon Presents . . . A Lifetime of Films*. London: Hutchinson of London, 1969.

Barr, Charles. *Ealing Studios*. Berkeley: University of California Press, 1998.

Baxter, John. *Stanley Kubrick: A Biography*. New York: Carroll and Graf, 1997.

Beatles, The. *The Beatles Anthology*. San Francisco: Chronicle Books, 2000.

Bell, Simon, Richard Curtis, and Helen Fielding. *Who's Had Who*. New York: Warner Books, 1990.

Bentine, Michael. *The Reluctant Jester*. London: Corgi Books, 1993.

Billington, Michael. *The Life and Work of Harold Pinter*. London: Faber and Faber, 1996.

Booker, Bob, and George Foster. *"Pardon Me, Sir, but Is My Eye Hurting Your Elbow?"* New York: Bernard Geis Associates, 1968.

Boulting, Roy. "Getting It Together." *Films and Filming* (February 1974).

———. "What Happened After the Cliffhanger." *Films and Filming* (March 1974).

Bourne, Stephen. *Brief Encounters: Gays and Lesbians in British Cinema, 1930–1971*. London: Cassell, 1996.

Brady, Frank. *Citizen Welles*. New York: Charles Scribner's Sons, 1989.

Bragg, Melvyn. *Richard Burton: A Life*. Boston, Toronto and London: Little, Brown and Co., 1988.

Braun, Eric. "Authorised Sellers." *Films* (August 1982): 30–31.

———. *Deborah Kerr*. New York: St. Martin's Press, 1977.

Briggs, Asa. *The BBC: The First Fifty Years*. New York: Oxford University Press, 1985.

Brossard, Chandler. "The Weird World of Peter Sellers." *Look* (January 28, 1964): M7–9.

Brough, James. *Margaret: The Tragic Princess*. New York: G. P. Putnam's Sons, 1978.

Brown, Peter, and Stephen Gaines. *The Love You Make: An Insider's Story of the Beatles*. New York: McGraw-Hill, 1983.

Brownlow, Kevin. *David Lean: A Biography*. New York: St. Martin's Press, 1996.

Bugliosi, Vincent, with Curt Gentry. *Helter Skelter*. New York: Bantam Books, 1976.

Bull, Peter. *I Say, Look Here!* London: Peter Davies, 1965.

Cain, John. *The BBC: Seventy Years of Broadcasting*. London: British Broadcasting Corporation, 1992.

Caine, Michael. *What's It All About?* New York: Turtle Bay Books, 1992.

Calder, Angus. *The People's War: Britain, 1939–1945*. New York: Pantheon, 1969.

Cameron, Ian, and Mark Shivas. "What's New Pussycat?: An Interview with Clive Donner." *Movie* 14 (Autumn 1965): 15.

Carmean, Karen, and Georg [*sic*] Gaston. *Robert Shaw: More Than a Life*. New York: Madison Books, 1994.

Castell, David. "Best Sellers." *Films Illustrated* (February 1976): 212–214.

———. "The Last Masquerade of Peter Sellers." *Films Illustrated* (September 1980): 466–469.

Chaplin, Charles. *My Autobiography*. New York: Simon and Schuster, 1964.

Chapman, Graham. "Reflections in Gray." *Mean* 1, 5, (September–November 1999): 42.

Clayson, Alan. *The Quiet One: A Life of George Harrison*. Cambridge: Black Bear Press, 1996.

———. *Ringo Starr: Straight Man or Joker?* London: Sanctuary Publishing Ltd., 1996.

Collins, Joan. *Past Imperfect*. New York: Simon and Schuster, 1984.

———. *Second Act: An Autobiography*. New York: St. Martin's Press, 1996.

Crowe, Cameron. *Conversations with Wilder*. New York: Alfred A. Knopf, 1999.

Crowther, Bosley. "Buying Sellers." *New York Times* (May 1, 1960): sec. 2, 1.

Cullum, Paul. " 'The Crew Was In Hysterics!' " *Mean* 1, 5, (September–November 1999): 37–41.

———. "International Man of Mystery." *Mean* 1, 5 (September–November 1999): 34–36.

———. "Maybe We Can Relieve Each Other's Boredom a Bit . . . ?" *Mean* 1, 5 (September–November 1999): 53.

Dangaard, Colin. "Call Clouseau! Peter Sellers Just Killed the 'Pink Panther.' " *People* (October 3, 1978): 64–65.

Danischewsky, Monja. *White Russian—Red Face*. London: Victor Gollancz Ltd., 1966.

Dempster, Nigel. *Princess Margaret: A Life Unfulfilled*. New York: Macmillan, 1981.

Dennis Kirkland, with Hilary Bonner. *Benny: The True Story*. London: Smith Gryphon Ltd., 1992.

Dick, Bernard F. *Joseph L. Mankiewicz*. Boston: Twayne, 1983.

Douglas, Melvyn, and Tom Arthur. *See You at the Movies: The Autobiography of Melvyn Douglas*. New York: University Press of America, 1986.

Draper, Alfred, with John Austin and Harry Edgington. *The Story of the Goons*. London: Everest Books, 1976.

Dunn, Clive. *Permission to Speak*. London: Century Hutchinson Ltd., 1986.

Durante, Hilda. "My Secret Love Affair with Peter Sellers." *Sunday Express* (October 2, 1994): 35–36.

Durgnat, Raymond. *A Mirror for England: British Movies from Austerity to Affluence.* New York: Praeger, 1971.

Ekland, Britt. "An Ill-Fated Affair with Inspector Clouseau." *Penthouse* (March 1980): 74–76, 146–154.

———. *True Britt.* New York: Berkeley Books, 1980.

Ellis, Lucy, and Bryony Sutherland. *Tom Jones: Close Up.* London: Omnibus Press, 2000.

Epstein, Edward Z., and Joe Morella. *Mia: The Life of Mia Farrow.* New York: Delacorte Press, 1991.

Evans, Peter. *The Mask Behind the Mask: A Life of Peter Sellers.* London: Leslie Frewin, 1969.

Evans, Robert. *The Kid Stays in the Picture.* New York: Hyperion, 1994.

Farnes, Norma, ed. *The Goons: The Story.* London: Virgin, 1997.

Fawcett, Ian. "I Died—And Now I'm Having a Baby!" *Photoplay* (January 1965): 51–52, 75.

———. "I want to start living again." *Photoplay* (April 1965): 46–49, 58.

Fein, Irving A. *Jack Benny: An Intimate Biography.* New York: G. P. Putnam's Sons, 1976.

Ferguson, Ken. "Sellers." *Photoplay* (June 1971): 18–23.

Fischer, Mary A. "Peter Sellers' Chance of a Lifetime." *Rolling Stone* (April 19, 1979): 63–64.

Fleischer, Richard. *Just Tell Me When to Cry.* New York: Carroll and Graf, 1993.

Fletcher, Tony. *Moon: The Life and Death of a Rock Legend.* New York: HarperCollins, 1999.

Forbes, Bryan. *A Divided Life.* London: Heinemann, 1992.

———. *Notes For a Life.* London: Collins, 1974.

Forster, E. M. *Marianne Thornton: A Domestic Biography, 1797–1887.* New York: Harcourt, Brace and Company, 1956.

Fox, Julian. *Woody: Movies From Manhattan.* Woodstock, N.Y.: Overlook Press, 1996.

Frank, Gerold. *Judy.* New York: Harper & Row, 1975.

Franks, Alan. "Peter's Friends." *Sunday Times Magazine* (London) (February 11, 1995): 7, 11.

Frischauer, Willi. *Margaret: Princess Without a Cause.* London: Michael Joseph Ltd., 1977.

———. *Will You Welcome Now . . . David Frost.* New York: Hawthorn Books, Inc., 1971.

Garel, Alain. "The Best Sellers." *Image et son* (November 1981): 105–122.

Geist, Kenneth L. *Pictures Will Talk: The Life and Films of Joseph L. Mankiewicz.* New York: Charles Scribner's Sons, 1978.

Geldray, Max, with John R. Vance. *Goon with the Wind.* London: Robson Books, 1989.

Gelmis, Joseph. *The Film Director as Superstar.* Garden City, N.Y.: Doubleday, 1970.

Gilchrist, Ellen. "Growth in the Spring." *Sight and Sound* 1, 5 (September 1991): 35.

Gilchrist, Roderick. "The Search for My Secret Daughter, by Peter Sellers." *Daily Mail* (April 3, 1980): 3.

Giuliano, Geoffrey. *Dark Horse: The Private Life of George Harrison.* New York: Dutton, 1990.

Glazer, Mitchell. "The Strange World of Peter Sellers." *Rolling Stone* (April 17, 1980): 42–46.

Goldman, William. *Adventures in the Screen Trade.* New York: Warner Books, 1983.

Gottfried, Martin. *Nobody's Fool: The Lives of Danny Kaye.* New York: Simon & Schuster, 1994.

Gow, Gordon. "The Urge of Some People." *Films and Filming* (July 1969).

Grade, Lew. *Still Dancing.* London: HarperCollins, 1987.

Graham, Sheilah. *Confessions of a Hollywood Columnist.* New York: William Morris and Co., 1969.

Grandinetti, Fred M. *Popeye: An Illustrated History of E. C. Segar's Character in Print, Radio, Television, and Film Appearances, 1929–1993.* Jefferson, N.C.: McFarland & Co., 1994.

Haining, Peter. *Goldie.* London: W.H. Allen, 1985.

Hall, William. *Arise, Sir Michael Caine: The Biography.* London: John Blake Publishing Ltd., 2000.

———. *Raising Caine: The Authorised Biography.* Englewood Cliffs, N.J.: Prentice-Hall, Inc., 1981.

Harris, Warren G. *Natalie & R. J.* New York: Doubleday, 1988.

———. *Sophia Loren: A Biography.* New York: Simon and Schuster, 1998.

Henderson, Scott. "Life in a Pink Panther Factory." *American Cinematographer* (July 1978): 670–671, 684–687, 689–699, 710.

Herrmann, Dorothy, and S. J. Perelman. *A Life.* New York: Simon & Schuster, 1986.

Higham, Charles. *Lucy: The Life of Lucille Ball.* New York: St. Martin's Press, 1986.

Hoare, Philip. *Noel Coward: A Biography.* New York: Simon & Schuster, 1995.

Holborn, Mark. "Bill Brandt portraits." *Aperture* 90 (1983): 3–5.

Holden, Anthony. *Prince Charles.* New York: Atheneum, 1979.

Hunter, Allan. *Walter Matthau*. New York: St. Martin's Press, 1984.

Hyams, Joe. *Mislaid in Hollywood*. New York: Peter H. Wyden, Inc., 1973.

James, Henry. *English Hours*. Cambridge: The Riverside Press, 1905.

Jameson, Fredric. *The Cultural Turn: Selected Writings on the Postmodern, 1983–1998*. New York: Verso, 1998.

Johnson, Nora. *Flashback: Nora Johnson on Nunnally Johnson*. Garden City, N.Y.: Doubleday & Co., Inc., 1979.

Johnson, Richard. "Peter Sellers: A Life in Pictures." *Radio Times* (February 11, 1995): 32–36.

Johnston, Richard J. H. "Sellers, En Route to Hollywood, Talks of His 'Work' (Not 'Art')." *New York Times* (April 23, 1962): 33.

Jordan, Ruth. *Princess Margaret and Her Family*. London: Robert Hale & Co., 1974.

Kanfer, Stefan. "The Prime Minister of Mirth." *Time* (August 4, 1980): 61.

Katz, David S. *The Jews in the History of England, 1485–1850*. Oxford: Clarendon Press, 1994.

Kemp, Philip. *Lethal Indifference: The Cinema of Alexander Mackendrick*. London: Methuen, 1991.

King, Greg. *Sharon Tate and the Manson Murders*. New York: Barricade Books, 2000.

Knezevich, Steve. "Making Nonsense from Madness." *Mean* 1, 5 (September–November 1999): 50–51.

———. "Timeline." *Mean* 1, 5 (September–November 1999): 34–52.

Krantz, Judith. "This Man Says He's Peter Sellers." *McCalls* (August 1963): 42, 150–151.

Landy, Marcia. *British Genres: Cinema and Society, 1930–1960*. Princeton: Princeton University Press, 1991.

Lawrenson, Helen. "The People Inside Peter Sellers." *Esquire* (November 1970): 121–123.

Lawson, Twiggy, with Penelope Dening. *Twiggy: In Black and White*. London: Simon & Schuster, 1997.

Lax, Eric. *Woody Allen: A Biography*. New York: Alfred A. Knopf, 1991.

Leaming, Barbara. *Orson Welles*. New York: Viking, 1985.

———. *Polanski: A Biography*. New York: Simon & Schuster, 1981.

Lehman, Peter, and William Luhr. *Blake Edwards*. Athens: Ohio University Press, 1981.

Leigh, Wendy. *Liza: Born a Star*. New York: Dutton, 1993.

Lejeune, C. A. "This Is Peter Sellers," *Good Housekeeping* (December 1959).

Lewin, David. "Enigmatic Peter Sellers: 'Behind Our Masks, We Comics Lead Very Sad Life.'" *Us* (April 29, 1980): 60–61.

————. "Peter Sellers and His Latest Lady Stalk Off After Royal Snub." *Photoplay* (April 1977): 38–39, 43.

————. "Sellers: What Went Wrong with my Four Marriages." *Daily Mail* (May 8, 1979): 3.

Lewis, Flora. "The Ubiquitous, Multifarious Sellers." *New York Times Magazine* (June 23, 1963): 20, 53–54.

Lewis, Roger. *The Life and Death of Peter Sellers.* New York: Applause Books, 1997.

————. *The Real Life of Laurence Olivier.* New York: Applause, 1996.

Lewisohn, Mark. *Radio Times Guide to TV Comedy.* London: BBC Worldwide Ltd., 1998.

Lidz, Franz, and Steve Rushin. "Here a Comic Genius, There a Comic Genius." *New York Times* (January 30, 2000): sec. 2, 1, 26–27.

Lightman, Herb A. "On Location with 'Revenge of the Pink Panther.' " *American Cinematographer* (July 1978): 652–653, 682–683, 719.

————. "Riding Herd on a Chinese Fire Drill." *American Cinematographer* (July 1978): 654–655, 696–697, 704–705.

Linderman, Lawrence. "*Playboy* Interview: Julie Andrews and Blake Edwards." *Playboy* (December 1982): 77–116.

LoBrutto, Vincent. *Stanley Kubrick: A Biography.* New York: Donald I. Fine Books, 1997.

Lownes, Victor. *The Day the Bunny Died.* Secaucus, N.J.: Lyle Stuart, Inc., 1982.

Loy, Myrna, and James Kotsilibas-Davis. *Myrna Loy: Being and Becoming.* New York: Alfred A. Knopf, 1987.

Luhr, William, and Peter Lehman. *Returning to the Scene: Blake Edwards, Vol. 2.* Athens: Ohio University Press, 1989.

Lydon, Peter. "The Goons and a Bomb on Broadway." *Sight and Sound* 5, 2 (February 1995): 39.

————. "The Return of the Pink Prankster." *Independent, Metro Supplement* (London) (February 10, 1995): 16–17.

MacLaine, Shirley. *My Lucky Stars.* New York: Bantam Books, 1995.

Macnee, Patrick, and Marie Cameron. *Blind in One Ear: The Avenger Returns.* San Francisco: Mercury House, Inc., 1989.

Mair, George. *Under the Rainbow: The Real Liza Minnelli.* Secaucus, N.J.: Brich Lane Press, 1996.

Mancini, Henry, with Gene Lees. *Did They Mention the Music?* Chicago and New York: Contemporary Books, 1989.

Marshall, Garry, with Lori Marshall. *Wake Me When It's Funny.* Holbrook Mass.: Adams Publishing, 1995.

Martin, Jonathan. *Cleese Encounters.* New York: St. Martin's Press, 1992.

Maslin, Janet. "Peter Sellers: 'I Just Can't Stand Amateurism.'" *New York Times* (March 26, 1980).

Mason, James. *Before I Forget.* London: Sphere Books, 1982.

Mathews, Jack. "Is There Ruhm for Another?" *Los Angeles Times* (August 22, 1993).

Mazursky, Paul. *Show Me the Magic.* New York: Simon & Schuster, 1999.

McAsh, Iain. "The Heavy . . . and the Comic." *Films on Screen and Video* (April 1983).

McCabe, John. *The Comedy World of Stan Laurel.* Garden City, N.Y.: Doubleday & Co., Inc., 1974.

McDaniel, Wanda. "Peter Sellers: The Subject Was Being Anywhere." *Los Angeles Herald-Examiner* (May 22, 1980).

McGilligan, Patrick. *Backstory 3: Interviews with Screenwriters of the 1960s.* Berkeley: University of California Press, 1997.

———. *Jack's Life: A Biography of Jack Nicholson.* New York: W. W. Norton & Co., 1994.

McKern, Leo. *Just Resting.* London: Methuen, 1983.

McVay, Douglas. "One Man Band." *Films and Filming* (May 1963): 44–47.

Mendoza, Daniel. *The Memoirs of the Life of Daniel Mendoza.* Edited by Paul Magriel. London: B. T. Batsford Ltd., 1951.

———. *The Modern Art of Boxing, As Practiced by Mendoza, Humphreys, Ryan, Ward, Watson, Johnson, and Other Eminent Pugilists, to which are added the Six Lessons of Mendoza, as published by him, for the use of scholars; and a Full Account of his Last Battle with Humphreys.* London, 1789.

Millar, Gavin. "Goonery and Guinness." *The Listener* (February 1983): 33.

Milligan, Spike. *The Book of the Goons.* London: Robson Books, 1974.

———. *The Goon Show Scripts.* London: The Woburn Press, 1972.

———. *More Goon Show Scripts.* London: Sphere Books, 1974.

———. *Peace Work.* London: Penguin Books, 1992.

Minney, R. J. *"Puffin" Asquith.* London: Leslie Frewin, 1973.

Morley, Sheridan. *A Talent to Amuse.* London: Heinemann, 1969.

Mortimer, John. *Clinging to the Wreckage.* London: Weidenfeld and Nicolson, 1982.

Mullins, Peter. "Strictly By Design." *American Cinematographer* (July 1978): 666–667, 703.

Nathan, David. *The Laughtermakers.* London: Peter Owen, 1971.

Naughton, John. "Goodness Gracious Me!" *Premiere* (May 1994): 106–112.

Neal, Patricia. *As I Am.* New York: Simon & Schuster, 1988.

Nelson, Thomas Allen. *Kubrick: Inside a Film Artist's Maze.* Bloomington: Indiana University Press, 1982.

Norman, Barry. "It's Not All Right, Peter." *Radio Times* (June 12, 1999): 48.

Norman, Philip. *Elton John*. New York: Simon & Schuster, 1993.

———. *Shout! The Beatles in Their Generation*. New York: Simon & Schuster, 1981.

Nowell-Smith, Geoffrey. *The Oxford History of World Cinema*. New York: Oxford University Press, 1996.

Oakes, Philip. "Desiring This Man's Art." *The Listener* (February 1984): 39.

O'Connor, Garry. *Alec Guinness: Master of Disguise*. London: Hodder and Stoughton, 1994.

O'Dowd, Brian. "My Friend Peter Sellers." *Hollywood Studio Magazine* 16, 7 (June 1983): 22–23.

Paris, Barry. *Audrey Hepburn*. New York: G. P. Putnam's Sons, 1996.

Parker, John. *Polanski*. London: Victor Gollancz, 1993.

Parkinson, Michael. "Classic Interview: Peter Sellers." *Comedy Review* (June 1996): 24–25.

Parrish, Robert. *Hollywood Doesn't Live Here Anymore*. Boston: Little, Brown and Co., 1988.

Paskin, Barbara. *The Authorized Biography of Dudley Moore*. London: Sedgwick and Jackson, 1997.

Payne, Graham, with Barry Day. *My Life with Noel Coward*. New York: Applause, 1994.

———, and Sheridan Morley, eds., *The Noel Coward Diaries*. Boston and Toronto: Little, Brown and Co., 1982.

Peary, Gerald. "Peter Sellers: The Costumes Made the Man." *American Film* 15 (April 1990): 54–56.

Peter Duchin, with Charles Michener. *Ghost of a Chance*. New York: Random House, 1996.

Petrucelli, Alan W. *Liza, Liza! An Unauthorized Biography*. New York: Karz-Cohl, 1983.

Phillips, Gene D. *Stanley Kubrick: Interviews*. Jackson: University Press of Mississippi, 2001.

Phillips, John, with Jim Jerome. *Papa John*. Garden City, N.Y.: Dolphin Books, 1986.

Pitt, Kenneth. *Bowie: The Pitt Report*. London: Omnibus Press, 1985.

Polanski, Roman. *Roman, By Polanski*. New York: William Morrow and Co., 1984.

Powell, Michael. *Million Dollar Movie*. New York: Random House, 1992.

Powers, James. "Dialogue on Film: Hal Ashby." *American Film* (May 1980).

Reemes, Dana M. *Directed by Jack Arnold*. London: McFarland & Co., Inc., 1988.

Ribalow, Harold. U. *Fighter From Whitechapel: The Story of Daniel Mendoza*. New York: Farrar, Straus, and Cudahy, 1962.

Rigelsford, Adrian, and Geoff Tibballs. *Peter Sellers: A Celebration*. London: Virgin Books, 1997.

Rivers, Joan, with Richard Meryman. *Still Talking*. New York: Random House, 1991.

Robbins, Fred. "Our Young Wives Club." *Woman's Own* (April 23, 1978): 20–23.

Robinson, Jeffrey. *Bardot: An Intimate Portrait*. New York: Donald I. Fine, Inc., 1994.

Roth, Cecil. *A History of the Jews in England*. Oxford: Clarendon Press, 1964.

Sanders, Coyne Steven, and Tom Gilbert. *Desilu: The Story of Lucille Ball and Desi Arnez*. New York: William Morris & Co., Inc., 1993.

Sanders, Ed. *The Family*. New York: E. P. Dutton and Co., 1971.

Sandilands, John. "Brilliant at the Character Parts He May Be, But It's Peter Sellers That Is the Problem." *Nova* (April 1969): 58–63.

Sarlot, Raymond, and Fred E. Basten. *Life at the Marmont*. Santa Monica, Calif.: Roundtable Publishing, Inc., 1987.

Sarris, Andrew. *Interviews with Film Directors*. New York: Bobbs-Merrill, 1967.

Schickel, Richard. "Sellers Strikes Again." *Time* (March 3, 1980): 64–73.

Sealy, Shirley. *The Celebrity Sex Register*. New York: Simon & Schuster, 1982.

Seaman, Frederic. *The Last Days of John Lennon*. New York: Birch Lane, 1991.

Sellers, Peter. "The Gesture of Creation: Peter Sellers Talks to Teens." *Seventeen* (July 1964): 92, 123.

———. "A Serious Look at Laughter." *Films and Filming* (March 1960): 7, 35.

Sellers, Victoria. "My Father, Peter Sellers." *Mean* 1, 5 (September–November 1999): 47.

Sennett, Ted. *Ted Sennett's On-Screen/Off-Screen Movie Guide*. New York: Simon & Schuster, 1993.

Sherrin, Ned. *A Small Thing—Like an Earthquake*. London: Weidenfeld and Nicolson, 1983.

Short, Ernest, and Arthur Compton-Rickett. *Ring Up the Curtain*. London: Herbert Jenkins, Ltd., 1938.

Silver, Alain, and James Ursini. *Whatever Happened to Robert Aldrich?* New York: Limelight, 1995.

Simon, Neil. *Rewrites: A Memoir*. New York: Simon & Schuster, 1996.

Sinclair, David. *Snowden: A Man for Our Times*. New York: Proteus Books, 1982.

Sineux, Michel. "Bye Bye Birdie-num-num." *Positif* (February 1981): 47–51.

Southern, Nile. "Grossing Out." *Mean* 1, 5 (September–November 1999): 48.

Southern, Terry. "Strangelove Outtake: Notes from the War Room." *Grand Street* (Summer 1994): 64–80.

Stamelman, Peter. "In the Lair of the Pink Panther—An Interview with Blake Edwards." *Millimeter* (January 1977): 20, 72.

Stark, Graham. *Remembering Peter Sellers*. London: Robson Books, 1990.

Steiger, Brad. "Peter Sellers Is a Medium." *Fate* (January 1970): 44–48.

Stempel, Tom. *Screenwriter: The Life and Times of Nunnally Johnson*. New York: A.S. Barnes & Co., Inc., 1980.

Stollar, Steve. *Raised Eyebrows: My Years Inside the Groucho House*. Los Angeles: General Publishing Group, 1996.

Street, Sarah. *British National Cinema*. New York: Routledge, 1997.

Summers, Sue. "Peter Was Always Cruellest to the People He Was Closest To." *Mail on Sunday* (February 5, 1995): 24–29.

Sylvester, David, ed. *Moonraker, Strangelove and Other Celluloid Dreams: The Visionary Art of Ken Adam*. London: Serpentine Gallery, 1999.

Terry-Thomas, with Terry Dunn. *Terry-Thomas Tells Tales*. London: Robson Books, 1990.

Thompson, Charles. *Bob Hope: Portrait of a Superstar*. New York: St. Martin's Press, 1981.

Thompson, Howard. "Pause for Reflection with Peter Sellers." *New York Times* (October 25, 1964): sec. 2, 7.

Thomson, David. "The Rest Is Sellers." *Film Comment* (September–October 1980): 30–32.

Tonkin, Boyd. "Mad or Bad?" *New Statesman and Society* (May 20, 1994): 40.

Took, Barry. *Comedy Greats*. Northamptonshire: Thorsons Publishing Group, 1989.

Torme, Mel. *It Wasn't All Velvet*. New York: Penguin, 1988.

———. *My Singing Teachers*. New York: Oxford University Press, 1994.

Tornabene, Lyn. "Lunch Date with Peter Sellers." *Cosmopolitan* (September 1962): 14.

Tynan, Kathleen. *The Life of Kenneth Tynan*. New York: William Morrow and Co., Inc., 1987.

Tynan, Kenneth. "The Antic Arts: The Nondescript Genius." *Holiday* (June 1961): 127–33.

———. *The Diaries of Kenneth Tynan*. John Larh, ed. New York: Bloomsbury, 2001.

Vickers, Hugo. *Cecil Beaton: The Authorized Biography*. London: Weidenfeld, 1993.

Von Dassanowsky, Robert. "Casino Royale at 33: The Postmodern Epic in Spite of Itself," *Bright Lights Film Journal* 28 (April 2000). http://www.brightlights film.com/28/casinoroyale1.html

Waggoner, Walter H. "Arrival of Sellers." *New York Times Magazine* (March 27, 1960).

Walker, Alexander. *Hollywood UK*. New York: Stein & Day, 1974.

———. *Peter Sellers: The Authorised Biography*. Oxford: Clio Press, 1991.

Wapshott, Nicholas. *Peter O'Toole: A Biography*. New York: Beaufort Books, 1983.

Weinberg, Gerhard. *A World at Arms: A Global History of World War II*. New York: Cambridge University Press, 1994.

Whicker, Alan. *Within Whicker's World*. London: Elm Tree Books, 1982.

White, Carol, with Clifford Thurlow. *Carol Comes Home*. London: New English Library, 1982.

Whitelaw, Billie. *Billie Whitelaw . . . Who He?* New York: St. Martin's Press, 1995.

Wiley, Mason, and Damien Bona. *Inside Oscar*. New York: Ballantine Books, 1987.

Wilmut, Roger, and Jimmy Grafton. *The Goon Show Companion: A History and Goonography*. London: Robson Books, 1976.

Wilmut, Roger. *Tony Hancock—"Artiste."* London: Eyre Methuen Ltd., 1978.

Wilson, Pamela. "Dr. Strangelove." (Book review). *New York Times Book Review* (December 15, 1996): 26–27.

Windeler, Robert. *Julie Andrews: A Life on Stage and Screen*. Secaucus, New Jersey: Birch Lane Press, 1997.

Woodward, Ian. *Audrey Hepburn*. New York: St. Martin's Press, 1984.

Wyman, Bill, with Ray Coleman. *Stone Alone: The Story of a Rock 'n Roll Band*. New York: DaCapo Press, 1997.

Yoakum, Jim, and Paul Cullum. "Inspecting Clouseau." *Mean* 1, 5 (September–November 1999): 48–49.

Yule, Andrew. *The Man Who "Framed" the Beatles: A Biography of Richard Lester*. New York: Donald I. Fine, Inc., 1994.

Zee, Donald. *Sophia*. New York: David McKay and Co., 1975.

Zetterling, Mai. *All Those Tomorrows*. New York: Grove Press, 1985.

Zinsser, William K. "A Young Man Riding High." *Life* (June 20, 1960): 64–70.

A C K N O W L E D G M E N T S

Biographers put their hope and trust in hundreds of friends and strangers, some of whom become friends, and who collectively turn the author's wishful thoughts into a book.

It was an honor to interview such generous and articulate people as Rod Amateau, Ian Carmichael, Hilda Parkin Durante, Peter Eyre, Kenneth Geist, Max Geldray, Gail Gerber, Kenneth Griffith, John Guillermin, the late Sir Alec Guinness, Gene Gutowski, the late John P. Hamilton, Anthony Harvey, Burt Kwouk, David Lodge, Herbert Lom, Salem Ludwig, Malcolm McDowell, Joseph McGrath, Dr. Jonathan Miller, Hans Moellinger, Angela Morley, Kathleen Parrish, the late Robert Parrish, Siân Phillips, Larry Pizer, Roman Polanski, Alvin Rakoff, Clive Rees, the late Walter Shenson, and Dame Maggie Smith. For reasons that will be obvious to anyone who has followed the course of Peter Sellers's reputation after his death, his immediate family declined to speak to me about him; I think I understand why, and I hope I have not hurt them further.

I drew quotations from Peter Sellers, Anne Levy, Michael Sellers, Victoria Sellers, Britt Ekland, and others from a variety of sources, most significantly Alexander Walker's invaluable *Peter Sellers*; Michael Sellers's equally worthy *P.S. I Love You*; Graham Stark's informative and funny memoir, *Remembering Peter Sellers*; Peter Evans's fine (and unduly criticized) *The Mask Behind the Mask: A Life of Peter Sellers*, and Britt Ekland's engrossing autobiography, *True Britt*. I drew additional quotations from Peter Sellers and his friends and colleagues from three fine documentaries: John Scheinfeld and David Leaf's *The Unknown Peter Sellers*; the three-part *The Peter Sellers Story*, which was produced by Arena and aired on BBC2; and *Sellers' Best?: An Introduction to the Channel Four Season of Peter Sellers' Films*, which aired on Channel Four. And I owe every person named in this book's admittedly lengthy bibliography my deepest gratitude.

Assistance, contacts, advice, factual corrections, interview transcriptions, and absolute kindness came my way from Mary Alexander, Nigel Algar, Lance Aston, David Boxwell, Darla Bruno and her fabulous fan website, Ron Caldwell, Aaron Clauset, Alice Crary, Paul Cullum and *Mean* magazine, Bruce Finlayson, Phil Geldray; Donna Gianarelli, Phoebe McReynolds, and the faculty of the Colorado College English Department; Barry Goralnick, Adele Greene, Sally Harrison, Walter and Dianne Harrison; Gary Hill, Janice Roland, and the staff of Falco Ink; Costas Karakatsanis, Marshall Kean, Rick Kot, Charles Kreloff, Dick Ray, Tom Rhoads, Ira Robbins, George Robinson, Pierre Salinger, Linda Sarro and the faculty and staff of Haverford College; Draper Shreeve, Sandra Skuse, Joe Smith, Ted Sorensen, Nile Southern, Peter Steinberg, Thom Taylor, Thomas S. Wilson, Bill and Sandy Woncheck, and Jim Yoakum and the Graham Chapman Archives.

Greg Meyer is the best, most thorough, and most responsible research assistant any writer could have, let alone an egocentric and anxious biographer like me. I owe him more gratitude than I could possibly afford. Adam Orman, Michael Kaniecki, and John Freed provided equally reliable research assistance as well, but it's easier for me to thank them because they worked fewer hours.

For making their extraordinary knowledge available, let alone their facilities, I thank Sandra Archer, Barbara Hall, and the other librarians and staff at the Academy of Motion Picture Arts and Sciences' Margaret Herrick Library; the librarians and staff of American Film Institute's Louis B. Mayer Library; the special collections librarians at the University of Southern California and the University of California at Los Angeles; the New York Public Library; the librarians and film archivists at the British Film Institute; the librarians at the Theatre Museum in London; Fred Zentner and Dejan Zamurovic at the Cinema Bookshop in London; and, as always, Ron Mandelbaum and the guys at Photofest in New York.

Any contest for the title "World's Greatest Peter Sellers Fan" must result in a tie between Maxine Ventham and Dimitris Verionis. Both of these marvelous and appreciative people provided access to rare materials and important contacts. They gave me support and solid friendship when I needed it most, not to mention critical observations about their favorite performer. Maxine and Dimitris are devoted to the life and work of Peter Sellers, and they each helped me to understand him much better than I could have on my own. There may be observations in this book that will upset those with whom they put me in contact. I can only say that I never meant this book to be mean.

I trusted my friends Christopher Bram and Matthew Mirapaul enough to let them read my first draft. They gently steered me away from my worst impulses; they suggested improvements kindly; and they told me they thought the book was funny, which is what I hope Peter Sellers himself would have appreciated. It was Chris who kicked me out of my writer's block by suggesting that I write Peter's life story as a sympathetic black comedy; Matthew suggested the title.

I love my agent, Edward Hibbert, as well I should, since I owe him my career. What could be better than to have a brilliant actor as your agent? Fans of *Frasier* know Edward as Gil Chesterton, the British food critic; I, however, am most fond of his stage performances as Lady Bracknell in *The Importance of Being Earnest* and Frederick Fellowes in the Broadway smash *Noises Off.* Edward's associates at Donadio and Olson—Neil Olson, Ira Silverberg, and Jesse Dorris—are kind enough to advise me, take my phone calls when Edward is out of town or in rehearsal, and hold my hand as often as I beg them to do so.

This book's genesis occurred in the offices of Hyperion when Jennifer Barth, the editor of my earlier biography on Billy Wilder, and Alison Lowenstein, her assistant, were discussing ideas for my next book. They, not I, came up with Peter Sellers, and I think they made a very good decision.

Peternelle Van Arsdale edited this book with a fine eye and a sharp pencil, two things every author needs. She's the greatest, and I'm forever in her debt. Thanks to Natalie Kaire, this book sailed smoothly through its transition from manuscript to print, and I am thrilled with the way it turned out. Thanks also to Donna M. Ellis, senior production editor; Laura Starrett, copy editor; and Phil Rose, art director.

My parents, Irving and Betty Sikov; my partner, Bruce Schackman; and all of my extended family make me appreciate, each day, how lucky I am in every way—not least of which is that none of us are famous.

INDEX

In this index, PS is used for Peter Sellers.